Unwin Education Books

PHILOSOPHY AND EDUCATIONAL FOUNDATIONS

Unwin Education Books

Philosophy and Educational Foundations

ALLEN BRENT
Lecturer in Philosophy of Education,
James Cook University of North Queensland

London
GEORGE ALLEN & UNWIN
Boston   Sydney

**George Allen & Unwin (Publishers) Ltd,
40 Museum Street, London WC1A 1LU, UK**

George Allen & Unwin (Publishers) Ltd,
Park Lane, Hemel Hempstead, Herts HP2 4TE, UK

Allen & Unwin, Inc.,
9 Winchester Terrace, Winchester, Mass. 01890, USA

George Allen & Unwin Australia Pty Ltd,
8 Napier Street, North Sydney, NSW 2060, Australia

First published in 1983.

British Library Cataloguing in Publication Data

Brent, Allen
    Philosophy and educational foundations. – (Unwin educational books)
1. Education – Philosophy
I. Title
370'.1   LB41
ISBN 0-04-370143-4
ISBN 0-04-370144-2 Pbk

0027005

Library of Congress Cataloging in Publication Data

Brent, Allen.
    Philosophy and educational foundations.
(Unwin education books)
Includes bibliographical references and index.
1. Education – Philosophy. 2. Philosophy, Modern – 20th century.
I. Title. II. Series.
LA133.B735   1983   370'.1   83-11772
ISBN 0-04-370143-4
ISBN 0-04-370144-2 (pbk.)

Set in 10 on 11 point Times by Fotographics (Bedford) Ltd
and printed in Great Britain by
Billing and Sons Ltd, London and Worcester

Contents

*For the sons and daughters of North Queensland and their
university, in this century and the next*

Introduction

This book is a sequel to my *Philosophical Foundations for the Curriculum* (Allen & Unwin, 1978) although its argument and new material stand on their own and can be followed in their own right. The question that I asked there was, in effect: what philosophical resources were available to us in formulating proposals about knowledge and the curriculum that would enable a rationally based and epistemologically defensible consensus to emerge between warring ideologies and their curricular factions. My answer was that there were certain transcendental (in the sense of 'transcultural' and, in a special sense, 'transhistorical') modes of understanding. I produced an epistemological defence of such a thesis and drew its implications for curricular decision-making.

I have found much of the public criticism of the thesis of my first book (in the form of book reviews and other sources) far from satisfactory and for reasons that I give in the course of my present work (see below, for example, pp. 292–97, 344–47). On reflection, however, I reached the conclusion that some points of my case required strengthening. What I have therefore done is to write a second book from a completely different direction but which nevertheless critically supports parts of the argument of the first. I have this time taken exemplifications of basic approaches to practical curriculum problems of such writers as Bloom, Bernstein, Hirst, and Whitty and Young and their associates. Then I have sought in great detail to expound the fundamental, social-science and philosophical models that underly such proposals, such as classical empiricism and behaviourism, Durkheim's consensus and Marx's conflict models, Wittgenstein's later philosophy and so on. In each case, moreover, I have explored the case for reformulation of classical models in terms that leave their fundamental framework intact, such as phenomenological reformulations of Marxism with their dependency on Freud or 'operant' reformulations of classical behaviourism. In the last analysis, however, I have found such reformulations that preserve the parameters of the original model unsatisfactory on grounds that I argue in detail. If such models are finally incoherent, whether in their classical or reformulated forms, then they cannot support the curriculum proposals which are derived from them.

Throughout my argument I have adopted a somewhat Aristotelian conception of the philosopher's role. Aristotle, in laying the foundations for the study of logic, saw the role of philosophy as one of grasping various patterns of coherence and incoherence within and between groups of statements that went well beyond the surface appearance of their agreements and disagreements. When we are presented with fundamental conflicts between models in the social sciences that guide educational practices, I have assumed, contrary to the prevailing later Wittgensteinian fashion, that it is the role of the philosopher not simply to describe and analyse the formal frameworks of such models. Rather, the philosopher's task is to go on to reduce such incoherences by reformulation of key concepts and procedures in order to work towards a new synthesised model. My argument has been therefore that some form of a theory of semantic universals, such as that advocated by Chomsky and Katz, can constitute the basis for such a new synthesis. Such a theory can shape a rule-following model of human action that does not involve the conceptual problems of rule-conforming reductions. Such a model can, in turn, incorporate disparate yet important insights of epistemologists such as the later Wittgenstein, psychologists such as Freud, and sociologists such as Durkheim. I have therefore made suggestions for reformulating formal frameworks presupposed by such theorists. In doing so I have suggested a more coherent and epistemologically viable model of human action which has critical implications for the curriculum.

Both therefore the ground covered by this my second book and the formal character of the argument are new. I am conscious, however, that in the argument of my first book I was somewhat cavalier both in my criticism of dialectical arguments and in my use of the perspectives both of Chomsky and the later Wittgenstein. Terms like 'semantic universals' and 'family-resemblance' were sketchily introduced and not applied in any detailed or systematic way, either to Hirst's theory of the forms of knowledge or to any other curriculum theory. In pursuance of the new arguments of this book applied to the new territory covered, I have therefore discussed and defended my understanding both of a theory of semantic universals and its relationship to family-resemblance. I have also expounded and criticised I hope far more incisively the dialectical presuppositions of Marxist frameworks. In propounding a new argument, I hope therefore to have critically strengthened my original one.

I regard the production of this, my latest work, to have been critically urgent owing to what are in my opinion two potentially disastrous developments in the philosophy of education. The first was the publication of *Experience and the Growth of Understanding* (Routledge & Kegan Paul, 1978) by Professor David Hamlyn, in which an account of the epistemological conditions of a viable social or psychological theory of children's development was outlined on the basis of a Wittgensteinian argument developed in self-conscious opposition to that of Chomsky. My reasons for regarding it as disastrous, I hasten to add, had nothing to do with the brilliance of an argument that I have found, in the last analysis, nevertheless to have failed. Rather my reasons were related to the curricular consequences of a brilliant yet misguided account, as I have endeavoured to show in Chapter 9, and to the way in which Hamlyn's conditions would provide a formidable obstacle to the development of a unified model of human action as the foundation for pedagogic practice, as I show in Chapter 8. The second development is the emergence in Australian philosophy of education of an intellectually powerful and articulate school of Marxist materialists exemplified in the writings of Jim Walker, and Colin Evers of Sydney University, and Kevin Harris and Michael Matthews of the University of New South Wales. Evers and Walker in particular, in using Quinean pragmatism and extensional logic in defence of a Marxist materialism, are the very theorists against whom my critical analysis of Quine's work throughout this book could have been directed had their work come into my hands before this book had assumed its final, finished form.

Since writing my first book, I have enjoyed the privilege of changing both country and institution. I have found the atmosphere of both North Queensland generally and of its recently founded university in particular both morally and intellectually invigorating in sad contrast to the higher education and national scene in the United Kingdom at this present time. I would like to thank therefore my colleagues at James Cook University for their intellectual support, and also my secretary, Mrs Ria Houston, for her painstaking labours in typing my manuscript.

James Cook
University of North Queensland
March 1981

Chapter 1

Behaviourist Foundations and Approaches to Pedagogy

This book is about theoretical models of pedagogy, the foundations of which are found in the social sciences. It is written in the conviction that basic conflict between contemporary theoretical foundations need not be final, and that such conflicts are reducible using the techniques of philosophical analysis. It is further written in the conviction that, because theory does affect practice whether consciously or subconsciously, there is great practical importance in at least attempting a synthesis of such models of pedagogy via some tentative moves towards a reconstruction and reconciliation between rival theoretical foundations. Our first principal theme will therefore be about the way in which theoretical models of pedagogy originate as explanations of and answers to certain particular classroom practices and problems and how, from such a base, they come to dominate answers to all such practices and problems. In the course of our discussion on this theme, we shall see how changes in the 'taken-for-granted', 'common-sense' views of classroom practices are produced by changes in the theoretical models themselves. Our second principal theme will be an exploration through an analytic critique of the foundations of such theoretical models of how they might be reformulated in order to tell a more consistent story of how men are in their natural or social world, and how, as adolescents or as children, they are introduced to such a world.

In this chapter, we shall be presenting with a view to analysis the first of several, admittedly stereotyped examples of common-sense approaches to the classroom, together with examples of common-sense views of such approaches. We shall then show how several major and conflicting theoretical frameworks have grown out of the discussion of such common-sense views and have been used to license some common-sense practices in preference to others. Having thus shown how setting theory against theory also sets practice against practice, we shall be showing in later chapters how the reduction of theoretical conflict will license a new more coherent model of pedagogic practice. Before, however, we launch into a description and a discussion of our first theory, namely, behaviourism and its origins in certain exemplified classroom practices, let us justify by means of a general example our claim which some may find controversial that theoretical frameworks develop out of common-sense judgements in such a way as to pronounce some common-sense judgements valid and others invalid, thus modifying or even drastically revising general, taken-for-granted approaches to situations. We shall leave for the moment whether such developments are justifiable and whether such pronouncements about validity are in fact valid.

Let us take as our simple though inevitably controversial example that famous description of Isaac Newton throwing an apple into the air, watching it fall, and either inventing or discovering thereby the laws of gravity. That the apple would fall was a common-sense prediction made on the basis of common-sense observation by millions of mankind before Newton. However, it was a common-sense observation and prediction which Newton suddenly and perhaps insightfully grasped to be at variance with other kinds of common-sense observation and prediction on this momentous occasion. The common-sense view of physical objects was and, I suppose, still is that objects are normally at rest and only (abnormally) move, when, for example, someone or something pushes or propels them. If I look at the objects around me in my room as I write, they all appear to be at rest. When one of them moves, it appears to be because some force propels it. If I push a book, a glass or a pen at rest at one end of the table towards the other end, then it appears from common-sense to move because of a force which I have brought to bear upon it, and, when it ceases its move, it appears to be because the force has spent itself and the object has returned to its normal state of being at rest. This was the common-sense view of objects and their motion, refined by Aristotle's (1932) physics, which regarded unmoving objects as no problem and held it to be only a *movement* of an object that required any explanation.

But let us go back to the good Sir Isaac throwing his apple into the air. 'If this common-sense view of physical objects and the forces that moved them were correct,' he thought, 'why doesn't the apple just stay put in the air?' He had, after all, thrown the apple, and the force which he had brought to bear upon it was now spent. Yet the apple did not simply stick there but had fallen to the ground! Supposing then for one moment, reflected Newton, that we were to make the breath-taking assumption that all things were normally in motion and that only when things came to a rest was any explanation required. Now we would have to change totally our common-sense, Aristotelian world view. We would now assume that all objects throughout the universe were in motion and only pause to look for an explanation when we found one that was at rest. We should then look, not for what started things moving but for what stopped them, and such theories as explain these phenomena are to be found in the theory of gravity, friction and motion that Newton went on to propound.

Now it is important for us to be clear from the outset from this example how theoretical models come to be constructed on the basis of a limited and highly selective range of common-sense experiences which somehow get the theory started. This will be particularly important for the argument which this book will be developing specifically about the nature and character of educational theory. Although rooted in one particular set of common-sense experiences, like apples falling, Newton's theory takes us beyond common sense and a 'taken-for-granted' view of the world. It sanctions some kinds of common-sense products against others, labelling some of our intuitions as real and others as mistaken. Furthermore, Newton's theory united piecemeal and discrepant descriptions of apples falling, rivers flowing downhill, satellites revolving around planets and so forth into a unified and coherent explanation. What they had in common, however, common sense could not detect whereas Newton's theory could. Theoretical frameworks therefore fulfil that general criterion of rationality described as 'the transcendence of the particular' (Peters, 1972, p. 59).

The social-science foundations of pedagogic theory which we shall be meeting in this book fulfil these two criteria: namely, (a) they sanction some items of common-sense experience against others, and (b) they transcend the particular in that they enable us to see items of experience which were, at the level of common sense, unrelated as part of a comprehensive and coherent view of things. For the Marxist, frustration with school subjects, rebellion in a classroom, a strike against an incomes policy, a manager's ulcers, though they appear unrelated at the level of common sense, form within his theory of the contradictions of the capitalist system and his conflict model of social change part of a clear pattern, the discernment of which leads to explanation and prediction. Furthermore, some kinds of common-sense within that theory will be sanctioned as real whereas other kinds of common sense will be dismissed as the illusion of false-consciousness, as we shall see (Chapter 5). For Durkheim and the structural functionalists (Chapter 7), however, we shall find that other and contrary common-sense insights are sanctioned by the contrary, consensual theory of social change, with a different pattern, involving a theory of social pathology, uniting the aforesaid disparate items of common-sense experience. Our subject for this chapter is however behaviourism, and the traditional, common-sense attitudes to teaching and learning of which, I shall argue, it represents a theoretical extension of the same type as that which I have been generally describing. Let us devise a typical example embodying common-sense attitudes of a traditionalist kind.

1.1 A TYPICAL CHARACTERISATION OF A TRADITIONAL CLASSROOM

We begin, then, with the first of our 'typical characterisations'. I would mention, however, from the outset that I am using such fictional constructs for the purpose of initial exposition, and would not like to be accused of trying to win my critical points too cheaply by reducing my opponents to gross caricatures. Once, however, I have secured my initial expositional objective, in a later section I will be listing and summarising actual curricular proposals that I will argue to have the theoretical presuppositions which I am analysing and criticising (in the case of this chapter, behaviourist presuppositions).

Let us imagine Julia, who is a student teacher, joining Mr Callaghan and his class, to which she has been assigned for her teaching practice. As the bell rings, the children pour through the door and Mr Callaghan begins to quieten the class, identifying potential sources of disorder. Jamie is blowing up a balloon and squirting air into Christopher's face to Christopher's annoyance but to the great delight of Vicki, Jaqui and Russell. Mr Callaghan demands the balloon, which Jamie with some appearance of resentment hands over. 'That's right Jamie!' says Mr Callaghan. 'You can play with that to your heart's content at playtime. But within the walls of this class you are here to work!' So saying, he takes a sidelong glance at Julia, winks fatherly, with a wise and self-contented look on his face.

Mr Callaghan whispers into Julia's ear: 'You must put your foot down from the word go. Once individuals start to get away with it, then things will go to pot. Insist on good standards.' And 'good' standards are precisely what Mr Callaghan proceeds to exhort, both by word and by deed as he takes his class through a first hour of arithmetic, a second hour of writing, a third of religion, and a fourth of reading, duly interspersed with usual breaks, planned diversions for momentary 'light relief' and so on. Tables are learned by rote and poems by heart, and the child who succeeds in reciting the nine-times table or 'London Bridge' successfully and before anyone else is held up as the hero to be praised by the teacher and admired by all. But Mr Callaghan is nevertheless an intelligent and perceptive man. In case praise combined with 'stars' for individual good work encourages too much a selfish and individualistic attitude, he rewards a great deal of achievement by a system of house-points by which he tries to foster a desire to work for the common good as a result of working for red house against green, or blue, or yellow. Those who lag behind in competition, whether it be for praise, stars or house-points, are chided caustically and reminded that their being last is a function of their moral values, for they are choosing laziness to industry. Mr Callaghan is, however, basically a sensitive and humane man, and his chiding more often than not is more in sorrow than in anger, despite the fault being basically the pupils' who have not paid attention, been lazy and so forth.

The class is not treated to a boring monologue, and for this Julia notes a pleasing contrast between Mr Callaghan and some of her lecturers in the University's Education Department who are always lecturing for fifty minutes or more on how bad lectures are as a means of communication. When he sees interest flagging and attention roaming, he raises his hands with a gesture like that of an orchestral conductor and chants, 'Once four is four!' to be joined by a loud chorus of response from children thus stimulated to proceed to chant the four-times table. Sometimes, however, he varies his approach and chants instead, 'Many hands . . .' to which the children respond, '. . . make light work but too many cooks spoil the broth', thus completing the maxim as they do with many other such maxims. Mr Callaghan is clearly aware that he is not simply responsible for his children's arithmetical education but for their moral education too.

As they write their essays (perhaps in the form of 'news' items), aided by his first selecting likely boys and girls 'to get things going' with oral contributions, individual boys and girls are called on to bring out their work for him and Julia to read and to mark. Work neatly written, grammatically well formed and interestingly (perhaps even imaginatively) written he rewards with a gold star, and work achieving some degree of approximation to one or all of these three criteria is accordingly given yellow stars, red stars, blue stars or green stars. Jamie produces an ink-stained and grubby offering at which Mr Callaghan scowls and sticks a large red label with 'KEEP-IT-CLEAN' written over it. As Jamie returns to his desk, there is a rustling of feet as many heads reach over to look at his book in order to witness the full horror of what the notorious Jamie has perpetrated!

Julia and Mr Callaghan, despite an initial antipathy, get on well together. Julia talks to him about the schemes of work that her tutors are keen for her to do and, after a period of initial vociferously expressed scepticism, he finally shows interest, having reflected how battle-scarred and out of touch with an oversized class he probably is.

He becomes enthusiastic, and so, with the head's permission, an approach is made to the Educational Technology section of the Education Department to come and see whether they have any suggestions to make to help to improve an already excellent situation. And so the bearded, besweatered group of jargon-spouting lecturers arrive. They talk about 'aims and objectives', 'learning packages', 'programmed texts' and 'positive reinforcement' in particular and actual curriculum areas that I shall specify in greater detail later (Chapter 4). Where Mr Callaghan is wrong, they insist, is in trying to teach a group of forty children all together at the same speed and at the same time. Learning packages of various kinds are produced which will enable children individually or in small groups to proceed at their own pace. Mr Callaghan's principle of reinforcement of successful learning with stars and house-points were a good idea but too haphazard and disorganised in their application. Only a few children received stars or house-points, and the consistency with which they were given was very rough indeed, with the result that those who received neither were likely to become apathetic and unmotivated. With learning packages, the learning units would be so spaced and organised that, at each successful accomplishment of a unit, reinforcement could be given regularly and consistently. Success in one unit would thus motivate progress to the next and a clearly thought out 'schedule of reinforcement' would secure the success of a clearly 'paced' schedule of learning. The 'keep-it-clean' labels could be safely thrown into the dust-bin. They were examples of 'negative reinforcement' which was proved to be a less economic aid to learning than 'positive reinforcement' by rat experiments (Skinner, 1953). In such experiments, rats would continue going through doors in mazes far longer when rewarded with food pellets than they would if encouraged to choose the door because all the others in the maze had given them electric shocks. 'Praise' rather than 'blame', therefore, was shown to be a far more successful method of achieving learning objectives. Now that each individual was regularly rewarded with praise, stars, lollipops and other incentives for having completed a unit of his own package (irrespective of what the rest had or had not done), there was no need of aversion stimuli. The absence of reward rather than positive punishment would be motivation enough, and positive punishment was precisely what blaming, scorning, shaming of children into action represented.

'Yes!' remarked Mr Callaghan to Julia. 'They are quite right. If you set up a "schedule" (as they say) of punishments, kids in my experience will simply do the minimum necessary to avoid punishment. If you tell them that anyone with less than four out of ten will have to stay in and write an essay, then there is a solid group of them that will just make sure that they get four out of ten and no more. But perhaps if I start reinforcing positively instead of negatively, then less numbers will rest content with only four and try to achieve more.'

Julia was to observe Mr Callaghan taking this lesson very much to heart. In fact he stopped his habitual tirades against unruly behaviour the morning after such somewhat trying experiences as games afternoons. He also stopped stern warnings about 'crime does not pay' and 'getting the police in' when money, scarves, pumps or other items went missing. Whenever games afternoons went well, he became fulsome in his praises, not only of the class in general but of the virtues of as many of the individual boys and girls as he could possibly enumerate. 'Blue and Red teams could have simply lounged around or been fighting one another while Yellow and Green were competing, but,' added Mr Callaghan with pride, 'they did not. They watched attentively, and cheered and encouraged their pals on!' The morning after an afternoon of near riot following two heats having to be run several times over again produced in Mr Callaghan complete silence. Likewise, when Jamie found a five-pence piece and handed it in to him, Mr Callaghan waxed eloquent with praise. 'Now pay attention!' he called to the class. 'I have something important to tell you. Young Jamie here has handed in this five-pence piece that Christopher lost. Now he could have put this in his pocket and spent in on an ice-cream for himself. But rather than do this, he handed it in.' Mr Callaghan had indeed been converted from 'blame' to 'praise', and though before he had been a 'good' teacher by getting things right by intuition, he was now becoming an even better teacher by articulating and generalising, on the basis of particular and individual judgements, formal rules and principles with which to guide himself. He was simply by such a process enabled to be more consistent to what in his heart of hearts he was really committed and to what for him was 'common sense'.

1.2 THE BEHAVIOURIST PERSPECTIVE: GENERAL PRINCIPLES

We saw in the opening paragraphs of this chapter that what a scientific perspective has done is to take certain common-sense insights, perhaps handed on through a community originally in the form of folklore, and to develop these particular insights into a formal and general system of considerable sophistication. In the light of this system, other common-sense insights have been declared to be misconceived and invalid, in fact to be just folklore. We saw that this was the case with Isaac Newton and the common-sense experience of an apple falling when thrown into the air. The insight gained from formulating this piece of common-sense knowledge had systematically led him to overthrow the validity of another piece of common-sense experience, namely, that objects are 'naturally' at rest and that it is their movement which requires explanation. For the moment, we are content to record such a procedure as a fact of history, although later we shall show the limitations of such a view of theory. Likewise, too, Mr Callaghan in our teaching example has begun to see that his folklore practices were based on inconsistencies in what he counted as common-sense knowledge. He has begun, with the help of an educational technology based upon behaviourist learning theory, to develop systematically some parts of his common-sense knowledge to a point where he had formed a general perspective in the light of which he rejected other parts of his common-sense knowledge. 'It's only common sense to tear kids off a strip whenever one of them steals or runs riot,' is a piece of 'common-sense' pedagogy rejected in favour of praising if they do well repeatedly and consistently, but simply remaining silent when they do not. The latter is nevertheless supported by another item of common sense, namely: 'If you repeatedly nag, they will take no notice of you.' Furthermore, Mr Callaghan's common-sense practice of encouraging with stars is developed into a full-scale theory involving schedules of positive reinforcement, whereas his other common-sense practice of using 'keep-it-clean' labels is rejected. Curricular subjects, moreover, are either given a clear structure (or their implicit structure is spelled out) by which clear learning steps can be mastered, thus eliminating haphazard guesswork.

It is interesting at this juncture to note, however, that, for all the innovatory and revolutionary appearance of the educational technologists in contrast to Mr Callaghan, both they and he share a common perspective derivable from the same set of common-sense experiences. Both see teaching and learning in terms of behaviour modification and control, stimulus and response, rewards and punishments, schedules of reinforcement and so on. In fact, this is why Mr Callaghan gets on so well with Julia and her college tutors in our example, since they share common presuppositions about the teaching situation. The educational technologists, for their part, would readily agree with my contention. This is why, they would be quick to argue, they deserve all the economic resources that they claim. They are trying to answer the 'real' problems of 'real' teachers based upon 'common sense'. Only, alas, as it will be argued further in this book, their 'common-sense' foundations are but a sub-set of the shared common-sense experience of men. We shall in subsequent chapters be seeing that there are other items of common sense which even Mr Callaghan would sometimes find commonsensical which run counter to those other items of common sense upon which Mr

Callaghan has chosen to erect his theoretical perspective. These other items, as we shall see, can produce a theoretical model by a process equally of strict logical deduction from them which conflicts with the behaviourist model. It is arguable, for example, that equally commonsensical is the view that, if unemployment is endemic in an economic order, then the failure of those who come out bottom is not a product of their laziness. If one-third of all school-leavers are unable to find employment, however hard they worked and however generally standards of performance in school subjects rose, one-third of school-leavers would still be unemployed. Irrespective of the smallness of difference in attainment between pupils, Mr Callaghan would still have to grade them, not because such grades corresponded to anything in reality, but to meet the requirements of the economic order. At this point, alternative 'common sense' would begin clearly to generate an alternative theoretical perspective in which such concepts as false-consciousness, alienation and so forth will occur. This is a perspective that we shall be exploring further in Chapter 5.

There is a second point that at this juncture it will also be important for us to note. I will not be subscribing to a view which holds that all theoretical perspectives when they conflict must be as acceptable as each other because each is equally derivable from conflicting sub-sets of common sense (Pring, 1977). At this point, however, I have preferred to leave this option open and only to close it in the light of subsequent discussion. I have been careful from the outset nevertheless to avoid prejudging this issue as was done in the philosophy of science by writers in the empiricist tradition (for example, Ayer, 1940). Such a prejudgement might have lead me to claim that only one set of common-sense experiences could logically and coherently give rise to a theoretically adequate and scientific perspective, following application of appropriate logical formulas to such experiences. Such formulas, it was believed, when applied to items which were factual and commonsensical (commonsensical *because* they were factual even) must necessarily and inevitably produce the true view of how things are. Thus the existence of an established, scientific world view somehow was held to guarantee the truth of the particular sub-set of common-sense experiences that generated it and vice versa, relegating all other items of common sense to the status of false belief, fantasy and illusion. I have preferred for the moment to leave matters open and simply to rest content with the possibility that different sets of conflicting common-sense experiences might logically generate different and conflicting theoretical perspectives. I shall want finally to argue a thesis about the ultimate coherence of what is logically derivable from all items of common-sense experience. For the moment, however, let us leave matters open until we have mapped out conflicting common-sense views and conflicting theoretical perspectives. Let us, then, examine our first perspective, the behaviourist perspective, in order to see how certain kinds of common-sense experience have been systematically developed both by reflection and experiment.

Classical behaviourism, which began with the work of such men as Watson (1924) and Pavlov (1927), represented a phenomenon in psychology that was considered by its adherents to be comparable with that of Newton's in physics. The behaviourists' strategy is to reduce all mentalistic concepts to physicalistic ones, which can be done, they argue, without loss of (real) meaning. Once this reduction has been accomplished, then cause and effect can be charted by psychologists. We observe those causes which invariably have produced past behaviour, and so we can predict future behaviour with all the certainty and consistency as that with which the physical sciences can explain and predict natural events. Classical behaviourism was thus to share belief in the certain and causal predictability of human behaviour in a way comparable with that in which classical (though not, as we shall see, modern) physicists thought possible with all physical events at the final completion of the scientific quest. A good pedagogic example of behaviourist presuppositions may be seen in Bloom's *Taxonomy* (Bloom *et al.*, 1956) and the practice of getting teachers to write down their 'aims' and 'objectives'. Suppose, however, I express my objective in a given unit of instruction (lesson) thus:

To get class 5a to see the relevance of theory x in the construction of diesel engines.

This for a behaviourist is a too imprecise and 'unscientific' formulation. Whereas 'construction' will pass the test since it is analysable in terms of a determinate number of skills and behaviours specifiable in terms of further objectives, 'to see the relevance of' fails the test. The latter statement is not behaviourally specifiable. The problem here is that the statement requires us to guess what is going on in people's minds, albeit in a way not really different from Mr Callaghan's original view of how work was to be marked. But such guesses typically vary greatly from one observer to another. Our imprecision, however, is created simply by the fact that our psychological thinking is still dominated by pre-scientific mythology. In reality, there is nothing going on in someone's head other than electrochemical or neurophysiological events. Re-express, therefore, what you mean in terms of overt behaviour and the subjectivity of guesswork will be transformed into objective description. Retranslate 'see the relevance of', which refers to non-existent mental events, in terms of what the student shall actually be able to do, perhaps as follows:

To get 5a when presented with engines of type A, B, C, D, E to select theory x when presented with theories s, t, u, v, x, y as representing what is common to the operations of A, B, C, D, E.

This, then, is a statement of what the individual student shall be able to do. As a performance, it can clearly at the close of the lesson be declared to be fulfilled or unfulfilled, achieved or not achieved, true or false, right or wrong against a description of how individual students were actually seen to behave. Guesswork, in the best traditions of scientific inquiry, claims the behaviourist, has been eliminated in favour of an objective description fulfilling clear and determinate criteria for truth and falsehood.

There are, however, implicit in the behaviourist accounts with which we shall be dealing two distinct positions between which, as we shall see, such accounts vacillate. We shall be frequently drawing attention to these vacillations as our analysis proceeds. Let us, however, spell them out from the outset. As they involve a weaker and a stronger claim, let us call them 'weak behaviourism' and 'strong behaviourism' respectively and define them as follows:

(a) *Weak behaviourism.* Because nothing goes on 'in someone's head' other than neurophysiological and similar events, and because the nature of these internal phenomena cannot at the present moment be tested and analysed, we must for the time being therefore rest content with the study of external behaviour produced by these events.

(b) *Strong behaviourism.* All phenomena, whether called 'internal' or 'external', are to be studied in behavioural terms. This requirement is an 'operationisability' requirement, that is, the requirement whose satisfaction makes any kind of objective test or measurement possible. Therefore the internal/external distinction is spurious and must thus be excluded on logical grounds from scientific description.

We may bring out the distinction between the weaker and stronger claim as follows. The first claim (a) is weak by contrast with the second (b) because it allows that there could be other ways of studying mental events other than in terms of overt behaviour. Since, however, no one has as yet produced any methods for determining what can be said truly or falsely, rightly or wrongly, about such events, at the moment there cannot be any scientific study of them. Yet this weaker claim does admit that there could be such methods discovered in the future. To be scientific, a hypothesis must be verifiable or falsifiable, that is to say, we must know how in principle we could show that it was true if it is true, or, at very least, we must be able to specify what would have to happen to make it false (Popper, 1959, pp. 27–48). The weak behaviourist is simply claiming that, at the moment, we do not have ways of verifying non-behavioural mentalistic hypotheses. Yet he admits that, in the future, this might be possible. The strong behaviourist rules this out *a priori*. His behaviourism represents, not simply practical advice to scale down our research to present practical necessity, but rather what is known as a 'principle of significance'. A principle of significance in philosophy of science is a rule which instructs us to treat data in one way only and claims that, if we are not bound by this rule, we shall only end up chasing fantasies. The much discussed, and recently much criticised, 'causal principle' is one such principle of significance in the natural sciences. This principle tells us to treat every event as though it were the result of some cause and, even though we are unable to find a particular cause of a particular event, we must go on looking. Thus to say the lightning bolt fell and nothing caused it, or that there was no cause but rather the purpose and design of the god Jupiter behind it, are explanations ruled out *a priori* by the causal principle as a principle of significance. Though we cannot as yet chart all the causes of every event, yet we know in advance that there must be an explanation in terms of causes for every event that occurs. The strong behaviourist is similarly using the principle that all mental operations be reduced to physicalistic ones as a principle of significance. He is instructing us that, unless we abide by this principle, we shall fail in our attempts to construct an objective and scientific account of an ordered psychological world. We cannot stipulate in advance all the new discoveries that psychology or physics (according to this view) will make, but we can, according to this stronger thesis, stipulate that whatever will be discovered in psychology will be expressible in behavioural terms, or in physics (controversially) in causal terms.

It is important, then, to appreciate that, for Skinner, behaviourism must be founded on a principle of significance which represents the strong version of the behaviourist thesis. It is on this point that we reach the real disagreement between Skinner and his critics, particularly Chomsky (1959). Chomsky's claim, as we shall see later and in greater detail, is that we need to understand the human mind in a way which preserves the internal/external distinction that the strong behaviourist regards as vacuous and as such an impediment to clear thinking. Chomsky's model of mind is a computer model rather than a neurophysiological model. When we compare the output of the model with the input (environmental stimuli, sensory-data and so on), we must infer mentalistic structures which act like a computer programme. Without such a programme, there could not be the kind of output in the form of mental operations that human beings exhibit. This is because such an output bears a completely different form from the input. This formal programme will require spelling out in terms of the neurophysiological process which creates it and composes its material structure. But whatever this process will be shown to be when we have the investigatory techniques for exposing it, the form of its functions can be expressed in the algebra of the new linguistics that we shall be considering later. Suffice it to say at this point that weak behaviourism is a non-starter on this view, and convincingly so, since Chomsky's work shows a way around the difficulty with which it insists that it is reluctantly stuck. If at any point Skinner can be shown to revert to a weak behaviourism, then his case arguably fails. What he and such of his supporters as Quine (1960) or Cooper (1975) must be committed to doing is not simply to produce empirical evidence against such an understanding of mental processes, but to rule such an understanding out of court from the outset of the inquiry as a meaningless model generated by pre-scientific methodology. As such, they must show that anything the computer, mentalistic model can explain, the behaviouristic theory can explain more clearly, more economically and more scientifically. Their claim, in other words, must represent a logical and methodological attack on the adequacy of non-behavioural approaches. That is to say, they must defend the strong thesis of behaviourism.

That the strong thesis is what Skinner is after may be seen from the following passage:

> We can follow the path taken by physics and biology by turning directly to the relation between behaviour and the environment and neglecting supposed mediating states of mind. Physics did not advance by looking at the jubilance of a falling body, or biology by looking at the nature of vital spirits, and we do not need to try to discover what personalities, states of mind, feelings, traits of character, plans, purposes, intentions or what the other pre-requisites of autonomous man really are in order to get on with a scientific analysis of behaviour. (Skinner, 1971, p. 20)

Here Skinner is arguing that, just as physics advanced by adopting a new procedural rule, namely, by refusing to search for inner qualities or essences like 'jubilance' or 'vital spirits' but rather by seeing all movements and change in terms of the action or effect of one body on another, so would psychology advance by removing from its frame of reference such 'inner' states as 'feelings', 'intentions' or 'purposes'. Thus the strong behaviourist is backing a principle of significance in terms of which 'we do not need to try to discover' such 'inner' states. Such 'explanations' of human behaviour, relying on an inner/outer distinction, are as much part of the metaphysical claptrap of a bygone age as talk of 'ghosts', 'spirits' and 'souls' as causes of human behaviour. They represent a vestigial remnant in the infant science of psychology comparable with similar vestiges which lingered on in physics and biology in the seventeenth and nineteenth centuries. Bodies which fell or bounced were thought to do so because of some kind of jumping force ('jubilance') within them. In connection with another science, Skinner says:

> Chemistry made great strides when it was recognised that the weights of combining substances, rather than their qualities or essences, were the important things to study. (Skinner, 1953, p. 41)

To search for 'inner' 'qualities' or 'essences' in the mind is therefore for Skinner to miss the true character of mental events in terms of observable and manipulable physical conditions produced by the interaction of human bodies with their environment.

Psychological theories such as McDougall's instinct theory exemplify Skinner's parallel here between rudimentary science and contemporary psychology. Early science's vain quest for 'inner' essences like 'jubilance' or 'vital spirits' is paralleled by explanations in terms of 'instincts'. People behave aggressively, fearfully, lovingly, hungrily and so forth, and the internal causes of these are said to be such instincts as aggression, flight, sex, hunger (McDougall, 1932). But it is arguable, I think in this case rightly, that all that such an 'explanation' amounts to is a logical equivalence masquerading as a factual discovery. For example:

John made love to Jane because he was moved by his sexual instinct,

says no more than:

John made love to Jane because John made love to Jane.

This parallels precisely:

Bodies x, y, z bounce because of their essence of jubilance,

but adds nothing by way of explanation to:

Bodies x, y, z bounce because bodies x, y, z bounce.

Thus it is important to see from what Skinner says here that his position is not what we have characterised as weak behaviourism. His method is not simply necessitated by our lack of knowledge or means of testing hypotheses about internal states. Rather it is a principle of significance which rules out references to internal states as confusions about the logic of scientific inquiry for which an inner/outer distinction of this kind is spurious.

However, Skinner is not consistent in his application of this principle. A typical statement is the following:

> The objection to inner states is *not that they do not exist* but that they are not relevant in a functional analysis. We cannot account for the behavior of any system while staying wholly inside it; eventually we must turn to forces operating upon the organism from without. Unless there is a weak spot in our causal chain so that the second link is not lawfully determined by the first, or the third by the second, then the first and the third links must be lawfully related. If we must always go back beyond the second link for prediction and control, we may avoid many tiresome and exhausting digressions by examining the third link as a function of the first. Valid information about the second link may throw light upon this relationship but can in no way alter it. (Skinner, 1953, p. 35)

Here, then, Skinner concedes that internal states might exist, but talk about them is rejected as irrelevant to functional analysis. But, as we saw in our previous quotation, his earlier comparison between pre-scientific essentialism and instinct theory suggested the stronger thesis, namely, that internal states do not exist simply because the inner/outer distinction is incoherent. There a description of neuro-physiological mechanisms was still a description in terms of behaviour, in terms of parts of an organism responding to stimuli, and description of them in terms of inner states was meaningless instead of merely functionless. We shall have later to pursue in greater detail the adequacy of either stronger or weaker claims. For the moment we shall rest content with a brief caveat. In this passage, Skinner makes use of a familiar rule of inference, namely, if A bears some (in this case causal) relation to B, and B bears some (causal) relation to C, then A is related (causally) to C. So long as we have a reasonably clear picture of A and a reasonably clear picture of C, all that we need to know is that both are connected causally to B and it will not matter how vague our knowledge of B is otherwise. But this begs the question. According to the strong thesis, B is a meaningless notion and what is meaningless cannot be causally related to anything. According to the weak thesis, B can be discarded because, though meaningful, it is irrelevant. But before it can be discarded it must at least be sufficiently known to be reliably described as causally related to A and C. Therefore Skinner must grant the possibility of investigation to establish at the very least the causal relationship of A to B and of B to C. But this is precisely what is at issue. Consider the following example of stimulus (A) eliciting response (C) through an unknown mechanism (B). The stimulus is a group of more than one goose associated with the description 'geese' (A). The response is for someone seeing such a group to say to himself or out loud, 'Geese' (C). The mechanism whose properties are both unknown and irrelevant to the weak behaviourist is whatever nervous or endocrine activity makes the response possible (B). If invariably when A occurs C also occurs, then perhaps the nature of B is not interesting. Even supposing we were to grant this, the nature of B will inevitably become interesting when an assumed causal link between A and C through B collapses because something other than C occurs. Children subjected to adult descriptions of 'geese' have been known to respond to the sight of more than one goose with the non-C response of 'gooses'. And at that point, the nature of the intervening mechanism (B) which breaks the chain of causation and instead follows the rules for the formation of plurals becomes interesting. And children, by imposing logical regularity on the illogical irregularity of adult speech, often exhibit powerful evidence against behaviourist explanations of behaviour in terms of a purely causal model (McNeill, 1972).

We shall have more to say, therefore, in criticism of Skinner's model of explanation in terms of overt behaviour. Before we do, however, we must explore in more specific terms the precise character of the model of psychological explanation that Skinner adopted and how he developed this to a high level of sophistication.

1.3 CLASSICAL BEHAVIOURISM: PAVLOV'S DOGS

Accepting in the main the strong thesis that no reference was to be made to internal states because these had no real existence, the behaviourists believed that they were able to produce a revolution in psychology similar to that of Newton's in physics, described at the beginning of this chapter. Newton, as we saw, adopted a methodological principle which was revolutionary in terms of Aristotelian physics. Newton, from his observation of the apple falling, adopted the methodological principle that we should start from the premise that every-thing is in motion, and then explain why some things are at rest, rather than from the premise that everything is at rest and then explain why some things move. In one sense, the behaviourists too proposed that we adopt the principle that all living things are in motion as well and that their movement is to be understood in terms of responses to stimuli. Instead of regarding the normal condition of living things as motionless, and then, when they move, looking for causes of their movement in terms of 'instincts', 'wills', 'desires' or 'choices', we should, it is argued, seek causes for absence of motion against a background of continuous motion. An amoeba is in continuous motion responding to the stimuli of sunlight, darkness, the presence of plankton or acid in the water. Its plasm lashes out in all directions throughout its unicellular structure, forming podia. So, too, is a new-born infant in perpetual motion, kicking, sucking, moving, crying and gurgling. When the new-born infant stops such motions or confines them to specific occasions or circumstances, it is at this point that explanation is required. The behaviourist explanation is that responses associated with the reduction of need get repeated and those that are not get extinguished. As such, the behaviourists, like the Newtonians, appeared to be moving beyond common sense. After all, human beings, according to the common-sense view, only move when moved, which is why we order, command, ask, request each other to do things. The behaviourists invite us to believe that such behaviour is the discriminating residue of an originally indefinite number of quite general indiscriminate and varied responses. Those responses made to environmental stimuli that are associated with the reduction of need either will be or tend to be (Skinner is ambiguous about this, as we shall see) repeated, whereas responses which are not will not be or will tend not to be repeated. Finally, a response after a long record of unsatis-fied need-reduction will be extinguished, however great the strength of the stimulus that once elicited it.

Let us look, therefore, at the classical experiments in conditioning which, when conducted by Pavlov (1927), were to lay the foundations of classical behaviourism. Pavlov experimented with hungry dogs and his experimental observations lead him to formulate the stimulus/response/associationist framework by means of which we can both explain past and predict future behaviour. Having kept a number of dogs chained in kennels, he measured carefully the quantities of saliva that they produced when hungry. During such periods of hunger, when red meat was brought within their sight and smell, the amount of saliva increased in anticipation of eating the red meat. Now this was a natural, every-day occurrence which could be explained within the behaviourist framework as a 'conditioned reflex'. No agent had designed or intended that the reflex should happen, but clearly the dogs would not have survived as a species had not the development of such an automatic reflex taken place within the context of quite fortuitous environmental conditioning. Yet, because of the fortuitous character of this conditioning, a conditioned reflex could not be described as 'learning'. Here Pavlov, in my opinion to his credit, was trying to go beyond a common-sense view of learning by means of his general theoretical perspective while maintaining useful common-sense distinctions. We do not, for example, in common-sense language describe a baby's blinking when light shines into his eyes as his 'learning' to squint, even though a condition of the reflex is the shining of the light so that it is a 'conditioned' reflex. However, a blink was a response to a stimulus. If, therefore, learned behaviour was to be distinguished from reflex behaviour in a way consistent with common-sense distinctions, responses which were describable as learned had to be distinguished from reflexes which were not so describable. Pavlov therefore described the salivation of his dogs as the 'unconditioned' response to the 'unconditioned' stimulus of the red meat. To be an example of what in ordinary language is described as 'learning', a response and a stimulus had to be describable as 'conditioned'. As such, it must be said, the distinction between the conditioning in a reflex and the conditioning in a stimulus/response could only be maintained with reference to the intentionality of the teacher/conditioner in the learning process in contrast to the unintended and fortuitous environmental conditioning of the reflex. This was, for the behaviourists, a rather unfortunate consequence, since 'intentions', 'choices', 'decisions' were the very concepts which they professed able to squeeze out of any psychological explanation warranting the description 'scientific'. But let us for the moment continue to allow Pavlov to present to us the behaviourist case. Suffice it to say that the nomenclature conditioned/unconditioned, stimulus/response enable him to make the reflex/learning distinction. By describing a reflex in terms of an *unconditioned* response and learning in terms of a *conditioned* response, he was able to distinguish two sets of behaviour by different adjectives while insisting that both had properties which were similar by using a common noun. To what extent the assumption of similarity was justifiable so that this amounted to something more than a verbal sleight of hand is the fundamental question that, as we shall see, behaviourism must answer, particularly in view of Pavlov's difficulties in disposing of intentionality from the outset. But let us grant him his assumption and see what is now to be made of learning in terms of a conditioning of stimuli and responses.

With what he did next with his dogs, Pavlov exemplified his view that a learning process involved the substitution of conditioned for unconditioned stimuli and responses. Every time the red meat was produced, he rang a bell and flashed a light. After a measured interval of time, he dispensed with the red meat and simply rang the bells and flashed the lights. The dogs produced almost exactly the same amounts of saliva as when the red meat had been present. Now, normally, when bells are rung and lights are flashed dogs do not salivate profusely. Their salivation response, argued Pavlov, must therefore now be termed a 'conditioned' response to a stimulus (lights and bells) which was also conditioned. What made both 'conditioned' was the experimenter's intentional association of the stimulus and thereby the response with the unconditioned stimulus of the red meat. Salivation as a response to lights and bells could be described as 'learned', in contrast to salivation in response to the red meat which was 'unlearned'. Learning could now, it was thought, be defined in a way consistent with the principle of significance of the strong behaviourist as: 'any change in behaviour, more or less permanent over time, which was not the result of maturation'. But here, once again, recurs the difficulty that we have mentioned before, namely, the absolute necessity of referring to intentions in order to make the distinctions required by the behaviourist model which seeks to exclude such references. 'Maturation' refers to what would normally or naturally develop without human intervention. The problem here is that it is difficult to see, using strictly the strong behaviourist's principle of significance, whether there can be any final distinction between maturational and learned changes of behaviour such as the definition requires. My reasons are as follows. A baby's eyes begin to focus or a puppy starts to salivate because this is how babies or puppies naturally grow or develop towards maturity (hence 'maturation'). But, within a strictly behaviourist framework, this can only be because, in the natural history of human or of canine evolution, the response of focusing or of salivating has lead to the reduction of the survival needs of the organism and its species. Nature as well as evolution is accidental and fortuitous. There can therefore be no final distinction between maturation and learning unless it is conceded that the act of bringing about learning involves, by contrast with maturation, human intervention which is unnatural in the sense of being, say, non-accidental or non-fortuitous. But intervention as such can only be understood in terms of such categories of explanation as 'purpose', 'intention', 'design' or 'choice'. And so we are here once more forced to use the language of decisions, choices, intentions and so forth with which the strong behaviourist insisted that we could safely dispense without loss of real meaning. But this, alas, is no hopeful beginning for a science which takes, as we have seen science must, certain common-sense assumptions and develops these into an overall framework in terms of which it tries to dismiss other common-sense assumptions.

Moreover, what a scientist does when he invents new technical terms is to take us beyond common sense by providing us with a vocabulary that is clearer and more precise than our common-sense vocabulary. When scientists renamed the common-sense word 'water' H_2O, they were making clearer and more precise that to which they were making reference. But without reference to intentions, the behaviourist, as we have seen, ends up obliterating rather than refining common-sense distinctions. In common-sense explanations, we distinguish between what our physiology or environmental circumstances cause us to do from what we choose or decide to do. The behaviourist depended on those distinctions when distinguishing what is learned and unlearned in terms of conditioned and unconditioned responses, but ended up with an explanation which undermined the very distinction on which his technical vocabulary depended. With the obliteration of such common-sense distinctions will also come the collapse of the technical distinctions within the behaviourist model itself which rest on such common-sense distinctions. The difference between conditioned reflexes and conditioned responses and between learning and maturation we have seen to be glaring examples of this case in point. At the very outset, therefore, the behaviourist is seen to have failed in the enterprise of constructing a framework of explanation logically derivable from a sub-set of common-sense experiences which it unites into a coherent whole while reformulating other items of common-sense experience so that they become consistent with the overall explanation, or otherwise simply rejecting them. Even the sub-set of common-sense experiences with which the behaviourist begins is, in the final analysis, inconsistent with the model that is meant to unify the experiences within an explanatory framework.

On such, to say the least, shaky foundations laid by Pavlov, the behaviourists were to erect their model of explanation. The examination of the precise extent of the 'more or less permanent over time' that characterised a learning rather than a maturational change was to lead to additions in behaviourism's repertoire of technical terms describing the learning process. It was found that, the longer that the ringing of the bells or the flashing of the light went on without reward ('reinforcement') of red meat, the less was the quantity of saliva produced, until finally bells and lights produced no saliva at all. Technically, such an outcome is known as the 'extinction' of a 'stimulus' in the absence of 'need-reduction'. In order to retain the learned behaviour, it was necessary (in terms of the theoretical base) to renew periodically the reinforcement. By measuring the points at which the salivation tailed off, it was possible to gauge accurately where reinforcement could most economically be applied. Such a measurement, which might most conveniently take the form of a graph, become known as a 'schedule of reinforcement'. Furthermore, having established the principle of 'stimulus substitution' (ringing bells and flashing lights substituted for red meat), the further principle of 'stimulus generalisation' can be experimentally established. Substitute for the bells a tuning-fork capable of producing a general class of varying pitches. First strike the tuning fork to make a pitch similar to that of the bells and the dogs will salivate in approximately similar quantities to that produced by the bells. Vary the pitch and, despite such variation, the saliva will continue to be produced in the same quantities. Thus, as a result of a planned series of stimulus substitution selected on the principle of similarity with the immediate prior stimulus in a temporal series, stimulus generalisation has been achieved. A similar response is elicited by a variety of stimuli.

Such a theory of learning has been used to prescribe new practices and to license existing ones in the curriculum, as we suggested earlier in our exemplification of the basic behaviourist approach in our description of the advice of Julia's tutors to Mr Callaghan. We shall be looking at specific examples of behaviourist licensing of teaching method and curriculum organisation later (below, Chapter 4). For the moment, we may briefly look at an example of a behaviourist explanation of language acquisition in explicit Pavlovian terms. According to Pavlovian behaviourists, words are simply conditioned responses to conditioned stimuli. Daddy takes Christopher for a walk and they see a horse. Christopher is babbling all kinds of noises indiscriminately in response to the sight of the horse. Daddy, hearing amid the babble the sound 'hor . . ', seizes upon this and cries: 'That's right. Hor . . . se, horse. You clever boy. You know what a horse is!' Christopher responds, 'Horse.' Daddy's voice and action constitutes the unconditioned stimulus and the reply 'horse' constitutes the unconditioned response. Daddy's praise reduces Christopher's need to feel praised. After a time, the mere sight of the horse without Daddy's voice, because it has become associated with the reduction of need, elicits the response 'horse'. The mere sight of the horse has now become the conditioned stimulus and the response 'horse' the conditioned response. Thus the conditioned response associated with the reduction of need gets repeated so long as there remains something like a reinforcement schedule. With language acquisition, the reinforcement schedule is present in the social environment, as, for example, when other people pay attention and respond in need-reducing ways when Christopher says, 'Horse.'

On these foundations, then, B. F. Skinner was to build his distinctive model of behaviourism. Let us now see what Skinner's distinctive additions and adaptations were.

1.4 OPERANT BEHAVIOURISM: SKINNER'S PIGEONS

Skinner saw that the problem with classical conditioning as a comprehensive explanation of human behaviour rested on too passive a model. For all the parallels that we have drawn between the behaviourist revolution in psychology and Newton's physics through an analogy with Newton's laws of motion, we may say that there are still elements of pre-revolutionary thinking which have left their debilitating traces on the classical model. Although classical behaviourism made its partial breakthrough by assuming that living things are normally in motion and that it is only at those points at which they stop moving that explanation is required, classical behaviourists were still trying to assign a general cause to the original state of indiscriminate motion in the form of the stimulating environment. It was, to preserve the physical analogy, as though Newton had asserted some general cause of bodies falling at the same rate instead of regarding such falling as axiomatic to physical explanation. The new-born baby might kick in all directions as the amoeba might lash with its podia in all directions, but they both only did so because of external stimuli (sunlight, light, warmth, touch and so on) which initially elicited an indiscriminate variety of responses before need-reduction made them more discriminating. Skinner was to dispense with the reliance of the classical model on a general cause of motion by placing the movement of the organism and the movement of the environment on an equal footing. Just as the environment could stimulate the organism, so could the organism stimulate the environment and would tend to repeat a stimulus associated with need-reduction. The organism's activity was not therefore wholly determined by the environment since the organism itself could provide the stimuli which determined environmental responses. By such a strategy, Skinner, as we shall see, was to provide behaviourism with a new way of solving the problem of retranslating common-sense categories such as 'freedom', 'choice' and 'intention' in terms of the causal, stimulus/response/associationist categories of the behaviourist explanatory model.

Let us, however, begin by seeing how a dissatisfaction with the classical framework arose to which Skinner offered his novel solution. Undoubtedly some examples of retranslating such terms as 'choosing', 'deciding', 'intending' in stimulus/response/ associationist terms in an explanation of the classical type was unproblematic. Let us take as a simple example tea drinking. If we are both cold and thirsty, we drink hot tea (response) because hot tea (conditioned stimulus) has been associated with feeling cold and thirsty (unconditioned stimulus) and their reduction in the past. Thus the common-sense description: 'I *chose* some hot tea because I *decided* to warm myself up', may be arguably retranslatable in terms which dispense with 'chose' or 'decided' without loss of real (= significant for the strong behaviourist) meaning. There is, it must be admitted, a problem with such an argument for retranslation of common-sense 'choice-explanation' into a technical causal explanation. The problem is the objection that the technical explanation only gives us the necessary but not the sufficient conditions which would explain the particular behaviour of tea drinking. In other words, it might be objected that the technical, causal description is not a true translation since it only tells us why the subject should have chosen something hot and not why he chose tea rather than, say, coffee, cocoa or soup. Moreover, so the objection continues, any attempt to go beyond the necessary to the sufficient conditions of tea drinking will involve reference to choices and intentions. But this objection only appears to be insuperable because it is levelled at one example extracted from the total picture of the subject's overall behaviour and the total behaviourist explanation of that picture. Further details in the case of examples such as tea drinking could be supplied which spelled out additional conditions which would both pass the strong behaviourist's criterion of significance and also make the explanation sufficient as well as necessary. Even an inveterate opponent of behaviourism, such as the present writer, would have to concede that, with examples of the tea-drinking variety, a complete description of both necessary and sufficient conditions within a behaviourist framework (stimulus/response/association) can stand as a complete translation of an account in terms of choice or decision. We can satisfactorily build into our explanation further items which will turn a necessary into a sufficient explanation. If, for example, in times past tea was more associated with the reduction of thirst and coldness than, say, coffee, cocoa or soup, then the subject would, according to the explanation, respond to tea rather than the others. The 'reasons' for this, the behaviourist would quite delightedly note, would be more appropriately described in terms of environmental causes which had, quite accidentally, produced this outcome, as when, for example, the subject's unfortunate previous experience of offerings of soup, coffee and cocoa had invariably been lukewarm. Here, then, by building into our explanation more information duly processed by behaviourist formulas such as 'previous reinforcement' we can finally make what was previously purely necessary finally sufficient.

But once we begin to look at other examples which do not fit easily into a stimulus/response framework, these shade into examples which, we shall argue, do not fit at all. There are examples of novel, unusual and especially creative acts in which human beings appear to break with prior patterns of stimulus/response/association. Let us look first of all at an example of unusual behaviour that appears to accomplish such a break. I am going to say to you: '2 + 2 = 5'. Note what happens and what does not happen when I say this. My vocal chords do not contort so that, try as I will to say '5' having put 2 and 2 together, I find myself forced by previous conditioning to say '4'. We *can* happily break the rules. In fact, sometimes (a cynic would say 'often') breaking rules can be quite fun. But note what such rule-breaking behaviour establishes. It establishes that the kind of rule-governed activity (a) in which rules followed *as the norm* are broken is in a different category from that kind of rule-governed behaviour (b) in which, because the rules are causally determined, the rules cannot be broken. Rule-governed behaviour (a) has been described as 'rule-following' behaviour (Peters, 1958, pp. 4–8) as opposed to rule-governed behaviour (b), which may be described as 'rule-conforming' behaviour. An example of rule-following behaviour (a) was my following the rules of computation when I added together 2 and 2 to make 4. The fact that I could *break* the rule by saying '5' guaranteed that what I did was an example of rule-following. An example of rule-conforming behaviour (b) with which rule-following contrasts is the rate at which my heart beats per second or the behaviour of my body in falling at a certain velocity if I slip from the roof of a very high building. While it may be true, then, that we frequently behave, as with tea-drinking behaviour, in ways predictable within the framework of the rule-conforming model of classical conditioning, it is arguable that such a model is too passive to be able to provide an adequate explanation of the vast category of rule-following behaviours in human beings.

Now, as we have already established, what any model of behaviourism must be able to do is to show how all examples of rule-following are chimerical and that the only real explanation of such activity must be in rule-conforming terms. As Skinner says:

Personal examption from complete determinism is revoked as a scientific analysis progresses, particularly in accounting for the behaviour of the individual. (Skinner, 1971, p. 26)

Remember what we have so far established as central to the behaviourist's thesis. He must establish his strong thesis, exhibited in this quotation, that all behaviour is explicable within his framework and that the use of mentalistic categories of choice and decision are expendable and necessarily expendable since they are the ghostly chimeras of a pre-scientific mode of thinking. A non-behaviourist (accepting that we have demonstrated weak behaviourism to be non-behaviourism) can, as we have seen, accept that we can often only examine mental events behaviourally because we have so far only the apparatus to examine matters in this way, although in the future it may be possible to conduct research differently. A non-behaviourist can, furthermore, accept that *some* kinds of human activity may and ought to be explained in behavioural (rule-conforming) terms, where other, rule-following categories of explanation in terms of choice or decision fail. For example, in common-sense language we speak of people doing things 'by *force* of habit' when it seems inappropriate to talk of conscious, rule-following at all and where 'force' captures the rule-conformity of causality. What is at issue, as we have seen, is the behaviourist's entitlement to generalise such a specific class of common-sense, rule-conforming examples into a principle of significance for the investigation of all human behaviour by analogy with the development of the Newtonian framework in physical science.

It will be well, therefore, if we develop in a little greater detail the problem which Skinner, to his credit, saw that classical behaviourism needed to solve, and which he was to try to solve with his concept of operant conditioning. The problem, as we have seen, was how to explain rule-following in terms of rule-conforming, given the ability to break with previous patterns of stimulus/response conditioning. It is a problem interestingly illuminated in passing in a monograph by Jonathan Bennett (1964) which was chiefly concerned with the analysis of the concept of rationality. Bennett's monograph suggests a way in which the adequacy of the behaviourist framework can be tested in comparisons between insect and human communication systems. We may apply the behaviourist framework to the communication system of bees and find that such a framework exactly fits the data and enables successful prediction of how future communications will proceed. But when we then try similarly to apply such a framework to the raw data of human languages, we run into problems. Predictions are not confirmed as they ought to be if such a framework is viable. Moreover, they do not fit the very category of rule-following behaviour with which, we have already indicated in general terms, behaviourism is likely to experience difficulties. Let us therefore use this specific strategy in order to test the adequacy of the behaviourist model. We can draw out the inadequacy of the model as follows. Having shown how the behaviourist model satisfactorily fits the communication system constituted by actual apian dances, we could then, employing Bennett's method, redescribe such dances to show what they would have to be like to possess features that paralleled those of a human communication system. If we find that, in the light of such a redescription, the behaviourist model ceases to fit the data, then the model will have been shown to be unsatisfactory as a means of handling scientifically the raw data of human language (Bennett, 1964, pp. 8–21).

Let us begin, therefore, with a description of the actual language of the bees, following, as Bennett does, Von Frische's description. Groups of bees are able to dance different varieties of dances and Frische's observations showed that a particular variety of dance was correlated with distance and direction of pollen-bearing plants from the hive. Moreover, a particular dance by one group of bees is correlated with other groups of bees going off in the direction and for the distance specified by the dance in order to find pollen. We might therefore claim that this was directly parallel with a group of human beings from a primitive tribe finding food and coming to tell their fellows that they have found food (= commencement of the dance) and pointing to the direction (= continuing the dance until it forms a determinate pattern) of where it is to be found. Furthermore, both the bees' communication and its human parallel can be explained in terms of classical behaviourism's stimulus/response/association model of explanation. A bee's eye under a microscope is shown to consist of millions of lenses set at various angles of incline, and the sun's rays on the horizon in conjunction with the presence of food might be reasonably claimed to set up a given set of responses corresponding to the distinctive features of individual dances. The activation of a given set of responses will thus be said to be controlled by the angle at which the sun's rays enter the lenses, and the responses will be different for different angles. Since, in the process of evolution, bees that failed to respond to stimuli of the sun's rays associated with the need-reduction of the pollen failed also to prolong the life of the hives upon which their own lives depended, the behaviour of the bees is shown to be explicable wholly in terms of a rule-conforming explanation of behaviour. So, too, it is arguable, the human parallel also holds. Had not, in the past, the giving of instructions (stimulus) about where the food was to be found produced, the behaviour of actually going there (response) and also finding food (reduction of need), the tribe itself would not have lived to tell the tale. Human communications at this level, too, may be argued to be causally determined in the way that the behaviourist requires.

But up to this point our comparison as a means of demonstrating the explanatory power of the behaviourist model does not take us very far. As yet, the description of the bees' language only bears direct comparison with a small part of the various kinds of propositions exhibited by human speech. For example, as yet the only correspondence between what the bees do with their dances and what humans do with their sentences is the ability to affirm a statement. The bees direction and distance indicating dance is like a human statement of direction, and the response of following the direction is like the response, 'Yes, let's go!' Let us now, as Bennett did, proceed to extend the analysis by devising a fable. Such a work of fiction will tell us nothing about the communication of actual bees, but it does tell us what the communication system of bees would have to be like to be directly comparable with a human communication system. If we rest content with the bees' actual language, we should only be able to compare human languages with it and find a delusive similarity because our attention is restricted to the equivalence of the total set of bees' communication with only a sub-set of human communications. If, however, we try to represent in stimulus-response terms bees communications which would parallel the total set of human communications, then we should be able better to compare bees' language with human language. If our attempt succeeded, and in our version of bees' language which provided an exact analogue of human language we were to find that the model of classical behaviourism (at least) could still be satisfactorily applied, then the validity of the model would be unquestionable. If, however, we found that to such an analogue the behaviourist model ceased to apply, as it clearly did in our description of the language of actual bees, then the adequacy of the framework is called into question. Its explanatory power will be considerably reduced, particularly in view of the claim of the strong behaviourist to present a comprehensive explanation which combines human and animal behaviour with that of all living things.

One thing that the bees in Von Frische's actual description are unable to do is to reject statements. In other words, though there is in the dances much that is analogous to human beings saying 'yes' in agreement, there is nothing analogous to human beings saying 'no' in disagreement. In our analogous example of a primitive tribe, a group may, when told where food is on a particular occasion, refuse to go there. This may be for a variety of reasons, like disbelieving their fellows' honesty, not trusting their judgement since food had never been found there in the past, or because they have chosen a new policy for food finding or for food production. With the bees, however, the pattern of dance which communicates the presence of pollen at a certain direction and distance from the hive invariably produces an affirmative or 'yes'-response from their fellows in their moving off in pursuit. To describe bees' dances in fable that were comparable with a human communication system, it is arguable therefore that a group of bees would, on some occasions, have to return to the hive, dance the pattern of dance which sent their fellows off to find pollen at a point to the south-east of the hive, while they themselves set off to the south-west to keep the pollen for themselves. It is arguable, in other words, that they would have to show that they could lie, since this would indicate that their behaviour was rule-following rather than rule-conforming because they would have broken the causal, stimulus-response nexus. They would be doing something analogous to what we did when we showed that we are normally rule-following when we say '$2 + 2 = 4$' by showing that we could, if we wished, break the rule by saying '$2 + 2 = 5$'. Now, I am aware that behaviourists might try to claim that lying can be explained within his framework as really rule-conforming behaviour, since the liar has been reinforced in his behaviour by past success or need-reduction. But this presupposes that lying can go on as the rule. But this cannot be so. The liar's behaviour must be rule-breaking in a context in which he too rule-follows because lying only has any point in a context in which, other things being equal, the truth is normally told. If consistantly and as the rule I lied, then you would simply translate what I said into its opposite and I would end up telling the truth. If I always said that my lecture will begin at nine but I *never* began until eleven, you would simply retranslate '9' as '11', and, for '11', '9' in my language, and it would be no lie that I told but the truth. The problem for my students if I, as a rule-follower rather than a rule-conformer, carry on in this way is that they must always show up at nine in case the lecturer actually comes. But here is the problem of representing lying in the unquestionably behavioural language of the dance. All that will happen when a south-west pattern is followed and unrewarded is that the communication will have been changed but the change not understood. A correct understanding of the pattern would produce an appropriate 'yes' response instead of an inappropriate one. In a regular pattern regularly altered, there could be no real dissimulation.

We see, therefore, that we cannot extend the fable of the bees to produce an unmistakably behavioural account of lying. The framework will not fit the phenomenon since it will not permit everything that is explicable non-behaviourally in terms of rule-following to be explained behaviourally in terms of rule-conforming. My objection, it will be noted, is a logical objection, that is to say, an objection about the coherence of the language in which the theory is stated. But were I not entitled to make such logical objections on any other grounds, I must be entitled on the behaviourist's own grounds since the strong behaviourist's principle of the reduction of the mental to the physical is, as we have seen, logical in the sense of a methodological principle of significance.

There is, however, a further problem for a strict behaviourist to explain within the confines of his framework, and one raised more precisely in terms of Bennett's account, with which I have dealt rather freely in the use of my example of lying (Bennett, 1964, p. 35). This is the problem of accounting in stimulus-response terms of what Bennett called 'tensed denials' (Bennett, 1964, pp. 67–86). Even if, as we shall shortly see Skinner was to suggest, behaviourist frameworks could be modified by the strategem of operant conditioning so as to account for the phenomenon of lying in causal, rule-conforming terms, there is still a problem. This is the problem of representing, in a fable about a bee's analogously human language, the distinction between present-tense and past-tense denials. At first sight, all that we require in behavioural terms to make the distinction between a present and a past tense is a different pattern of dance. But, on closer analysis, we see that we require more, namely, a stimulus in the environment that will elicit the response. Supposing the bees were to discover traces of pollen at point x where there had been pollen yesterday, but there was no longer any pollen today. The pollen traces may be said to activate a pattern of dance which recorded this fact and actually modified some habitually repeated flight to that spot in search of pollen. So far, then, there would remain a stimulus-response explanation of two types of dance giving present and past-tense information on the basis of different kinds of stimulation of the olfactory organs. But what such dances, wedded to particular sensations, cannot do is to express the existence of general classes of past things. They cannot take us from the recording of present pollen, and then the recording of a trace left by the pollen, to the recording of the presence of pollen once in past time even when all traces of pollen have faded. Existence of pollen in the distant past cannot be expressed. The existence of past things *generally* must also be emphasised here. Sometimes, when a hive has been removed from, say, a rotten beam and replaced with a sound one, bees will return and continually fly against the sound beam as if they remembered that their home was there. It would, however, be false to deduce from this that the bees were making a judgement to the effect that, 'Our home is always (generally) to be found there'. As Kant grasped (Bennett, 1966, pp. 87–9), the ability to identify and re-identify the same particular over time is related to the ability to subsume particulars within general classes, to form enduring concepts and so forth. There is a logical gap between a bee being caused by habitual past reinforcement to fly into a beam where once its hive was fixed and a bee making the judgement that, 'My home was once there'. The latter, though not the former, requires the presupposition that, 'My hive is to be found there consistently, and as the rule that hives are places that can be flown into, that since beams cannot and this is a hive and not a beam, I can fly in . . .' The bee, as it repeatedly batters itself against the beam, shows that it has no understanding that rules can be broken, and shows thereby, as we have seen, that its behaviour is rule-conforming and not rule-following. A human being, who has in his language, which he shares with others, a repertoire of past experience, is not dependent on immediate sensory acquaintance. He can break the stimulus-response nexus, not simply in mathematical statements breaking rules for computation, but by making judgements that some other general state of affairs now prevails, that other men (of whom he need have no personal, sensory acquaintance), for example, sometimes remove rotten beams, since houses with rotting beams generally collapse . . . What human languages represent, in other words, is what Peters (pp. 209–10) describes as the 'transcendence of the particular', and this 'transcendence' is to be seen particularly in relation to the ability of human beings to make general judgements in terms of classes of events, particulars and so on. It is also to be seen in the ability of human languages to make judgements about the remote past which presupposes the ability to make general classifications. As we shall see in the next chapter, and what will be one of the major themes of this book, a behaviourist framework, in being unable to cope with these two aspects of human linguistic judgements, reflects two general defects in empiricist philosophy on which behavourism is based. The first will be the general inability of empiricist philosophy to give an account of universal terms that does not regard them as deducible from strings of particulars. The second will be empiricism's failure to give a satisfactory account of historical knowledge which relies on being able to record the remote past and which, as such, falls foul of empiricism's difficulties with the concept of memory. Memory, after all, is fallible, yet what is explicable in terms of stimulus-response, sensory stimulation ought not to be. The act of recall can be as rule-breaking as lying.

So far I have therefore set out in great detail my objections to classical behaviourism by focusing attention on what is by common consent the most difficult set of items to explain within its framework, namely, certain basic features of human languages. I have done so because, if Skinner is to succeed convincingly in reformulating the behaviourist framework as a more adequate instrument of explanation and prediction, this will be the ultimate hurdle that he must be able to surmount. As we shall find, such writers as Chomsky see, in their analysis of a structure of human languages, the critical and conclusive case that not only classical behaviourism but behaviourism in any form cannot answer. In terms of the argument of this chapter, however, let us remind ourselves precisely what the problem has been. It is the problem that explanatory frameworks in science in general share with behaviourism in particular. To be valid, a scientific framework, deducible in the case of classical behaviourism from examples such as tea drinking that we discussed earlier, though based upon some set of common-sense experiences, must be able to take us beyond common-sense experience so as to provide us with a quite general and total explanation of all phenomena within its sphere of interest. Such a general framework validates some common-sense experiences rather than others. Furthermore, hitherto disparate items of common-sense experience are unified into a common and general pattern of explanation. In our example taken from physics, disparate common-sense occurrences such as falling apples, streams flowing downhill or satellites encircling the earth were unified into a comprehensive theory of explanation, namely, Newton's theory of gravity. When, however, we begin to explain such examples as tea-drinking behaviour within the framework of classical conditioning and try to bring other more disparate items of behaviour within this general framework, we begin to run into trouble. We saw, as an extreme example, the inexplicability of certain features of human language behaviour within this framework. There are, however, others which, while being still to some extent amenable, yet cumulatively test the framework to its breaking point. As some of these provided Skinner's starting point for his reformulation of the behaviourist framework, we shall discuss certain of them in order to show how he succeeded in explaining them within his reformulated framework, but ultimately came to grief on the rocks of the (for any kind of behaviourism) intractable problem of language. Here the framework will finally be shown to have failed to achieve a comprehensive explanation unifying the total set of phenomena, and thus the death-knell of strong behaviourism will be sounded.

Some kinds of behaviour, as we saw with tea drinking, might admit of a total and sufficient explanation within the framework of classical behaviourism. But there are other examples in everyday life, though not as conclusive as our analysis of the fable of the bees, which are not so amenable to the classical behaviourist's explanations. There are countless examples in everyday life of people doing things that are out of character, novel, unpredictable or even creative. In technical, behaviourist terminology, sometimes people do not behave in accordance with what their schedules of reinforcement lead us to predict, nor does a stimulus which appears to us to be similar, say, in pitch or appearance to another stimulus eliciting a type of response invariably elicit the same type of response. A classical behaviourist would have, I think, to explain such examples as imperfect conditioning, as he might try to do with lying. But such an explanation would be unsatisfactory for Skinner, since some such creative, unusual behaviours do lead to new solutions to problems which as such are need-reducing. They do not show up as the kind of aimless irritants that an understanding of them as the results of imperfect conditioning would require them to be.

Let us, then, take some specific examples that, while falling short of the absolute objections raised by features of human languages, nevertheless were sufficiently intractable within the framework of classical behaviourism for Skinner to have modified that framework in order to take account of them. Here is a list of four such examples:

(a) An adolescent has been strictly brought up not to drink alcohol but he decides to try his first drink.
(b) A person decides that, though he likes his job, he should nevertheless try something new.
(c) I decide to try drinking Bovril when I am cold instead of my usual tea.
(d) Galileo decides to abandon the Ptolemaic system of geometry.

A classical behaviourist might try to explain (a) in terms of alcohol advertisements where the conditioned response of drinking lager is made to the conditioned stimulus of a cool, blonde drink associated with the unconditioned stimulus of a cool, blonde lady. He might then go on to explain (b) in terms of the aversion-stimulus of a routine, although his explanation becomes weaker here because it involves arbitrarily ruling out of court, in the interests of preserving the validity of the framework, the person's protest that he *was* happy in his job. ('He simply could not have been! He must have been pretending...'). It might be possible for (c) to be explained in terms of stimulus generalisation since both tea and Bovril are steaming hot, only someone had to discover the Bovril in the first place and for him it was not just the fact that liquid (like tar or oil) is hot that one drinks it. It is therefore the problem of how to explain the discovery in classical, stimulus-response terms. But when one then passes from these examples, finding one's framework shaking all the more uncertainly as one goes, to (d), one finally finds oneself in classical behaviourism's impasse.

The problem with (d) is as follows. Although the Ptolemaic system of astronomy appears grotesque to us today, in its own time it lead to the reduction of such needs as the need to calculate the months of the calendar and the need to be able to steer one's ship by the stars. In fact this was the very case made by Urban VIII and Bellarmine to Galileo in their attempts to get him to abandon his new system of geometry, or at least to teach it in Latin, unread by the masses, as a purely mathematical speculation. The existing schedule of reinforcement leading to need-reduction was perfectly adequate to secure the learning of the Ptolemaic system. Yet Galileo broke out of his stimulus-response nexus of reinforcement to propose a new and completely different system of astronomy. The formulation of a new conceptual framework for astronomy shares much with our example of the ability of human languages to make general judgements in contrast with the 'language of the bees'. Old patterns of reasoning are broken with, some rules (such as the symmetry of movement of the heavenly spheres) are broken, all of which we saw to be characteristic of rule-following as opposed to rule-conforming behaviour and to that independence of immediate sensory inputs that is the transcendence of the particular. Furthermore, we have in our Galilean example an example of what, as we shall see later, Kuhn described as a 'paradigm revolution' in science. Within a classically behaviourist framework, we would have to predict the development of science as a progressive and evolutionary movement from the caves to the stars. One set of positively reinforced responses to environmental stimuli would give rise to another; the process of stimulus generalisation, stimulus discrimination and so on would all combine to produce a set of responses of increasing complexity and effectiveness to the environment. But, according to Kuhn, the history of science does not progress in this way but rather by a series of revolutionary breaks with classical scientific traditions. Kuhn's paradigms are therefore part of those groups of human linguistic phenomenon that prove powerful counter-examples with which the framework of classical behaviourism is unable to cope (Kuhn, 1970).

We have therefore exemplified in great detail how classical behaviourism, while being able to cope with some phenomena, found others increasingly difficult until it arrived at those phenomena in the area of general, tensed judgements in human languages that were completely intractable. Skinner's originality lies in his reformulation of the classical behaviourist model in an attempt to enable the model to cope with the indispensability of concepts like freedom, choice and intention in human behaviour generally, and in language in particular, as what as we have seen to be regarded by his opponents as the conclusive counter-example. It is to the details of this framework, characterised by the name of 'operant conditioning', already briefly sketched at the beginning of this section, to which we now must turn.

As we saw at the beginning of this section, Skinner dispensed with the reliance of classical behaviourism on a general cause of motion, namely, environmental stimuli producing behavioural responses from an otherwise passive organism. Skinner placed the movement of the organism and the movement of the environment on an equal footing. Sometimes behaviour is the result of a response associated with need-reduction to an environmental stimulus, but equally, sometimes behaviour is also the result of the organism's stimulation of the environment to respond – a stimulation that tends to be repeated when the response is associated with the reduction of need. The organism's activity was not therefore wholly and passively determined by the environment, since the organism itself could provide the stimuli which elicited environmental responses. The organism, as part of the environment, both operated on (hence 'operant') and interacted with the environment. By such a strategy, Skinner was convinced that he could provide classical behaviourism with a new way of solving the problem of retranslating common-sense categories such as 'freedom', 'choice' and 'intention' in terms of the causal, stimulus/response/associationist categories of the behaviourist's explanatory model. Skinner therefore proposed the new concept of 'operant' conditioning which would supplement that of 'classical' conditioning. Classical conditioning could still be left to explain some phenomena, but need not be stretched any longer to explain examples of creative, novel or unpredictable behaviour such as that exemplified above in the examples (a), (b), (c) and (d). Operant conditioning explains such examples in terms of the organism itself initiating a stimulus which elicits an environmental response, just as some of the random movements of a baby, its kicks, cries, screams, are to be understood, not as responses to light or noise, but as stimuli which lead to the need-reducing responses of parental attention, concern and care. A stimulus that has been met with a need-reducing response will tend to be repeated, whereas one that has not will tend not to be repeated; and novel movements sufficiently repeated so as to become part of a significant change in the direction of the history of the organism are thus to be explained in a manner faithful to behaviourism's original perspective. As Skinner says, contrasting classical with operant conditioning:

> Pavlov himself called all events which strengthened behaviour 'reinforcement' and all resultant changes 'conditioning'. In the Pavlovian experiment, however, a reinforcer is paired with a

stimulus; whereas in operant behavior it is contingent upon a *response*. (Skinner, 1953, p. 65)

As operant conditioning therefore appears at first sight to offer a promising, behaviourist explanation of unusual, creative behaviour which seems to warrant such descriptions as 'he chose', 'he decided', 'he wanted', let us specifically examine in the light of this new concept our problem: counter-examples for classical behaviourism. In example (a), we can explain the behaviour of the youth from a non-alcoholic home background in taking his first drink in terms of a general tendency of organisms not simply to respond to environmental stimuli but themselves to provide the stimuli that elicit environmental responses. Some such stimuli are never repeated because the one-off environmental response is not need-reducing. Such stimuli, never repeated, do not become part of the remembered history of the organism. The youth's asking for a glass of alcohol constitutes a stimulation of the environment, the provision of the alcohol an environmental response, and the stimulus was repeated perhaps because the youth found it pleasant or because it was pleasant to have now been accepted by his peer group. Likewise with example (b). The man who decides to change his job though he likes his present one has not really decided or chosen anything. While classical behaviourism could not plausibly dispel this illusion of free will successfully, Skinner's 'operant' behaviourism, it is contended, can. The 'choice' is simply a stimulus operating upon the environment that leads to a need-reducing response (he was offered a new job) and so became a significant and remembered part of the overall behavioural pattern that constituted the man's history. We need, moreover, to look no further for an explanation of the 'choice' of hot Bovril to hot tea in example (c). Another random stimulus from the organism has been positively reinforced and so will tend to be repeated. Finally, with Galileo's break with the Ptolemaic system (d), all that Galileo has arguably done is to have found a set of random stimuli positively reinforced so that they get repeated as a pattern. His proposal for a new astronomy produces the need-reduction of a man who finds certain problems solved that were intractable within a Ptolemaic system, and clearly 'solutions' and 'need-reductions' are to be regarded as the same sorts of things. If, then, operant behaviourism solves within a purely behaviourist framework examples of type (d), it cannot be far from solving too, within such an explanatory framework, problems with the linguistic phenomena with which we argued such examples to be connected. Our rule-breaking example of lying, for example – implying rule-rollowing as opposed to rule-conformance – might be explained in terms of a stimulus that appeared to break with previous conditioning only because organisms characteristically make such moves, and when their consequences are need-reducing, they tend to get repeated. That lying cannot be universalised might then be explained purely as a function of the social environment that could not reinforce all lying, and the more it reinforces some lying, the less healthy it is. At this point, then, it might appear as if operant behaviourism has succeeded in explaining all cases of rule-following in terms of rule-conformance.

It will be my contention that this conclusion is unwarranted and that the rule-following/conformance distinction must stand. But to make my case I want first to analyse more carefully Skinner's concept of operant conditioning, basing my analysis on his famous pigeon experiments and the conclusions that he drew. Pigeons, when strutting around in cages, tend to bob their heads up and down indiscriminately within a given range of such movements. What Skinner wished to do was to explore experimentally his notion of operant conditioning by seeing whether the environment could reinforce some of these stimulus movements rather than others, with a resultant change in the way in which the pigeon bobbed its head as it walked. We may observe, therefore, an example of operant conditioning,

> by sighting across the pigeon's head a scale pinned on the far wall of the box. We first study the height at which the head is normally held and select some line of the scale which is reached only infrequently. Keeping our eye on the scale we then begin to open the food tray very quickly whenever the head rises above the line . . . In a minute or two the bird's posture has changed so that the top of the head seldom falls below the line which we first chose. (Skinner, 1953, p. 64)

Thus the process in which the pigeon's own operating on the environment produces a self-initiated behaviour change is known as operant conditioning. The behaviour of the pigeon looks like what is meant by a 'choice' or an 'intention' to raise its head higher in order to get at the food. It appears as such to be self-initiated and independent of environmental stimulus or cause, since it cannot be a reinforced response to some previous environmental stimulus. However, such explanatory concepts as 'chosen', 'designed' or 'intended' only look plausible if we ignore other quite random stimuli (initial quite random bobbings of the pigeon's head) which, because they are not subsequently reinforced, do not emerge as part of the final pattern of behaviour. Once we include these 'purposeless' movements into our account, as strict, scientific observation must, then they are seen to be of the same type as those movements in the final pattern which are considered to merit the description 'chosen', 'designed' or 'intended'. All the movements, whether designated 'purposeful' or 'purposeless', are contingent upon reinforcement. In the case of the former this contingency was satisfied, but in the case of the latter it was not.

There is, however, an important distinction to be drawn between the operant conditioning exemplified in Skinner's pigeon experiments and the classical conditioning exemplified by Pavlov's dogs, despite the similarities over contingency upon reinforcement. With Pavlov's dogs, the quantities of saliva were *causally determined* by the ringing of the bells and flashing of the lights combined with such factors as the temporal recency of reinforcement. The explanation regards the stimulus as a particular cause (bells, lights) which produces as its event a particular response, namely, salivating. With Skinner's pigeons, on the other hand, it is a *class* of occurrences that constitutes the stimulus and not any one particular occurrence. The pigeon's head still continues to bob at a variety of heights after operant reinforcement and does not fix on any one particular height. It is, rather, the *range* of a *class* of particular bobs that has been raised to a higher point on the scale of measurement so that Skinner can say that 'the top of the head' not invariably but 'seldom falls below the line which we first chose'. Classical conditioning therefore deals with particular causes of particular events, while operant conditioning deals with the production of recurrent *classes* of events. Both, however, Skinner (questionably as we shall see) regards as constituting a single and unified framework of behavioural explanation. Together they exhaust all possible categories of explanation. As Skinner says:

> We note ... that these two cases [of operant and classical conditioning] exhaust the possibilities: an organism is conditioned when a reinforcer (1) accompanies another stimulus or (2) follows upon the organism's own behavior. Any event which does neither has no effect in changing a probability of response. (Skinner, 1953, p. 65)

We are now, I think, in a position to assess whether operant behaviourism is able to surmount those hurdles at which its predecessor in the purely classical form was seen to have faltered, and to succeed in producing a unified and comprehensive explanation of human behaviour. We saw that it must succeed in satisfactorily closing the logical gap between rule-following and rule-conforming behaviour, and in so doing to deal with the related problem presented by the 'transcendence of the particular', that apparent ability that humans have of breaking stimulus-response bonds. Let me summarise here the substance of my argument which will follow. Instead of having closed the logical gap between rule-following and rule-conforming by means of the concept of operant conditioning, Skinner has simply re-expressed this distinction in a different form. The logical distinction between rule-following and rule-conforming is replaced by a distinction between a description in terms of cause and a description in terms of statistical tendencies or probabilities, and between the two parts of this re-expressed distinction there remains an identical logical gap. Causal explanations, as we have seen, are reserved for phenomena explicable within the framework of classical conditioning, while statistical or probabilistic descriptions are reserved for those explicable in terms of operant conditioning. Yet, if there still remains a logical gap of a kind that I will demonstrate between the two types of conditioning, Skinner cannot have succeeded in defending behaviourism by anything more than a sleight of hand. I will be arguing further that Skinner has only managed to persuade himself that he has closed the gap between rule-following and rule-conforming because he has failed to grasp just how radical the shift is between causal and probabilistic explanations in contemporary physical as well as biological sciences. The probabilistic model does not represent a logical extension from the causal model with suitable clarifications, as Skinner appears to think from the misleading way that he represents them.

Skinner began with the intention of producing an explanation of human behaviour wholly in causal terms. That it cannot be doubted that Skinner believed causal explanation to be the test for the virility of any science is demonstrated by the following quotation:

> Science . . . is a search for . . . lawful relations among the events in nature . . . By predicting the occurrence of an event we are able to prepare for it. By arranging conditions in ways specified by the laws of a system, we not only predict, we control: we 'cause' an event to occur or assume certain characteristics. (Skinner, 1953, p. 13)

Furthermore, there can be no doubt that such 'prediction', based upon the charting of particular causes of particular events, must lead to the complete determinism of the behaviour of the individual. Freud, in his approach to psychology, had built into his explanations reference to albeit unconscious intentions and desires, but with the progress of a 'proper' scientific study of psychology such references could and ought to be removed. As Skinner says of Freudian psychology:

This escape route is slowly closed as new evidences of the predictability of human behaviour are discovered. Personal exemption from *a complete determinism* is revoked as a scientific analysis progresses, particularly in accounting for the behaviour of the individual. (Skinner, 1971, p. 26; my italics)

Here Skinner represents an attitude towards the explanation of organic behaviour identical with that which, as we shall see in Chapter 3, was the attitude of classical physics to the behaviour of inorganic matter.

Regarding his description and definitions of operant conditioning, however, Skinner appears to reject the quest for 'complete determinism' which, in any interpretation, would be the very 'all-or-nothing' venture that he denies in the following passage that he is concerned with:

If a given sample of behavior existed in only two states, in one of which it always occurred and in the other never, we should be almost helpless in following a program of functional analysis. An all-or-none subject matter lends itself only to primitive forms of description. It is a great advantage to suppose instead that the *probability* that a response will occur ranges continuously between these all-or-nothing extremes. We can then deal with variables which, like the eliciting stimulus, *do not 'cause a given bit of behavior to occur'* but simply make the occurrence more *probable*. (Skinner, 1953, p. 62; my italics)

Indeed, operant conditioning cannot be understood in terms of reinforcement causing an invariant stimulus which makes the response that it elicits also invariant. Classical conditioning can be so understood because the *response* of the organism which comes *after* the stimulus is what is reinforced. But, in operant conditioning, the initial stimulus that comes from the organism does not occur because of past reward. Yet how can a stimulus in operant conditioning be possibly described as determined when the reinforcement is *subsequent* and not prior to it? In Skinner's own words:

it is not correct to say that operant reinforcement 'strengthens the response which precedes it'. The response has already occurred and cannot be changed. What is changed is the future probability of responses in the same *class*. It is the operant as a class of behavior rather than the response as a particular instance, which is conditioned. (Skinner, 1953, p. 87)

Here Skinner is seeking, then, an explanation no longer in terms of causal determinism but in terms of *'probability* of responses' in terms of tendencies exhibited by a 'class of behavior'. As Skinner said when he originally defined operant behaviour:

> A response which has already occurred cannot, of course, be predicted or controlled. We can only predict that *similar* responses will occur in future. The unit of predictive science is, therefore, not a response but a class of responses. The word 'operant' will be used to describe this class. (Skinner, 1953, p. 65)

Skinner has therefore introduced the notion of operant conditioning (based upon a probablistic model) as a complement to classical conditioning (based upon a causal one). In doing so, however, he has failed to grasp just how radical a reversal of the concept of empirical explanation and prediction is constituted by the substitution of a probablistic for a causal model. As we shall see in Chapter 3, this was also not always clearly grasped by early evolutionary theorists, with whom Skinner on this point will be seen to express agreement. If we go for a probablistic model which both explains and predicts in terms of classes of events, we shall have revoked the notion of 'complete determinism' on which Skinner's case rests.

Let us take two examples which exemplify the two types of prediction:

(*a*) If I fire a bullet into your heart, you will die (causal prediction).
(*b*) If I shake the dice 1,000 times, 'six' is likely to come up more than ten times.

At first sight it might appear that these statements are of an identical logical type on the grounds that both make predictions of future events. Furthermore, both statements (*a*) and (*b*) appear at first sight to be about causing something to happen, even though statement (*a*) predicts a series of particular events in a certain combination, whereas statement (*b*) predicts a class of events (a class in which the number six occurs more than ten times). But closer examination will show both these appearances to be wrong.

The difference between type (a) and type (b) statements is as follows. Given the fulfilment of the conditions in (*a*), given than I have a loaded gun, I pull the trigger and the bullet hits your heart, then the event that is your death must follow from a combination of these individual causes. The basis of the prediction is that, on grounds of past experience, one or a particular series of causes must necessarily produce a certain event. If this outcome is uncertain, it is because some cause is missing. There may be a series of causes that are necessary but no one of which is sufficient, or a series of causes that are sufficient but no one of which is necessary (Mackie, 1974). In the absence of both necessary and sufficient conditions, the outcome in question will cease to be invariable and certain and becomes merely probable or possible. Type (a) statements might therefore include statements of probability or possibility, but such statements would be classifiable as such because we can envisage a scale by which such statements are measured. The scale for type (a) type statements is one in which there is certainty at one axis and uncertainty or doubt at the other, while each point in between is marked by varying degrees of probability or possibility. While, however, type (*a*) probability or possibility statements are merely those lacking vital necessary or sufficient conditions by which, once they are observed and incorporated into the statement, the statement will be made certain, the probability or possibility of type (*b*) statements is of a radically different kind. There is no axis of certainty/doubt between which their probability can be measured since they can only ever be probable, however much to a very high degree their probability might reach. With type (*b*) statements, there is no certainty to which degrees of probability can finally attain.

At first sight, however, it might appear as if the more you shake the dice the more certain that you make it that the number 'six' will come up until finally all uncertainty is excluded. But a moment's reflection will show that this is not the case. If I say, for example, that there is a one-in-six probability of the side with 'six' on it coming up, do I mean that, if I throw the dice six times, on one of the six throws it will invariably show up 'six'? This would be false, and it would be false precisely because I would be unwarrantedly assimilating predictions in terms of statistical probability with predictions in terms of causes. On however many particular occasions one shakes the dice, there is always the possibility that 'six' will never come up, however unlikely that may be. It is the fact of this principle having been grasped at the level of common sense that keeps people purchasing premium bonds and engaging in other speculative games of chance despite the probabilistic odds against them. There remains, therefore, a logical gap between measures of particular events in terms of their causes which have certainty and doubt at their axes, and measures of statistical classes of events in terms of tendencies that have no such axes. Skinner is quite wrong to talk as if these two distinct measures could be synthesised so as to unify classical and operant conditioning into a unified theory, as he does when he says:

The terms 'cause' and 'effect' are no longer widely used in science.

They ... mean more than scientists want to say. The terms which replace them, however, *refer to the same factual core.* (Skinner, 1953, p. 23; my italics)

Or:

something essential to scientific practice is missing in almost all current discussions of human behaviour. It has to do with our treatment of the causes of behaviour. (The term 'cause' is no longer common in sophisticated scientific writing *but it will serve well enough here.*) (Skinner, 1971, p. 13; my italics)

He has simply closed the logical gap between causal and probablistic explanations by sleight of hand.

We shall have to look more closely in Chapter 3 at the implications for the philosophy of science of the survival of the logical gap between rule-conformance and rule-following in the form of the logical gap between causal and probablistic models of explanation. We shall also see there how these implications will affect not only our approach to the philosophy of science, of which Skinner's 'science' of human behaviour will be shown to constitute a highly confused part, but also our general view of the nature of argument and of definition in any kind of human language. Let us for the moment briefly demonstrate our conclusion that Skinner's description of operant conditioning represents simply a restatement masquerading as a solution in terms of statistical probability of the problem of rule-following behaviour, including the problem of the concepts of 'choice', 'decision', 'intention', the 'transcendence of the particular' and so forth. We shall carry out our demonstration with particular reference to the examples with which we have argued his revised behaviourism must cope, concentrating particularly upon his failure to close the causal/ probablistic, rule-conforming/rule-following logical gaps, neither of which, as we have seen, admit of closure.

Our first example, that of lying, can be redescribed in the categories of statistical probability, as required by the concept of operant conditioning. The problem with lying, it will be remembered, was that lying cannot take place as the rule, otherwise it will either be ineffective or become transmuted into a peculiar kind of truth-telling. Yet classical conditioning required lying to be of an invariant, rule-conforming kind. Operant conditioning, which deals, as we have shown, with probabilities, can now be used to redescribe the phenomenon of lying. People as a class generally tell the truth, just as generally, when a dice is thrown a hundred times, 'six' will come up at least five times. But as we are dealing with statistical probabilities, there can always be particular exceptions. Individuals can as the exception to their own general patterns of behaviour as well as that of their social group tell lies, just as sometimes, albeit very infrequently, one can throw the dice a hundred times and 'six' come up less than five times and, on very rare occasions, even not at all. Particulars, whether they be instances of lying or instances of 'six' coming up, can, as it were, drop in and drop out of general classes while the general pattern of behaviour exhibited by their class remains the same. But all that Skinner has succeeded in doing with this redescription masquerading as an explanation is to show how the 'complete determination' of rule-conformance is not essential to an account of human behaviour, despite the fact that, as we have shown, the concept of operant conditioning was intended to demonstrate that it *was* essential.

Our further examples with which Skinner's unified models had to cope were, it will be remembered, concerned with the general phenomenon of the 'transcendence of the particular' of which we have seen lying to be one particular example. This we saw to be the ability to break particular stimulus-response bonds and to make general judgements which were not tied to immediate sensory perceptions. Once, however, we concede that probablistic as opposed to causal models of explanations can properly be applied to human behaviour, then the view that particular stimuli generate by a strictly causal process certain responses need not apply. Any breaking of a stimulus-response bond which we have argued to be the criterion of rule-following as opposed to rule-conforming, can be explained, albeit partially, in terms of an aberration from a general class that represents a statistical tendency. But here we must object to Skinner that, in that case, it is not the aberration of the particular that he has explained, but that he has rather ruled it out as of no importance because the focus of his attention is on the behaviour of classes. But in claiming that he needs to explain 'intention', 'choice', 'decision' and so forth, it is precisely *individual* instances of behaviour that he has claimed to be able to explain. In other words, once again we see that Skinner cannot admit that certain kinds of behaviour are not caused since this would leave open the logical gap between rule-following and rule-conforming that he is determined to close, even at the expense, as we have seen, of muddling distinct categories of empirical explanation and prediction, namely, causal and probablistic categories. He has failed to close that gap and once again only succeeded in re-expressing it in different terms.

There is, moreover, a further reason why Skinner's solution to the problem of general judgements in terms of general classes which transcend particular sensory experiences is unsound. Let us recall what the problem was. The problem was that, whereas bees could be said to dance a dance in the presence of pollen traces which was different from their dance in the presence of pollen, such a dance could not be logically equivalent to the general judgement that 'there used to be pollen there'. This is because such a human judgement presupposes the ability to unite a whole series of particulars into a single, general class that is independent of the presence or absence of any one particular item. Even the pollen trace may have faded, and yet it is still possible for human beings to make the judgement that at a number of previous times, as part of the same temporal series, there was pollen there, and for this judgement to be verified. Skinner's 'operant' solution is presumably, then, that this phenomenon is explicable in terms of general classes of events in which individual particulars may or may not be included. The 'transcendence of the particular', therefore, Skinner might argue, simply records the way in which general classes (that to which the concept of 'operant behaviour' refers) can be understood apart from any one particular that is subsumed within them. General classes, moreover, cannot, as we shall demonstrate in greater detail in the next chapter, be defined in terms of some exhaustive string of particulars. But Skinner's problem now is this. The behaviourist psychologist, in order to observe the phenomenon of operant conditioning, must therefore possess the very ability that he is claiming that the concept explains, namely, the ability to make judgements in terms of classes of particulars without requiring the presence of any one particular within that class. But if human behaviour is to be defined in terms of operant conditioning, then, by definition, it must be described in terms of classes which in turn by definition transcend their particulars. In other words, the method of explanation (explicans), namely, operant conditioning, and what is to be explained (explicandum), namely, judgements in terms of general classes, are one and the same thing. When this happens, the so-called 'explanation' is a logical fallacy. But as our reference to the logic of classes and judgements of probability raises far greater questions about the logic of inquiry in general and the nature of classification, we must now turn to the broader context of argument, definition and related matters in our next chapter, and then to scientific method, in which Skinner's misunderstanding occurs, in Chapter 3.

Chapter 2

Behaviourism and the Philosophy of Language

We have frequently referred to behaviourism as being derivable from an empiricist view of the philosophy of science. Moreover, as we shall be showing in this chapter and the next, general problems of language in philosophy of language and their proposed solution are similar formally to specific problems and their proposed solution in the philosophy of science. Such a formal similarity is, after all, hardly surprising, since both philosophy of language and philosophy of science are concerned with the relation between language and the world, whether it be the relation of ordinary language or the technical language of scientific description and explanation. We therefore propose in this chapter to examine both the historical antecedents of behaviourism in classical empiricism so as to expose fundamental and, we shall argue, erroneous assumptions that are formally similar and held jointly with contemporary behaviourism. We shall thus show that Skinner's problems with language are reflections of general problems with empiricist theories of meaning and truth. In our next chapter, we shall look specifically at Skinner's philosophy of science, to show how errors about language show up specifically in his conception of psychology as a science, in which he fails to break loose from a Newtonian model. We thus turn for now to general problems in the philosophy of language raised by Skinnerian behaviourism and its antecedents, pursuing in greater detail the themes of Chapter 1.

It is particularly important to be clear about the empiricist foundations of behaviourism, particularly in view of the behaviourist claim to have solved the fundamental defects in classical empiricism. Moreover, it will also be important for us to have studied Skinner in this way in view of the way in which the philosophical aspects of Chomsky's work will prefigure in our later argument (Chapter 8), developed as those aspects were in self-conscious opposition to Skinner. We shall see that Chomsky avows a rationalist epistemology in conscious opposition to Skinner, and it is perhaps the most fundamental task of this book to try to show ways in which the rationalism represented by Chomsky can be regarded as complementary to the sort of 'intersubjectivism' (see Chapter 7) represented by the later Wittgenstein. We shall argue that both Hirst and Hamlyn have failed to grasp this complementary character (Hirst, 1974a; Hamlyn, 1978). We shall content ourselves here with a brief description of the contrast between rationalism and empiricism as an introduction to what is our immediate objective at this point, namely, a discussion of the background to Skinner's empiricist assumptions.

It is often claimed that the problem of knowledge raises two different types of question, namely: (a) how do we come to acquire knowledge of what is true? And (b) how do we confirm that what is thus acquired is true? (a) is a question about the origins of ideas, behaviours, practices, whereas (b) is a question about their justification. Both empiricists and rationalists treated answers to (a) as though they were answers to (b) or, to put matters more favourably to their case, they grasped that type (b) questions were really type (a) questions. Whether they were right to treat the two as equivalent will not detain us now, since the intersubjective view of truth, which argues that they were not, will be our concern in Chapter 8. It will, however, be of importance for us to observe in what follows that behaviourism is an attempt to answer both types of question, both psychological (a) and logical (b). Skinner, we shall see, is primarily concerned with behaviourism as an answer to the psychological problems raised by the empiricists, whereas Quine is concerned with behaviourism as an answer to their logical problems. Traditionally, then, however warrantedly or otherwise, such empiricist writers as Locke (1975) or Hume (1969) took their stand regarding the justification of truth claims on a particular thesis about the origins of ideas against the counter-thesis about such origins of rationalists such as Descartes (1911) and Leibniz (1968) (Stich, 1975, pp. 37–67). Let us therefore look first at classical empiricism as an account of the origins and justification of claims in language.

2.1 LOCKE, UNIVERSALS AND INNATE IDEAS

'Empiricism' therefore describes an epistemology or argument about the nature of knowledge which holds that all knowledge originates in experience *and* that experience is to be defined in terms of sense-perception. How have men built up an ordered, coherent picture of the world into which they incorporate some things because they are true but from which they exclude others because they are false? The empiricists' reply was that nature itself is orderly and consisted of stable and enduring objects changing in accordance with fixed laws and principles. The way, therefore, that men acquire a mind that thinks orderly and logically is by the order of nature, the law-like behaviour of its objects and their relations and so on, becoming impressed upon the mind through its sense-organs. The mind is a *tabula rasa*, a blank sheet upon which nature writes its objective account of how the world is.

The rationalist retort was that this was a false view of how knowledge was acquired. It was a mistake to describe the problem in this way. There was no logical and law-like order of nature 'out there'. The child is not confronted by a natural order of things external to himself and which he passively receives, but rather by a booming, buzzing chaos. On to this chaos the mind actively imposes order and law-like relations in accordance with its own, innate principles. The chaos which confronted us as children would have remained as such unintelligible had not our minds actively imposed order upon it, as when, argued the rationalist, we insisted that certain things be regarded as causes and others as effects of causes (events). Such principles, which were, according to Descartes and Leibniz at least, innate, were therefore principles like, 'Every event has a cause', and 'Two objects cannot exist together in the same space and at the same time' (Cooper, 1972). These, the rationalists asserted against the empiricists, could not have been learned from experience since they are not immediately derivable from experience. Yet they appear to be indispensible for any organisation of experience.

There are, moreover, many examples of events which appear to have no cause. Let us take as an example a sub-fertile male whose sperm count is shown on examination of a specimen to be low. X-ray examination reveals no abnormalities in the genital organs. A surgeon might then perform a biopsy and discover that his hormone count is in perfect balance. Here, it might be argued, is an example of an event without a cause. But the surgeon consciously rejects such a solution and insists that, even though we do not yet know the cause, there must be *some* cause. Perhaps biochemical techniques of analysis are not yet sophisticated enough, so that what shows up as one healthy hormone is in fact three different types, only two of which are sound. He, to use the idiom of our previous discussion, transcends particular and immediate experience and insists against what appears to be no cause that there must be some cause. We may say that, for the rationalist, without prejudice to our discussion in the next section of problems with the causal principle, if a scientist were to accept for one moment that there might be an event which had no cause, then at least part of experience would become chaotic and therefore unintelligible. There could be no general and unified framework of scientific explanation such as we argued at the beginning of this chapter that it was the task of the scientist to construct. Without the causal principle, the rationalists contended, it would not be an alternative world that came into existence, but, if no world at all, at least an only partially intelligible world that was otherwise chaotic. Yet the problem for empiricism, as the rationalists saw it, was that, having only as yet discovered a few causes of a few events, how can we assume on the basis of experience that not just some but *every* event has a cause? Because we could not have derived the principle from experience, the rationalist contentiously claims it must therefore be innate.

The way in which the empiricists countered arguments for the innate character of the causal principle or the spatio-temporal framework was to treat them as generated by the problem of general terms or universals. After all, 'Every event has a cause', and, 'All objects exist in a general relation to space and time', were general statements referring to the total class of all objects throughout the universe (Staniland, 1972). What the empiricist sought to do, therefore, was to show that universals had no real existence, either as objects, as Plato had thought, or as predetermined, innate categories of thinking, as Descartes and Leibniz had thought (Brent, 1978, pp. 14–48). Rather were universal or general terms a fiction of language which made reference to particular things more easily manageable for certain purposes. 'Cause', 'space' or 'time' was therefore to be placed in the same category as 'table' or 'white', which are general terms because there is more than one (particular) table or (particular) white thing in the world. How, therefore, did these convenient linguistic fictions that were general terms get produced in a world which consisted only of particular things? Locke's answer was that such words are symbols or 'sensible marks' (Locke, 1975, p. 159) of ideas in men's minds. They are produced when the human mind *abstracts* features of sense-impressions (one sense of 'idea' in Locke). Tables come in all sorts of shapes, sizes and colours. Many white objects exhibit degrees of whiteness. The cause of a match burning is different from that of a bridge collapsing. The space in which I stand is different from that in which you stand. The time for breakfast is different from the time for lunch. General classes of such things were produced by abstraction and this makes them no more than general ideas in the minds of men that use them (Locke, 1975, p. 145).

Locke's empiricist account of general terms is, however, flawed in a fashion similar, as we shall see, to the behaviourist account which sought to succeed it. There is, first, the problem of how particulars come to be identified as instances of universals on Locke's account. Does Locke mean that we identify one particular with others because they are the same? He cannot mean *that*, since particulars are individual things and words that refer to them are like names that individuate individuals. They refer to one particular thing, just as 'Plato' refers to one particular man. As Leibniz pointed out, indiscernables are identical so that no two particulars could be identical and logically be *two* (and not one) particular. This is why particulars occur as subjects of subject/predicate sentences and why, if there is any doubt about whether reference is being made to a particular or to a general term that can also occupy such a position, a prefix such as 'this' is used to indicate the former. For example, 'table' stands for a universal when one says:

1 This tree-stump is a table.

It stands, however, for a particular when one says:

2 This table is red.

But both,

1A This tree-stump is this table; and
2A This table is this red,

would be not only badly formed sentences, but, if they mean anything at all, would not mean what their counterparts in 1 and 2 mean. 1A is certainly nonsense and breaks the logical principle of non-contradiction, and 'this red' in 2A, if it means anything at all, is an ellipsis for 'this kind of red' and as such refers to a universal, a sub-class of red things, and is not a particular. When I say therefore:

3 The fire caused the bridge to burn; and then
4 The water caused the sugar to melt,

I cannot mean either that 'cause' as a universal term is identical with a collection of *identical* particular causes since, similarly, the causes are not identical. By trying to explain at least some of the principles which the rationalists regarded as innate as part of the problem of how language arrives at general terms in a world that consists only of particular objects, Locke is thereby running into problems which are in need of resolution.

Locke's later reflections (Locke, 1975, pp. 535–6) undoubtedly changed the meaningless 'universals from *identical* particulars' to the possibly meaningful 'universals from *similar* particulars'. Particular causes, particular reds, particular tables and so forth could, as subjects, be subsumed under general predicates, not because they were identical ('the same'), but because they were similar. But if he does this he runs into at least two problems. First, as Russell (1912, pp. 1–24) pointed out, there must be on this account at least one real universal existing in the world and not simply in language. The relationship of 'resemblance' itself, which holds between particulars, could not itself be a particular. As such the 'resemblance' would not be a creation of the mind's abstracting or associating particular things, but it would have to be what was detected as relating particular objects. Different causes, different reds, different tables and so on would be bound together into general classes by identical *general* properties of resemblance, different in kind though that resemblance might be for different groups. It would be the detection of such different *kinds* of resemblance and not different *particular* resemblances that constituted general classes. With the requirement that there be one real universal, namely, resemblance, the basis of Locke's theory is undermined since an explanation of universals in terms of abstraction requires, as its starting-point, that there exist only particulars in the world.

Adequately defining 'resemblance' as combining particulars into a general class is a problem, too, at least for classical behaviourism. As we saw, what united particular responses into a general pattern of response in stimulus generalisation was similarity in stimuli substituted for the original stimulus in a temporal series constructed in accordance with degrees of similarity. Yet, when one looks at actual classes of response, particulars which exemplify one class on one occasion are not identical with particulars which exemplify the class on another. This is why the alleged solution of 'operant conditioning' relies on the notion of statistical probability. Yet, on such a view, we have given grounds and will give further grounds in our next chapter as to why the enterprise of explaining how general terms are formed simply by stringing together determinate particulars is grossly misconceived. Yet such an enterprise represents behaviourism's essential *raison d'être*, with the result that such an admission must critically undermine their whole theory in a way of which behaviourists seem generally unaware.

There is a second objection to Locke's abstractionism, and this is that, since we can never receive the general idea of something from particular things, what particular features we pick out to form universal ideas must be arbitrary. As Staniland says:

One might easily imagine Locke to be saying that when we perceive a particular man, for example, we receive the idea of man along with a bundle of others, which we then discard to get the idea of man in its pure form. And this is not what he wants to say for according to his theory we never receive the idea of man as such from experience at all. (1972, p. 35)

Moreover, we might add that not only does his account require that 'we never receive the idea of man *as such* from experience', but that we construct the idea of man from certain other experiences, experiences of particular things, in conformance with some general law. Otherwise, all general terms might be arbitrary constructions, and this they cannot be, given Locke's assumption that his account explains how men build up an orderly and coherent picture of the world that is veridicial. To what extent Locke here requires a rule-conforming, causal explanation of human thinking in a way that mirrors Skinner's requirement that the rule-conforming/rule-following logical gap be closed, is something that we shall deal with in a moment when we come to consider his account of primary and secondary qualities.

It does not, of course, follow that the rationalists' case for a theory of innate ideas is established simply because Locke ran into problems with an account of how, without recourse to such a theory, universal terms like cause, space or time could be explained in terms of particular instances. Certainly, from our exposition of Locke's problem, we can see that he has at least established that the problem of such allegedly innate principles are part of the general problem of universals. To have established this is of importance for the discussion, since certainly Descartes and Leibniz did not want to subscribe to the principle that *all* general ideas were the result of some kind of innate, mental pre-patterning. We shall see in Chapter 8 how Chomsky claims that the ability to use sentences of the subject/predicate form implies an innate knowledge of semantic rules for the formation of general terms. In so doing, Chomsky is arguably coming to terms with the full implications for a thesis about innate knowledge of language as affecting our understanding of the formation of all, and not just some general terms in a way that Locke showed to be necessary but which Descartes and Leibniz never clearly grasped. For the moment, it is interesting to compare from our account so far how the problems which Locke's psychological abstractionism (or 'associationism' as this, in the context of his total account, came to be called) parallel to some extent the problems of abstractionism's successor, behaviourism.

2.2 QUINE'S LOGICAL BEHAVIOURISM AND CLASSICAL EMPIRICISM

We saw that the strong behaviourist sought to expunge all internal, mental mechanisms from his description and to show how human understanding and interpretation of the world could be more realistically described in stimulus/response terms. The only capacity which was required was the general capacity to respond to stimuli (classical conditioning) or to initiate stimuli within a given, statistically measurable range, some of whose members had met in the past with a need-reducing environmental response (operant conditioning). Such a capacity could hardly be described as 'innate' since stimulus/response activity was the defining characteristic of all living things and the description would not, in that case, differentiate between external and internal events, as does the term 'innate'. 'Innate' both in classical and Chomskyan rationalism does, after all, characterise that in men's minds which external experience, observation, stimuli and so on could not have put there. This being the case, both Locke and Skinner are seen to share similar problems. The problem for Skinner was to show how, without the intervention of innate predispositions which the strong behaviourist's principle of significance had ruled out, particular stimuli and particular need-reducing responses could produce a coherent pattern of behaviour which corresponded to the mentalists' allegedly more inferior description of a coherent picture of the world. We have seen how with Locke a world of general ideas constructed from particular ideas proved problematic. We have seen, too, how general patterns of behaviour, quantified statistically by the requirements of Skinner's theory of operant conditioning, proved impossible to build up from particular stimuli and responses as the commitment of the model to the causal principle required.

At this point I am aware that it may be objected that a logical behaviourist like Quine has accepted the requirements of innate mechanisms for behaviourist theory. As Quine says:

For, whatever we may make of Locke, the behaviourist is knowingly and cheerfully up to his neck in innate mechanisms of learning-readiness. The very reinforcement and extinction of responses, so central to behaviorism, depends on prior inequalities in the subject's qualitative spacing, so to speak, of stimulations. If the subject is rewarded for responding in a certain way to one stimulation, and punished for thus responding to another stimulation, then his responding in the same way to a third stimulation reflects an inequality in his spacing of the three stimulations; the third must resemble the first more than the second. Since each learned response presupposes some such prior inequalities, some inequalities must be unlearned; hence innate. Innate biases and dispositions are the corner-stone of behaviorism. (Quine, 1975, p. 201)

We shall be returning in Chapter 8 to a fuller discussion of the themes of this passage in relation to our account of Chomskyan innatism. Suffice it to say here, however, that, in the light of our preceding account of Skinnerian behaviourism, it represents a fairly significant retreat from behaviourism as a principle of significance or, in other words, 'strong' behaviourism. Quine's admission amounts to what we earlier described as 'weak' behaviourism, the acceptance of which we argued, and will further argue later in this chapter, represents a serious undermining of the whole behaviourist position. For the moment, let us pursue Locke's side of the associationist/behaviourist dichotomy by considering further the second objection to Locke's 'abstractionist' solution to the problem of universals. We turn therefore from our commentary of the first objection, namely, that abstraction, by using the principle of resemblance, is as self-defeating as that of identity, to the second objection, which required abstraction to take place in conformance with some rules, otherwise general terms simply describe arbitrarily constructed categories.

Locke's solution to the problem of arbitrariness in the construction of general terms (descriptions) will repay some consideration at this point, especially in view of its influence upon associationist psychology against which early behaviourists such as Watson and Pavlov self-consciously revolted. Such a consideration will help us further to augment our case that behaviourism as a conscious attempt to surmount the problems with general empiricist epistemology was as much a failure as its predecessor. Locke believed that he could give an account of experience in terms of certain basic or 'simple' ideas which have come to be constructed into complex ideas. The problem of universals as complex ideas was therefore seen to be similar to that of ideas of particulars that, too, were complexes, though a proper analysis of what he was saying ought to have put him on his guard against talking as though 'complex universal idea' and 'complex particular idea' were equivalent to 'idea of a universal' and 'idea of a complex particular'. These simple ideas in turn would, if they were to be more than mere arbitrary guesses about the world, have come directly from the world. Locke therefore began with what he described as 'primary qualities' which he regarded as adhering to matter (or 'substance'), and these qualities were solidity, extension, figure, motion, rest and number (Locke, 1975, p. 140). Since introspection or the process of looking at one's own ideas could not reveal any mental image corresponding to primary qualities, Locke proposed that their existence could only be inferred from those secondary qualities that they produce as they bombard our sense-organs. 'Secondary qualities' therefore describe the effect of primary qualities upon our sense-organs and describe our perceptions of colours, sounds, smells and so forth. From our introspection of these sensations or 'secondary qualities', we form simple ideas such as 'yellow', 'white', 'heat', 'cold', 'hard', 'soft', 'bitter' and 'sweet' (Locke, 1975, p. 105).

As we saw, then, Locke's problem is to show how a human being builds up an orderly and coherent picture of the world. If such a picture of the world requires for its understanding such notions as 'cause', 'space', 'time' or, to select from Locke's actual list, 'extension', 'motion', 'rest', of which we cannot form mental pictures, this is because, to use a modern metaphor, the blank film in our heads cannot register their precise images, rather than because they represent innate mechanisms for organising raw data. What does show up upon the photographic plate, namely, the secondary qualities, enables their existence to be inferred. The inference, moreover, is causal. Primary qualities cause secondary qualities which in turn cause sensation which in turn causes simple ideas. And as Locke says:

> It is not in the power of the most exalted wit, or enlarged understanding, by any quickness or variety of thought, to *invent* or *frame* one new simple idea in the mind ... nor can any force of the understanding *destroy* those that are there. (Locke, 1975, p. 40)

Simple ideas, therefore, whose production is connected by an unbroken causal chain to the external world, are passively received in sensation and as such are incorrigible. As such, Locke's account shares with Skinner a quest for an account of human psychology purely in terms of rule-conformance which he, more so than Skinner, beset by the further problems raised by the 'solution' of operant conditioning, sees purely in terms of a causal relationship between objects in the external world (primary qualities) and the production of simple ideas (from secondary qualities) in sensation. But Locke, no less than Skinner, has a problem, of course, and that is that, on his account so far, since no one can at will 'invent', 'frame' or 'destroy' simple ideas, all human affirmations about the world describing ideas would have to be veridical. Yet this is impossible, since men come to different and mutually contradictory conclusions about the world. Some, for example, claim that there are mermaids, which others deny. How, given this causal account of how an orderly picture of the world is built up, can the phenomenon of human error be explained? Locke's answer is that the fault must lie somewhere between where the simple ideas are passively received in sensation and where they are built into complex ideas through reflection, since ideas, by contrast with simple ideas, can be invented, framed and destroyed.

This process of reflection must provide therefore the source of the error. In reflection, the mind introspects its own operations and, by copying how it combines simple ideas to form complex ideas of real objects, it is able to fashion complex ideas of non-existent objects. Somehow, therefore, when falsehoods are asserted, the simple ideas have been incorrectly put together, as when the complex idea of a mermaid is formed. Simple ideas, say, of green, soft, moist, webbed and so on have been put together correctly to form the complex idea of a fish's tail, and the simple ideas of, say, white, yellow, blue, skin (?), hair (?), eye (?), dry and so on have been put together correctly to form the upper part of a woman's body. But their further combination was inaccurate. The mind in reflection, having introspected how it had formed correct complex ideas when it joined tails with fishes' heads, and top halves of women's bodies with legs, had somehow copied this act of combination to produce the fictitious complex idea of the mermaid.

We see, then, in Locke's account a further parallel with Skinner's need to close the rule-conforming/rule-following gap. Just as there was a collapse in the causal chain between particular stimulus-response acts and general patterns which 'transcend the particular' (rule-breaking, tensed-denials and so on) observable in behaviourist theory, so, too, in Locke's account. There is a chain of causality beginning with primary qualities and continuing through secondary qualities and simple ideas at the stage of sensation which is somehow interrupted at the stage of reflection. Locke's and his successors' problem was how to restore the causal link so that errors of reflection were eliminated and a true and incorrigible picture of the world could be built up. Thus the location of the source of error in the faculty of reflection lead logicians to seek for appropriate logical formulas which, when applied to simple ideas about which we could not, as we have seen, be mistaken, could not help but produce a series of propositions which gave a complete and true account of the world. Furthermore, it lead psychologists to look for the causal laws by which ideas are associated in normal human beings in the light of which psychological abnormality (for example, illusions of mermaids) could be diagnosed and treated. This latter view of psychology is known as associationism and is, as we have said, the view to which classical behaviourism rose in direct opposition. The principle by which complex ideas were correctly or incorrectly built up was 'resembance', and the problem of how this term could be given the required, non-arbitrary function we have more than once commented upon. The failure in the last analysis of the theory to give an account of non-arbitrary resemblance so that universal terms are not arbitrarily constructed out of particulars is a failure lethal to the theory. As we have seen, it was precisely such an account that the whole apparatus of primary and secondary qualities, simple and complex ideas, was erected to demonstrate.

Locke is, as we have seen, often charged with confusing psychological questions about the origins of ideas or propositions with their justification. We shall see in Chapter 8 that the distinction on which this charge is based has been unsatisfactorily drawn by Hamlyn and others. The nature/social distinction on which it is based cannot represent the final disjunction that many relativist, intersubjectivist theses demand. It is at least questionable that fundamental social agreements, constituting Wittgenstein's interpersonal backcloth of objectivity, are not critically conditioned by certain, arguably linguistic features of man's nature. However, without prejudging at this stage whether the implied distinction between interpersonal backcloth and psychological origin is at all final, it would nevertheless, on either view, be true to say that Locke's account did give rise to two distinct kinds of problem, namely, problems about it as a psychological theory and problems about it as an epistemological theory, however much we may want finally to argue that the two kinds of problem are interconnected. If it could be shown that the causal theory of perception worked, that introspection in reflection could lead us to discover the infallible formula by which we constructed complex from simple ideas when we did so in correspondence with reality, there is still the problem of how we test independently that the complex ideas have been constructed according to this formula and how we know that the formula itself is reliable. How we know that a man has used the right formula when he makes a true statement is a psychological question. How we know that the formula is the right formula is an epistemological one.

Let us take the psychological question first. Supposing that a man makes statements whose truth he asserts about women and fishes but not about mermaids. Supposing that he does this consistently and as the rule. How, first of all, can we be sure that he has the same mental images of simple ideas as we have? Even if we grant that he does on the basis of inference (he calls things 'red', 'hard' or other qualities when we do), how can we confirm that he is using the same method as we do to construct complex ideas? Is it not possible for a man to produce a true proposition, even if the method that he used was different from the method that we use? Locke implies that there is only one method, that a statement not formed using that method cannot be true, and that he must discover for himself by introspection whether he had used that method. The method of psychological investigation had therefore to be one in which the researcher asked his subjects to introspect their internal mental states. Such states, according to Locke's associationist followers, must be similar for all men, as must the formula used to organise them. But, notoriously, associatist psychology failed to obtain any general, clear-cut and consistent account of mental organisation from such researches, with the result that Locke's psychology failed to provide an adequate and scientific account of how human beings come to construct a true picture of the world.

We come secondly to the epistemological question, namely, how can we confirm that what someone says that they 'know' to be true is in fact true. In traditional logic, for example, a conclusion can be true even if both premises are false if those premises have been invalidly put together. Then there are the famous Gettier examples (Gettier, 1963) where someone claims to know something, what he knows is true, but his grounds for believing what he does are unfounded. Supposing that I am in Switzerland and I want to discover the exchange rate for the pound sterling. I pick up a newspaper and I misread the date. The paper is dated 24 July 1976, having been left in a cupboard and simply placed accidentally upon the coffee table where my Swiss relatives usually deposit today's newspaper. I pick up the paper on 24 July 1979, but I misread the date and think that it is today's. I therefore read that the exchange rate is 3.70 Swfrancs to the pound. Now, as it happens, on both 24 July 1976 and 24 July 1979, the exchange rate was 3.70. I therefore, having read the wrong newspaper, would have reached the true conclusion that the rate was 3.70. Can we possibly deny that I knew the exchange rate because my belief was a true belief even though my grounds for so believing were unjustified? If method is all, as Locke implies that it is, then a wrong method ought to produce a false picture of the world. Locke's solution to the problem of knowledge was, as we have seen, the psychological assertion that primary qualities produce the same secondary qualities in all men. We agree in our linguistic labels for the secondary qualities, and the isolated examples of individual men not conforming to this general pattern can be explained in terms of physical or psychological derangement of the sense-organs. The problem, therefore, of how we can be certain that the simple idea that one man receives is identical (it refers to the same particular) that another man sees, becomes of epistemological as well as of psychological importance. Without this assurance of identity, the existence of a world independent of human thought confirming statements or denying them could not be held as certain. Yet how, if there are no independent ways of studying primary qualities, can we be certain that the secondary qualities that they produce bear the causal relationship with them that the theory requires? Furthermore, as the theory presupposes that the problem of knowledge is essentially one of how an individual can, in isolation, build up a picture of a world of objects and other persons, this is a problem that the epistemologist as well as the psychologist has to face, namely, how can we be certain that the simple ideas that one man perceives are identical with those that another perceives?

Locke here is hostage to the ultimate empirical verifiability of the foundations of his epistemology. His thesis requires that it be a fact that there are certain, causally acquired, simple ideas that as such are unalterably fixed in and identical throughput the consciousness of all men. It is, after all, a fundamental requirement of his thesis that only complex ideas can be altered, albeit idiosyncratically, in reflection. We shall also see in Chapter 8 how Chomsky claims that Skinner's theory is also hostage to the empirical verifiability of its ultimate foundations. In Locke's case, the form that the shaking of the empirical foundations takes is the comparative study of different cultures by the anthropologists (for example, Wright Mills, 1963). Different societies appear to have different colour schemes so that simple ideas produced by introspection of secondary qualities appear to differ from one culture to another. And yet the foundations of the theory require that such simple ideas, passively received, are unalterable and received as such by all men. Once we admit of cultural differences, we are near to admitting also that reflection can alter simple ideas and we cannot do this while leaving Locke's theory intact. Moreover, the Eskimoes have ten different words for 'snow'. How, as epistemologists, are we to settle the dispute as to which of the following two statements are true:

(*a*) We have one word for ten different things and this word is 'snow'; and
(*b*) The Eskimoes have ten different words for the same thing, namely snow?

Is there, in other words, only one simple idea or many simple ideas for snow, or is snow a complex idea and different complexes called by this word constructed out of different simple ideas? Even if psychologically this question could be answered with reference to, say, physiological differences in receptor organs of different races, the epistemological question would remain, namely, how do we determine which of two conflicting world views is correct? Only, according to Locke, by reiterating the very psychological theory of how complex ideas are built up which anthropological investigation has called into question. Moreover, this objection applies *a fortiori* to the existence of different versions of epistemological justification both logically sound but both radically different because the foundational concepts of the system are different.

We have already explored earlier in this chapter how behaviourism sought to solve the problems of Lockean psychology while remaining fundamentally within an empiricist frame of reference. We must simply dispense with the notion that psychology should be studied in terms of ideas or sense-impressions which required introspection of our reflection on them. If we adopt the strategy of what we have defined as 'strong' behaviourism, then the problem of subjectivity in descriptions of colour words or words for snow is dissolved. Translate all such ideas in terms of overt behaviour, and the problem of differing ideas, their fomulation, association and disassociation will be shown to have been a pseudo-problem. We need not, according to the strong behaviourist, subscribe to the thesis that, because one man's ideas were different from another's, the study of human psychology could not be placed upon a firm footing. The study of human thinking could still be objectively described, since all that matters is overt behaviour, how a person responds or does not respond to a given stimulus (classical conditioning) or what general class of stimuli tend to get repeated following need-reducing environmental responses (operant conditioning). Let us, however, briefly examine how behaviourism seeks to solve the problem of Lockean epistemology, taking as our example the monumental work of Williard Quine (1953, 1960 and 1973).

2.3 QUINE AND OBJECTIVITY: THE INDETERMINACY OF TRANSLATION

As we have seen, the epistemological problem raised for Locke's thesis was the existence of two different world views, both of which are constructed by a method that appears at least to be logically valid on the basis of what appears to be radically different schemes of simple ideas. Locke's theory postulates, of course, the logical impossibility of the existence of two such views. We saw, moreover, that this process of construction was closely related to the problem of universals, namely, how general descriptions of classes of things come to be formed in language on a theory that claims that only particular things exist in the real world. The construction must furthermore take place in a way that must not simply be non-arbitrary but, for Locke as well as Skinner, in a way that is rule-conforming or causal. Quine begins at the level of directly observable behaviour instead of at the level of primary and secondary qualities in his description of the role of universal terms in language. Opposing, as did Locke, the view that universals are entities existing in the world, Quine also opposes the view that they are entities which exist in the mind as faded memory traces left as simple ideas to which such terms refer. Instead, as a good behaviourist he rejects the adequacy of mentalistic descriptions and begins at the level of directly observable behaviour. As Quine says:

> The problem of explaining these adjectives 'significant' and 'synonymous' with some degree of clarity and rigor – preferably, as I see it, in terms of behaviour – is as difficult as it is important. But the explanatory value of special and irreducible intermediary entities called meanings is surely illusory. (Quine, 1953, p. 12)

Quine regards the classification of individual objects as 'red' or 'snow' as explicable in terms of general classes of pointing behaviours that mark general tendencies to point at the objects so named in regular ways. If a child does not know what 'snow' or 'red' means, we do not explain their meaning in words but simply point to appropriate objects, and that is what it means to say that such terms are defined 'ostensively'. Thus Quine might have been replying to Locke's mental entities as well as Plato's 'essences', when he attacks the notion that the meaning of 'square' is either a universal essence in which all square particulars participate or a mental image left by bombardment of the sense-organs by large numbers of square things. As Quine says of the level of immediate, behavioural experience:

> Actually there is no need, up to this point, to suppose such entities as attributes at all in our ostensive clarification of 'square'. We are clarifying, by our various pointings, our use of the words 'is square'; but neither is an object squareness supposed as object pointed to, nor need it be supposed available as reference of the word 'square'. No more need be demanded, in explication of 'is square' or any other phrase, than that our listener learn when to expect us to apply it to an object and when not; there is no need for the phrase itself to be a name in turn of a separate object of any kind. (Quine, 1953, p.34)

Thus it is at a behavioural level that high degrees of certainty can be expected, but these degrees of certainty are merely a statistical function of the likelihood of classes of responses to classes of stimuli. The objects that demand our attention, that we are caused to point at by psychological drives towards need-reduction, that stimulate our response or elicit general classes of response because they are members of general classes of stimuli, are those on which men are more likely to reach common agreement. Whatever our scientific, moral, religious or political understandings of the world (which themselves have yet to be cashed in behavioural terms), we do, despite such differences, share the language of tables and chairs, of colours and so forth. What is happening when we call an object 'red' is not that we introspect a common idea but that our behaviour is part of a common class of responses. I respond 'red' to a range of stimuli (there are, after all, shades of red), and you respond 'red' to a range of stimuli, and there is a considerable overlap or intersection of my classes of response and your classes of response. Quine is here at his most subtle. Because he can talk of classes of stimuli rather than an individual stimulus using statistical notions of class, he gives the appearance of being able to cope with the problem that, when we learn the meaning of 'red', we must be able not only to classify actual objects of past experience but also future ones too that may not be quite like them. Probability of future response describes the flexibility and adaptability of language to encompass new experiences within existing schemes. Whether, as with the similar case of Skinner's description of operant conditioning, such a statistical redescription of the problem of 'transcendence of particulars' amounts to an explanation, we have already challenged and will be challenging in further detail in a moment. For the moment, let us allow Quine to continue to make his case. What we assert when we say that we 'know' the meaning of a sentence such as:

This object is red,

is, then, that we observe the object to be such that it is a member of a class of stimuli that would elicit the verbal response of 'red' in the speech community under observation. As Quine says:

> Consider . . . the affirmative stimulus meaning of a sentence s: the class Σ of all those stimulations that *would* prompt assent to s . . . Certainly it is hopeless nonsense to talk thus of unrealised particulars and try to assemble them into classes. Unrealised entities have to be construed as universals. (Quine, 1960, p. 34)

Whether 'probability of response' as the key to universals which appear to refer to unrealised particulars is an explanation rather than simply a redescription of the problem is something that we will leave for now, as we have said.

There may, however, be social groups where such general patterns of pointings, stimulations, responses and so on radically diverge from our own so that the general classes exhibited by our stimulations and responses in no way intersect with theirs. There will then be between our social group and this one a radical divergence of stimulus meanings. This is how, presumably, Quine would propose redescribing the problem of cultural divergence of colour schemes or of different words for snow in the language of Eskimos, although he thinks he has an explanation rather than a mere redescription. Thus we have a behavioural retranslation purporting to be an explanation of differences in simple ideas between cultures that Locke would have found so difficult. Moreover, the advantage of Quine's account here to the behaviourists' case is that it tries to do justice to language as a social phenomenon in a way that neither Locke nor Skinner succeeded in doing. Language is not simply a response to, or a tendency to elicit responses from the natural environment, nor is it simply the product of the introspection of secondary qualities whose formation in the mind is caused by the natural environment. The individual does not build up his stimulus/response patterns (or his picture of the world) in isolation. Rather we may say that the majority (at least) of his sentences interact with one another and with those of other people in a social context, so that such stimulus/response patterns (or pictures of the world) are collective products. To say that sentences interact with one another in a social context is, however, to use shorthand. It is, of course, the speech-behaviour of one language-user (or group of language-users) upon another language-user (or group of language-users) that constitutes the interaction. The result is that human assertions get further removed from direct experience, though they are albeit remotely joined to such experience by chains of stimulations. This interaction of speech-behaviour is what Quine means when he talks of the 'interanimation of sentences' in such passages as the following:

> What we are doing when we amass and use circumstantial evidence is *to let ourselves be actuated* as sensitively as possible by chain stimulations as they reverberate through our theory, from present sensory stimulation, via the interanimation of ensuing interplay of chain stimulations. (Quine, 1960, p. 18)

Since, as we shall see in the next chapter, as scientific patterns of reasoning (induction) are never conclusive (tightly deductive), all scientific evidence is circumstantial, and Quine would argue, more contentiously and in a special sense, so are mathematical patterns of reasoning (Quine, 1953, Chapter 5).

As we are concerned in this section with cause and probability as concepts in a general theory of meaning, we will leave the implications of our account so far for Quine's philosophy of science to our next chapter, where those implications will receive their proper consideration. Let us say at this point in connection with a theory of general meaning that it would be a mistake to regard the whole process of the interanimation of sentences as powered almost mechanically by a small number of behaviours which, standing in the place of simple ideas, are indubitable. It would be a mistake because, as the behaviours which stand closest to experience are defined in terms of statistical patterns of recurring probability, Quine grasps in a way that we have shown that Skinner with his operant behaviour does not know how such behaviours can never be clearly determinate. There is about them an indeterminate character. We would agree with this indeterminacy within a framework that we have characterised as rule-following in connection with our analysis of the logical discontinuity between bee-dances and human communication systems, though our argument has been and will be that 'rule-following' constitutes an explanation that takes us beyond the redescription of statistical indeterminacy. But let us pursue further Quine's characterisation of indeterminacy as it prefigures in his important thesis of the indeterminacy of translation.

As we have seen, 'the affirmation meaning of a sentence s is the class Σ of all those stimulations that would prompt assent to s'. If this is the case, the act of identifying a colour in the form of a subject-predicate sentence would not be a particular response to a particular stimulus, but, as we have seen, part of a general pattern of responses. As individual identification, a colour word would therefore in itself be indeterminate, since any slightly different response within a given range would count as well as such an identification. The indissolubility of Locke's simple ideas therefore, just like the invariance of a conditioned response in classical behaviourism, has given way in Quine's reinterpreted empiricism to descriptions in terms of classes of stimuli similar to what happened in the case of Skinner's operant conditioning. This indeterminacy of conditioning, even where sentence meanings are closest to direct experience, means that we cannot approach the problem of knowledge as did classical empiricism by looking for a number of privileged sentences causally produced from primary qualities through secondary qualities and on to simple ideas produced by introspection. Experience is related to sentences, but circumstantially and not directly to certain foundational sentences. Experience confronts, as it were, the whole corpus of sentences in a language organised to explain and assert. Evidence, as we shall see in the next chapter, is never direct but only circumstantial, so that no sentence in the corpus can be refuted against experience in isolation. The result of this is that it is possible to have two languages that so radically diverge that any translation from one language to another fails to represent even an approximate meaning to the other.

Now, remember what Quine has so far argued. Colour schemes and schemes for snow are to be cashed in terms of classes of stimulations, as are all universals whose particulars may, as such, not be realised. Now you cannot have a class of stimulations without responses to at least some members of the class, since a stimulus gets described as it does because it is a member of a class of things that get responded to. But what produces both individual and, through the interanimation of sentences, group responses? It is need-reduction, and particular social and individual needs in some cultures and at some times and places will be different from those at others. This, as we shall see, leads Quine to a pragmatic view of knowledge which is one that asserts that the practical use of a system of thinking (cashed in terms of stimulus/response/need-reduction) is sufficient for its epistemological validity. There is therefore no guarantee that classes of stimulations in one culture will overlap with those of another, particularly in view of the indeterminacy of conditioning. If there happens to be an intersection between one class of stimulations in one society constituted by its pursuit of its own pragmatic ends (cashed in terms of need-reduction), and another class of stimulations in another society similarly constituted, then by this happy accident we can translate one another's languages. But let us suppose for one moment that, by an unhappy accident, we meet with a new tribe whose classes of stimulations have no common members. We may find ourselves constructing a manual of translation which correlates first sentences and then expressions and words with our own language as if there was an intersection between classes of stimulations. And yet, because there is no intersection, we fail totally to assign the individual items of particular behaviours that we observe to their appropriate classes, which are at all events unknown to us. Thus we had not even begun to represent what members of the tribe meant by what they uttered, however coherent and meaningful our translation of what they uttered might appear to us. As Quine says,

> there can be no doubt that rival systems of analytical hypotheses can fit the totality of speech behavior to perfection, and can fit the totality of dispositions to speech behavior as well, and still specify mutually incompatible translations of countless sentences insusceptible of independent control. (Quine, 1960, p. 72)

In order to exemplify this thesis, Quine, in a much discussed passage, imagines a member of an alien tribe pointing to what we would call a 'rabbit' and saying the word 'gavagai'. Quine continues:

> Consider 'gavagai'. Who knows but what the object to which this term applies are not rabbits after all, but mere stages, or brief temporal segments, of rabbits? In either event the stimulus situations that prompt assent to 'gavagai' would be the same as for 'rabbit'. Or perhaps the objects to which 'gavagai' applies are all and sundry detached parts of rabbits; again the stimulus meaning would register no difference. When from sameness of stimulus meanings of 'gavagai' and 'rabbit' the linguist leaps to the conclusion that a gavagai is a whole enduring rabbit, he is just taking for granted that the native is enough like us to have a brief general term for rabbits and no brief general term for rabbit stages or parts. (Quine, 1960, pp. 51–2)

The thesis of the indeterminacy of translation in general and this passage in particular has been much criticised. We have tried to work out in detail in our discussion how that thesis rests upon the postulate of the indeterminacy of conditioning, an indeterminacy necessitated by the presence in the theory of responses that are responses to *classes* of stimulations. Yet what Quine here postulates in this passage is three quite *determinate* classes, namely, the class of whole rabbits, the class of 'brief temporal segments of rabbits', and the class of 'sundry undetached parts of rabbits'. Now this determinacy of classes surely weakens Quine's earlier thesis of the indeterminacy of conditioning on which we have shown the thesis of the indeterminacy of translation to depend. The basis of that indeterminacy was the probabilistic character of what open classes record, in which not only possible but even actual particulars need not be so classified in the future, even though they had been in the past. The class of six throws of the dice, we saw, need not in future contain an instance of the number six even though it has done so in the past. Quine is caught, therefore, in the dilemma that we saw that Skinner's operant conditioning was to be found. Classes which predict probable responses are recording general tendencies to which there might always be particular exceptions, yet the thesis assumes that possible and actual members of the class can somehow exhaustively be spelled out.

A similar point to the one that I am making here was made less formally by Yudkin (1979, pp. 93–6). She charges Quine in this passage with attributing to the tribe 'a passion for exactness that only someone familiar with metaphysical hairsplitting in our own language could manifest'. She then quotes Leach's example of asking whether the sketch of a car upon a blackboard is a Ford or a Cadillac.

Leach compares this with someone putting a question like, 'Do ants have legs?' to a Kachin who, while killing a pig, says, 'I am giving it to the ants.' It is arguable that it is the vagueness (or imprecision) of a special kind exhibited by the sketch of the car or a Kachin's sketch of an ant that constitutes their communicative strength. This special kind of imprecision enables communication to go on without commitment to any distinct picture, presuppositions or discovery which one side may have but the other not about what the terms describe is precisely like. This special kind of imprecision, therefore, allowing new discoveries to be incorporated into existing schemes (or open-classes), is that which arguably enables cross-cultural under-standing and rules out the problem which Quine holds there are about radical translation. It is, moreover, arguable that Quine's example fails to make his case since the classes,

$$\{\text{whole rabbits}\},$$

$$\{\text{brief temporal segments of rabbits}\},$$

$$\{\text{sundry detached parts of rabbits}\}$$

represent a range of possibilities of speaking about rabbits that do overlap and criss-cross with one another. As such, we can discern some kind of boundary between them as open classes or general terms without which any kind of language would fail to classify (or predicate) and hence become chaotic. Whether the ability to so bound without closing such classes is to be understood as one of those innate dispositions that Quine, as we have seen, admits into his theory, must await our discussion in Chapter 8. Suffice it to say here that it is this ability to bind without closing certain classes that the later Wittgenstein had in mind when he contrasted genuine universals as open-class concepts with closed-class concepts, under-standing the constitutive principle of the former in terms of 'family-resemblance' (Bambrough, 1968, and Wittgenstein, 1974, pp. 31–2).

It is arguable, therefore, that Quine is left hanging on the horns of a dilemma. If he maintains that we can define classes of stimulations precisely (and thus their members exhaustively), then he undermines the indeterminacy of conditioning upon which the indeterminacy of translation rests. If, on the other hand, he makes the classes open-ended, then he makes his thesis of the impossibility of radical translation void, since he points to ways in which men recognise cars, ants and rabbits without recognising them as Fords or Cadillacs, things with legs, or whole rabbits in contrast with temporal rabbit stages. We shall in a moment be spelling out in greater detail how Wittgenstein began with problems similar to those of Quine but dealt with them in a radically different way, in the course of which we shall flesh out in more precise detail the notion of 'family-resemblance'. Suffice it to say here that it is arguable that, contrary to Quine, the ability of human beings to construct open-class concepts in terms of family-resemblance is precisely that which makes it impossible that there could ever be a problem of radical translation that would make the thesis of the indeterminacy of translation credible.

Thus, at the end of our initial discussion of Quine, we see that we have returned to the point at which we left Skinner with our criticism of his concept of operant conditioning. We saw there that operant conditioning as a psychological theory is beset by a similar problem to that which must be faced by Quine's indeterminacy of classes of stimuli as the foundation for an epistemological theory. Talk of 'classes of stimulations' (Quine), like talk of 'probability of response' (Skinner), simply retranslates the concept of following a rule as opposed to conforming to a rule into statistical terms, without explaining anything at all. As we have seen, the ability to discern statistical patterns exhibits that transcendence of the particular which itself makes behaviourism incoherent since it exemplifies the very rule-conforming/rule-following distinction that the behaviourist is using it to close. The discernment of statistical patterns is rather like the discernment of 'family-resemblance'. It reflects an ability to ignore a particular or group of particulars that have hitherto been assigned to a general class (not, in other words, to stimulate them or respond to them) so that general tendencies can be studied. Now we can justifiably explain either statistically or causally events in the world other than the acts of human understanding, explanation or judgement. This is because, when we do so, we are explaining one thing (the explicandum) in terms of another (the explicans). Because of the success of statistical explanations in the natural sciences and even in many parts of sociology and psychology, it is understandable how the psychologist has gone on to apply such explanations to the acts of understanding, explaining and judging themselves (Lonergan, 1957, pp. 53–128). It is also understandable that an empiricist like Quine should be involved in a similar enterprise, since he wishes to see epistemology grounded on such foundations. But both Skinner and Quine's move is invalid since, in the matter of acts of understanding, explaining and judging, the explicans and the explicandum merge with one another.

We see, therefore, that we require now an account that clarifies the role of general terms in language, their formation and justification, that will lead us out of the impasse in which we are now found. What I propose doing is showing how Wittgenstein originally began looking for a solution to the problem of universals in ways that bear comparison with Quine's work, but later in life was to adopt a radically new solution for which, as we shall argue later (Chapter 8), the rule-following/rule-conforming distinction has to be axiomatic.

2.4 THE EARLY WITTGENSTEIN AND LOGICAL BEHAVIOURISM

Let us begin, therefore, with some general reflections on the problem of universals or general terms in language. We shall see in our next chapter how the problem of induction in an empiricist view of science is related to the overall problem of how we come to make general classifications. The behaviourist, when he focuses upon the meaning of such terms, has to explain how, by observing particular things, we assemble such observations into general classes. When, moreover, he turns his attention to induction a similar problem arises. How specifically does a scientist move from the observation of particular phenomena to the framing of general laws? Keeping therefore to our brief for this chapter, let us now confine ourselves to questions of general meaning.

Let us take as an example of the summation of a particular under a universal the statement:

This (particular) is a table.

The statement invites us to include a particular object in the general class of all things that are tables. Yet how is it possible to explain how we are able to make such general classifications? Tables come in all sorts of shapes, sizes and colours. By what right do we select certain features of an object, say that these are similar to features selected from certain other objects and bind them together within the same class? Hume concluded that there was no such justification ('right'), but that sensible particulars such as particular tables bombarded our sense-organs and left general impressions. The more particular features recurred, the more persistent would be the memory traces left by them. General terms are simply the linguistic symbols of faded memory traces. We have already seen problems that were raised by such an account for Locke's secondary qualities. But even as a psychological account, this view of universals is highly implausible since it implies that positive identification of a particular within a general class is accompanied by a psychological operation involving some basic, essential cognitive map on which the particulars are read off. Yet what essential features do all tables hold in common that constitute such a basic, cognitive map? Must all tables be square, round, flat or be either one of these or another? The moment that one thinks that one has at last some essential, exhaustive list, a counter-example invariably comes along. Nor will it do to talk of uses that any object must have to count as a table since there are similar problems with general and particular uses.

We have, of course, seen what is behaviourism's solution to Hume's problem with sense impressions as also with Locke's simple and complex ideas. It was to dissolve the problem by substitution of precise behavioural descriptions for imprecise mentalistic ones. We have seen how this proposal of strong behaviourism tended to go awry since it had to revert to statistical redescriptions of rule-following behaviour which were indeterminate (Skinner). Sometimes it took the form of a theory that tried both to recognise the indeterminacy of classes of stimulations while reasserting a deter-minacy of concepts that made radical translation impossible (Quine). But there arises here a new problem for a behaviourist account of how words get their meaning. What classical behaviourist account would prescribe as the way in which noises or marks on paper acquire meaning is that such noises or marks are need-reducing responses made to stimuli. But this prescription of classical behaviourism is falsified by the imprecision of natural languages, particularly in respect of general classes. The prescription requires that, for every word in a language, there would be one and only one corresponding object, an object which, having produced need-reduction, invariantly elicits a clear and determinate response. But this would then imply that human languages consisted only of descriptions of particular things and not of general classes. Furthermore, there could not be one word designating several different concepts. A 'swan' can designate an animal swimming on a lake, a public house or a young man in his prime.

The behaviourist now succumbed to the temptation of regarding his problem of meaning as the problem of the vagueness of general terms or classes. The classical behaviourist tried to regard general terms as simply equivalent to sets whose component elements were decided by process of induction. Skinner and Quine, aware of the problem of induction, both proposed versions of statistical explanations of the meaning of general terms as distinct from their particulars, but, as we have seen, succeeded only in re-expressing the problem in different terms as opposed to solving it. To explain general terms statistically was simply to exercise one's ability to make judgements which are more than the linking together of a string of particulars. But that was then simply a fresh exemplification of the problem to be explained rather than an explanation. The persistence, therefore, of the problem of adequacy of explanation of any behaviouristic view of meaning therefore centred on the problem of universal terms. We shall now consider an account of meaning which took its point of departure from a similar position to that of behaviourism, with opposite conclusions.

The early Wittgenstein, like Quine, may, I think not unfairly, be regarded as representing a version of logical behaviourism (Kenny, 1973, p. 184). Sentences and their basic constituents get their meaning by being isomorphic with what they describe beyond language in the world. 'Mental events', echoes the behaviourist, must be shown to be isomorphic with physical events, and in the stimulus-response interaction there must be an isomorphic relation between cause and effect, stimulus and response. Because universals cannot be defined in terms of closed classes of particulars, because, in other words, one table can be round and still be a table, one square and still be a table, it seemed plausible to conclude that ordinary language is defective, because it is not isomorphic with what it describes. Its imperfection lay in its lack of imprecision which universals share with some particulars, examples of which we have given in the case of 'swan' and 'bachelor'. A behaviourist might talk of 'imperfect conditioning' or the indeterminacy of classes of stimulations as explanations of ordinary language containing universal terms which are not exhaustively definable in terms of closed classes of particular objects. As such, we have seen him to have fared no better than Locke's account in mentalistic terms requiring basic sensory data or simple ideas which could be understood as cognitive maps giving bare essentials that an object must have in order to be admitted into the general classes that describe them. The early Wittgenstein, sharing a concern with both the behaviourist's and the classical empiricist's problem, looked for an ideal language whose parts lay buried in the indeterminacy of our present one whose sense would be clear and determinate because it could precisely mirror or picture what it was in the world that it described (Wittgenstein, 1961).

But how could it become possible for ordinary language to be so revised that its propositions became 'articulate' and expressed their meaning in 'a determinate manner' (Wittgenstein, 1961, p. 13)? Wittgenstein's answer lay in his picture theory of the proposition. As we have seen, Wittgenstein's requirement, like in one sense that of the behaviourists, is that language (like a pattern or responses) must be isomorphic with what it describes (the stimulating conditions). Thus a proposition if it is to be 'clear' and 'determinate' must be in some way a picture of what it describes. To begin with, each particular word in the proposition must be correlated with each particular object in the world without one word, as in the case of universals, standing for a collection of objects. But this is not enough. If the picture is true, it must show how the objects in the world are, in fact, joined together in patterns or 'configured' (Wittgenstein, 1961, p. 9). A true proposition, therefore, would have corresponding to the objects in the world, primitive signs (or 'names') joined together (in a 'concatenation of names') so that it accurately pictured such objects and their configurations in the world. In ordinary language, however, words cannot be construed as primitive signs or 'names' that picture what they describe. First, there are general terms like 'red' or 'table' that are applied to more than one object so that there is no one-for-one correlation between word and object. Such terms therefore fail to name or picture. Furthermore, several terms are used to describe the same object when it is called both 'red' and 'table'. But, in an ideal language, the necessity for composing such indeterminate descriptions marred by the presence of universals would be removed (Wittgenstein, 1961, p. 17). The removal of universal terms is therefore the key to producing an ideal language.

Secondly, in ordinary language, only *some* words *approximate* to being like elements in a picture that 'is attached to reality' and 'reaches out to it', even words for particulars (Wittgenstein, 1961, p. 16). Words which linguists call 'signs' (as opposed to 'symbols') represent such approximations. A 'bang' or a 'splash', for example, sound like the sounds that they describe, but only approximately. An ideal language for Wittgenstein would be one where every word was an individual and precise picture of what it described. Such a language would only have references therefore to particulars, with universals, in all their vagueness, excluded.

Although Wittgenstein could give no example of even one such primitive sign, perhaps we can at least make his argument clearer by looking at what would follow for universals from the conclusions of the argument of the Tractatus. Universals would be reformulated, as we have seen that both classical empiricism and Quine's and Skinner's behaviourism required them to be, as strings of particulars within closed sets. In fact, that is also what the formulations of modern symbolic logic, employed in the Tractatus, require them to be on the assumption of a fixed number of objects in the universe. The rules of universal quantification are rules of quantification which men have devised to compensate them for the vagueness of ordinary language which fails to mirror reality precisely. When, for example, we say:

All swans are white,

we are showing the vagueness of ordinary language which has no distinct concept for each particular swan that makes immediately obvious both its similarity with every other particular swan and its dissimilarity with every other particular non-swan. If we had such a particular and clear concept, the general terms 'swan' and 'white' would become superfluous and in the following way. If this particular and clear concept were also to distinguish a particular and clear colour as well as shape, size and so forth, then each concept in our new language would name, signify or picture its exact object so that general terms like 'swan' and 'white' would be superfluous. The formation of classes and the subsumption of some inadequate 'picture' or 'name' for an object within such classes and the exclusion of other inadequate 'pictures' or 'names' of objects from them would be superfluous. Logic as the 'scaffolding' (Wittgenstein, 1974, p. 21) of language would become therefore the equivalent of pointing, gesturing, looking around the object, the point of which cannot be explained ('said') but only 'shown'. As such, the early Wittgenstein's view of logic made it amenable to the kind of behaviourist development that prefigures in Quine's work. To say what the point of logic, understood as gestures and so on, was would involve using the very gestures which would only be intelligible to someone who already knew what they meant, with the result that one could not use them to 'say' anything. This lead the early Wittgenstein to postulate that, for a language to have sense, there must only be a limited number of objects in the world which could be depicted or encapsulated in elementary propositions which met the criteria for being a language with clear and determinate sense. If it were possible for simple objects (atoms) to come into existence *ad infinitum*, then there could be no clear and determinate language which could give a complete account of all actual and possible states of affairs. His quest for an ideal language presupposed, therefore, that the number of simple objects in the universe was limited. An ideal language would be thrown into perpetual chaos if such objects were not so limited, since it could only for one moment succeed in mirroring the word and thus expressing its actual and, by negation, possible states of affairs, but at another moment, with new, simple objects (atoms) coming into existence, it would fail to mirror. To every simple object, therefore, there must, if language is to function precisely, exist a corresponding 'name' or 'primitive sign' that describes it and it alone. Such 'names' are strung together in chains ('concatenations') in order to represent actual or possible states of affairs. The primitive names in advance of an ideal language we cannot exemplify, but they would need, as we have seen, to depict each positive and negative feature of objects in a finite universe which ordinary language obscures by its imprecision. That ordinary language at least enables us to see that propositions must be either true or false, that it also is possible to deduce from the bi-polarity principle the nature of its imprecision, shows us that somehow, embedded in ordinary language, must be the materials from which a new and precise structure could be formed.

As we have seen, Skinner similarly followed classical behaviourism in looking for an account of human behaviour in general, and of language acquisition in particular, in which 'personal exemption from complete determinism is revoked as scientific analysis progresses' (Skinner, 1971, p. 26). We saw, furthermore, that this was at variance with his description of operant conditioning in statistical terms, even though Skinner thought that such descriptions 'refer to the same factual core' as do causal ones. We saw also that Skinner's account ran into trouble on using a human ability to explain the same human ability, namely, the ability to 'transcend the particular' exhibited in the use of universal terms or open-classes in language, of which statistical classes are examples. In our immediately preceding discussing we have furthermore seen that the early Wittgenstein shared Skinner's desire to give an account of language that was 'clear and determinate' and that could be explained in terms of causal interaction between men, the world and the representational form of language in which, in an ideal language, the world would stand mirrored. This involved Wittgenstein in an attack upon the validity of universal terms and a desire to make such terms redundant in an ideal language which need have no open-classes in a universe whose simple objects were fixed in number. As such, Wittgenstein may be credited with having tried to dispense with that category of explanation, namely, statistical description, which is such an embarrassment to Skinner's putatively causal account. Quine, as ever, handled the data so problematic for their accounts far more subtly than either Skinner or the early Wittgenstein – a subtleness into which he had been educated no doubt by the developments in theoretical physics and the philosophy of science that we will briefly record in the next chapter.

Let us, however, briefly outline here how specifically Quine's solution to the problem of universals that we have already discussed contrasts with that of the early Wittgenstein.

2.5 QUINE AND THE LATER WITTGENSTEIN ON UNIVERSALS

Quine's solution, basically, as we have already seen, was to treat universals as classes of statistical possibilities or probabilities as Skinner had done, while maintaining by means of the indeterminacy of classes of stimulations that there could never be in language so privileged kinds of particles of meaning (or 'names') that mirrored reality in a determinate manner. As Quine says:

> We can improve our conceptual scheme, our philosophy, bit by bit whilst continuing to depend on it for support; but we cannot detach ourselves from it and compare it objectively with an unconceptualised reality. Hence it is meaningless, I suggest, to inquire into the absolute correctness of a conceptual scheme as a mirror of reality. Our standard for appraising basic changes of conceptual scheme must be, not a realistic standard of correspondence to reality, but a pragmatic standard. (Quine, 1953, p. 79)

Yet Quine does follow the early Wittgenstein in understanding universals as formed in a way analogous with complex particulars, since the distinction for him between the particular/universal description is a difference between different orders of *quantification*. When we include an object within a class ('This object is a table', 'This object is red'), we simply point to a large number of individual objects and expect that our hearer, by a process of induction, will deduce the sort of things to which we are referring in a way analogous (but not, of course, identical with) the way in which we proceed with concrete particulars.

Remember Quine's story about the anthropologist, the rabbit and its rabbit stages. Quine gives a similar example of a river which we may, if we like, describe as a complex particular composed of simple elements that are spatially and temporally located river stages. It might be argued that, on the account of the early Wittgenstein, it is far better to talk of river stages, and that, as such, complex particulars suffer from the same problem of imprecision as do universals. Why should we refer to a river as a complex particular ('This river is . . .') rather than to its river stages ('These river stages are . . .')? The early Wittgenstein believed this latter course to be preferable, as it would lead, as we have seen, to a clear and determinate language. But Quine rejects this possibility. Instead, he invokes the principle of Occam's razor, which is that one should not multiply entities without justification. His point is that Wittgenstein was wrong to look for entities such as primitive signs which could stand as the basis for any kind of discourse. Whether we use a so-called complex particular or a so-called simple one is relative to the pragmatic purpose of the particular discourse that we are using (Quine, 1953, p. 70). 'Pragmatic purpose', moreover, is understood by Quine behavioristically, as we have seen (Quine, 1953, p. 76).

We have quite frequently criticised Quine's account of universals as a statistical redescription of the problem of rule-following behaviour masquerading as an explanation in terms of rule-conformity. It is time to fill out this criticism in greater detail with particular reference to the later Wittgenstein's refutation of his own earlier account. Quine, as we saw from our criticism of his example of radical translation, has a clear and determinate version of universal terms, albeit quantified differently from references to particulars. When we point to a particular thing, we are behaving differently from when we point to some members of a general class of things and invite a different (statistical) kind of inference. But, from our discussion of his account of radical translation, we can see that in one respect it is still very closely related to Wittgenstein's original position. Although universals are no longer distinguishable from particulars because of the 'garbled reference' of the former ('river' from the standpoint of 'river stages' is as garbled as a general term like 'red'), universals nevertheless are determinate as a result of the quantifier 'class of'. Hence the indeterminacy of universals is simply the indeterminacy of given individual members from which a class of stimulations, duly determinately quantified as such, is composed. Moreover, the general class of things can still be determined by an inductive process.

There are some general problems with the notion of induction that we shall set out briefly in our next chapter. For the moment, let us pursue them, our central theme, namely, the later Wittgenstein's account of universals in which he radically diverged from his earlier account in a different and arguably more satisfactory direction than that of Quine's. One of the problems with Quine's account is that there is a kind of arbitrariness about how universals are formed that, as we saw, Locke's account as well none too successfully tried to avoid. Quine might seek to reply to such a criticism that his account is not arbitrary since universals are so quantified in accordance with pragmatic principles. Hence Eskimos (like our tribe discovered by our hapless translator) may form universals for snow by circumscribing ten distinct groups of particulars (rather like 'rabbit stages') rather than just one according to the pragmatic concerns of their particular social group. The problem with such a strategy is that it is itself arbitrary because it appears to say that, whatever reduces the tension of inquiry for a particular individual or group, then that is true for that particular individual or group. This represents a psychological rather than a logical criterion for the truth of a statement. But this is not the only nor the really basic problem with which we are here concerned. A far more critical problem for Quine's pragmatism regarding universal terms is one that we uncovered in our analysis of Quine's indeterminacy of translation. We saw in connection with Yudkin's criticism of that thesis that there was arguably a kind of imprecision about general terms that drained them of their pragmatic force but which contributed to their communicative strength as a basis for transcultural translation. It is with this second problem that we shall be basically concerned in our discussion of the later Wittgenstein's solution to the problem of universals in terms of family-resemblance.

The problem with which both Skinner and Quine wrestled with in their explanations in terms of operant conditioning and classes of stimulations was, as we saw, the problem of creativity in language, the way that language is able to change and adapt itself to new situations. This phenomenon, the later Wittgenstein was to claim, requires the concept of rule-following to be regarded as axiomatic to any explanation of human language. As our account so far has been supportive of such a claim in its demonstration that operant conditioning and indeterminacy of classes of stimulations simply redescribe in terms of rule-conformance the problem that they are seeking to explain, Wittgenstein's axiom may be now accepted without further argument. A purely mechanical view of how a language could be built up from primitive signs mirroring the world by means of strictly deductive formulas was falsified by the later Wittgenstein's analysis of how a language dependent upon universal terms could not produce genuine universal terms by such a method. The later Wittgenstein came to see that, far from a language formed from such primitive signs being communicatively superior to our present one, such a language would be virtually unworkable because of its inability to adapt itself to new discoveries and new concerns. If an ideal language was so because its meaning was 'clear and determinate', universal terms would have to be closed classes exhaustively definable in terms of their particulars. Once the last particular had been listed and enclosed within the class, there was an end to matters, just as with a Quinean quantification as 'a class of' applied for reasons of pragmatism. But both an early Wittgensteinian and a Quinean account miss the creative character of language to be seen in the way the universals as open-class categories cannot be defined exhaustively since instances of new particulars, possible instances, can *ad infinitum* be added to them. The later Wittgenstein saw this process as classification of universals because of the detection of family-resemblances between members of open-classes rather than simply because of the circumscribing of clusters of particulars according to principles of pragmatism. By means of the notion of 'family-resemblance', therefore, Wittgenstein was to argue that the creative, rule-following, adaptive character of language, comprising new discoveries within known schemes, could be more adequately explained, even surmounting, as we have suggested, the problem of radical translation.

What was, then, the later Wittgenstein's account of 'family-resemblance' as a solution to the problem of universals? As we have seen, his concern to explain the creativity of language lead him to reject his earlier account of language in terms of a fixed number of particles of meaning with rules for deriving propositions from them. He was assisted, as we shall argue in the next chapter, by changing perspectives in theoretical physics which suggested an expanding universe as opposed to a universe of limited and determinate objects to which such limited and determinate particles could correspond. The thesis by which he believed, then, that he could solve the problem of creativity and adaptability was his account of definition by family-resemblance of universal terms to explain conceptual creativity, and his theory of 'language-games' with which 'family-resemblance' was inextricably linked in explanation of propositional creativity. We begin with his account of family-resemblance believing that we can show this to be critical for his views on language-games. His account of definition in terms of family-resemblance enabled him to account for how it is that learning a language makes us capable of recognising not just actual classifications of universal terms like 'table' but also possible classifications. Tables come in all sorts of varieties of colours, shapes and sizes. We cannot make an exhaustive list of features of actual tables which could form some kind of paradigm for a table constructed from a fixed number of basic particles of meaning. If we did so, what we would produce would simply be the combination of strings of particulars, which, if learned as such, would bear no relation to how a language learned with true universals operates. As Bambrough says:

> A pupil does not have to consult on every separate occasion on which he encounters a new object, and if he did consult us every time, we should have to say that he was not *learning* the use of the word. The reference that we make to a finite number of objects to which the word applies, and to a finite number of objects to which the word does not apply, is capable of equipping the pupil with a capacity for correctly applying or withholding the word to or from an *infinite* number of objects to which we have made no reference. (Bambrough, 1968, pp. 200–1)

Closed-classes are artificial and stipulative concepts which have no place in natural languages where general terms cannot be defined exhaustively. In an artificial language where all universals represented closed-classes, new instances of, for example, new kinds of tables could never be recognised. But if new possible instances could never be added to existing classes because of their closure, then linguistic usage would be in a state of perpetual revolution, the anarchic character of which would make it almost impossible to say anything at all. Far from the early Wittgenstein's ideal language being 'clear and determinate', the very strategy for producing it would be self-defeating. To account for the phenomenon of language, therefore, we must account for its creativity, which must necessarily be related to open-class concepts and their operation. The explanation of this operation is to be found in the human language-user's ability to dispense with some paradigmic apparatus of exhaustive definition or of determinacy of quantification and instead to grasp that classes really are family resemblances (Wittgenstein, 1974, pp. 31–2).

Let us take as our example of a universal term the well-worn 'table' and let us show how tables may also be said to 'form a family'. Bambrough describes classification by family resemblance thus:

> We may classify a set of objects by reference to the presence or absence of features A, B, C, D, E. It may well happen that five objects e, d, c, b, a are such that each of them has four of these properties and lacks the fifth and that the missing feature is different in each of the five cases. (Bambrough, 1968, p. 189)

Table a may have three legs (A), be round (B), have a flat top (C) and be made of wood (D). Table b may have four legs (E), be square (F), have a curved top (G) and be made of plastic (H). Table c may have a curved top (G), have three legs (A), and be made of plastic (H). How can we say that a and b are tables when $a = A, B, C, D$, and $b = E, F, G, H$? Defined exhaustively we should have to say that, if a is a table then b cannot be so since they have no features in common, not even essential as opposed to accidental features. What entitles us to do so is our classification of c as a table since $c = A, H, G$ which links a to b through G. This is why Wittgenstein sometimes uses the metaphor of a chain rather than a family to characterise open-classes since it is the fact that their features are *linked* in a certain way that makes them what they are and also that new objects for classification are so linkable. But whether we describe them as 'chains' or 'families', 'tables' are shown by our discussion to represent 'a complicated network of similarities overlapping and criss-crossing: sometimes overall similarities, sometimes similarities of detail', with no exhaustively definable, fixed, determinate list of particulars that can be 'quantified over'.

If, however, universal terms are not simply constructed arbitrarily in language but as the result of rule-following which, because it follows rules for family-resemblance, cannot be regarded as rule-conformance, it may well be asked where do such rules come from? Such rules cannot constitute the causal conformance of men to what the order of nature impresses upon either their minds in sensation or through the stimulus–response nexus on their behaviour, or upon the representational form of utterances and writing. They involve that transcendence of the particular which enables some features of what is observed to be ignored (for example, absence of the Churchill scowl or forehead) in favour of other features (the Churchill nose) that are allowed to override such absences so that the family-resemblance identification can be made. Can, therefore, such rules be considered innate and/or part of the basic form of any example of human social life? We shall see in Chapter 8 how Chomsky accepts the first part of this dichotomy and in Chapter 7 how Durkheim accepted the second. Wittgenstein, however, is perhaps by the majority of his interpreters regarded as accepting neither part of this dichotomy, wrongly as I shall argue. Although there is, I believe, an ambiguity in Wittgenstein's account, he is often regarded as claiming that the rules by which family-resemblances are detected and so classified come from the interpersonal backcloth of rules that we learn as a result of our initiation, usually as children, into a particular social form of life (Hamlyn, 1978, pp. 17–18). It is thought that we can invoke Wittgenstein's notion of a culturally relative 'language-game' to explain how we go about making classifications in terms of family-resemblances. There are many questions here about the nature of objectivity to which we shall have to give our more detailed attention when we deal with them critically in Chapter 8 when we re-examine critically the epistemological backcloth to Hirst's curriculum theory. Suffice it to say for the moment that such a culturally relative interpretation of Wittgenstein's notion of a language-game would go as follows. We are born into a social situation in which certain language-games are being played in which all kinds of new, creative moves are allowed. New examples of instances can be added to existing general terms, for example. But such moves are not arbitrary but are rule-governed. They are governed by certain, basic ground rules. In order to have disagreement in opinion, in order to propose new ideas, classifications and so forth which conflict with existing prejudices and so on, we must, paradoxically, have achieved a prior agreement, an agreement in a form of life. We can have a disagreement over whether 'blue' is really a 'sound' rather than a 'colour' or vice versa, but only by leaving most of the remaining rules for the meaning of concepts in our language unchanged, otherwise we cannot even communicate the substance of our disagreement. Without such an agreement about those remaining rules ('agreement in form of life') it is impossible, therefore, to have disagreement in opinion let alone agreement.

Sometimes, therefore, Wittgenstein is interpreted as having in his later work espoused a culturally relative position in explaining rules for forming general classes as originating from 'language-games'. The general classes that we construct are grouping of particulars in accordance with rules whose open-ended and ambiguous character reflect the shifting interests and consensus of the social group. Certainly, explanations of fundamental moral concepts as arising in this way exemplify the weaknesses as well as the strengths of such a position. It is arguable that both 'lieing' and 'murder', albeit defined in some minimal sense, must be norms that hold generally across human societies (Brent, 1978, pp. 119 ff.). Wittgenstein's actual words in the *Philosophical Investigations* on this point are notoriously vague. If language-games are to be regarded as culturally relative frameworks of rules, then he can be making a point which is little different from that which is made by Quine's thesis of the indeterminacy of translation. To paraphrase the familiar slogan: 'The meaning of a concept (universal or general term) is its use in the particular language-game that is being played.' Different cultures play different language-games, and the use that the concepts that make up such games have is relative to the pragmatic concerns of the particular culture. A given culture may thus play a language-game that diverges so radically from another that both sets of players, having no agreement on basic ground rules, have no means of intelligible communication. Thus interpreted, the Quine/ Wittgenstein thesis appears to support more or less the culturally relative view of science that we shall discuss in greater detail in the next chapter and that is associated with Kuhn's paradigms. Scientific frameworks of explanation are, on this view, like language-games that communities of scientists play among themselves.

Let us, however, develop this point briefly here. We may say that Isaac Newton in the incident with the apple mentioned in Chapter 1 acted in a way that was analogous to a footballer running with the ball. Supposing, Newton argued, we reconstruct the ground rules of the game of Aristotelian physics that we have been playing for centuries. Supposing we cease to regard all objects throughout the universe as normally at rest and cease to look for the causes of motion as though motion were abnormal. Thus we break the rule that instructs us to regard rest and not motion as that which requires explanation. As the principle is fundamental to the system, we may say that a new language-game has come into being. Likewise Kuhn argues that we are to similarly understand Newton's eventual super-session in Einstein's physics. Space and time are now to be regarded as continua. What Kuhn describes as a 'paradigm revolution' has taken place and the two conflicting paradigms of explanation in contemporary physics are explicable (according to this interpretation of Wittgenstein) in terms of two different language-games that are being played.

So runs one interpretation of the later Wittgenstein which makes his thesis run parallel to Quine's indeterminacy of translation. We have already suggested that this interpretation is incorrect. Now I wish to transform this suggestion into a full-blown criticism. My criticism is that such a view of 'language-games' runs counter to that fundamental insight of the later Wittgenstein that interprets universals in terms of family resemblances. Problems of interpretation of Wittgenstein's later work abound, principally because his object in that work was not to propose a new, systematic account of epistemology but rather to expound some insights about the nature of language for philosophers to develop how they will. That, however, his view of family-resemblance is critical to his understanding of a language-game may be seen from the passage in which he originally expounded his view of family-resemblance using the very example of 'games' (Wittgenstein, 1974, pp. 31–2).

The fundamental problem of assimilating language-games to Kuhn's paradigms is, I submit, that such an assimilation misses how much games are to be understood in terms of family-resemblances. Such as assimilation presupposes that Newtonian physics as a language-game can be exhaustively defined, compared with the language-game that is Einsteinian physics, and declared not to be part of the same paradigm or language-game. But the notion of 'paradigm' is, as such, too 'clear and determinate' to make it a satisfactory key to an understanding of the later Wittgenstein's view of language, which regards a special kind of vagueness as constituting the communicative strength of language. There are 'groups of games', as we saw in the passage just quoted, and Newtonian and Einsteinian physics, I submit, can be regarded in the same group where 'similarities crop up and disappear'. We saw, moreover, in our discussion of Yudkin's criticism of Quine's view of radical translation, that there was a special kind of imprecision in the example of a blackboard sketch of a car that enabled communication to go on without commitment to a distinct picture, presuppositions, discoveries or frameworks making sophisticated metaphysical distinctions. Human communication and explanation, understood by analogy with language-games characterised by family-resemblance, allows such 'games' to incorporate new discoveries (like 'rabbit stages', 'whole rabbits', 'Cadillacs' and so on) into existing schemes (or open-classes) which enables cross-cultural understanding and therefore translation to go on. There is in this respect no great difference between Quine's anthropologist and the native talking about 'rabbit stages', and the child in Bambrough's example learning the universal 'table'. The new, possible instances of tables are like new possible instances of rabbits, cars or tables ('Is this rabbit stage a rabbit?', 'Is this Cadillac a car?', 'Is this coffee table a table?'. . .). Likewise it might be argued that the new Einsteinian instances of explanation, and spatio-temporal events are to be understood as part of the same 'group of games' expanded and developed by an evolutionary rather than a revolutionary method. Such an evolutionary method of development involves an examination of 'a complicated network of similarities overlapping and criss-crossing: sometimes overall similarities, sometimes similarities of detail'. Language-games ought therefore, I submit, to be understood in terms of family-resemblance and are thus an alternative to revolutionary paradigmatic explanations rather than equivalents.

We see, therefore, where Wittgenstein's analysis of the open-class character of genuine universals has led us that enabled not simply actual but possible new instances to be subsumed under them. 'Family-resemblance' was his explanation of the creativity of language that enabled him to explain why we did not have to create continually new concepts and with them new languages. It is on this view a strength rather than a weakness of ordinary language that it does not have to have a name or primitive sign for every distinct, particular table, swan or rabbit in the world, as Wittgenstein had originally thought. Likewise a proper association of family resemblance with language-games has taken us one stage further and accounts not merely for the conceptual but for the propositional creativity of language. Because the notion of a language-game is therefore an open-ended notion, a language-game cannot be exhaustively defined so as to give it a clear and determinate paradigmatic form. The famous building-site passage (Wittgenstein, 1974, pp. 83–93) emphasises the creative, open-ended character of language, the infinite variety of uses to which it can be put, the new, possible descriptions and explanations which it can develop. Far from Wittgenstein's notion of a language-game being usable therefore as an account of how there can be paradigmatic revolutions, we have here an account of language which disposes of the need for such changes. Language in terms of 'language-games', like universal classifications in terms of family-resemblance, shows how there can be a progression from actual to possible classifications and descriptions without the need for revolutionary displacement. Because language-games cannot be exhaustively defined, their classes cannot be closed as the early Wittgenstein and Kuhn appeared to desire to close them. Had the early Wittgenstein and Kuhn succeeded in producing accounts of descriptions of the world whose general terms were exhaustively definable closed-classes, then such descriptions could not cope with new instances of particulars. When, to speak metaphorically, such closed-classes were bombarded with new particulars, they would have to be broken up and discarded and language would be in a state of permanent and anarchic revolution. But, as we have seen, Wittgenstein later denied that exhaustive definitions of universal terms were possible, so that, between different versions of language-games, we ought, on the basis of family-resemblance, to see that there is a basic continuity between such apparently differing versions.

How, then, were both the early Wittgenstein, Quine and Kuhn lead astray regarding the nature of the language of inquiry? Undoubtedly it was because the former two were influenced positively and the latter negatively by what we shall see in the next chapter to have been an empiricist view of science. Science and mathematics appeared both to be seeking and to require either a clear and determinate picture of the world or a clear and determinate (mathematical) language in terms of which such a picture could be quantified. When, therefore, the philosopher of science or mathematics came across either non-technical expressions or even technical expressions which were indeterminate in a given scientific or mathematical system, then he strove to revise such expressions in order to make them clear and determinate. This revision, to use the terminology that we have adopted so far, involved replacing open-class universal terms with closed-class ones. Take, for example, the common-sense term 'water'. Now, 'water' is rather like 'table' in that there is a very wide and indeterminate variety of things that are described as 'water' and novel instances can always possibly be added to this open-class. Then the scientist comes along and constructs a technical term for 'water' which turns it into an exhaustively definable closed-class. He turns it into what the early Wittgenstein described as a 'concatenation of particulars'. 'Water', in the scientist's ideal language, is written H_2O, and when it is so written it has a clear and determinate sense because it now consists of a closed string of particulars, namely, two atoms of hydrogen and one of oxygen, no more and no less. Further classifications of novel items of experience become impossible other than in terms of these indeterminate features (H, 2 and O). If a sample of what in ordinary language is called 'water' is now produced and analysis reveals more than the string of particulars H_2O, then ordinary language must be displaced. When to the particulars H_2O further particulars are added, such as $MgCl_2$, a new term is devised, namely, 'carbon tetrachloride' and exhaustively defined

H_2OMgCl_2. As exhaustively definable 'concatenations of particulars', such closed-classes can be broken up and reformulated in accordance with the needs and interests of the scientific community. We have seen, moreover, that both Quine and Kuhn, both in their own different way, seek to produce an account of how such concepts come to be broken up and reformulated. Thus the philosopher of science on the basis of what has happened with the formation of technical descriptions for 'water' (H_2O) proceeds to try to generalise his principle of clarity and determinacy over every concept in the total framework of scientific explanation. But when he finally reaches the ground rules of the framework, he begins to run into trouble because of the very failure to recognise how definition by family-resemblance operates that we have noted in connection with Kuhn's work. Let us take such ground rules to be what Hirst calls 'categorical concepts' in contrast to clear and determinate substantive concepts (Brent, 1978, pp. 101–10). 'Cause', for example, as we shall see in the next chapter, produced enormous difficulties when philosophers sought to define this concept exhaustively, and as we have already seen, it was one of those open-class universal terms that was very difficult to explain on Locke's account. It is arguable (as we shall further argue in Chapter 8) that this is because instances of causes can only be defined in terms of family-resemblances without precipitating the linguistic chaos that Kuhn thought to be unavoidable. Likewise, in the case of mathematics, we may be able to give exhaustive definitions of 'square root' (a substantive concept) as we could give exhaustive definitions of 'water'. But what happens with such ground rules (categorical concepts) of mathematical systems such as 'calculus', 'operation' or 'proof'? As Waismann, a mathematician heavily influenced by Wittgenstein's thinking on family-resemblance, says:

> This [*sc.* definition by family-resemblance] is also valid of the expressions 'arithmetic', 'geometry', 'calculus', 'operation', 'proof'. 'problems', etc. They all designate families of concepts, and it is of little value to start a controversy regarding their exact definition. In wishing to explain the concept of arithmetic, we will point to examples and allow the concept to reach as far as the similarity reaches in these examples. The very openness, nonclosure, of these concepts also has its good points, for it gives language the freedom to comprise new discoveries in a known scheme. (Quoted in Richardson, 1976, pp. 96–7)

We have seen how the later Wittgenstein found such a quest for a clear and determinate description of a language-game not only difficult but logically impossible. We shall demonstrate in detail in Chapter 8 that, though substantive concepts are able to be exhaustively defined, categorical concepts in those language-games that may be called 'forms of knowledge' cannot be so defined. We shall pursue there our theme that the later Wittgenstein saw that his earlier quest had been founded upon a complete misunderstanding of how the language of science and mathematics is connected to common-sense language that is open-ended. One consequence of this conclusion was that Wittgenstein reinstated forms of inquiry other than the scientific and the mathematical which the empiricists rejected – a reinstatement that has given rise to the curriculum theory of Paul Hirst which I discussed in a previous volume (Brent, 1978) and which I will be discussing further in this context in Chapter 8. Perhaps, however, it will be in order for me to outline briefly this consequence here, particularly as it will illuminate further the epistemological position that we have here established regarding the nature of universals as open-classes definable in terms of family-resemblance.

It was believed by the empiricists that the possibility of mathematical and scientific descriptions being clear and determinate gave them an epistemological superiority to, for example, historical inquiry which could never be clear and determinate. Historical inquiry requires the use of such general terms as, for example, 'Christian' or 'Marxist' in order to, for instance, predict, explain, evaluate historical events, influences on currents of opinion and so on. Yet the problem for the early Wittgenstein as for the empiricist (as for many empiricist-minded Marxists and Christians) was how to define the 'true' Marxist or the 'true' Christian. The *Tractacus* stipulation that language requires a clear and determinate sense with all general terms exhaustively defined appears elusive regarding the 'true' Marxist or 'true' Christian. Is the 'true' Christian the first-century millenarian looking for the imminent apocalypse, the third-century trinitarian seeing divinity in terms of substances and essences, the seventeenth-century Puritan and so forth? Is the 'true' Marxist to be found in the Eastern European communist, the Latin American guerrilla or the left-wing member of the Labour Party? What exhaustive list of particular features do Christians and Marxists throughout the world and throughout the ages hold in common in virtue of which they are so classifiable? There are none. Instead there are 'a complicated network of similarities overlapping and criss-crossing'. When we try to make such descriptions of classes of people clear and determinate closed-classes we end up with the absurdity of sectarian Christians and sectarian Marxists arbitrarily stipulating that only a certain group (of which they, of course, are members) possess the appropriate and closed list of particular features. Their stipulations would, if accepted, of course throw into turmoil the structure of historical analysis and evaluation based upon the use of these terms as open-classes, however unaware the professional historian may be of the way that family-resemblance functions in the language of historical explanation. Like the later Wittgenstein's classic reference to 'games' that we quoted earlier, there is no exhaustive list of features whereby the historian recognises 'Christians' or 'Marxists'. Identification proceeds by family-resemblance.

The early Wittgenstein, in his *Tractatus* period, was influenced by what we shall see in greater detail in the next chapter to have been an empiricist philosophy of science. When scientific and mathematical discourse were analysed by contrast, the early Wittgenstein though, ideally, they would be exhaustively definable, and an ideal language would be like the language of mathematics and science, but unlike the language of literature and history in this respect. The later Wittgenstein was to grasp, as we have seen, that only some of the concepts in which scientific and mathematical discourse is conducted are exhaustively definable, and these are concepts which, in Chapter 8, we shall be trying to give a formalised account of in terms of what Hirst describes as 'substantive' concepts. In our next chapter we shall see that what Hirst calls 'categorical' concepts were, on analysis shown to be intractable in terms of exhaustive definition. This will emerge as not simply the replacement in some part of modern physics of Newton by Einstein, but the failure even in classical physics to produce a satisfactory account of causation which could survive what we shall see was Hume's criticism of the causal principle. We shall focus on a critical example of this in empiricism's failure to carry through its programme of finally explaining induction in terms of deduction. Suffice it to say here that we shall see how the exhaustively definable definition of 'cause' became as elusive as the exhaustively definable definition of a 'Christian' or of a 'Marxist'. The negative results of the quest for an ideal language containing universals which were but concatenations of particulars prompted, as we have seen and described in detail, an original mind like Wittgenstein's positively to pursue a new strategy in understanding language which was to make no distinction between the validity of different kinds of inquiry.

It is now clearly time to look more deeply at changing views on the philosophy of science, important as these have been shown to have been for corresponding changes in the views of both Skinner and the early Wittgenstein. Before, however, we do, let us summarise where our discussion has lead us so far. We have seen how Skinner's putative revision of a science of human behaviour ran into great difficulties regarding the nature of 'operant' conditioning, for which Skinner was forced by his fundamental presuppositions to continue to demand a causal basis for behaviour. The problem was that an explanation of behaviour in terms of statistical probability (on which 'operant conditioning' is based) is part of the general problem of universals that are open-class concepts, namely, that there is involved in their formation that 'transcendence of the particular' that behaviourism seeks to deny. Quite frequently we have drawn attention to the way that both Skinner and Quine use redescriptions in statistical terms of rule-following behaviour in terms of rule-conforming behaviour without being able to account for the rule-conformance that now appears in the redescription. We have looked at two further attempts to deal with the problem of universals in either causal or behavioural terms: that of the early Wittgenstein, who sought to dispense with universals altogether, and that of Quine, who sought to explain their formation arbitrarily or, as he would prefer to say, 'pragmatically'. Finally we have followed Wittgenstein's later insights on language-games towards a new account of universals in terms of family-resemblance to which rule-following is irreducible to rule-conformance and axiomatic. We have, moreover, briefly pointed to ways in which our account will help us in future with curriculum issues, particularly those raised by Paul Hirst. We shall be seeing in Chapter 4 how the problems with general behaviourism that we have outlined apply also specifically to behaviouristically inclined curriculum proposals. For the moment, let us complete our criticism of behaviourism by looking in greater detail at those changing perspectives in the philosophy of science with which we have so far only dealt briefly and sketchily.

Chapter 3

Skinner's Conflicting Paradigms of Science

In our last chapter we considered general problems of the relationship between language and forms of human experience, noting the phenomenon of the transcendence of the particular. We saw that rule-following was both irreducible to rule-conforming and indispensible to grasping how it is possible to grasp the operations of open-class concepts through the family resemblances of their particulars. We now turn to the relationship between forms of scientific inquiry and their language, and forms of human experience. Whereas empiricism sought to revise language and its functions in the light of what it falsely believed to be an inductivist paradigm for natural sciences, we shall see that the new physics shows in its model of inquiry a mirroring of forms of human experience in natural languages rather than an allegedly more logical imposition upon them.

3.1 EMPIRICIST APPROACHES TO SCIENCE

So far we have spoken of scientific enterprises as being rooted in a particular set of common-sense experiences, but as taking us beyond at least certain of such experiences as they progress towards becoming general frameworks of explanation encompassing every event throughout the universe. Frameworks of scientific explanation, we said at the beginning of Chapter 1, sanction some kinds of products of common sense against others, labelling some of our intuitions as real and others as mistaken. We have presented this picture of the scientific enterprise as a purely factual description of how scientists generally proceed, leaving until now the question of to what extent they are entitled to make such assumptions. Thus empiricists such as Locke undoubtedly saw the nature of the scientific enterprise in such programmatic terms as these. Mistaken common sense items ('Beware of mermaids') could be explained in terms of misconstructions of other common sense items, namely, Locke's 'simple ideas'. The followers of Newton, as we saw also in Chapter 1, interpreted the role of scientific explanation similarly, as one which was able, beginning with a number of quite specific common-sense observations (apples falling, for instance), to construct from these observations a general and universal framework in terms of which all events could be explained in terms of their causes and future events thereby predicted. It was a mechanistic view of science in which the universe could be likened to a vast and complex clock. Once the mechanisms of nature, their operations and interrelations were understood, then the task of science would be complete since the workings of the clock would be completely understood. We have seen how the work of the early Wittgenstein bears the impress of this caste of thinking in his belief that once we had a complete list of primitive signs that depicted clearly and determinately each particular object in the universe and applied to them appropriate logical formulas, then we could give a complete description of the universe, past, present and future. Skinnerian like the classical behaviourists reflected this empiricist philosophy of science. As Skinner said:

> Science ... is a search for order, for uniformities, for lawful relations among the events in nature. It begins, as we all begin [*sic*!], by observing single episodes, but it quickly passes on to the general rule, to scientific law.

and:

> By predicting the occurrence of an event we are able to prepare for it. By arranging conditions in ways specified by the laws of a system, we not only predict, we control: we 'cause' an event to occur or assume certain characteristics. (Skinner, 1953, pp. 13–14)

Thus explanations of human behaviour could become part of our scientific explanations of the behaviour of animate as well as inanimate matter. Curriculum proposals based on such an empiricist view of science reflect, as we shall see in the next chapter, a similar desire to 'begin ... by observing single episodes' in the learning of school subjects and to quickly pass 'on to the general, to scientific law'. 'By arranging conditions of the laws of' behaviourally defined 'laws of' a curriculum, we not only predict, we control: we 'cause' students to learn subjects. We shall see also in Chapters 5 and 6 how formally a similar view of the nature of theoretical frameworks is held by Marxist curriculum theorists.

It is now time for us therefore to challenge this approach in the form of a specific challenge to an empiricist philosophy of science. We have already seen some general problems for this view of science as it is a version of the unsatisfactory, empiricist solution to the problem of universals. It involves us being able to construct a general picture of the world from strings of particular observations, and being able to close this picture of the world when the last particular object has been observed and duly classified.

3.2 EMPIRICISM AND THE PROBLEM OF INDUCTION

Let us begin with what was a critical problem in science for this point of view, namely, the problem of induction. The problem of induction is a particular example of the general problem of universals, namely, how does one pass from a sentence of the form 'In every observed instance of x . . .' to statements of the form 'In all cases of x . . .'. But by what right, having observed only a given number of x's, do we proceed to make such general statements as, 'In all cases of x . . .'? How many observations and of what sort would give us this right? The question poses the problem of induction. We have seen, moreover, that behaviourism too had its own particular problem with induction in its description of stimulus generalisation. Classical behaviourism thought that it could show how, by a series (one might even say a 'concatenation') of unbroken particular steps, stimulus generalisation takes place from substitutions of one stimulus for another in a temporal series in which one stimulus succeeds another on the principle of similarity. We saw, moreover, that the quest for a complete determinism implied by such an inductive method and accepted by Skinner was implicitly and self-contradictorily revoked by him in the statistical explanation implied by operant conditioning. Skinner was, we argued, unaware that the requirements for the concept of operant conditioning were the very requirements for a more radical alteration of the inductive model than Skinner himself wished to allow. It is now time, therefore, for us to explore in greater detail the implications of the disjunction between cause and probability for science in general and for a science of human behaviour in particular.

Induction was seen to be problematic because it is, to say the least, extremely difficult to specify at precisely what point particular empirical observations convey the right to frame general laws such as those about water boiling. Hume, for reasons that we shall discuss in a moment, was extremely sceptical that, in principle, such a right ever existed. The assertion of such a right, as we shall see, implied the justifiability of the causal principle. For the moment, let us see what logical justification empiricism might give for such a claim that there must exist such a mechanical method of scientific investigation as the inductive method which, when clearly explicated, would lead to some final and true clear and determinate picture of the world. It might be argued first of all that statements such as 'x is possibly water', 'x is probably water', are parasitic or polar concepts (Hamlyn, 1970, pp. 16–22), and as such are only explicable against a backcloth of judgements, some of which are more than merely possible or probable. It is only on this view possible to make probability judgements because we can also make judgements that are more than probable (that are certain) by comparison and contrast with which we understand the 'merely probable' character of the former. If, therefore, to use the early Wittgenstein's expression, we lack a 'clear and determinate' identification of a given concept, it is only because we need to do better research, to find out more things about the world, to achieve between reality and our linguistic classifications a better alignment and so forth. On this view, therefore, we might say that inductive arguments are poor relations of deductive ones. When the premises of an inductive argument have been all spelled out in a clear and determinate fashion, when a large and exhaustive collection of all relevant premises has been made, then certainty will replace possibility or probability and deduction will replace induction or inference.

This quest for certainty which lead to the demand that induction be explained in terms of deduction was part and parcel, therefore, of an empiricist view of the nature of science. Science was to be seen as a progressive and evolutionary enterprise from the caves to the stars. Early man begins on this view with a vague and provisional picture of a world populated by gods, ghosts and demons and similar entities. By slow degrees and by the slow development of an accurate scientific method, men obliterate from the picture such falsehoods, they write in clearer lines and colours where these are inaccurate, vague or obscure until, at the last, the universe is completely described and explained. But the fundamental lynchpin of this view of science was the causal principle. As we have already remarked earlier, the principle 'every event has a cause' arguably points to a view of the universe as a clockwork mechanism in which, once one has charted every single event, then one can quite mechanically explain the past and predict the future. We can do this as mechanically as the early Wittgenstein thought that, given an exhaustive list of primitive signs or names and the appropriate logical formulas, we could produce a complete description of the world. Clearly, then, a view of induction as the poor relation of deduction was, together with the causal principle that sustained such a view, integral to an empiricist frame of reference. But within such a frame of reference, doubts began to be felt about how causal descriptions of the world could be justified as early as the great empiricist philosopher, David Hume.

Hume was sceptical about the causal principle (Hume, 1969, pp. 117–29). His problem, put simply, was as follows. Scientific descriptions of the world which followed the Newtonian paradigm presupposed the causal principle even if they did not speak of causes, as they quite frequently did. Talk of causes, then, fairly riddles scientific descriptions as when we say, 'Heat causes metal to expand', 'Sucrose must have been present since only it causes Millean's reagent to turn orange.' Yet what does it *mean* in all such statements to say that 'A caused B'? Clearly it means far more than that, whenever event B occurred in the past, it was preceded by event A, or that whenever event A occurred in the past, event B followed it. When I say that, 'The lighted gas caused the water in the kettle to boil,' I mean something more than whenever kettles in the past were put on lighted gas-burners, they boiled. I mean that not only have these events happened in the past, but that the connection between these events was such that they must also occur again in the future. Granted that we make distinction between conjunction ('A *and* B occurred in the past' (A. B)) and implication ('*If* A occured *then* B also occurred' (A → B)), how can we justify this distinction? Our only justification, claims Hume, is greater frequency of conjunction in the past on the basis of which the stronger claim of causal implication is made. Whenever (*a*) kettles full of water have been conjoined with gas-burners in the past, the water has boiled, whereas (*b*) lightning has only on a few occasions illuminated the closing words of a witch-doctor's curse.

The frequency of conjunction in the case of type (*a*) observations has deceived us, according to Hume, in claiming more for such observations than we ought. The notion of 'cause' is a psychological illusion and we are in no way entitled to conclude that kettles will boil in the future simply because they always have done so in the past. ''Tis by no means impossible', in Hume's famous words, 'that the sun should not rise tomorrow' (Hume, 1969, p. 122). The practitioners of Newtonian science did not, of course, take Hume seriously. His problem appeared (before Einstein, as we shall see) an academic quibble of no practical consequence to the day-to-day running of scientific inquiry. The assumption of the causal principle had lead to great practical strides in science, and so its lack of justification appeared to be of no practical consequence. Kant, however, did take Hume's objection to the causal principle seriously, and sought to show that it was misconceived. Kant pointed out that Hume's objection to the causal principle presupposed the very causal principle that it sought to deny in a way that interestingly parallels Skinner's presupposition of the transcendence of the particular in statistical explanations that he, too, sought to dispense with. If we only believe that there is a stronger association between events than conjunction because habitual recurrence of conjunctions causes a psychological illusion, then we require the very notion of 'cause' to explain why we are wrong in thinking that some things are the causes of others. Kant's positive solution (Kant, 1939), to a form of which we shall return in Chapter 8, was to claim that the causal principle, together with categories of space and time, did not exist in the world (in 'things-in-themselves') but were the product of our mental apparatus through which we construct the account of the world that we do (in terms of 'things as they appear'). Our picture of the world is constructed from two sources and not from one, as both Locke (direct experience produced in sensation) and Plato (knowledge of pure Forms or Ideas) had both tried to suggest from widely differing standpoints. Those external objects which register themselves upon our receptor organs in sensation would appear to us as completely chaotic unless our minds actively sorted them out within a causal, spatio-temporal framework. A framework of this sort both the empiricist Quine and the neo-rationalist Chomsky would regard as innate and might attribute to Kant an innatist standpoint and details of which they would nevertheless wish to modify drastically. Such an innatist interpretation of Kant is to be considered with care. Kant would not have regarded the causal or spatio-temporal principles as part of our innate *knowledge*, as Descartes and Leibniz had done. They only become part of our *knowledge* when they are employed in actual experience. For Kant, our knowledge of the world comes not from innate ideas in isolation from sensation, nor from sensation (Locke's 'simple ideas', for example) apart from innate categories. Only in combination can sensation and a pre-existing, innate framework produce knowledge of the world.

As we said, Hume's scepticism was not taken seriously by his contemporaries who practised Newtonian science. But the Einsteinian revolution in physics has shown Hume's doubts about the causal principle to have great practical importance indeed. Let us briefly now recount why. Whether they were the product of innate dispositions as Kant may have thought (and as Quine certainly thinks), or innate knowledge as Descartes had thought, or in some way the result of impressions left upon the sense-organs by particular objects as Hume thought, certain definitions of space, time and cause were the foundations of Newtonian science. Kant believed them to be *a priori*, Locke somehow learned in experience and therefore *a posteriori*, Descartes *a priori* because they were *known* innately. But whatever the empiricists (for example, Locke, Hume), the rationalists (for example, Descartes, Leibniz) or a 'constructionalist' (like Kant) might believe about the origins and epistemological justification of such principles, they were within Newtonian physics regarded as for whatever reason unchangeable. What Einstein was to do was to produce a framework of physical explanation which changed all three principles and thus threw into doubt both empiricist, rationalist and constructionalist accounts of such principles. Let us now explore how this came about.

3.3 EINSTEIN'S PROBABILITY AND SKINNER'S DETERMINISM

In Newton's system, space and time were absolutes against which all changes in physical objects could be measured. This character of Newtonian space and Newtonian time is exemplified in the statement: 'Two objects cannot exist together in the same space and at the same time.' Space for Newton had the same quality throughout the universe so that, if millions of miles away in outer space two objects change places at a given distance apart, then the distance between them is identical with the two pencils that I have just changed places between identical points in space. Time, moreover, has the same quality throughout the universe for any object in any space and at any speed. As such, time is the measure of the ageing of matter throughout the universe. That half an hour has passed since I began writing this page simply measures the ageing of my body and all other objects around me and throughout the universe. A few more hairs have fallen out, a few more teeth gone that much badder, a few more wrinkles in my face, an undetected but sure drying of the ink and paper on which I write and so forth. The ageing process is also, for Newton, identical for any piece of matter throughout the universe at any speed. Now, it is this absolute character of space and time within the Newtonian framework that makes these categories capable of acting as a measure. A measure must itself be a constant if it is to be capable of measuring variables. An elastic ruler, for example, could not measure anything.

In 1905, Einstein, from the obscurity of his patent office in Zürich, published two papers which were to overthrow at least large parts of the Newtonian system. Having renewed his interest in mathematics, which he had lost when in this subject he only achieved sufficient grades for entry into Zürich Polytechnic (and in the subsequent dreary routine of that institution), Einstein produced a mathematical argument to the effect that space and time were relative to either one's position in the universe (space) or to the speed at which one was travelling (time). Einstein explained gravity, not in terms of a force which attracted objects, as Newton had done, but in terms of the distorted or warped character of space relative to the nearness of a given point in space to an object and its size. Planets revolve around the sun, or get pulled towards its surface because they proceed through curved space like trains on a curved track. If you therefore were to take two objects which occupy two different points in space in Newton's universe the same distance apart and then to transpose them into an Einsteinian universe with warped space, you would find that they would now be different distances apart, depending upon how warped or curved was the particular space at the particular points in Einstein's universe at which we chose to locate them. Regarding time, since matter ages relative to its speed through space, identical objects going at different speeds age differently (Schilpp, 1969).

The spatio-temporal framework could therefore no longer function as the absolute measure for which Newton used them. A measure necessarily must be fixed. An elastic ruler would never succeed in providing a standard of comparison between objects. How, then, could cause and effect be measured in Einstein's universe where no events were in any absolute sense prior to others with the result that the various parts of the universal clock could not interact in any determinate way? Einstein's answer was to provide one absolute measure in terms of which the elasticity or relativity of times and spaces could be accurately measured and compared. This absolute measure was the speed of light. But here a problem arose which directly supported Hume's scepticism regarding Newton's understanding of the causal principle. In a second paper, published betwixt the processing of Swiss patents in 1905, he argued against the wave theory of light in favour of the particle theory of light in which light was considered not to consist of waves but of particles called 'quanta' or 'photons'. But subsequently, in the 1920s, it became clear that the behaviour of photons could only be described in statistical terms. Such a conclusion revolted Einstein, who declared of such a view that: 'An inner voice tells me that it is not the true Jacob', and, in a classic reference to the God of Spinoza no less than of Abraham, Isaac and Jacob: 'The Old One would not have planned it that way nor does He play at dice!'

We saw at the beginning of this section that it was its acceptance of the causal principle as axiomatic that lead to empiricism's demand that inductive arguments be explained as the poor relations of deductive ones. With the mention of statistical explanation (which were the only kind that worked for photons), we find a proposal made for a third kind of argument which is neither deductive nor inductive. Let us take as an example of statistical or probablistic argument the following:

75% of Texans are oil millionaires (Major premise)
x is a Texan   (Minor premise)
_____
Therefore, x is (possibly, probably) an oil millionaire (Conclusion)

This syllogism differs from our example of a deductive syllogism about swans in that the major premise does not consist of a closed-class exhaustive of its particulars. But neither is it dependent upon any one particular object either becoming or remaining a member of the general class, as in inductive argument. One or more particular Texans can go bankrupt and cease to be oil millionaires, but, so long as these are replaced by an identical number of Texans who become oil millionaires, then the statement remains true. Likewise, as we saw earlier, in connection with the predictions about dice games, in a statistical argument no prediction is made about the behaviour of any one in particular thing in the general description of the behaviour of classes of things. When I say that there is a one-in-six probability of the number six coming up, I am not making any prediction about a particular series of throws. I am not predicting that, when I throw the dice for six particular successive throws, the number six will invariably come up once and not more than once. I am only establishing a possibility or probability based upon recurring patterns discerned in a large enough sample of random throws. Past conjunctions of events when repeated on a large enough scale exhibit a pattern, and this pattern justifies possible or probable convictions about what will happen in the future. But there is no more certainty about such patterns of statistical recurrence than there was for Hume a certainty based upon some causal chain of events that the sun will rise tomorrow. The example of the sun illuminating the morning was happily chosen by Hume in this connection since, by a fortunate accident, it links Hume's thinking with Einstein's. Light beams, as we have seen, consist of photons, and it is only general patterns of recurrence that can be studied. Individual photons may pop in and pop out of the general class just as individual Texans may become or cease to be oil millionaires. What matters is the general pattern of past conjunctions established with a large enough sample which yields probability but not certainty.

It is interesting to develop for a moment a line of speculation from the sufficiency of probabilistic explanations of a kind that may have given Einstein his alarming vision of God as a cosmic dice-player. We saw the causal principle to be exemplified by: 'When kettles full of water are placed upon gas-burners, the water boils.' Now Einstein was a philosopher as well as a scientist and he had read Hume. As Einstein himself said:

Hume saw clearly that certain concepts, as for example that of causality, cannot be deduced from the material of experience by logical methods. Kant, thoroughly convinced of the indispensibility of certain concepts, took them – just as they are selected – to be the necessary premises of every kind of thinking and differentiated them from concepts of empirical origin. I am convinced, however, that this differentiation is erroneous, i.e., that it does not do justice to the problem in a natural way. All concepts, even those which are closest to experience, are from the point of view of logic freely chosen conventions, just as is the case with the concept of causality, with which this problematic concerned itself in the first instance. (Einstein, 1969, p. 13)

Now Einstein's equivalent of the Humean dilemma may be stated as follows. Supposing for one moment we were to concede that we had been deceived, as Hume thought, about going beyond 'mere' conjunction to postulating a stronger, causal connection between certain events. An account of kettles boiling in a universe without causes might go as follows. In the past, every single observed instance of a kettle placed on a gas-burner has recorded the boiling of water at a certain air pressure and temperature. Yet we may in a universe without causes also say that even if every instance of a kettle boiling has so far exhibited these features, nevertheless, all such instances of actual occurrence are only a sub-set of possible instances in some of which it is both possible that a kettle be placed on a gas-burner *and* that it does not boil. We see here, moreover, a parallel between a comparison of Newton's with Einstein's physics and a comparison of Wittgenstein's earlier view of language in general with that which he came latterly to hold. Newton's view of the universe is like a closed system of individual atoms, indivisible and fixed in number, whose spatio-temporal and causal relations join them together into a clearly definable, fixed, complex mechanism. Likewise, as we have seen, for the early Wittgenstein language consisted, or ought to have consisted, of a fixed number of primitive signs corresponding to a fixed number of particular objects in the world. Einstein's universe, on the other hand, is an expanding universe in which atoms are not fixed in number nor are they indivisible. They can be broken down and further divided, and such subdivisions, like photons, follow statistical rather than causal laws. In such a universe there are possibilities and probabilities yet to be actualised which, while they 'resemble' patterns of past conjunctions of particulars into patterns or configurations, are not equivalent to them. Following Lonergan (1957, pp. 120–21), we may describe such patterns or configurations as 'schemes of recurrence'. With such a description of the physical world we may compare the later Wittgenstein's view of how universals are employed and constructed in language. Universals are not closed-classes of actually observed particulars as they must be on an empiricist (Newtonian) view of how the world is described in language. Rather universals are open-classes and are related to the ability of language users to form classes of things as the result of detecting family resemblances between them. Observations of how we and others have configured past groups of particulars (for example, tables) enable us to pass on to possible, new classifications according to the principle of family resemblance. Our actual classifications give rise to possible new ones, not because the new ones are equivalent to the old but because they bear a family resemblance. There are, therefore, formal similarities between Newton's physics and the early Wittgenstein's view of language, and between Einstein's physics and the later Wittgenstein's view of language.

It is, moreover, interesting to compare how such a statistical model of explanation, taken to extremes, would deal with the subject of miracles in comparison with a causal one. An earlier, empiricist account of the best-way-to-treat accounts of the miraculous was for those who believed in them to try to show that there were no (natural) causes of such events, whereas for those who disbelieved them to try to show that, to the contrary, there *were* perfectly clear, natural and causal explanations. Belief in miracles arose because causes were confused with coincidences – just as in our example of the witch-doctor who was illuminated by the lightning flash, mere juxtapositions of events (A. B) were mistaken for causal relations (A→B). Skinner interestingly describes superstitions as originating similarly as a result of an accidental association of a non-reinforcer with a reinforcer. As he says:

> A neutral stimulus which has merely happened to accompany a fearful event may subsequently evoke an emotional response, and the effect may survive for a long time in spite of repeated presentations of the neutral stimulus alone. In operant behavior a single instance of a response which is followed by a reinforcing event may be strengthening, and the effect may survive for a long time even though the same consequence never occurs again. Verbal behavior is especially likely to show this sort of 'magic' because of a lack of mechanical connection between response and reinforcement. (Skinner, 1953, p. 89)

But, once again, we see that Skinner is presupposing causal determination of human behaviour in connection with operant conditioning, the model for which, as we have seen, is statistical and not causal. Something – a neutral stimulus – became a cause since it 'has merely happened to accompany a fearful event', and in operant conditioning such neutral stimuli will tend to get repeated in the future even though no accidental and contingent reinforcement accompanies them. But the appeal in support of the principle of operant conditioning to those statistical models of explanation substituted by the post-Einsteinians for Newton's causal principle deny him the very cause/conjunction distinction on which his fact/ superstition distinction rests as well as his account of its psychological generation. When we saw the witchdoctor's final words illuminated by the lightning flash we ought to have been caused to respond as though the events were simply conjunctions without regarding one event as implying the other. Thus if Skinner is saying that, if we are superstitious, we have been caused to treat a conjunction as a (causal) implication, then the validity of his distinction rests upon the disjunction between conjunction and causal implication. But, as we shall now see, an explanation using a new, statistical strategy of putative miraculous events would dispense with any conjunction/causal explanation of the distinction between superstitions and facts in order to remain consistent with its fundamental presuppositions in a way that clearly Skinner failed to do.

If our entitlement to expect future recurrences of past events is related purely to probability of recurrence established by observation of patterns or classes of particulars, then causal explanations will not apply to alleged miracles any more than anything else. Take, for example, the case of the Liverpool docker, James Goad, who provided the test-case which lead the Vatican to make into a saint the sixteenth-century Catholic martyr, Richard Ogilvy (ITV report, 1977). All medical evidence after a long illness pointed to the fact that Goad had only a few more hours to live. His lungs were in an advanced state of disintegration as proven by X-rays vouched for by non-Catholic and non-believing doctors. Yet, it was claimed, as a result of many months of intercessions to the blessed Ogilvy, a miraculous cure was the explanation of Goad's sudden recovery. Now the scepticism created by the classical empiricist tradition would have insisted still that every event has a cause and that there *must be* some material cause for Goad's recovery since the progress of scientific discovery has been almost universally accomplished without requiring the postulate of divine intervention. In, however, a universe governed by statistical as opposed to causal laws, a different and seemingly fantastic alternative explanation presents itself. If the recurrence of patterns of events are merely probable, and the measure of their recurrence one of statistical probability, then however probable the recurrence of a pattern on configuration, there is always a possibility that on one or more occasions the pattern or configuration will not recur or will recur in a radically altered form.

The failure of the pattern of recurrence which generally holds more or less for instances of organ decay is, it could be argued, exemplified in Goad's recovery, statistically against the odds though this may be. A random universe in which laws of probability rather than cause apply is all that is required in order to explain away Goad's miraculous recovery! No wonder, therefore, that an Einstein, overwhelmed by the implications of quantum mechanics, should have been highly disquieted by the thought of a cosmic dice game! All that so-called 'miraculous' events amount to on this view is an inevitable feature of a random world. We may, as we saw earlier, concede that kettles have generally (we could even grant 'always') boiled in the past when heat has been applied to them, but this does not imply that this *must* happen in the future, even though the degree of probability is high. If one shakes the dice 10,000 times, it is highly unlikely that '6' will never show up at least once, yet if one could go on shaking the dice long enough, there could always occur a succession of 10,000 throws in which '6' never recurred. The number of occurrences of an event are always a sub-set of the total number of possible occurrences, and it is in that possibility that the validity of predictive strategies resides and not, as the empiricists thought, in the realised or actual occurrences described in the sub-set.

We have repeatedly drawn attention to the failure of Skinner's psychology to maintain the disjunction between causal and statistical models of explanation. Skinner's determination to assert the possibility of a 'complete determinism . . . particularly in accounting for the *behaviour of the individual*' (Skinner, 1971, p. 26) is thus shown by our account to be pure dogma generated by confusing two quite different models of scientific explanation. Where classes of behaviour whose patterns of probable recurrence are being charted are the focus of attention as in operant conditioning, there can be no 'complete determinism . . . in accounting for the behaviour of' any one 'individual'. Earlier in this chapter we criticised in this connection Skinner's failure to close the gap between explanations of human behaviour in terms of rule-following and rule-conformance. The substitution of statistical descriptions for rule-following ones in the case of human behaviour amounted to a redescription masquerading as an explanation. We have seen here that even if we allowed Skinner his redescription, he has failed to produce a coherent scientific methodology. There are, of course, two questions regarding the nature of causality, both of which are related in a way that Skinner has arguably failed to understand. The first question is whether there are causes *and* conjunctions existing in the world. The second is whether knowledge of (or appropriate patterns of behaviour towards) causes and conjunctions is acquired by distinct causal processes which have different features which distinguish the two cases. But Skinner cannot answer the second affirmatively (as he clearly wishes to do in the passage quoted above) unless he answers the first affirmatively too. He simply cannot make the point about different, causal processes of conditioning, one of which is the result of natural reinforcement of a positive stimulus, and the other of which represents a stimulus naturally neutral that has been accidentally and arbitrarily reinforced without claiming that there is, in the nature of things, a distinction to be made between caused events and conjoined events. It is precisely the validity of this distinction in what is observed, acted upon (stimulated) or responded to on which the distinction between the two processes of acquiring right behaviour (towards facts) and wrong behaviour (towards superstitions) rests. It is, however, a rather strange incongruity in Skinner's account that he should have failed to distinguish causal and statistical models. I say this because, as I want now to bring out in greater detail, the statistical methodology of quantum physics bears striking comparison with the statistical character of arguments and explanations in biology, particularly in evolutionary theory. Skinner, as we shall now see, relies heavily on evolutionary theory in order to try to eliminate the last vestiges of 'choice' and 'decision' from the classical, Pavlovian account of behaviourism.

3.4 BEHAVIOURISM AND EVOLUTIONARY THEORY

The first systematic attempt to produce a scientific description that dispensed with the notion of cause is to be found in Darwin's theory of evolution. If we ask the evolutionary theorist how it has come about that living things are of the kinds and with the features that they are, his answer is 'natural selection'. The use of the concepts 'nature' and 'selection' here are, however, unfortunate. 'Selection' implies 'choice', 'decision' (about one option rather than another), the attainment of excellence by what is selected and so on, and 'nature' cannot according to the theory be held to operate in such a rational way. Instead of looking for purpose or design in nature, even of a material or causal kind, Darwin instead took as his principle that of randomness. Once the principle of random possibility or probability is understood, there does not have to be a reason or a cause of anything happening simply because there can, on the other hand, be no reason or cause of it *not* happening. Let us take as our example a large number of billiard balls, and let these stand for a large number of objects (atoms, for example, or the energy of which they are composed, or biological cells). Let us now set the billiard balls in motion, and imagine, with Newton, that motion is their natural condition and is perpetual unless prevented by special circumstances (gravity, curvature of space or whatever). The balls are now spinning around colliding, travelling together, spinning apart in a random manner. Now, given that the movement of the billiard balls is random, that is to say, unplanned, fortuitous, accidental and so forth, could there be a state of affairs in which the billiard balls never collided? The answer is that, although anything is possible in a random universe, the longer the billiard balls exist and move randomly, the more unlikely this becomes. Their non-collision, non-combinations and so on would be the remarkable thing about them, not their collisions and combinations. If we were to see the billiard balls never colliding or combining, always, say, moving in straight lines which never intersected with one another, then our universe of billiard balls would no longer be random, but instead exhibit some kind of order, design or plan. For the universe of billiard balls to be genuinely random, sometimes some balls would collide and sometimes not. A few balls might escape collision entirely and, assuming the process could go on for millions of years and that we could live to watch it, the continuous collisions, bouncings together and falling apart would produce varieties of configurations, sometimes repeated with one configuration recurring in a series of realisations each bearing some degree of resemblance to one another. For the configurations and their recurrences, no explanation in terms of cause, design, purpose is necessary. Given that the universe is genuinely random, and given sufficiently large numbers of billiard balls and a sufficiently long enough time-span, then all sorts of patterns will emerge, very many of them occurring and persisting.

Now, evolutionary explanations of the origin of life and of the species are founded upon a similar random principle. Natural selection follows from (A) the limited amount of natural resources combined with (B) the ability of the species to reproduce themselves without limit. From A and B there necessarily follows C: there is a competitive struggle for survival among the species. Another way of expressing C is C.1, which tautologously reads: whatever survives in a given situation is *ipso facto* the fittest to survive. Now, it is important to impute no design or ethical value to C.1. It is simply that, given certain contingent and random circumstances, certain creatures with certain types of organ which happen to give them certain advantages in such circumstances survive at the expense of others. We can imagine different circumstances in the natural history of the human race which would have resulted in certain creatures different in kind from those of today occupying our planet. For example, if the world were covered by water, then certain extinct fish like creatures could have survived at the expense of the ancestors of *Homo sapiens*. We can imagine, to preserve our analogy with the billiard balls, all sorts of different possible patterns which have never been realised but, given the randomness of their movement, could well have possibly been realised. That the particular evolutionary pattern that has emerged has been realised is the result of purely random, accidental and fortuitous combinations of events. As such, it must be noted, evolutionary biology and quantum physics share common pre-suppositions to any model based upon the sufficiency of statistical probability to scientific explanation. It would be fallacious, for example, to argue that either in biology or in physics the concept of being random is undermined by the reflection that, given a long enough period of time, all possible patterns would be realised. Once, in other words, all possible patterns had worked themselves out, then the total design of everything could emerge. As one pattern invariably has given way to another and all possibilities have been exhausted, the concept of randomness no longer has any purchase. The fallacy in our argument would have been generated by the undue influence of the analogy of the billiard balls which were fixed in number. As we have seen, Einstein's universe, the universe of the quantum physicist, is an expanding universe, which is the reason for its probable character. The principle of explanation that is statistical probability presupposes that the number of objects existing in the universe is unlimited. Thus the substitution of probability for cause is once again seen to be part of a major shift in perspective that evolutionary biology and quantum physics share with Wittgenstein's shift from his earlier to his later position regarding the nature of language. As we have seen, his *Tractatus* view of language, presupposing a universe with a fixed number of objects in which all classes were closed and exhaustively definable, conflicted with his later views on open-classes in terms of family-resemblances which presuppose unlimited objects in an expanding universe.

Given the randomness of natural selection, it is, therefore, impossible to discern any clearly determinate causes of the persistence of one configuration of events such as a pattern of biological interaction between a given species and its environment. Like Skinner's principles of operant conditioning, randomness, statistically quantified, yields tendencies, possibilities, probabilities, though not the causal determinism for which Skinner hankers. In evolutionary biology, the principle of randomness, thus statistically quantified, becomes the principle of *adaptation* or *adaptability*. When incorporated into a behaviourist scheme of explanation, adaptability becomes the principle that those organisms with a greater genetic susceptibility to reinforcement will survive, since their needs are more likely to be reduced even when environmental contingencies change. As Skinner says:

> New practices arise, and they tend to be transmitted if they contribute to the survival of those who practice them . . . A culture evolves when new practices further the survival of those who practise them . . . A culture survives if those who carry it survive, and this depends in part upon certain genetic susceptibilities to reinforcement, as the result of which behaviour making for survival in a given environment is shaped and maintained. (Skinner, 1971, p. 142)

There is a problem with the notion of 'genetic susceptibilities to reinforcement'. It is perhaps an example of a general problem with evolutionary arguments. What purports to be an explanation of the emergence of cultural practices really only follows from the way that the process of emergence is defined. We would not say that the explanation of someone being a bachelor is that he is an unmarried man, since the so-called explanation follows tautologically from the meaning of 'bachelor'. Whether needs are reduced by the environment is surely accidental and contingent, so that whether or not an organism reduces its needs by means of certain kinds and varieties of reinforcer depends not upon 'greater genetic susceptibilities'. The concept of 'greater genetic susceptibility' simply describes the fact that the right kind of environmental reinforcers chanced to occur at the same time that organisms existed that happened to be reinforced by them. We cannot therefore say that behaviours were reinforced because of ('depended upon') certain genetic susceptibilities to reinforcement. Environmental factors are only describable as 'reinforcers' because they 'reinforce', and the 'because' is a 'because' of definition and not of explanation. It is important to grasp, therefore, how difficult it is for Skinner to ally his principle of operant conditioning with an evolutionary theory that contains the concept of genetic mutation. This is because at this point evolutionary theory employs a computer model, likening genetic possibilities and their realisation to a computer programme. Genetic possibilities are realised because of genetic 'pre-programming'. We have already seen how, as a 'strong' behaviourist, Skinner must eschew such a computer model of mind since it would license reference to internal states. We shall, moreover, be seeing how a computer model has lead Chomsky into an account of language diametrically opposed to Skinner's 'strong' behaviourism. Let us, however, allow Skinner for the moment to continue in his endeavour to wed his 'strong' behaviourism to evolutionary theory.

Stimulus-response patterns of behaviour, reinforced and persistent throughout the history of a culture, owe their origins and persistence to the process of natural selection. As Skinner says:

> Just as we do not need to explain the origin of genetic mutation in order to account for its effect in natural selection, so we do not need to explain the origin of a cultural practice in order to account for its contribution to the survival of a culture. The simple fact is that a culture which *for any reason* induces its members to work for its survival, or for the survival of some of its practices, is more likely to survive. (Skinner, 1971, p. 134)

When, therefore, we are confronted by examples of cultural practices which appear to be monuments of human 'choice', 'intention', rule-following and so forth, we are as mistaken as the pre-Darwinian biologist, who saw design and intention in the natural order because he had failed to grasp the randomness of natural selection. As Skinner says:

> No one saw that the environment was responsible for the fact that there *were* many different kinds of organism (and that fact, significantly enough, was attributed to a creative Mind). The trouble was that the environment acts in an inconspicuous way: it does not push or pull, it *selects*. For thousands of years in the history of human thought the process of natural selection went unseen in spite of its extraordinary importance. (Skinner, 1971, p. 22)

And we have already seen that the concept of 'selection' is a misnomer, since the principle of randomness means that we can squeeze the language of choice and decision out of the system of explanation.

Skinner's incorporation of an evolutionary perspective into his behaviourist model, it might be argued, enables him to overcome the inconsistency which we detected in Pavlov's original formulation of conditioning. Remember what this inconsistency was that we detected at the very outset of our account of behaviourism. Pavlov distinguished between conditioned stimuli and responses and unconditioned stimuli and responses on the grounds that the latter were straightforward reflexes whereas the former were the intentional products of the teacher who had managed to associate need-reduction with the behaviour that she/he was trying to shape. Dogs do not normally salivate when bells are rung and lights are flashed nor associate such stimuli with need-reduction. The salivation in response to the red meat was, however, for Pavlov's dogs the natural, unconditioned response to an unconditioned stimulus. For there to be a conditioned stimulus (the lights and bells), someone had to associate unconditioned stimuli (red meat) with what they had not previously been associated with in order to produce responses to such conditioned stimuli by themselves which normally they would not have elicited. There remains, therefore, within Pavlov's account, a designer whose intentions and decision are responsible for conditioning, in the form of the teacher or experimenter. Pavlov's model still rests, in the last analysis, upon presuppositions expressed in terms of 'design', 'purpose', 'intention' and 'decision' without which the conditioned/unconditioned distinction cannot be made. Such descriptions record interventions outside the conception of human nature within which the explanatory model otherwise tries to remain. What Skinner wishes to do by means of an evolutionary perspective, therefore, is to explain conditioned stimuli and responses without reference to intentions of the conditioner while maintaining the unconditioned/conditioned distinction. He wishes to do this by seeing the conditioner's behaviour as the product of an evolutionary process. The transmission (or conditioning) of cultural practices exemplifies one aspect of the adaptability of our species. Had not such practices been reduced by the reduction of our survival needs, then there would be no culture to exhibit those practices whose features we so misleadingly describe in the language of 'choice', 'intention', 'decision' and 'design'. That reflex represented by the salivation of Pavlov's dogs at the flashing of the lights and the ringing of the bells differs from salivation in the presence of meat on the grounds that the former (conditioned) reflex differs from the latter (unconditioned) reflex in that the former represents the evolutionary principle of adaptability. There is no adaptability represented by salivation at the red meat at this moment in time (though it may presumably have so been represented by it at some point in the evolutionary history of the canine species). Adaptability is, however, represented by the transference of the salivatory response in conditioning to the flashing of the lights and the ringing of the bells and in the process of stimulus generalisation that follows from this. Adaptability-in-action thus enables us to make the conditioned/unconditioned distinction between different pairs of stimuli and responses. Likewise, then, outside the artificial setting of a laboratory with a child learning or being taught a cultural practice, the child responds to stimuli such as hot coals by avoiding them, and if he did not do so, if the sight of the burning coals (conditioned stimulus) did not cause him to avoid them (conditioned response), then the child would not have exhibited that adaptability in his behaviour necessary for his evolutionary survival. No one has 'chosen' or 'decided' that he survive. It is simply that, had he not exhibited adaptative behaviour, he could not have been around to have exhibited non-adaptative behaviour. Likewise, when a teacher teaches a child how to weigh or measure things, it is similarly an illusion that this is by the 'choice' or 'design' of the teacher/conditioner. The fact is that, according to Skinner, the teacher's conditioning activity merely represents the mechanism of adaptation which enables the culture to survive and flourish by developing such adaptations of behaviour as weighing and measuring that, in evolutionary history, gave the culture the decisive advantage in the struggle for survival. The teacher's behaviour is thus simply the product of evolutionary forces and is part of and not apart from the scientific, natural order.

There are, however, problems with Skinner's account thus reinforced by evolutionary theory, some of which will be specific applications of general criticisms already previously outlined and some of which will be new to us at this point. To begin with, Skinner believes that his account gives rise to a technology of teaching (Skinner, 1968, Chapter 4). His Baconian account of scientific knowledge (reformulation in terms of stimulus-response behaviour) is intended to provide not simply an understanding of human nature but also to provide the means of controlling (human) nature. But the introduction of evolutionary theory in order to squeeze out of his description the need to talk about the 'decisions', 'choices' and 'intentions' of teachers does not serve his purpose very well. Skinner resembles in this connection those who have sought to use evolutionary theory as the foundations of a theory of ethics. The proposal represents a violation of the principle that one cannot deduce judgements of value from statements of fact (Flew, 1967). Let us see what is involved here from an argument which bears striking resemblance to that used by that distinguished fellow of All Souls turned politician, Sir Keith Joseph. Our social arrangements, or, as Skinner would prefer to say, our 'design of a culture' are defective because they are interfering with the laws of natural selection. Imagine as an example of the stereotype of the conservative propagandist an unemployed Irish (with respects to my paternal grandfather) labourer in Registrar General's categories IV or V. He draws for himself and for his large family (to which he keeps adding) both unemployment and social-security benefits while he luxuriates in the comfort of his subsidised council house. Now, Joseph's argument is that we are wrong to treat our unemployed labourer in this way since we are interfering with the laws of natural selection. But the problem with this argument is that all that the theory of evolution establishes in this instance is that the Irish labourer, having survived in a certain situation, was *ipso facto* fittest to survive in that situation. If a teacher or a manager, by contrast, are developing ulcers or sterility because of the pressures of their social situation, then all that follows from evolutionary theory is that, in the same social situation, they are lacking those natural features necessary for them to have the decisive advantage in the struggle for survival. We can neither speed up nor retard the process of evolution, which is random, haphazard and accidental. Yet Skinner wishes, having laid bare his evolutionary presuppositions, to speak as follows:

> The task of the cultural designer is to accelerate the development of practices which bring the remote consequences of behaviour into play ... Explicit design promotes that good by accelerating the evolutionary process and since a science and a technology of behaviour make for better design, they are important 'mutations' in the evolution of a culture. (Skinner, 1971, p. 142)

How is it possible to 'accelerate the evolutionary process' since this is something which simply happens on its own random principle?

Skinner, therefore, has failed in his attempt to solve the Pavlovian dilemma, which was that the conditioned/unconditioned distinction presupposed the intentioned/unintentioned distinction that strong behaviourism claimed could be ruled out *a priori*. His solution was that the 'intentions' of the teacher/conditioner can be explained in terms of adaptation and natural selection. But if this is so, then the teacher/conditioner cannot be instructed to change his behaviour in order to follow more closely the process of natural selection. If the practices of the teacher/conditioner, anyway, are the product of natural selection, then such practices will change or fail to change in accordance with the contingencies of adaptation and survival. Yet the very notion of a 'technology of teaching' implies that nature can be directed in that way. We see here once again that Skinner's pretence at closing the rule-following/rule-conforming gap in order to achieve a so-called 'science of human behaviour' is an illusion created by confusing rather than transcending that distinction.

There are, furthermore, general problems that a specifically psychological thesis incorporating evolutionary theory and statistical models must face. Psychology is a discipline which purports to deal with the thinking, behaviour, therapy and so on of individual people. Statistical models by their very nature can only deal with general classes of events. Skinner reflects, as we have seen, empiricist assumptions about the nature of (true) classes in requiring that these be treated as consisting of exhaustively definable strings of particulars. But we have also seen such empiricist assumptions to be invalid on the later Wittgenstein's analysis of universals in terms of open-class concepts not exhaustively definable but formed in the detection of family-resemblances. Thus predictions in terms of probable patterns of recurrence of classes of events says nothing about the behaviour of any one individual than can simply be included or drop out of a general class quite randomly and, *as an individual*, quite unpredictably. Thus a statistical model could not yield technological directions of how to deal with individuals at a psychological level, as Skinner seems to think that the theory of operant conditioning does. There is a parallel problem with the wedding of operant conditioning with the statistical underpinnings of the concept of evolutionary adaptability. It is a mistake frequently committed by evolutionary moralists like Sir Keith Joseph that adaptability can, as a principle, be applied to the treatment of individuals such as our Irish labourer. Adaptability and natural selection do not refer to the survival of the individual but of the *species*, since their basis is one of tendencies or probabilities to be observed in the behaviour of *classes* of events. Skinner frequently, as we have more than once brought out, thinks that from describing classes of operant stimuli he can be certain about individual behaviour. As Skinner says:

> The application of operant conditioning to education is simple and direct. Teaching is the arrangement of contingencies of reinforcement under which students learn. They learn without teaching in their natural environments, but teachers arrange special contingencies which expedite learning, *hastening the appearance* of behavior which might otherwise never occur. (Skinner, 1968, pp. 64–5; my italics)

'Making sure' reflects his belief, which we have shown to be inconsistent with a statistical model, of the possibility of a 'complete determinism' of behaviour. But this rests upon a misunderstanding of the nature of statistical models which, in turn, is generated by a misunderstanding of the nature of classes as exhaustively definable in terms of a fixed number of particulars. It also reflects, as we have also seen, a confusion between two distinct paradigms of scientific explanation, the Newtonian and the Einsteinian.

As translated into the practical demands of a technology, nowhere is Skinner's deduction about the treatment of individuals from the behaviour of classes in all its confusion better represented than where he talks about the responsibility for students failing. As he claims to provide a solution to students failing, a student's failure becomes not the responsibility of the student but of the teacher who has failed to provide the relevant technology. As a result, on some occasions

Skinner claims that students never fail but rather it is the teachers who fail *them* (Skinner, 1968, Chapter 5). If the student fails to learn, then it is because the teacher has failed among other reasons to construct the appropriate schedules of reinforcement, to get the contingencies right. 'Nature', as Bacon said, 'to be commanded must be obeyed.' If the teacher wishes therefore to get the student to learn, he must first follow a scientific understanding of human nature. Only by following such principles as those of environmental conditioning, adaptation, reinforcement – by, in other words, obeying nature – can nature be commanded in the learning process. At first sight, this appears to be a most liberal strategy undeserving of the critical attacks made upon Skinner's views by political radicals. Instead of simply accepting the inevitability of student failure as following from some innate inadequacy such as IQ or irremedial social background or upbringing, Skinner appears to be committed to the liberal principle of the reformability – indeed, even the perfectability – of human nature. If the mind has no innate mental structures, as the strong behaviourist (in contrast to a weak behaviourist like Quine) must, as we have seen, assert, then behaviour is plastic and malleable with any number of new patterns of stimulus response possible, with the achievement of ever-increasing levels of complexity made more clear and determinate. If a pigeon can be made to turn a 'figure of eight' by a process of operant conditioning, then surely children who fail to read or to count can, by a similar method, be lead to succeed. As Skinner says:

> The application of operant conditioning to education is simple and direct. Teaching is the arrangement of contingencies of reinforcement under which students learn . . . Programmed instruction also made its first appearance in the laboratory in the form of programmed contingencies of reinforcement. The *almost miraculous* power to change behavior which frequently emerges is perhaps the most conspicuous contribution to date of an experimental analysis of behavior. (Skinner, 1968, p. 65; my italics)

It appears at first sight, therefore, that Skinner's account advocates a rejection of things simply as they are and the proposal of a positive programme of educational failure. But whereas this may have been what classical conditioning implied, namely, the possibility of producing a more equal society through the equality of attainment and rewards, the remedy for the inadequacy of that classical theory presented by operant conditioning does not allow such a deduction to be made. A 'technology of teaching from which one can indeed *deduce* programs and schemes and methods of instruction' (Skinner,

1968, p. 27, my italics), is impossible on a view of operant conditioning that makes repetition of a stimulus only ever merely probable. Furthermore, if the repetition of a stimulus is only probable, and if such probabilities vary in a degree as they must in a statistical sample, then, at the end of the day, there will still be a curve of attainment represented by any group of individuals in terms of which success or failure will be defined. Moreover, even if the majority of groups submitted to operant conditioning show some rise in attainment, that this will in future be generally the case can only be probable and some groups will therefore always be exceptions to such a general statistical tendency. Skinner's premises therefore lead to opposite conclusions from those which he intends. A teacher cannot be blamed for failing since it is always possible to argue that the teacher deployed the right technology but that his particular class or school is the random exception to a general statistical tendency. We have already noted that statistical explanations of rule-following behaviour are really simply redescriptions of the phenomenon requiring explanation and not true explanations. Skinner's views on teaching as a technology and on the teacher's responsibility for learning failure is thus shown to be one particular instance of a general fallacious argument.

I am aware that the criticism of the last paragraph may appear to be carping. After all, it may be argued, if we raise the general level of achievement represented by a more satisfactory learning curve, is not this a worthwhile achievement, even though it still leaves some students at the top as learning successes and others at the bottom as failures? It is, however, important for us to grasp precisely what Skinner's argument amounts to on this point, particularly in view of attacks on Skinner's particular position here from such Marxist pedagogues as Mose whose work we shall be considering in greater detail in Chapter 5. Basically their charge will be that Skinnerian behaviourism, while claiming to be a revolutionary means of changing the level of educational attainment, in fact leaves the individual in the same predicament as before at the bottom of a more satisfactory learning curve. Furthermore, by regarding educational failure purely in terms of the failure of a causal or quasi-causal (statistically understood) conditioning process, Skinner neatly side-steps the role of rule-following explanations in accounting for educational failure by retranslating rule-following into the language of operant conditioning. If, for example, 40 per cent of one's class fails to read, is it because the teacher has not provided an adequate schedule of reinforcement? The schedule might be quite adequate, but the student fails to follow it because he sees that there is 40 per cent unemployment in his age group and that improvement in reading at the bottom of the scale commensurate with those at the top will still leave him unemployed. To describe his problem in terms of the statistical probabilities of operant conditioning merely redescribes his problem without either explaining or remedying it. It will be clear that the present writer has great sympathy with the radical case at this point. Where that case is defective is that, as argued by the writers with whom we shall be meeting in Chapter 5, it can be easily rebutted by the Skinnerian riposte that this is how things are and shown to be by the way that conditioning determines behaviour and as established by scientific study. It is my argument that Skinner's case simply does not add up, that it rests upon confusions between distinct models of scientific inquiry, and on obfuscations of rule-following and causal descriptions of human behaviour.

There is, however, a still more critical objection to Skinner, and at a far more fundamental level than that discussed so far, namely, the suitability of either physical or biological models in order to give an adequate psychological account of human understanding. We have briefly touched upon the kernal of this objection when we pointed out that the behaviourist psychologist, to observe the phenomenon of operant conditioning, must possess the very ability that he is claiming that the concept explains. He must be able to make judgements in terms of classes of particulars without requiring the presence of any one particular within that class. We saw, however, that, if human behaviour is to be defined in terms of operant conditioning, then by definition it must be described in terms of classes which in turn by definition transcend their particulars. In other words, the method of explanation (explicans), namely, the theory of operant conditioning, and what is to be explained (explicandum), namely judgements in terms of general classes, are one and the same thing. When this happens we saw that the so-called 'explanation' is a logical fallacy. We shall now demonstrate the relevance of this point to our discussion of Hume's problem of induction and cause, and the role that this problem played in the creation of quantum physics with which we are arguing that the problems of behaviourism are related.

3.5 HUME'S PROBLEM OF INDUCTION AND EINSTEIN'S REVOLUTION

We saw that Hume was a great sceptic regarding the causal principle. Just because A had been invariably conjoined with B in the past, with B invariably following A in a temporal sequence, this was no guarantee that this would recur in the future. Yet, as Kant pointed out, to give a psychological explanation of how we come to use the concept of 'cause' about a world which, in reality, contains no such relation, he had to use the very principle that he was seeking to deny. We see things in terms of the illusions of cause and effect because we are *caused* to do so by the constant conjunction of events. There was, however, some truth in Hume's account, albeit garbled, which Kant tried unsuccessfully to articulate. The justification of a given psychological account on the grounds that it explains how men arrive at understanding, at a true account of the world, must not already contain within it an assumption of the truth of the claim about the world that it is trying to justify. Both Kant and Hume might be united in the claim that a world of mere conjunction, of what Kant described as 'things-in-themselves', was unintelligible in a period before both evolutionary biologists and post-Einsteinian physicists showed that nature could be made intelligible by a statistical method based upon the notion of random conjunctions. But their account had the virtue of keeping distinct the world of conjunctions and the mental mechanisms, causal in character, by which an understanding of the world was reached. Basically, therefore, we may say that both were trying to show how that description of the psychological mechanisms by means of which what is true about the world is acquired must be made logically independent of the descriptions of the world built up by means of them if either type of description is to function as an explanation. 'Why do we grasp the world in terms of causal relations?' is not answered by: 'Because there are causal relations there to be grasped, otherwise we should not be caused to grasp them.' This would make the explicans part of the explicandum. 'The world is causal (explicandum) because we come to know it by a causal process' would not constitute an explanation of anything as opposed to a mere redescription which should perhaps read, 'The world is causal *and* we come to understand it by a causal process.' Hume's distinction between the truth about the world (conjunction) and the psychological mechanism by means of which we acquire that truth (causal) did therefore at least have the virtue of trying, however feebly, to produce a possible candidate for being an explanation as opposed to a mere repetition of a description, albeit in different words.

It will now be interesting for us to compare Skinner's account of operant conditioning with that for which Hume sought with feeble awareness. We shall, however, expunge from our account of operant conditioning all of Skinner's frequent injections of causal inconsistencies which we have already demonstrated to have vitiated his discussion. If we do so, we shall see that Skinner has simply reproduced in a way that we have frequently described the fallacy of confusing the explicans with the explicandum, by contrast with Hume, who, albeit unsuccessfully, sought to avoid that fallacy in psychological discussion. The theory of operant conditioning, as we have seen, ought to be grounded upon statistical and not upon causal premises. The pigeons were not *caused* to bob their heads in a new pattern of behaviour at a greater height than the original one. Their behaviour at the new height was simply made more probable. We have not here a view of knowledge (translated in terms of stimulus-response behaviour) that states that knowledge is acquired, as Hume albeit unconsciously presupposed, by a causal process. Skinner is saying (or ought to be saying) that objects that tend to be conjoined in nature constitute stimuli that tend to elicit responses similarly conjoined. Stimuli that, in operant conditioning, are initiated by the organism and tend to occur together are met, as a rule, by need-reducing environment responses that also tend to recur together. But in this case we are left with an explicans/explicandum in a new and as we have seen distinctly Skinnerian form. Instead of: 'We understand the world in terms of causes and effects because there are causes and effects and these cause us to see them', we have: 'We see the world in terms of recurrent random conjunctions because there are only conjunctions and these conjunctions are accompanied frequently but not invariably (for that would make them causal) similar conjunctions in our behavioural stimuli and responses towards them.'

It is, however, arguable that, if the world consisted purely in terms of probably recurring random conjunctions (as quantum physics and evolutionary biology requires), then on behaviourist premises we could never achieve any understanding of the order of physical or biological nature. Although both causal and statistical accounts in application to the phenomenon of human understanding may fall foul of the explicans/explicandum fallacy, it is arguable that at least a Humean or Lockean causal account of the acquisition of knowledge makes sense as a description of the problem of how we come to understand the world, though not as an explanation. The statistically based model of human understanding that is operant conditioning, in the last analysis, we shall now argue, in behavioural terms cannot even make sense as a description, let alone an explanation. Although there are no insuperable logical problems with descriptions of physical or biological nature in statistical terms (even when they may be redescriptions of non-statistical accounts), there are nevertheless serious problems in extending such accounts in such terms to acts of human understanding of such accounts. The root of the problem is this. When our senses are bombarded by numbers of particular things (or statistically random, stimulus-response patterns are set up between the organism and its environment), then to make sense of the world in terms of probable patterns of recurrent particulars, we have to be able to disregard some particular features of objects while paying attention to others. Now, even if we substitute for 'disregard' in the last sentence something like 'break a stimulus-response nexus', we are still compelled by the logic of our description to represent what we have already argued to be the phenomenon of the 'transcendence of the particular' which we have demonstrated to be irreducible to categories of rule-conformance. This rule-following ability which, by contrast with rule-conformity, enables particular features of objects to be disregarded, must therefore be central to our understanding of how human understanding can grasp an account of a world of randomly recurring statistical probabilities. We saw that this ability was presupposed by Wittgenstein's description of how we describe the world in terms of open-classes by means of family-resemblances, since classes of probable recurrences are likewise open-ended.

Consider the well-used example of the universal 'table'. Tables come in all sorts of colours, shapes and sizes. If we learned to recognise instances of such general classifications by a process of strict causation, then a square-topped wooden object with two side supports could not be identified with a round-topped plastic object with four legs in the class of things that are tables. If classes consisted of exhaustive descriptions of closed strings of particulars, then we could explain our descriptions of them in language as resulting from sensory bombardment by features of particular objects accomplished in whatever form. But we have seen that the actual form of human language does not support that account of how general classifications in language are made. Because universals are *open* classes, they cannot be understood as articulated in language as a result of a clear and determinate sensory bombardment, whether we describe such bombardment as mentalistic, as did Locke, or behaviouristic, as did Pavlov and Skinner. Such an analysis of the open-class character of universals in language points to a data-processing ability, understandable in terms of the analogy of computer pre-programming, in terms of which some particular features of particular objects can be accepted and others ignored.

We could, therefore, describe a causal world as reproducing itself by causal means upon human receptor organs as both empiricism and classical behaviourism demanded. But were this to be so, our language would have to function in a completely different manner from that in which it does. A statistical world cannot, however, be so reproduced on our receptor organs and also be understood, since where all events are only statistically probable, the act of understanding such a world cannot be causally described. Moreover, a world of statistical probability requires for its understanding the ability to transcend the particular, to break the hold that particulars would otherwise exercise upon a conceptual order which would not be able to generate open-classes and would thus be thrown into the kind of chaos exhibited by an imaginary language that had to devise a new word for every particular new thing or new feature of an old thing. But it simply does not make sense to talk of an understanding of such a world as generated (caused?) by an order of nature governed by such statistical laws.

We thus see how questionable are the strong behaviourist's premises that require us to describe the process of human understanding in terms of the same categories that we apply to physical nature as the object of that understanding. Such an order could never be perceived by human beings unless they were pre-programmed to receive it. Such programming will be present in such mental structures whose basis is as yet undisclosed but whose formal properties must be describable in terms of rule-following, the transcendence of the particular and other logically related operations. If the order and organisation of the human mind took place by a process describable as identical formally to the order and organisation of the physical and biophysical world, then, although there might be an interaction between men and the world of the random, probabilistic kind proposed by the operant behaviourist, such orders and their interaction could never be understood by human beings. The concepts of knowledge and understanding could gain no purchase on such descriptions. Such interactions in random and probable schemes of recurrence would simply be things that happened to us and the reflections upon them that is the subject matter of psychology would be impossible. We could certainly not, being unable to reflect upon them, be able to, in Skinner's words, 'hasten the appearance of' such patterns of behaviour, to 'make them sure' and so forth.

In the final analysis, Kant may have the last word, for Kant argued that 'things-in-themselves' might exist, though of them we could have no knowledge but only as they were processed by our innate mental order. Kant mistakenly thought that 'things-in-themselves' could only be made intelligible in causal terms. The post-Einsteinians have, in the light of this, claimed that empiricism has been vindicated in that the replacement of causal by statistical models shows that there is no pre-existence structure, no necessary *a priori* truths which can be known in advance of experience (*a priori*). As Reichenbach says:

Kant believed himself to possess a proof for his assertion that his *synthetic a priori* principles were necessary truths: According to him these principles were necessary conditions of knowledge. He overlooked the fact that such a proof can demonstrate the truth of principles only if it is taken for granted that knowledge within the frame of these principles will always be possible. What has happened, then, in Einstein's theory is a proof that knowledge within the framework of Kantian principles is not possible . . . It is fortunate that the scientist . . . looked for ways of changing the so-called *a priori* principles . . . It is to the philosophy of empiricism, therefore, to which Einstein's theory of relativity belongs. (Reichenbach, 1969, p. 309)

But although Einstein may have showed that the causal principle as an example of an *a priori* principle is misconceived, it does not thereby follow that any *a priori* principle is misconceived. Einstein may have been an empiricist in that he was revolted by his vision of a cosmic dice-player and looked for determinacy in a scientific theory, but my argument about the consequences of the acceptance and intelligibility of a description of the world in terms of statistical probability leads to a completely opposite conclusion to empiricist arguments about the nature of mind. If the post-Einsteinians have demonstrated against Kant that causal descriptions are not indispensible to any scientific account of the world, then, in the final analysis, in exhibiting their ability to understand the world in terms of statistical ability, they are demonstrating their possession of a statistical processing capacity that mere interaction with their environment could never have given them. They are, in other words, making *a fortiori* a version of the Kantian case that they are seeking to deny.

A world of statistical probabilities would not be intelligible without a statistics-processing capacity, for reasons that we have given. The case for some kind of invariant framework implicit in the claims to knowledge that men make is curiously, therefore, to be made even more strongly by the phenomenon of human understanding of the world in terms of probabilistic rather than causal explanations in science. We see, therefore, that a causal description of the way in which human beings come to understand the world as causal might just about make sense as a description though such a description would not amount to a justification of the causal principle. No rule-following, no transcendence of the particular so as to form open-classes in language ought to be possible if the relation of understanding of the world and the world itself was accurately described by such an account. We have seen how empiricists such as the early Wittgenstein was unhappy with ordinary language as a result which led him to yearn for the elements of an ideal language somehow hidden within ordinary language. The description would certainly not be justified by the actual form and actual functions of actual human languages, but at least the causal description would make sense. However, a statistical description of how human beings come to understand the world in terms of probabilistic patterns of interaction (as in operant conditioning) could not, however, even make sense as a possible description. As we have seen, the kind of understanding represented by operant conditioning involves the ability to process environmental stimuli or responses, to disregard particular features of particular objects when including them within open-classes and so on. Without such an ability, we could not even reflect upon probabilistic patterns of interaction and so understand them.

Thus we conclude our criticism of Skinnerian behaviourism. We have traced how Skinner's account of operant behaviourism fails to squeeze out of a description and explanation of the psychology of learning the language of choice and intention. We have argued that this failure is related to a number of deep-seated confusions about the nature of different models of scientific explanation. These confusions about models of scientific explanation, moreover, have been shown to interrelate in a number of highly complex ways with general questions about logic and language, and the relationship between language and the world. Skinner's incoherence we have therefore argued is not simply an incoherence about a particular psychological model. Rather does Skinner's general approach reflect a number of strands of questionable assumptions which subtly interrelate in many complex ways and which connect his work to general empiricist assumptions about the nature of language and scientific inquiry. We have seen the connection between Skinner's work and general empiricist views on the nature of language as exemplified in the work of Locke, and more recently in the early Wittgenstein and in Quine. The relationship between views on language and scientific inquiry has been demonstrated by showing how that an understanding of the logic of classes is interconnected with a view of universals in language. Skinner's understanding of both has been shown to be founded on a view that definitions of universals, to be adequate, must be exhaustive, and that this view in turn underlies Skinner's general empiricist error about the nature of induction. His failure, moreover, to understand the nature of universals in terms of open-class concepts we saw to have infected his use of statistical models in operant condition, which in turn reflected his failure to grasp the nature of statistical probability which underlies the evolutionary theory upon which the theory of operant conditioning is made by Skinner to depend. In the final analysis, we have detected that the common strand which underlies these seemingly disparate collection of errors is a failure to acknowledge the rule-following/rule-conforming distinction which the use of statistical models in science or open-class concepts in language generally implies. Skinner has sought unsuccessfully to close this distinction in order to provide an allegedly scientific account of human behaviour, and all that has resulted from his lack of success is incoherence. Let us therefore summarise the general conclusions which the critical account of these chapters have yielded, drawing out some positive conclusions for our subsequent argument.

3.6 SUMMARY AND FURTHER CONCLUSIONS: QUINE'S WEAK EMPIRICISM

We began our first chapter by describing the general features of the construction of frameworks of scientific explanation in terms of the scientist taking certain items of common-sense experience and deriving from these a general theoretical perspective in the light of which other items of common-sense experience are declared invalid. The derivability of a complex of concepts and principles from such a basis in stipulated items of common sense, taking us as such complexes do beyond a common-sense view of the world, are held to guarantee in some way their validity. Such a procedure has been shown to be invalid by an analysis of its failure to assist rather than restrict understanding both in the physical and in the human sciences. Our account has therefore pointed to reasons why attempted constructions of total world views, founded upon one sub-set of common-sense experience, can only ever succeed to a certain point in producing overall and comprehensive frameworks of explanations. This is because, in the process of an inquiry trying to be comprehensive on the basis of a sub-set of common-sense experience, other kinds of principles, derived from other kinds of common-sense experience, assert themselves. Moreover, the 'can' and 'cannot' in our description is arguably a logical 'can' and 'cannot' since different kinds of common-sense experience are mutually irreducible, in a way that we argued in an earlier work to be the case with the foundations of Hirst's forms of knowledge. To our strengthening of our argument on this point we must wait until Chapter 8.

Both Kant and Locke illustrate, each in their different ways, the operations of the kind of logical imperialism that we have been criticising. Not only is common-sense experience of nature evaluated within their systems with some items declared valid and others invalid, but common-sense experience of art morality, religion and society is ruled out of being capable of constituting knowledge. Hence Kant came to the conclusion that things-in-themselves could not be known, and that only things-as-they-appear could be known. Within a causal (Newtonian) framework, 'chance', 'fate', 'destiny' were thus ruled out of the sphere of significant discourse.

Now, such concepts as 'chance', 'fate', 'destiny' prefigured and still do prefigure in many common-sense reflections upon life and in many common-sense judgements on how to proceed. Yet Kant, within his Newtonian framework, asserts that one such sub-set alone is valid because it describes the form of human sensibility, that order in nature which the mind imposes upon nature (space, time, cause), and rejects such common-sense reflections on life and decisions for the future in terms of 'chance', 'fate', 'destiny' or whatever. It is curious, we may confidently and uncontroversially say, that at least 'chance' should have been in Kant's list in view of the centrality of random probability to quantum physics. But there are, in common-sense experience, areas of life and decision where one cannot be certain, where one has to weigh up options and plump for one rather than another without being able to determine one end rather than another. As we have seen, both the early Wittgenstein and Skinner shared the Newtonian demand for such determination. The causally based Newtonian framework could brook no rival to its favoured sub-set of common-sense experiences from which it was in all its complexity and sophistication derived. The result was that such activities as games of chance or human activities involving apparently indeterminate choices come to be investigated, sometimes with a theoretical and sometimes with a practical end in view, in order to show that the processes involved can be causally determined, as with the Monte Carlo gambler who thought that it must be his 'system' that accounted for his random success. The tables really and simply cannot operate by chance since 'chance', though used in common-sense discourse, is not part of the privileged sub-set stipulated by the Newtonians.

We have seen, however, in the development of evolutionary theory in biology and in quantum physics, that there exists a whole new framework of explanation derived, not from Newton's favoured sub-set of common sense in terms of cause, but from Kant's rejected sub-set in terms of chance. 'Chance' is, after all, a principle derived from experiences which enter the warp and woof of any human form of social life and without which social life is inconceivable. When goods are exchanged, for example, in the simplest forms of barter, or simplest collective decisions are made 'chance', indeterminacy of outcomes that nevertheless requires judgements between outcomes and so on are features of common-sense experience that are here exemplified. A sub-set of common-sense experiences, therefore, ruled out by the Newtonian framework of explanation which has been successful in leading to understanding of some parts of the physical and biological world, is rehabilitated by the requirements of explanation for other parts of the physical and biological worlds.

It will be further argued in later chapters that our account will logically require the rehabilitation of the validity of other sub-sets of common-sense experience ruled out by Kant and the empiricists, such as those of aesthetics, morals and lastly religion. Our argument will forge links with those both of the later Wittgenstein and of Chomsky. Their work has in part shown the imperialistic rejection of other sub-sets of common-sense experience on the basis of scientific understanding to be invalid. In the last analysis, the enterprise we have argued to fall short of the goal of providing a total explanation of the world in which physical and biological nature yields total explanations of the human agent, morality, religion and so forth. Now we must note precisely what sort of claim it is that we are making when we say that, 'It falls short of the goal of providing a total explanation.' Ought we not rather simply to say not that generally and universally such total explanations must be unobtainable, but simply that, in the past, we have failed to obtain them? Note, however, that, on the contrary, our point has been a logical one. The *form* of common-sense experience from which, for example, Newtonian physics is derived in the causal principle (things fall over because they are pushed or pulled or whatever) is logically different from the *form* of common-sense experience from which Einstein's physics is derived (experience of judging odds in institutionalised games of chance and so on).

It is therefore arguable that we need to look at other possible forms of common-sense experience from which other kinds of metaphysical, aesthetic, moral or religious frameworks may be both logically and significantly derived. There were, after all, other items in Kant's invalid sub-sets of common-sense experience other than 'chance', such as 'fate' and 'destiny', that have their place in religious discourse. But we have seen how the enterprise of classical empiricism, even in its Kantian form, was itself invalid. Classical empiricism in both its Lockean and Kantian forms claimed a method that ruled out religion as significant on the grounds that common-sense notions of fate and destiny were at variance with common-sense notions of cause, space and time that had produced such successful and far-ranging general explanations of nature. As God is eternal, God cannot be experienced within a temporal framework; as He is infinite, He cannot be experienced within a spatial framework. Kant was in this respect, however, a typical Protestant rather than a typical atheist in that he wished to assert that religion was a question of *faith* rather than of knowledge. Religion belonged to the realm of things-in-themselves, which could not be known, as opposed to things-as-they-appear, which could. Religious statements, in other words, did not conform to the basic form of human sensibility which was understood in terms of the Newtonian spatio-temporal framework. But we note once again that for Kant, in so far as he is to be regarded as a classical empiricist (Bennett, 1966), religious ways of thinking, characterised by such concepts as 'fate', 'destiny', 'God' or 'eternal', could be systematically excluded, just as in Newton's causal system the question whether event x was miraculous could be systematically determined by an inductive process that was in principle perfectable. It is the whole enterprise of systematic exclusion, dependent as this is on the stipulation that only one sub-set of common-sense experience is valid, that our account has been challenging.

Skinner, moreover, in what we described as his 'strong' behaviourist moments, also subscribed to the view that stimulus-response explanations can systematically distinguish between true belief and what he called 'superstition', despite the implications, undetected by him, of the operant conditioning thesis. But operant conditioning implied a 'weak' behaviourism in accordance with which other sub-sets of common-sense experience, such as the religious, could not be thus systematically excluded. If statistical redescriptions of psychological phenomena were limited in their explanatory power so that they could not exclude descriptions in personal terms as valid explanations, then, arguably, so might quantum descriptions of the physical world be also limited, with similar consequences. But the existence of probabilistic explanations belied behaviourism as a psychological theory in other ways too. The classical empiricist's view was that all knowledge is acquired through the senses without the mediation of innate mechanisms. There is, moreover, a behaviourist analogue of the classical view in Skinner's rejection of instinct theory in an account of mind in terms of stimulus-response patterns set up in interaction between the organism and its environment. Yet, to acquire understanding of a statistically governed universe, to operate with the principle of probability in classes of events which has its analogue in classifications by family-resemblance in ordinary language, we require to be able consciously to blot out certain features of items of sensory experience, to transcend the particular in rule-following as opposed to rule-conformance. Regarded in this light, Reichenbach's view that Einstein's description of the universe refutes Kant's quest *in principle* for *a priori* categories, however false Kant's particular examples of such categories may have been, is patently false. Consciousness of a quantum universe that rests on an understanding of what it is to be a probable scheme of recurrence requires Chomsky's concept of innate categories understood by analogy with computer pre-programming.

We saw, moreover, that Quine, a leading contemporary empiricist, took the rationalist argument for innate principles sufficiently seriously to produce a weak behaviourist position which accepts the possibility of innate mechanisms, albeit explained dispositionally (above, p. 52–3). Quine thus accepts a weakening of an empiricist epistemology on a second count that we have discussed here in detail. He accepts what Skinner appeared to be reluctant to accept, that an empiricist epistemology cannot give an account of the map of knowledge that systematically excludes some forms of discourse derivable from some kinds of common-sense experience in favour of others. Quine describes this logical imperialism of classical empiricism as the 'dogma of reductionism' (Quine, 1953, pp. 40–41). But Quine wishes still to remain within the empiricist camp so that his next move is to claim that sensory experience is the final arbiter, not of the validity of a number of foundation statements of a form of discourse considered individually, but of the discourse as a whole. Sensory experience affects a form of significant discourse by touching it at the edges and its effects 'reverberate' throughout the interrelated structure of propositions as a whole without altering any one proposition in a piecemeal fashion (Quine, 1953, p. 41).

Because 'our statements about the external world face the tribunal of sense experience . . . only as a corporate body', sensory experience can impinge upon a framework of scientific explanation only at the edges. Thus also there can be no unbroken logical chain linking particular experiences with particular statements so as to determine indubitably the truth of any one particular claim about the world. But Quine's admission leaves empiricism without teeth, since such a version of its epistemology can no longer systematically and methodologically determine what kinds of discourse can in principle be true or false. Religious claims, to use one example, which is, however, perhaps the limiting case for claims to knowledge, can no longer be systematically ruled out. If, as Quine asserts, sense experience confronts the total corpus of propositions in a given form of discourse and not each individual proposition in isolation, then the failure of certain religious experiences to confirm particular items of religious discourse in a tightly deductive way (for example in the theology of the sacraments) in no way sets religious discourse apart from scientific discourse. Quine admits this point when he concedes that 'in point of epistemological footing . . . physical objects and . . . gods differ only in degree and not in kind. Both sorts of entities enter our conception only as cultural posits' (Quine, 1953, p. 44). Quine, however, endeavours to save himself from complete epistemological relativism by claiming that one culturally relative system can be 'epistemologically superior' to another in that 'it has proved more efficacious than other myths as a device for working a manageable structure into the flux of experience'. Quine's ultimate test for the validity of a form of discourse is therefore a pragmatic one.

At this point, however, Quine arguably involves himself in a circular argument of the kind that causes problems for cultural relativism, even in the modified form in which he propounds such a thesis. The general problem for the cultural relativist is this. For his thesis that 'all bodies of knowledge are culturally relative' to hold, the cultural relative has, in effect, to admit at least one cultural invariant within his scheme of explanation, namely, that all bodies of knowledge, irrespective of culture, are culturally relative. For Quine, this means that pragmatism is the one non-amendable, non-adjustable principle. But if pragmatism is itself culturally relative, then Quine has no grounds on which to assert that modern physics '*has proved* more efficacious' than the myths of Homer.

We arrive, therefore, at the fundamental dilemma of Quine's weak empiricism, namely, how he can abandon the systematic strategy of the logical imperialism of classical empiricism and then finally escape from the kind of culturally relativist position which rules out not only any empiricist but any kind of coherent epistemological position? Rule-following, involving the transcendence of the particular, the ability to break stimulus-response connections, to ignore particular features of particular objects so that they can be subsumed within general classes and so on may seem thus to be the essence of a human creativity that can construct and reconstruct frameworks of explanation without limit. The concept of creativity unpacked in terms of the concept of rule-following may thus appear, deceptively as we shall argue, to license a view that pictures of reality can be broken down and built up in community by human beings in any way that they, in their particular social groups, appear to like or that strikes them for their own peculiar reasons as fitting. Such a view makes human freedom and epistemological demands incompatible with one another since epistemology requires basic forms of knowledge which to some extent bind and discipline human thinking, whereas freedom and human creativity, it is argued, require the absence of such bounds. It will be our thesis later in this work that, on the contrary, in Chomsky's words, human creativity requires a certain kind of 'rigid preprogramming'. It was a thesis that we explored in a way that we now see was inadequate in a previous book (Brent, 1978, Chapter 4). It will require us to spell out the connection between Chomsky's theory of certain semantic universals shared by all human languages and the later Wittgenstein's notion of family-resemblance. We shall in the process also see how, when Hirst's curriculum theory of basic forms of knowledge, derived by applications to propositions of reducibility as irreducibility criteria, is combined with such a perspective, we arrive at an account of an invariant framework, implicit in knowledge, which nevertheless gives adequate space to human creativity.

For the moment, however, let us examine in specific detail some behaviourist curricular proposals and how these are affected by the errors exposed here.

Chapter 4

Behaviourism: Curricular Deductions

In Chapter 1, we saw that those who tried to transform traditional practices within the framework of a behaviouristically based educational technology were in reality perpetuating a fundamentally traditionalist approach. Skinner himself and at least some of his followers (Bloom among others) do not see themselves in such a role. They argue that the results of conditioning trials, involving praise rather than blame, are liberalising in their practical effect in that they require the abolition of corporal punishment as inefficient 'negative reinforcement'. Moreover, the specification of syllabuses such as those of the Technician and Business Education Councils (TEC and BEC) in the United Kingdom, or of ROSBA in Australia, in terms of objectives can be seen as freeing teachers from strict syllabus requirements in terms of specific subject matter legislated from on high. For the moment, however, let us record that Skinner realises that there are at least three models of teaching which he downgrades to the status of 'metaphors' rather than 'models' in his quest for an allegedly scientific status for his 'technology' of teaching. These metaphors or models he describes as (i) growth or development, (ii) acquisition and (iii) construction.

The acquisition model (ii) is what educational philosophers nowadays broadly describe as the 'traditional' or 'subject-centrist' model (Perry, 1965). The child is an empty vessel who 'acquires' knowledge (Skinner, 1968, p. 2). On the other hand, in the growth model (i), we have what is usually called the 'child-centrist' mode, according to which schools are gardens of children (*Kinder* Garten) like gardens of flowers (Skinner, 1968, p. 1), with the teacher like a wise gardener watching over their growth points and assisted by his technical knowledge of such growth. Regarding the construction model (iii) Skinner says:

> To teach is to edify in the sense of to build. It is possible of course to say that the teacher builds precursors such as knowledge, habits, or interests but the metaphor of construction does not demand this because the behaviour of the student can in a very real sense be constructed. (Skinner, 1968, p. 4)

It is difficult to see precisely why Skinner at first sight should think that the construction model (iii) differs to any significant degree from the acquisition model (i). But I think that Skinner's retort would be that he does not describe (i), (ii) and (iii) as 'models' but as 'metaphors'. Metaphors by their very nature overlap one another and cannot be stressed literally. The only viable model, therefore, to replace such metaphors in a thoroughgoing 'scientific' analysis of teaching and learning would be a behaviourist model that incorporates in a revamped form the concept of 'operant conditioning'. As Skinner says, 'Any serious analysis of the interchange between organism and environment must, however, avoid metaphor' (Skinner, 1968, p. 4). It would seem, therefore, that Skinner was not unduly perturbed by lack of fine distinctions between what, by contrast with his science, was purely metaphorical. Perhaps, however, Skinner found the construction 'metaphor' relevant because it appears to introduce a synthesis between acquisition and growth. 'Construction' gives equal weight to both genetic endowment that is there to be developed *and* the acquisition of socially acquired knowledge that gives the endowment '*Form* or shape' (Skinner, 1968, p. 4). Whether our ability to synthesise x with y means that x and y cannot be metaphors but must be models is a criterial consideration that never appears to have occurred to Skinner. The Skinnerian synthesis we have seen to be the theory of operant conditioning. This theory, in attempting to cope with the rule-conforming/rule-following distinction in a way more satisfactory than that of classical behaviourism, might seem to suggest a reconciliation, therefore, between the ideas of the 'traditional', 'authoritarian' and 'free' schools. Operant conditioning tried in behaviourist terms to account for the 'natural' curiosity and interest of the learner, his taking the initiative in producing stimuli to which the environment responds and which, when the response is beneficial, tend to get repeated. Skinner himself has frequently criticised traditional teachers for their negative reinforcement, the way in which traditionally teachers have got their way by 'beating up' their pupils (Skinner, 1978). The operant conditioner can, in a certain sense, be said to 'respect the child', to follow (at least some of) his needs and interests, and to strengthen positively reinforcement when (real or beneficial) needs are expressed. Skinner would therefore argue that his modifications of behaviourism really point to a new, scientifically based, liberal consensus.

We have extensively criticised the whole basis of Skinner's synthesis in our general critique of behaviourism with which our last three chapters have been concerned. We have sought to attack it neither on political nor primarily on ethical grounds, but upon epistemological ones. The underlying philosophical basis for his proposed liberal consensus simply does not add up. By looking for an empirical basis in overt behaviour on which what he regards as three metaphors rather than models can be reconciled, he has ignored important philosophical distinctions regarding different foundations to different versions of the scientific enterprise. We have shown that operant conditioning rests upon a non-inductive view of science at conflict with the deterministic account of Newton. Such a view makes impossible the reduction of rule-following to rule-conforming behaviour that Skinner falsely assumes possible, and so shatters the philosophical basis of his synthesis. But we have also detected a related flaw in Skinner's empiricist strategy, namely, the view that general terms arise out of descriptions of their observed particulars, and we shall now see this general flaw embodied specifically in proposals for curricular aims and objectives.

4.1 AIMS AND OBJECTIVES: BLOOM'S TAXONOMY

For the traditionalist or what Skinner calls the acquisition metaphor, mere catalogues of subjects can suffice as general educational aims. Reading, writing, arithmetic, mathematics, history, science, art may describe traditional general objectives or 'aims' as the long-term educational objectives that are 'aimed at', albeit with many false starts or misses. Specific objectives or specific performances in such subject matters that are immediately obtainable correspond with chapters in textbooks of such subject matter graded in accordance with the age and aptitude of the learner. The Skinnerian tradition in which Bloom seeks to provide an educator's manual is, however, as we have stressed, one that believes itself to be liberal within scientific disciplines. Aims are not described in terms of behaviours that relate to specific subject matters but rather to 'liberal' aims. As Bloom says:

> This area, which we named the cognitive domain, may also be described as including the behaviours: remembering; reasoning; problem solving; concept formation; and, to a limited extent, creative thinking. (Bloom, 1956, Vol. 1, pp. 1–2)

Thus it would appear that Bloom believes that any subject matter, so long as it is capable of producing 'behaviours' such as 'remembering', 'reasoning', 'problem-solving', can be validly included within the curriculum. Traditional subjects could be taught as means to these ends, but other types of activity presumably could be found and used instead. There is, however, a limit on such activities, however open the search for them might otherwise appear. The overall plan which connects individual behaviours which are specific objectives together in complex ways so that they lead to the fulfilment of general objectives or aims must be behaviourally specifiable. Bloom calls such a plan a 'taxonomy' for reasons that we shall shortly explain, and makes the following stipulation:

> In one sense, however, the taxonomy is not completely neutral. This stems from the already-noted fact that it is a classification of intended behaviours. It cannot be used to classify educational plans which are made in such a way that either the student behaviours cannot be specified or only a single (unanalysed) term such as 'understanding' or 'desirable citizen', is used to describe the outcomes. (Bloom, 1956, Vol. 1, p. 15)

We shall be seeing in the course of this chapter how both the belief that aims such as 'remembering', 'reasoning', 'problem-solving' are not logically independent of specific subject matter in the way that Bloom implies. We shall further be seeing that the behaviourist stipulation distorts the nature of the subject matters themselves.

For the moment, however, let us expand in greater detail how the taxonomy is worked out and to define more clearly what in fact the term 'taxonomy' means. Bloom calls his book a 'taxonomy of' rather than a 'classification of educational objectives'. In a classification, individual items are related to one another in a way that the classificatory term implies. In a taxonomy, on the other hand, there is rather a hierarchical arrangement between different classes within the taxonomy such that certain basic classifications can be grasped far more easily than more complex classifications which depend on them and which are further up the hierarchy. Thus Bloom summarises the six major classes of the taxonomy and their subdivisions as follows:

1.00 Knowledge
1.10 Knowledge of Specifics
1.11 Knowledge of Terminology
1.12 Knowledge of Specific Facts
1.20 Knowledge of Ways and Means of Dealing with Specifics
1.21 Knowledge of Conventions
1.22 Knowledge of Trends and Sequences
1.23 Knowledge of Classifications and Categories
1.24 Knowledge of Criteria
1.25 Knowledge of Methodology
1.30 Knowledge of Universals and Abstractions in a Field
1.31 Knowledge of Principles and Generalisations
1.32 Knowledge of Theories and Structures

2.00   *Comprehension*
2.10   Translation
2.20   Interpretation
2.30   Extrapolation
3.00   *Application*
4.00   *Analysis*
4.10   Analysis of Elements
4.20   Analysis of Relationships
4.30   Analysis of Organisational Principles
5.00   *Synthesis*
5.10   Production of a Unique Communication
5.20   Production of a Plan, or Proposed Set of Operations
5.30   Derivation of a Set of Abstract Relations
6.00   *Evaluation*
6.10   Judgments in Terms of Internal Evidence
6.20   Judgments in Terms of External Criteria

(Bloom, 1956, Vol. 1, pp. 18 and 78–207)

In a moment we shall try to clarify what it means to proceed through this hierarchy or 'taxonomy' of educational objectives with reference to, as an example, a pupil learning the process and ramifications of photosynthesis in biology and thus see in detail what is being proposed. We have, we shall argue, in this outline of the taxonomy represented a basic empiricist, inductivist scheme. We travel from knowledge of specifics and specific facts rather as did the scientist in the empiricist's inductivist legend when he went in an unbroken chain of logical succession from incorrigible simples of observation to the complexities and abstractions of universal laws. Moreover, general empiricism has in Bloom assumed the specifically behaviourist form that we saw in our second chapter was its historical transformation, as we saw in our previous quotation.

Thus we see from the very outset that behaviourist presuppositions are made and that the seemingly mentalistic appearance of the taxonomy is to give way to a physicalistic specification since, as Bloom warned us, 'it cannot be used to classify educational plans that are made in such a way that . . . the student behaviours cannot be specified'. If they are so reduced such mentalistic statements become objective and capable of precise and measured fulfilment without losing thereby any real meaning. We have already in this work exposed the error in such a point of view. In an earlier work, moreover, we expounded some commonplace objections to such a behaviourist theory of meaning (Brent, 1978, pp. 50–55). In Chapter 2 of our present work, we pointed out that the determination of objectives in such behavioural terms as we see here in the taxonomy implied the possibility of an ideal language in which every term could be given a clearly specifiable and exhaustively definable meaning. Clearly the taxonomy needs such a language and has not quite got there yet, since many of its key concepts, such as 'knowledge', 'interpretation', 'analysis' and 'judgment', are mentalistic terms. 'Knowledge', in Skinner's own words, 'is a meaningless term – it has no physical properties or dimensions' (Skinner, 1978). We showed, however, in Chapter 2 that such a definitional strategy would reduce natural languages to chaos since a given language would require a new term for each new object that came within human experience. The result would be that human linguistic activity would be reduced to a state of permanent and chaotic change. Our charge was that such a view neglected the creativity of language – what Wittgenstein regarded as that special kind of vagueness that enabled new discoveries to be incorporated within known schemes.

We saw, too, how that classification in terms of what Wittgenstein described as 'family-resemblance' helped unravel what is involved in 'new discoveries' that are 'incorporated within known schemes'. We showed how the ability of language users to form classes in natural languages in terms of 'family-resemblance' was related to the rejection of induction as a valid philosophy of science. The ability to form general classes was not simply the ability to string together particulars based upon common properties or relations as induction implies. What was a common error in empiricist theories of meaning in general was instantiated in behaviourism as a particular form of empiricism. We saw that the bottom of 'stimulus generalisation' was a particular behaviourist error about the nature of universals. Let us, therefore, begin our critique of Bloom's taxonomy with an example of how this would guide a programme in science in order to substantiate in a curriculum context our charge of inductivism.

4.2 TEACHING SCIENCE: THE TAXONOMY OF LEARNING PHOTOSYNTHESIS

Human understanding of the process of photosynthesis and its role in biological science must presumably proceed thus. We begin with knowledge of specifics (1.10) when we mentally record and recall such items as a plant, the fact that it is green like some other plants but not like others, that animals feed off green plants, that the green plant only grows in certain types of soil, that in such soil there is, among other things, water and mineral salts. Here we are at the Lockean level of simple ideas, the basically incorrigible givens of perception. When we begin to differentiate between such incorrigible givens by, for example, labelling the green substance as 'chloryphyl', describing mineral salts by specific terms, calling the basic building-bricks of the leaf's structure 'cells' and so forth, we have proceeded to knowledge of terminology which can be changed, even though that to which it applies must be regarded as remaining constant (1.11). We then proceed to knowledge of specific facts (1.12) when we learn that the cells have different shapes and sizes, that chloryphyl has certain properties, that the cells' shapes at certain points in the leaf structure causes them to close when a maximum amount of water has been imbibed. When water is described as H_2O to show that it contains one atom of hydrogen to two atoms of oxygen and similarly other items, we have reached knowledge of conventions (1.21). Knowledge that green plants take in carbon dioxide during the day and give out oxygen but reverse the process at night exemplifies for us knowledge of trends and sequences (1.22). We then proceed to classify the various types of cell structure and green plants into general classes and types so that we have knowledge of classifications and categories (1.23). When we then start deploying methods of testing the presence of chloryphyl, the way that it converts the sun's light into energy, the use of Millean's reagent in order to detect the presence of starches, we have grasped what it is to have knowledge of criteria (the change of colour of the reagent is a criterion for the presence of starch) (1.24) and the methodology (test-tubes, burners, microscopes and so on) (1.25). As we begin to see a general pattern emerging in nature in the form of the carbon cycle, our understanding has reached the level of principles and generalisations (1.31). Our understanding of carbon as the basis of all life that we know and possible speculation about other bases (for example, silicon) for living matter represents the taxonomic level of knowledge of theories and of structures (1.32).

The first taxonomic classification in comprehension (2.00) is translation, and this level of the hierarchy is reached when we are able to explain the process of photosynthesis in other ways, for example, when we can describe the process purely mathematically (in the form of biochemical equations) or purely empirically (2.10). We reach interpretative behaviour (2.20) when we show that we can give general mathematical descriptions or general empirical descriptions of biological processes regularly and interchangeably. Next we begin to extrapolate (2.30) when we begin to see gaps in our descriptions of biochemical reactions or parts of our descriptions which sometimes do not agree with the general pattern as once happened when the formula for photosynthesis had to be rewritten. In fact it differs between 'O'-level and 'A'-level texts where the latter fill the gaps in the former. At the level of application (3.00), we show our ability to apply our knowledge to new situations as when we discover that what applies to carbon applies also to nitrogen in that the limited amount of both substances in nature requires a natural recycling process.

Items 4–6 of the taxonomy and their subdivisions lead to greater abstraction. Under the ability to recognise unstated assumptions (4.10) might go recognition of the causal principle at the back of the description of photosynthesis or the general evolutionary theory from which the emergence of the carbon cycle follows almost necessarily and deductively, given the principle of randomness and given the principle of the survival of the fittest. Related to this performance, both logically as well as taxonomically, is the ability to grasp relationships between assumptions and their conclusions (4.20). The emergence of the carbon cycle follows from the assumptions of both randomness and the survival of the fittest. Underlying such sets of assumptions there are organisational principles (4.30), such as the principle of statistical randomness that underlies evolutionary theory as opposed to the logically quite distinct causal principle that underlies classical physics. Presumably at the stage of production of a unique communication (5.10) we have a further complexifying of what was earlier generalised (1.31) when new laws are produced, new experiments worked out to confirm such laws (5.20) and new abstract relations, logically continuous with the earlier organisational principles (4.30), are derived (5.30). By 'evaluation' (6) is presumably meant testing the new, unique communication for internal consistency (6.10) and trying to falsify it against new data that might challenge its adequacy (6.20).

Thus we see exemplified what is involved in the taxonomic classification of educational objectives. From the outset, however, it must be asked whether the programme of the taxonomy is one of logical or of psychological analysis. There is a distinction to be made between an ideal picture of the operations of the mind given us both by logicians and the new linguistics and actual operations of individual minds that might, over whole areas of thought and discourse, fail to conform to such an ideal picture. So we would do well to pose this question of the taxonomy in order to keep logical and psychological issues distinct.

Undoubtedly at many points Bloom claims to be giving us a psychological account. As Bloom says:

> So long as the simpler behaviours may be viewed as components of the more complex behaviours, we can view the educational process as one of building on the simpler behaviour. (Bloom, 1956, Vol. 1, p. 16)

But it is well at this point to ask what is the force of the 'must' in this quotation. Is it a logical 'must' or an empirical 'must'? The quotation assumes that the taxonomy is a factual description of how human beings learn, of how, in fact, they acquire the behaviours that they do when they learn so that unless they first acquire some behaviours they cannot in fact go on to acquire others. But we would do well to ask how Bloom has arrived at this knowledge of how human beings learn. He has not discovered this by observation but rather by analysing what is presupposed by the terms used to define his ultimate objectives. For example, interpretation (2.20) must *logically* presuppose having knowledge of universals and abstractions (1.30), classifications and categories (1.23) and knowledge of principles (1.31). What it *means* to 'interpret' is to 'assign to categories', to 'instantiate a general principle', to recognise something as a particular occurrence of a general class or 'universal'. A second example may be seen in our exemplification of analysis (4.00). The ability to grasp the relationships between assumptions and conclusions (4.20) must logically follow and not logically precede the recognition of assumptions (4.10). But note that in both these examples the priority must be *logical* and not *temporal*, since:

(a) In the first example one could not know that one was instantiating, classifying and categorising if one did not know that their object was interpreting.
(b) In the second example one could not recognise an assumption as an *assumption* without and before being able to recognise what it was for an assumption to give rise whether inductively or deductively to some conclusion.

What it means for x to be an assumption is that x stands in the relationship of a premise to its conclusion.

The empiricist problem in insisting that logical priority is equivalent to temporal priority leads therefore to an insistance that what is logically prior must also first be learned in a temporal sequence (Hamlyn, 1978, pp. 37–9). But that this is nonsense has been shown by the fact that we cannot learn what premises are before we learn what conclusions are, nor can we learn what abstractions, principles, categories and so on are before we learn what interpreting is. Premising, abstracting, categorising and so on may *logically* precede concluding and interpreting. They are part of the logical rules by which we sort out what we are doing and instruct ourselves in how to argue, interpret and so forth. But although we may apply one before the other in a temporal sequence, we cannot *learn* to do one before the other in such a sequence. The fact that at t_1 we know (that is, have learned) that we categorise, abstract or premise, shows that we already know (that is, have learned) what we shall be doing when at t_2 we shall be concluding or at t_3 we shall be interpreting.

When we survey the taxonomy as a whole, we can see that it exhibits the apparatus of inductivism in an only partially realised behavioural form. We start with observations of (it ought, of course, to be 'responses to' or 'stimuli of') specifics (1.10) and, having responded to such stimuli, we move by an unbroken succession to stimulus generalisation (for example, 1.30 and 1.31).

Groups of particulars are increasingly classified and then classes are subsumed within wider classes until the final synthesis is reached (5.00), where the sum total of cognitive behaviour stands defined as a curriculum objective. In the taxonomy, there can be no classes left open. Each class must be exhaustively filled and in the order of a strict progression. The open-endedness of classes such as 'space', 'time' and 'cause', related to what we saw in Chapter 3 to be concerned with Wittgenstein's view of classes in terms of family-resemblances, is ignored. Nor should the fact that it is ignored strike us by this time as in any way strange. We saw that inductivism as a view of science was related to causal models of explanation which in turn was related to the idealisation of closed, exhaustively definable classes, and that this was the error that the later Wittgenstein exposed.

From this point there follow others which have been made against the plan of the taxonomy (Pring, 1971, and Sockett, 1971). We have seen that at one level the ground-plan of the taxonomy appears to sanction the allegedly 'liberal' goal of fostering such general cognitive styles as 'knowing', 'analysing', 'synthesising', 'comprehending', 'translating' or 'extrapolating' without legislating on curriculum content. Whether one teaches subjects, or chooses projects or topics instead, or any other alternative form of integrated curriculum that may be devised, it is still considered possible by means of the taxonomy to measure what is achieved in such curriculum material in terms of the achievement of these cognitive styles. But the problem with regarding curriculum objectives in this light is that to so regard them rests upon a misconstruction. The misconstruction is known as the essentialist fallacy in the particular form in which the later Wittgenstein detected it. It is to claim that different types of cognitive activity detected in different subject matters have some common, essential form because they bear similar names. Yet to take as our example the cognitive activity described as 'analysis', it is arguable that mathematical analysis is different from empirical analysis, which is different again from historical analysis, the analysis of literature and so on. The difference between mathematical analysis and empirical analysis may be brought out thus. Mathematical analysis, issuing in deductive proofs, operates within axiom systems which makes mathematical systems, even on a classically empiricist point of view, highly complex, non-trivial tautologies (Russell and Whitehead, 1962). Such deductive analysis is different from the inductive analysis of the natural sciences. Moreover, it is arguable from a later Wittgensteinian point of view, as we saw in our earlier discussion of a quotation of Waismann's, that even within the discipline of pure mathematics itself there is no one type of activity that is mathematical analysis. Bloom, I submit, is not entitled to perpetuate his basically empiricist error in the philosophy of science.

Not only, however, with science and mathematics, but also in history and aesthetics, ethics and so on must the essential forms of 'knowledge of specifics', 'universals', 'analysis', 'translation', 'extrapolation', for instance, be held to be shared with each other and held in common with empirical and mathematical knowledge. Let us exemplify both the proposal and its fallacious character once again from 'Analysis of Relationships' (4.20). One illustrative item under this head is: 'Ability to distinguish cause-and-effect relationships from other sequential relationships' (Bloom, 1956, Vol. 1, p. 147). This clearly refers to empirical science. But note that it is assumed that analysis of cause and effect in a historical account will consist of a similar cognitive operation, for we read another illustrative item in 4.20 as follows: 'Ability to recognise the causal relations and the important and unimportant details in an historical account.' Now we see here the presupposition that the analysis of cause in a scientific account must be similar in form to the analysis of cause in a historical account. Once again the similarity must result from an identity of essential form or basic structure of each. Yet partly for reasons that we have already seen, an assumption not only distorts the nature of scientific inquiry but succeeds also at the same time in distorting the character of historical inquiry. We saw in our first chapter that there is a logical disjunction between rule-conforming and rule-following models of explanation. We argued that human action was an inappropriate area for the application of rule-conforming models. Human understanding of rule-conformance in terms of statistically probable patterns of recurrence presupposes the ability to transcend the particular that characterises rule-following and sets such under-standing itself apart from rule-conformance. Thus the very act of human understanding of rule-conformance in the physical world is inconsistent with any explanation of understanding itself in rule-conforming terms.

Notwithstanding this absolute prescription on the distortion of the human sciences by the imposition upon them of an invalid, empiricist methodology, it will be interesting to observe from some examples the way in which an empiricist epistemology in general and then in a specifically behaviourist form infected and distorted methods of historical inquiry in a way that Bloom's taxonomy reflects. As our example of the influence of general empiricist epistemology, we take first historical criticism of the gospel records of 1930s vintage.

4.3 EMPIRICIST HISTORIOGRAPHY AND THE JESUS OF HISTORY

As we have already seen in Chapter 1, the movement from general empiricist stances to specifically behaviourist ones became inevitable and this was true also when an empiricist methodology was applied to human sciences, of which we take the study of history to be a part. We saw that classical empiricism regarded the problem of knowledge as the problem of how certain simple ideas, formed infallibly in sensation, from the perception of primary qualities, became or failed to become combined into veridicial descriptions of the world. We saw, moreover, that the problem of producing objective descriptions from introspective descriptions by individual subjects of their own internal states was one that behaviourism sought to overcome. To illustrate how this development was mirrored also in historical research, we exemplify classical empiricist historiography in this section and behaviourist historiography in the following.

Let us take any standard analysis of descriptions of Christ's walking on the water in biblical criticism up to the 1930s (Guy, 1973). The miracle is explained as a hallucination produced by a combination of factors such as the fear of the disciples, the charismatic character of Jesus, a misunderstanding of the original description of the event as it was handed down by word of mouth. One particular feature of the account is fastened on to, namely, that the Greek word for 'upon' in 'walking upon' can also mean 'along the side of' (*epi*). It is therefore plausible that an ambiguity in the description of the original eyewitnesses was the cause of later corruption in the oral transmission of the story. There was originally observed a storm, and it really did provoke fear in the disciples, or so it is maintained. Christ's personality really was able to quieten fear and panic. But what they saw that quietened their panic was not his figure walking *upon* the sea but *alongside* the sea-shore.

Note precisely what is assumed by the method of the empiricist historian who attempts to reconstruct the probable account of a series of historical events in such terms as these. Everything has to be accounted for in terms of observation statements that went wrong. Certain observations must have taken place, but they have been put together to give an incredible picture of an event. Sometimes the account is regarded as having been generated by a misunderstanding of the word for 'alongside' as 'on', sometimes in terms of a hallucination provoked by fear in which a man walking beside the sea was actually thought for one moment to be walking upon the sea. Someone at the commencement of the oral tradition which preceded the writing of the gospels must have seen something, and the basic ingredients of what they saw, like Locke's simple ideas, must be incorrigible – the product of an unbreakable causal nexus between such ideas and primary qualities. The 'problem of historical knowledge' is seen as the problem of explaining how such primary and incorrigible observations were combined and reinterpreted so as to produce distortions.

Now, what was intended to be the use of a general empiricist epistemology in strengthening and refining historical methodology was arguably a hindrance to the progress of historical inquiry. It is, furthermore, possible to argue two quite contrary reasons why classical empiricism created such an obstacle. The first, which will be our more detailed concern in the next section, is the behaviourist reason. Because no consistently objective account can be produced between different historians in the form of specific descriptions of the intentions, desires, interests, sense-impressions that caused simple observations to go wrong in specific historical situations, then the classical methodology failed to achieve objectivity in historical judgements. Because no consistent formula was discovered for sorting out descriptions of internal mental states, it was concluded by behaviourists that the language of mental states was itself defective and must undergo translation into the language of overt behaviour. We have already criticised such a general behaviourist strategy in our first chapter, though we shall have more to say about the form that it takes in the study of history in our next section. For the moment, let us take the second objection, namely, that the rule-conforming model is in any form wrong, both generally, as we argued in Chapter 1, and in a specifically historical form, as we are now going to argue here.

The preponderance of a rule-conforming over a rule-following model of historical explanation leads to the failure of historians to study the way in which rule-following human activity creates and re-creates new orders of meaning through which and not apart from which the historian must somehow be able to work. The reason why, for example, the gospel writers describe Jesus as walking upon the waters is because this is how the Creator is described as operating in both Hebrew and pagan mythologies.

God or the gods in such mythologies are regarded as moving over the waters of the primeval chaos and creating universal order by, among other things, stilling their tumultuous raging. Now, in the task of reconstructing the historical Jesus, if this is to have any possibility of success, there must be some relationship between the man who actually lived and such schemes for interpreting his significance. But the relationship between fact and interpretation is by no means as simple as the empiricists maintained. There is no strictly causal chain of events, precisely describable in terms of a definite formula, that would bind the writer's interpretative schema to a value-free description of historical facts. Interpretation cannot be understood as a causal process, and neither for that matter can perception, in explanation of which the empiricists also produced causal theories. Interpretation cannot moreover be assimilated to perception. The isolation in analysis of certain raw observation data uncontaminated by later, community interpretation proved therefore as illusive in this particular instance as the isolation of general foundations of knowledge in terms of sense-data has proven in contemporary empiricism. Progress towards knowledge of the historical Jesus can only take place through a methodology that grasps how human beings in community judge persons and events and in a rule-following way without being tied to extra-linguistic sensations constituting an objectivity beyond language. To say this is not to rule out the possibility of any kind of objectivity or to make all knowledge, including historical knowledge, culturally relative. It is, however, to locate the possibility of objectivity within human languages and specifically within those common semantic features shared by all human languages to which Chomsky's work point and which makes rational consensus between men and the translation of their languages possible. But this is to anticipate our later discussion (Chapter 8), which is to pursue our earlier critique of Quine's thesis of radical translation.

For the moment, let us look at the first objection to classical empiricist methodology in specifically historical inquiry which we saw to have specifically behaviourist presuppositions. As such we shall illuminate the distorting effects of an empiricist programme upon historical inquiry, this time as it assumes a specifically behaviourist form. We take our example from David Irving's attempt to acquit Hitler of any knowledge of the programmes for the mass-extermination of the Jews in Nazi Germany.

4.4 BEHAVIOURIST HISTORIOGRAPHY AND HITLER'S 'FINAL SOLUTION'

Irving states his major contention quite early in his book in the following passage:

While Hitler's overall anti-Jewish policy was clearly and repeatedly enunciated it is harder to establish a documentary link between him and the murderous activities of the SS 'task forces' (*Einsatzgruppen*) and their extermination camps in the east. (Irving, 1977, p. 12)

At first sight such a claim appears fantastic and one which runs counter to the received interpretation. The received interpretation is that Hitler needed utmost secrecy in the 'Final Solution' of the Jewish question. If mass-extermination had been openly carried out in major population centres, then not only might serious resistance have been provoked which might have drawn men away from fighting the war, but widespread moral revulsion and public sympathy for the plight of the Jews might have broken out among the civilian population. No doubt a man of Hitler's character would have regarded such sympathy as weakness on the part of the general population and as evidence of their natural duty to serve him and of his natural right to lead them. But nevertheless a strategy of deceit was required on the part of the strong leader, and so a secret policy is evolved whereby Jews are transported to the East away from centres of population, ostensibly to resettle them for work in their own communities with their own culture but in reality for their own extermination. The world is encouraged to think that 'final solution' means a 'cultural solution' in which the 'cultural problem' is solved by simply distancing the Jews geographically from the centres of Aryan culture. 'Special treatment' is intended simply to convey such a relatively benign message. In fact, behind such euphemisms other intentions are at work which Hitler knew full well that these euphemisms were intended to conceal.

It is important to grasp that Irving's objection to this received interpretation is that it is not supported by a sufficiently rigorous methodology. He makes clear that we require a 'documentary link' of a special kind without which we are not entitled to deduce that Hitler had any knowledge of the true nature of the 'final solution'. It is not sufficient simply to inquire into Hitler's probable 'state of mind', 'his purposes' or whatever from the savage metaphors of his speeches and the character of the man revealed in his various writings. The 'documentary link' between what is written and our historical descriptions cannot be of this kind. For Irving, such hypotheses (he would regard them as 'speculations') the historian is not entitled to accept. Instead of producing accounts of 'intentions', 'designs', 'deceits', the mentalistic character of which enable only loose and subjective links to be drawn with documents, we must instead have objective, behavioural evidence in the form of marks on paper. The 'marks', moreover, must be of such a kind that the 'savage plan' must necessarily follow from them if it is to be regarded as the product of Hitler's own 'mind'. The 'documentary link' must therefore exhibit on paper marks which represent strictly translatable behavioural descriptions of, say, Hitler's 'mind', 'character', 'intentions'. That this account represents Irving's methodological requirements and not simply an espousal of the laudable principle that no one is so bad that we are entitled to tell lies about them may be seen in the following description of Hitler on military campaign:

> Hitler's positive enjoyment of the battle scene was undeniable. He visited the front whenever he could, heedless of the risk to himself and his escort . . . He enjoyed meeting his troops and, *for all we know*, was exhilarated by the smell of cordite and the sight of blood. (Irving, 1977, p. 16; my italics)

Irving's reluctance here to interpret Hitler's state of mind, reasons for acting and so on ('for all we know') evidences the behaviourist requirements of his methodology. The behaviours must be specifiable, with direct links of logical inference established between them and historical interpretations, so that the one must necessarily follow from the other. It is, furthermore, important to grasp what 'must necessarily follow' implies for Irving's account. The necessity cannot simply imply a psychological impression left firmly upon the historian from a combination of his reading of the texts and his general awareness of human characteristics, his skill at forming generally reliable impressions of people which are generally more or less confirmed in the light of subsequent behaviour, for instance. Irving writes as if, to the contrary, precise correlations between (*a*) marks made on paper and (*b*) descriptions of Hitler's character, intentions and so on could be established with (*b*) following from (*a*) by strict canons of *logical* inference. Yet we are once again, if we try to follow Irving in this matter, beset by all the problems of inference and quantification in a specifically historical form with which we met in a general form in Chapter 2. Problems of spelling out a precise formula for inference combined with a quest for an illusive system of exhaustive quantification we argued there to present insuperable obstacles to behaviourism in any form.

We see, therefore, that Irving is sceptical about a model of historical inquiry that has no strict rules of logical inference. Yet what makes such a model implausible, quite apart from fatal objections for empiricist models of inference in general, is that it becomes impossible to assume that perfect dissimulation is ever possible. If someone carried off a perfect charade and managed to conceal their true motives completely, then historical methodology would be precluded by Irving's longed-for canons of historical inquiry from ever uncovering them. Such practical problems as these, underscored as we have shown by basic theoretical flaws in the methodological strategy, have lead to many historians objecting to what they regard as the imposition of an inappropriate 'scientific' paradigm of inquiry upon their discipline. The thinking about history is not formally comparable with thinking about physiology or chemistry. Rather the historian must have the ability both to understand and interpret attitudes, feelings, states of mind, to be able to see not only what sorts of premises would lead a given individual to what sorts of conclusion, to gauge what characteristics of a person might lead him not to behave strictly in accordance with the canons of syllogistic logic. Without these kinds of skill, progress in historical inquiry cannot proceed, and yet it is precisely such skills that behaviourist canons rule out.

Our objections to such behaviourist canons apply equally well to the proposals of the taxonomy that imply that historical methodology be taught in that way. What we have argued here is, first, that such a paradigm is empiricist rather than 'scientific' since it implies an inadequate view of science. Secondly, we have argued that an empiricist paradigm would distort the character of historical inquiry (and has in fact done so) irrespective of its adequacy as a valid account of the logic of scientific inquiry. Thirdly, moreover, in framing specifically curricular objectives for history, the behaviourist Bloom is advocating the perpetuation of such methodological distortions, albeit in a behaviourist reformulation.

In what we have argued so far we have endeavoured to show how the influence of empiricism in a specifically behaviourist form has distorted the character not simply of scientific but also of historical inquiry. We saw, moreover, that an essentialist strategy was involved in so doing and that in Bloom's taxonomy also what was presupposed was that 'knowledge', 'comprehension', 'application', 'analysis' and so on would possess the same essential form irrespective of the particular subject area. Indeed, it was precisely this presupposition which also underlay both the claim of Skinnerian behaviourism and Bloom's taxonomy to be proposing a programme that was 'liberal' in the sense that it was not tied to specific subjects. We have begun to see with reference to the specific examples of both biochemistry and history not simply that there are different forms of inquiry but that the quest for common features shared by these different forms is at least in this case a quest for a non-existent unity that Wittgenstein described as the 'philosophic disease' (Wittgenstein, 1974). But having given some account of how history and science fare with both empiricist epistemology in general and Bloom's taxonomy in particular, it is perhaps now time to look at aesthetics, morals and religions in such a context.

4.5 MORALS, RELIGION AND AESTHETICS: BLOOM'S 'AFFECTIVE' DOMAIN

It is interesting to observe from the outset that general empiricism expunged morality, religion and aesthetics from the map of knowledge on grounds that were somewhat different from behaviourism. This difference has, we shall see, lead Bloom to be somewhat ambivalent in tending to place such models of inquiry within the 'affective' in separation from the 'cognitive' domain, while insisting that there be no final distinction made between the two. As Bloom says:

> We recognise that human behaviour can rarely be neatly compart-mentalized in terms of cognition and affect. It is easier to divide educational objectives and intended behaviours into these two domains. However, even the separation of objectives into these two groups is somewhat artificial in that no teacher or curriculum worker really intends one entirely without the other. (Bloom, 1956, Vol. 2, p. 85)

Bloom appears initially therefore anxious to absolve himself from the charge that, having stretched an empiricist paradigm of knowledge from scientific inquiry, where it had initially though deceptively an application, to history, where it had not, he found as did the classical empiricists that he could stretch the domain of what could be known no further. Aesthetics, religion and morals could not be considered legitimately to be within the domain of knowledge (cognitive domain). As they stand, they simply represent behaviour expressive of emotions (affective domain). Bloom, however, as we have said, avoids, as in the passage that we have just quoted, this pitfall by asserting that there is no radical disjunction between the cognitive and affective domains. It is well, however, for us to inquire on what precise basis he would seek to avoid such a radical disjunction.

Let us ask Bloom, therefore, on the basis of this passage, on what basis he makes this distinction or any distinction throughout the taxonomy? Sometimes he describes the distinction as purely 'arbitrary', but sometimes he alleges other bases. We here come very much to the crux of what Bloom proposes, since we are concerned with a fundamental question about the purpose with which Bloom writes. Does Bloom intend:

(a) To give us a detailed description of educational objectives simply on the basis of what a large enough sample of teachers claim those goals to be; or

(b) To stipulate what some goals ought to be rather than others, arguing therefore that some teachers who could be either the majority or the minority are wrong?

If, moreover, his purpose has been (b), we are entitled to ask him on what grounds he claims that teachers ought to follow his preferred objectives. On this question, Bloom is frequently ambivalent as between (a) and (b), as the following passage discloses:

> Insofar as possible, the boundaries between categories should be closely related to the distinctions teachers make in planning curricula or in choosing learning situations. It is possible that teachers make distinctions which psychologists would not make in classifying or studying human behaviour. (Bloom, 1956, Vol. 1, p. 6)

At first sight, therefore, it appears that Bloom intends simply to take teachers' claims about planning categories and simply to formalise and organise these (a). Thus his denial that there is any final disjunction between cognitive and affective behaviour may simply be a result of the fact that 'no teacher or curriculum worker really intends one without the other'. However, he goes on to say almost immediately following the passage just quoted that 'the taxonomy should be consistent with relevant and accepted psychological principles and theories'. Thus he implies that he *is* entitled to stipulate the objectives that teachers *ought* to seek and his intentions are as described conversely in (b). Moreover, the grounds for his stipulation he is claiming to be the grounds proffered by empirical psychology and governed by the prior stipulation of behaviourist reformulation. Perhaps, therefore, he is wishing to argue that empirical evidence could establish relationships of an empirical kind between cognitive and affective behaviour that teachers feel intuitively to exist there. Yet we have already seen that some relations at least between items in the taxonomy (in our discussion of the cognitive domain) are logical relations, and, though Bloom claims that 'the taxonomy should be a logical classification', he did not seem to grasp that such relations cannot sensibly be regarded also as empirical relations such as those of time. In other words, logical questions are not simply a question of making every effort 'to define terms as precisely as possible and to use them consistently' so that the cognitive/affective continuum should rest on an accurate defining and conceptualising of what could be empirically observed (Bloom, 1956, Vol. 1, p. 14).

We do well, therefore, to ask Bloom whether, in dividing the cognitive from the affective domain while maintaining no final distinctions between them, he is entitled to do so on empirical or on logical grounds. We have, after all, established that the empirical/logical distinction is of far greater concern for Bloom's account than he supposes. At one point he implies that the connections between the cognitive and affective domains are logical connections. He says:

> The fact that we attempt to analyze the affective area separately from the cognitive is not intended to suggest that there is a fundamental separation. There is none. As Scheerer puts it, '... behaviour may be conceptualized as being embedded in a cognitive-motivational matrix in which no true separation is possible. No matter how we slice behaviour, the ingredients of motivation-emotion-cognition are present in one order or another' (Scheerer, 1964, p. 123). (Bloom, 1956, Vol. 2, p. 45)

There are no empirical observations which could establish behaviour as being either motivational *or* emotional *or* cognitive on the one hand, or, on the other, all three of these together. Rather by definition and therefore necessarily is behaviour to be described in terms of the cognitive-motivational matrix – that is, what 'behaviour' means and therefore how it is to be conceptualised. At other points, however, the continuum is established against the disjunction on empirical grounds when Bloom says:

> In some instances the joint seeking of affective and cognitive goals results in curricula which use one domain as the means to the other on a closely-knit alternating basis. Thus a cognitive skill is built and then used in rewarding situations so that affective interest in the task is built up to permit the next cognitive task to be achieved, and so on ... Thus alternating between affective and cognitive domains, one may seek a cognitive goal using the attainment of a cognitive goal to raise interest (an affective goal). This permits achievement of a higher cognitive goal, and so on. (Bloom, 1956, Vol. 2, p. 60)

Here it does make sense to talk of affective and cognitive behaviours as distinct objectives and it is a purely contingent matter that the acquisition of one as a matter of fact does assist the acquisition of the other.

Given Bloom's ambiguity, therefore, over the nature of the distinction between the cognitive and affective domain, it will be well for us to inquire what lead either Bloom or those psychologists upon whose categorisations he is dependent first to posit this distinction and then to conclude that there was a continuum between its two poles. At the close of our last chapter we saw what we described as the imperialistic character of classical empiricism which extended its definition of knowledge to include mathematics, science and history within its domain, but which found that morals, religion and aesthetics could not be remodelled in accordance with its definition and so sought to exclude them. There is, therefore, one way that Bloom could have insisted on a radical distinction between the cognitive and affective domains, and that would have been by pursuing a route mapped out for him by classical empiricism. We shall see that, desirous though he may have been of taking such a route, this was foreclosed to him by his acceptance of the strong behaviourist principle that empiricism must assume a behaviourist form. We shall argue, moreover, that if Bloom's obliteration of the cognitive/affective distinction made in the form of a disjunction by classical behaviourism is done on inadequate, behaviourist grounds, then he will have missed important conceptual relations that a different model would have suggested. We shall, in conclusion, see that one practical outcome of inadequacy of theoretical grounds for bringing out the nature of this distinction has made Bloom, against his better judgement, allocate subjects in a classically empiricist fashion, with music, tolerance and moral education considered as decidedly affective kinds of activity that rules them out as forms of knowledge.

Let us begin with the classical empiricist route which he appears to disavow theoretically but whose practical conclusions he nevertheless appears finally to accept. Classical empiricism sought to dispose of morals, religion and aesthetics by what might be called 'emotivism'. The emotivist theory of ethics (Urmson, 1969), for example, sought to explain ethical statements in terms of emotional arousal in one way or another produced by the key concepts of such statements. Key concepts such as 'good', 'right' or 'ought' were considered the logical equivalents of pro-attitudes towards those kinds of behaviour to which a given individual or group applied them whereas 'bad', 'unjust' or 'wrong' were considered as the logical equivalents of anti-attitudes. Ethics as such was regarded as a subjective enterprise and not therefore as a form of knowledge. Any 'knowledge' there could be about ethics was simply knowledge about either the 'pro' or 'anti' attitudes of various cultures and subcultures towards various kinds of behaviour, or knowledge of the particular endocrine activity within an individual's bloodstream when he made his moral judgements. Classical empiricism treated aesthetics and religion similarly to morals so that all three thus became reduced to the psychology, social-psychology or even physiology of the person making moral, aesthetic or religious judgements. These as forms of inquiry in their own right were to be accordingly removed from the map of knowledge. In doing so, classical empiricism made morals, aesthetics and religion similar kinds of enterprises in contrast with those within the domain of knowledge. The words and concepts in which they were expressed represented affective psychological states.

We have, moreover, seen in Chapter 3 what lay behind the classical empiricist claim that the map of knowledge, founded on a scientific and mathematical paradigm, be extended to cover history, but should be cut short at the areas of morals, religion and aesthetics. The classical empiricist was always impressed by the way in which scientific claims could be settled in one way or another, whereas moral, religious or aesthetic claims could apparently not be so settled. But we have seen, however, that in a post-Einsteinian phase in the philosophy of science, such a position has become difficult to sustain. We cannot simply object to moral, religious or aesthetic forms of inquiry on the grounds that these, in contrast to science, generate so many different schools of thought, founded upon mutually conflicting presuppositions, with great difficulty (if not impossibility) of settling conflicts between them. There is at least a strong argument in the current debate about the nature of science, exemplified in the thesis of Kuhn's paradigms, that scientific inquiry is liable to the same charge of having no unshakeable method of deducing the truth or falsity of scientific propositions from some basic set of observation statements. Hume's ancient charge assumes in such a context some degree of new life that induction was unable to be rationally supported so that scientific inquiry rests upon some 'marvellous instinct'. It can sometimes therefore look as though the basis for regarding science/mathematics/history as capable of being known, and therefore capable of cognition, and distinguishing such cognitive enterprises from morals/religion/aesthetics, which can only be felt, is a distinction difficult to sustain.

It is also arguable that religious and aesthetic statements, as well as moral ones, have a similar logical form to general truth statements, despite a failure of nerve engendered in their proponents by over 150 years of empiricist argument (Brent, 1978, Chapter 3). Truth claims are set apart from subjective preferences by this logical requirement: what is 'sweet for me' is not necessarily 'sweet for you'. But what is 'true for me' is necessarily 'true for you'. As such, then, moral claims have a similar logical form to general truth claims in that 'moral for me' does necessarily imply universalisability into the prescription 'moral for you'. In religion also the psychological impression that religious disputes can never be settled whereas (Newtonian) scientific ones can, has recently been in some measure dispelled by the emergence not only of a general atmosphere of ecumenism, but also such propositional agreements as those represented by joint Anglican/Roman theological statements on the Eucharist and the ministry. Such an agreement, moreover, is epistemically based, as can be seen from the social and psychological forces that prevent its general acceptance and thus reveal the agreement not to be not simply the product of those forces. The possibility of such an epistemically based consensus, moreover, was arguably guaranteed from the start by the logical impossibility of assimilating the objective claim: 'I believe in God the Father, the Almighty, maker of Heaven and Earth'; to the subjective expression: 'When I think to myself – what a wonderful world!'

The distinction therefore made by classical empiricism between the cognitive and the affective, between what could be known objectively and what could only be felt subjectively cannot lead to any absolute distinction between different kinds of curricular subject matter. Since, however, Bloom eschews so radical a disjunction in some passages that I have quoted, it may well be asked why I have taken such pains to draw out and criticise the classical empiricist's argument on this point. The reason is that the way in which Bloom exemplifies certain specific cognitive and affective curricular goals appears to represent the very disjunction between different forms of discourse made by classical empiricists that he claims to deny. Such an ambivalence is, of course, not surprising, given Bloom's lack of clarity that we have documented regarding the grounds for making the cognitive/affective distinction anyway. But the ambivalence, I contend, does place great question marks about the coherence of Bloom's underlying philosophy in a way that parallels Skinner's ambivalence between opposing views on the nature of science that we documented in Chapter 3. We shall now therefore substantiate this charge in detail that a discredited classical empiricism is reflected in the different ways in which moral, aesthetic or religious concerns are described as 'cognitive' or 'affective', rather than the behaviourism that Bloom ostensibly espouses.

4.6 COGNITIVE AND AFFECTIVE AIMS AND CLASSICAL EMPIRICISM

Let us first set out the categories and subdivisions of the affective domain in order to see how the individual and particular statements of objectives which I will be citing fit into them. Bloom summarises his affective taxonomy as follows:

1.0 Receiving (attending)
1.1 Awareness
1.2 Willingness to receive
1.3 Controlled or selected attention
2.0 Responding
2.1 Acquiescence in responding
2.2 Willingness to respond
2.3 Satisfaction in response
3.0 Valuing
3.1 Acceptance of a value
3.2 Preference for a value
3.3 Commitment (conviction)
4.0 Organization
4.1 Conceptualization of a value
4.2 Organization of a value system
5.0 Characterization by a value or value complex
5.1 Generalized set
5.2 Characterization

(Bloom, 1956, Vol. 2, p. 95)

We shall now substantiate our charge by showing from selected items that any moral, aesthetic or religious item in the cognitive domain reflects a classical empiricist reduction to the history of moral opinions, the social-psychology of religious belief or knowledge of techniques of literary criticism practised historically by different aesthetic schools. When, however, such items are listed in the affective domain, I shall argue that they refer to religious convictions, moral convictions or aesthetic experience proper, which we have argued to rest upon propositions which must be considered as real propositions because they bear the same logical form as general truth claims. We shall juxtapose such cognitive and affective items with some brief comments, using the device 'x/?y' to stand for 'x actually but Bloom seems to think y'.

Example 1: Aesthetics
Cognitive: '1.11 Knowledge of the fine arts sufficient to be able to read and converse intelligently [aesthetic criticism/?aesthetics].' (Bloom, 1956, Vol. 1, p. 65)
Affective: '1.1 Develops awareness of aesthetic factors in dress, furnishings, architecture, city design, good art, and the like [aesthetics].' (Bloom, 1956, Vol. 2, p. 100)

We see here Bloom's empiricist tendency to regard anything that is cognitive about art to be a kind of non-emotive reading and discussing of what others regard as great art and by which they have been moved affectively. The cognitive statement in 1.11 does not, however, require that the reader or conversationalist is moved himself. He is therefore a kind of psychologist or historian of other people's aesthetic experiences, and art can therefore only be allowed as cognitive if it is reduced to empirical or historical forms of inquiry. For other comparisons, compare such cognitive items as, '1.23 Becoming familiar with types of literature' (Bloom, 1956, Vol. 1, p. 65), '2.10 The ability to translate non-literal statements (metaphor, symbolism, irony, exaggeration) to ordinary English' (Bloom, 1956, Vol. 2, p. 92) and '4.30 Ability to analyse in a particular work of art the relations of materials and means of production to the "elements" and to the organization' (Bloom, 1956, Vol. 1, p. 148) with such affective items as, '1.2 Develops a tolerance for a variety of types of music' (Bloom, 1956, Vol. 2, p. 100), '2.3 Enjoys reading books on a variety of themes', or '2.3 Responds emotionally to a work of art or musical composition' (Bloom, 1956, Vol. 2, p. 132).

Example 2: Morals
Cognitive: '1.32 Recall and recognition of what is contained in particular cultures [historical/?moral]'. (Bloom, 1956, Vol. 1, p. 77)
Cognitive: '2.30 The ability to estimate or predict consequences of courses of action described in a communication [historical/?moral].' (Bloom, 1956, Vol. 1, p. 96)
Cognitive: '3.00 The ability to relate principles of civil liberties and civil rights to current events [historical/?moral].' (Bloom, 1956, Vol. 1, p. 124)
Cognitive: '4.10 The ability to distinguish factual from normative statements [historical/?moral].' (Bloom, 1956, Vol. 1, p. 146)

Whether any of these is to count as moral as opposed to historical/ sociological depends upon an important distinction that Bloom has not made clear. The distinction is between what Wilson calls the 'inverted commas' sense of 'morals' and what is properly called moral. In the basic logical form of moral statements, part of which I have described in the last section, we find such a phenomenon as being able to say without internal contradiction: 'Although x was in accordance with the morality of his social group, he ought not to have done x, i.e. it was not moral.' Factual descriptions of *social mores* are therefore logically distinct from moral judgement, both arising from different bases. Descriptions of social *mores* belong to historical-sociological forms of inquiry since they are a branch of that inquiry known as social anthropology. When we ask in what category of inquiry these statements of cognitive objectives are to be placed, we are put into a quandary. 1.32 clearly implies that purely factual, non-evaluate objectives are in mind. As for 2.30 and 3.00, they are susceptible to either a factual or an evaluative interpretation. If 2.30 refers to a judgement that, by doing x the outcome will be an increase of the greatest happiness of the greatest number, then according to one view of moral reasoning, 2.30 refers to a procedure of moral inquiry. If, however, 2.30 refers instead to a historian's ability to weigh up the relations between outcomes and the intentions of the performers of acts, then the character of the objective is quite distinct. Likewise 3.00 can simply refer to a lawyer's ability to discover and apply the particular principles of his particular social group without reference to a moral form of inquiry which would determine the genuine morality of such principles. When we come to 4.10, there seems to be no longer any confusion. The implication here is that we can observe cognitively people stating facts and making value judgements and describe the psychology or social-psychology of both. But the actual value judgement itself, being a kind of gut-reaction, belongs emphatically in the affective domain where we shall find moral behaviour in a non-inverted-commas sense described by Bloom, as we shall now see:

Affective: '1.1 Awareness of the feelings of others whose activities are of little interest to ourselves.' (Bloom, 1956, Vol. 2, p. 100)
Affective: '1.2 Increase in sensitivity to human need and pressing social problems.' (Bloom, 1956, Vol. 2, p. 108)
Affective: '3.1 Grows in his sense of kinship with human beings of all nations.' (Bloom, 1956, Vol. 2, p. 141)

Of course, the mere statement of such allegedly affective objectives challenges the validity of the distinction between the cognitive and affective domain. Cognitive elements come inevitably creeping in, and for reasons unbeknown to Bloom that we shall discuss in greater detail in our next section. Cognitive appraisals are, after all, necessarily involved in assessing, for instance, that the feeling of x towards an activity is of one kind rather than another (1.1), that there is some aspect in terms of which a problem can be recognised as problematic and a person's lack to in fact be a need (1.2), that the feeling of kinship is in some way an appropriate feeling for people of other nations (3.1). The purpose of the cognitive/affective distinction, since it is hard to sustain with any clarity, becomes therefore difficult to divine unless it is, as we have suggested, a survival of a shadow of a classical empiricist frame of reference which Bloom as an avowed behaviourist ought to have succeeded in superseding. Regarding the third form of inquiry, namely, religious inquiry, that empiricism sought to expunge from the map of knowledge while unreduced to an appropriate psychological or historical form, Bloom has no cognitive examples. His affective example is, '3.1 Acceptance of the place of worship in man's life' (Bloom, 1956, Vol. 2, p. 141). But here, once again, there is a 'cognitive' element that belies the 'affective' label.

We therefore see that the case is made that the cognitive/affective distinction in the way that it is presented in specific objectives presupposes both a classical empiricist view about the nature of knowledge and the form of curricular subjects and not a behaviourist view. It may yet again be suggested that I have been unfair on Bloom, that he saves his account from my charge by insisting on the basic continuity between the cognitive and the affective domains that my account has itself merely demonstrated. My reply is as follows. If, as we saw in some places, Bloom is arguing that the relationship between cognitive and affective goals is that the acquisition of an affective goal provides the means for the acquisition of a cognitive goal and *vice versa*, then the relationships between the cognitive and affective domains are contingent. They are like, as Bloom says, the relations between higher and lower rungs of a ladder in which the attainment of one allows for the attainment of the other. One may need to 'feel' in order to 'grasp' and to 'grasp' in order to 'feel', but 'feeling' remains one thing and 'grasping' another. Although this would imply that affective and cognitive objectives were connected in causal and in other empirical ways, there can be no logical connection (such as a 'continuum') between them. But we have seen, to the contrary, that there are such logical connections. On Bloom's 'ladder' view of the relationship between the cognitive and affective domains, we ought to be able to use: (*a*) 'sensitivity to human needs' (1.2) as a means of motivating the student to: (*b*) 'relate principles of civil liberties ... to current events' (3.0) without (*a*) being either equivalent to or part of what (*b*) *means*. Yet we have indicated that part of what individual statements of affective objectives *mean* is to be cognitive appraisals. We will therefore side with the position which Bloom quotes from Sheerer, the importance of which we must charge him with failing to have grasped, namely, that 'behaviour may be conceptualized as being embedded in a cognitive-motivational matrix in which no true separation is possible' (quoted above, p. 145). What we require to be clear about educational objectives is a logical analysis that will bring out symmetrical relationships between so-called 'cognitive' and 'affective' objectives such as will belie the distinction. So far we have briefly seen some aspects of those relations in our argument that part of the meaning of so-called 'affective' objectives is that they involve cognitive appraisals. We shall be arguing further this case in the next section and showing how such an argument will lead us beyond behaviourism and Bloom's incoherent curriculum programme.

For the moment, it will be well for us to inquire why Bloom, having set out to analyse clear behavioural objectives, should have confused the very character of the objectives that he states, clear though they would have been, however mistaken, against a backcloth of classical empiricism that rigorously maintained the cognitive/aesthetic disjunction. The reason lies in what we have already observed about Skinner and Quine in earlier chapters (Chapters 2 and 3) and the process of trying to retranslate classical empiricism into a behaviourist form. We must now therefore seek to locate in such a process Bloom's ambivalence over the grounds for and nature of what he sees as either the cognitive-affective distinction or continuum. We shall see in our search what lead both Bloom and the psychologists upon whose theories he is dependent to posit this distinction and then to conclude that there was a continuum between its two poles.

As we saw (Chapter 3), Quine was lead by his behaviourist revision of classical empiricism to deny that there was any final distinction between the gods of Homer and the concepts of quantum physics, since 'in point of epistemological footing the physical objects and the gods differ only in degree and not in kind' (Quine, 1953, p. 45). It is clear, therefore, why Bloom, lead by similar behaviourist yearnings and influenced by similar behaviourist theories, should have had problems with maintaining that religion was to do with feelings and therefore to be assigned to the affective domain whereas science was to do with knowledge and therefore belonged in the cognitive domain. His defence would, no doubt, be similar to Quine's.

An earlier generation of empiricists, as we saw (Chapter 3), had distinguished scientific world views from mythological ones on the grounds that the former represented pictures formed more or less correctly by a logical formula of induction (which was yet to be adequately articulated) from indubitable basic items of sense-perception. We saw, moreover, that behaviourism as represented by Quine could not make such a distinction since it sought to query the possibility of objectivity given the mentalistic descriptions involved in the process of inquiry in question. In, however, making the behaviourist move which required the reduction of all mentalistic descriptions to physicalistic ones, Quine was forced to relativise his notion of truth by the adoption of a pragmatic standard which flatly contradicted the purpose of his original, behaviourist strategy to produce an objectivist epistemology. Bloom might, therefore, pursue a defence against the charge of abscuring distinctions on the grounds that we have not yet an adequate language for stating behavioural objectives, but, unless we seek one, we shall be lost in the quagmire of failures that was classical empiricism. Ideally we ought to be able eventually to revise the imprecision of ordinary language so as to produce a clearly stated and determinate learning – that is to say, a behaviour-modification programme. If Bloom is confused, therefore, it is only because ordinary language is so imprecise. We need to explain concepts in language, as Quine said, 'with some degree of clarity and rigor – preferably, as I see it, in terms of behavior' (Quine, 1953, p. 12). Yet Bloom's defence then becomes subject to the kinds of objections that I have raised, both from within such a sophisticated behaviourist framework such as Quine's as well as from the general difficulties raised in principle by the framework itself. Such a framework can only by its very nature be deceptively precise as Quine's phrase '*with some degree of* clarity and vigor' frankly admits. Yet precision was what was intended to commend behaviourism in general and the taxonomy in particular to both the hard-headed scientist and the teaching practitioner. We have given reasons for claiming, moreover, that the illusion of precision remains in the behaviourist model because Skinner clung to a Newtonian view of the function of a science of human behaviour while accommodating into his system non-Newtonian probability methods as in operant conditioning. Yet the imprecision of operant responses, because it was based upon observations of statistical patterns of probable responses, could only ever make such responses likely or probable and never certain. Quine furthermore admitted that imprecision in such phrases as 'indeterminacy of translation' (above pp. 62–6).

We have, moreover, charged operant behaviourism with being a redescription of a problem masquerading as a solution. Operant conditioning was required as the putative solution that classical behaviourism failed to furnish to the indeterminacy of that kind of human behaviour that had, within a behaviourist explanation, to go proxy for such mental events as choices, intentions, purposes and decisions and to be explained in terms of statistical probability. Yet, to grasp statistical schemes of probable recurrence, we had to presuppose a human ability that was different from law-like conformity to statistical laws. To understand statistical laws governing physical or biological events required a rule-following ability whose fundamental feature was the transcendence of the particular. Unless, therefore, we could give an account of human beings as rule-followers in a sense distinct from that in which they are rule-conformers, we should have been unable to specify valid curriculum objectives. Such objectives would have to look quite different from those that Bloom would have liked to have formulated, could an adequate behaviourist language have ever been developed.

It might, of course, at this point be argued in Bloom's defence that his original work on which our discussion has heavily relied was programmatic. Moreover, his *Taxonomy* was developed over a quarter of a century ago. As such, we should arguably regard it as a first, faltering attempt, however seminal and central it has been in relation to a vast amount of literature and curricular programmes since its first appearance. But if that were to be the case, then subsequent work would have been expected to have refined Bloom's categories. In such work, there would have been further written out what we have shown to be his classically empiricist taxonomic descriptions in favour of more rigorous and consistent behaviourist ones. What therefore I have argued as in principle impossible might subsequently have been shown to be possible, and my logical and a-priorist objections shown thus to be unfounded. However, some brief discussion of two recent works within the behaviourist and taxonomic tradition (Popham, 1975, and Shipman, 1979) will exemplify my general charge against this curriculum movement, namely, that no such fulfilment of Bloom's programme has taken place. Bloom's original framework, with its behaviourist pre-suppositions, have stood as the unexamined and undeveloped dogmas perpetuated in statements of curriculum aims.

Let us take Popham (1975) as our example. My argument has been that Bloom (*a*) perpetuated the inductivist legend by maintaining that it was possible to spell out general objectives in terms of exhaustive strings of particulars and that (*b*) it was possible to describe the achievement of objectives in terms of overt behaviour. How does Popham record the success or failure of such a programme? First, let us take (*a*) in conjunction with the following quotation:

> There was a belief in the early sixties that the more specific an objective was, the more useful it would be. Yet as educators went about devising superspecific objectives they ended up with encyclopedic lists of these detailed statements. Those who generated such elongated lists of instructional goals soon discovered another instance where *more is less*. Evaluators began to realize that the most useful sorts of instructional objectives would be those that described a set of desired learner behaviors, not just one. Sometimes these are referred to as *content-general objectives*. (Popham, 1975, p. 51)

But we have seen that the 'discovery' here is a logical and *a priori* discovery about the nature of open-class universals ('content-general' 'set of desired learner behaviors'). As such, the whole enterprise was doomed from the start as resting on a misconception. Regarding (*b*), however, if, as Popham continues, a 'content-general objective attempts to describe a more generalizable class of learned behaviours', he does well to say 'describe' and not 'explain'. As we have frequently seen, once it is admitted that inductive determinism that regards going in an unbroken chain from particular to general observations fails, then so do general objectives thus built up. The failure, moreover, is one of explanation and not just description. Yet it is precisely explanation and not simply redescription of why a student performed in a certain way that the teacher requires and that the taxonomic approach assumes. Redescriptions of open-classes or 'content-general learning behaviours' in terms of learner classifications of schemes of statistically probable recurring particulars we have argued to be, unlike their failed inductivist predecessors, redescriptions that only masquerade as explanations.

We have seen, moreover, that the application of the notion of 'technology' by behaviourists illegitimately obscured important ethical considerations, usually by wedding the theory to evolutionary inevitability (above, pp. 102–203). Popham also reflects but does not clarify such obfuscations when he says:

A technology consists of a related set of tested rules for behavior. Putting it another way, a technology is made up of a set of verified guidelines for practice. People who use the rules for action that constitute a technology will, in general, function more effectively than those who do not adhere to the technology's guidelines. (Popham, 1975, p. 16)

There is, of course, an implicit assumption made here, namely, that the taxonomic tradition merely gives us morally neutral means for achieving our desired ends that as such can be used for good or ill. Different political and religious views can simply be allowed to stand without even Skinner's proviso about choosing that which is more likely to contribute to a society's survival than not, inconsistent as that exhortation was within a causal framework. Being 'more effective' can apparently, in Popham's opinion, stand as an end in itself without further discussion.

What Popham fails in common with the behaviourists to grasp is the way in which the means that he is espousing are not logically independent of their ends. We have argued that the reduction of rule-following to rule-conforming in planning a learning programme in fact distorts the product by distorting the process. Not only therefore was the retranslation of the mentalistic concepts of classical empiricism in behavioural terms only partially successful, but where it was successful its issue was that pathological development of reducing teaching and learning to indoctrination and conditioning. The behaviourist programme of obliterating the rule-following/rule-conforming distinction by translating the latter into terms of the former can therefore be seen in certain general problems for educators which have been masked where the taxonomy has been slavishly accepted. One such problem is the identification of an act of teaching which behavioural definitions are supposed to make precise, but which in fact they make more obscure for reasons that Hirst points out (Hirst, 1974, pp. 104–5 ff.). Hirst points to the overt behaviour of someone who pours liquid from one beaker into another and asks how we can discern whether this is an example of (*a*) a cabaret act, (*b*) a scientific experiment, (*c*) a religious ritual, (*d*) teaching or (*e*) demonstrating. It is only by deducing the intention of the agent in each case such as (*a*) entertaining, (*b*) proving, (*c*) receiving grace, (*d*) bringing about learning or (*e*) publishing a procedure. Without using a rule-following concept like 'intention', therefore, the distinction cannot with clarity be made. We thus require to understand what teaching is not an account of purely behavioural rule-conformance but a study of a rule-structure and the way such a structure influences action describable only in terms of such fundamental rule-following concepts as 'intending', 'choosing', 'deciding', 'acting'. To ignore such concepts, far from producing clearer language for a theory of instruction, obliterates distinctions and produces general obfuscation. Yet this is the outcome of rule-following retranslations in terms of rule-conformities, despite the fact that the function of retranslations in philosophical analysis has point only if it clarifies previous obscurity. But it is not simply how to distinguish teaching from other general activities over which behaviourism is unhelpful, but also about how to distinguish teaching from seemingly cognate activities such as indoctrination. As we have argued, the distinction between learning and conditioning is also obscured. We shall now turn our attention to the implications of our critique of behaviourism for our understanding of conditioning and indoctrination.

4.7 CONDITIONING, REDUCTIONISM AND EXHAUSTIVE QUANTIFICATION

We have previously mentioned in connection with our discussion of Skinner's work that the purpose of retranslating ordinary language terms into technical terms in a form of inquiry such as empirical inquiry is to clarify and make more precise concepts that are vague or obscure in ordinary language. When, for example, the first chemist retranslated the ordinary language term for water as H_2O, he was clarifying our term for water by specifying that it must be pure, consist of two atoms of hydrogen and one of oxygen and so on. The problem that we saw therefore for the behaviourist definition of learning that 'all learning is conditioning' was that it obscured distinctions in ordinary language rather than drew them out and articulated them more clearly (above, pp. 19-21). Certainly there is a problem for educators who wish to distinguish sound from pathological learning processes if they are to conform to the stipulation of behaviourism that all such processes be understood as conditioning. Indeed, exponents of behaviourism like Skinner recognised the inability of classical behaviourism to deal adequately with such phenomena as 'intention' or 'choice' by claiming that there were two kinds of conditioning process, namely, classical and operant. Instead of a distinction between learning and conditioning, therefore, we are left with a distinction between two different kinds of conditioning that might be called conditioning *a* and conditioning *b*. It might, however, be objected that if we have a perfectly adequate word for conditioning *b* that clearly distinguishes it from conditioning *a* in ordinary language, and that word is 'learning', we can by now clearly see what Skinner's response will be. The concept of *b* as *conditioning* is essential to a science of human behaviour that, by definition, must be able to rewrite rule-following activities such as learning in terms of rule-conformances. Yet such a rewriting amounts merely to a statistical restatement of the problem and no explanation, for reasons that we have seen. Once again we see here obliterations of 'distinctions which teachers actually make' rather than the clarification of these that Bloom professed to be seeking.

There is, however, a lesson to be learned regarding the character of the process of conditioning itself from our preceding discussion, and this from the character of the empiricist/behaviourist error itself. For a further logical development from the general empiricist strategy of reductionism and logical imperialism was, as we saw, an obsession that quantification be exhaustive and that universals or open-classes be defined in terms of strings of particulars and duly closed (above, pp. 74-8). We traced, furthermore, the links between such a view and the empiricist view of induction as the poor relation of deduction. Now, given that such was the character both of classes and induction, then we would have to concede that learning the nature of things could be characterised as a conditioning process of the kind that behaviourists imply. But we have argued that learning cannot be like that because what is learned is not like that. We noted that the position of logical imperialism on the nature of language and thought presupposed a metaphysical commitment about the nature of the world, namely, that there was a fixed number of objects in the universe. Our discussion of certain issues both in the philosophy of science and in the philosophy of language showed such a metaphysical presupposition to be at least contentious. Einstein's universe, with its descriptions and predictions in terms of schemes of recurring probabilities, is necessarily an expanding universe of, in Lonergan's words, 'emergent probability' (Lonergan, 1957, pp. 121–7). But an understanding of such a universe, we have argued, cannot take place through a process of conditioning. By insisting, as Bloom does, that goals be exhaustively quantified, there follows also the requirement that the learning process itself be given a fixed and determinate form. As each individual objective is exhaustively quantified by the teacher, therefore, *pari passu*, so must the process of acquiring each objective become reduced to a conditioning process. We have not simply argued that this is the case, but why, on epistemological grounds, this is wrong. There are, of course, moral objections to conditioning too, but these are related to epistemology in the way that truth-telling is related to truth and lying to what is false.

But what of that counterpart to conditioning as a pathological form of learning, namely, indoctrination as a pathological form of teaching? How can indoctrination be shown to exhibit a similar logical profile as logical imperialism characterised *inter alia* in terms of reductionism and a strategy of imposing an exhaustive scheme of classification on open-class concepts in natural languages? To this question we must now turn.

4.8 INDOCTRINATION, REDUCTIONISM AND EXHAUSTIVE QUANTIFICATION

Let us take as our example a programme of religious indoctrination based, say, upon a religious account of the world such as that contained in the book *Omphalos* by P. Goss (1857). Goss was a Christian fundamentalist and an eminent biologist whose career at its height coincided with the Darwinian controversy over the theory of evolution. Goss sought to dispose of the challenge to biblical fundamentalism posed by the discoveries of fossils which testified to the former existence of now extinct species and to the age of the earth. Adam, so the hypothesis ran, would have been created after each species of living thing reproducing itself 'after its own kind' on the sixth day. As he rose, then, majestically to life full-grown on the day of man's creation, what would have been one of his first observations? He would have observed that he had a navel that testified to an umbilical cord that attached him to a mother that he never had. As he proceeded to tend to the garden, he cut down a tree and saw that it had rings that in turn also testified to a non-existent past history. Likewise the earth would be found to have within its own counterpart to Adam's navel or the rings in trees, namely, fossils that witnessed to a non-existent past history, with records of extinct species that had never lived any more than had Adam's mother or the tree's ancestors.

Now Goss, according to classical empiricism, was an indoctrinator because he maintained a point of view contrary to the evidence and tried to persuade others of such a view by non-rational means. Only a closed, Newtonian universe, mechanistically conceived in which one could get from basic observation statements of basic entities through a series of causal deductions could represent an account of the world that was either true or had the possibility of being made true by further investigation. But there is here a problem for empiricism, namely, that whatever items of sensory data we cite from which to make deductions against Goss, Goss is able to explain away such items in terms of his own hypothesis. Goss is in his own way a religious version of a logical imperialist who takes some areas of human experience, namely, religious areas, and proceeds to reduce all discrepant observations to the categories of his own system of thought.

It is interesting, therefore, in the light of our preceding account to ask precisely how someone who followed Goss's argument and taught it in the classroom could be charged with indoctrination? He cannot be so on grounds of classical empiricism since there is no disagreement over observation statements, nor can he be so charged in terms of Quine's neo-empiricist form of behaviourism. After all, if there are no differences in kind between myths such as the gods of Homer and those myths that describe subatomic particles in quantum physics, then there can surely be no differences in kind between explanations in terms of creation and explanations in terms of evolution. If in any scientific framework of explanation, as Quine says,

Any statement can be held true come what may, if we make drastic enough adjustments elsewhere in the system. Even a statement very close to the periphery can be held true in the face of recalcitrant experience by pleading hallucination or by amending certain statements of the kind called logical laws (Quine, 1953, p. 43) then Goss is entitled to his 'true' statements derived from 'drastic enough changes elsewhere in' his 'system'. One strategy that might nail Goss as an indoctrinator might be Popper's criterion of falsifiability devised by Popper in the light of the failure of the empiricist criterion of verifiability to gain purchase on this problem. Goss is unfalsifiable because he cannot specify how the universe would have to have come into being if it had not been created within seven days in 4004 BC. Would it, for example, have in that instance contained fossils which testified to the existence of species now extinct millions of years before the appearance of men . . .?

The problem with Popper is not his principle of falsifiability as such, with its corresponding valuing of descriptions that are open to refutation, but rather the way that he limits such falsifiability and openness to scientific inquiry. The nub of the problem in the light of our earlier discussion (Chapter 3) is this. If science is to be distinguished from other forms of inquiry on the grounds of the falsifiability of its statements, then this can only be on the grounds that 'falsification' can be cashed in terms of numerous methods that are capable of being spelled out and defined exhaustively in ways in which methods in other forms of inquiry cannot. It is, after all, possible to point to methods of falsification in other forms of inquiry so that falsification *per se* cannot isolate science in this way. It is possible, for example, to prove in religious inquiry that God cannot be a material being by means of implications drawn from fundamental categories that characterise religious thinking (Brent, 1978, pp. 197–8). Furthermore, we saw in Chapter 2 that categories fundamental to a mode of inquiry could not be exhaustively defined but were detectable in terms of what Wittgenstein called 'family-resemblance'. In mathematics, for example, Waisman quoted 'calculus', 'operation' and 'proof' as examples of such open-class exhaustively non-definable categories. Elsewhere we have argued that what Hirst calls 'categorial concepts' in his thesis of the forms of knowledge are to be understood in terms of family-resemblances guaranteeing a basic continuity between different historical and cultural versions of the forms and also guaranteeing a basic irreducibility of one form to another (Brent, 1978, Chapter 3). This claim, roughly sketched and alluded to in an earlier work, will be fleshed out in greater detail in Chapter 8.

But granted, therefore, that there are varieties of tests and procedures that will characterise other forms of discourse as well as scientific discourse in terms formally similar to falsifiability, Popper's general point against Goss's account may nevertheless be seen to hold. What constitutes both an unexamined biblical fundamentalism and an unexamined empiricism (should we even in both cases say 'unexaminable'?) as indoctrination is that lack of open-endedness which, in accordance with the programme of logical imperialism, tries artificially to close classes. Classes, as we saw earlier, always in natural languages and now, in a post-Einsteinian era, even also in the technical language of models of explanation in terms of statistical probability, ought to be left open so that their natural function of incorporating new discoveries within known schemes can be fulfilled. We have argued, moreover, that knowledge of an expanding universe in terms of statistical schemes of recurring probabilities could never be transmitted by conditioning. There could be no consciousness of such a universe of probablistic schemes of recurrence if such a consciousness were the product of a conditioning process in which regular stimuli produced regular responses in a way that, by definition, must be rule-conforming. An understanding of probability in terms that exclude limiting cases that are certain presupposes the ability to transcend the particular, to break fixation upon particular observed instances that are exceptions to general probablistic classes and so forth. Bodies of knowledge built up by falsification procedures characterised by categorial concepts presuppose therefore an account of innate and pre-existing schemas of interpretation in man's mind that could never have been derived from observations of the behaviour of classes of objects in the world.

Such a view of the distinction between learning and what is learned on the one hand and between conditioning into what cannot properly be regarded as conditioned or exhaustively determined on the other reveals an isomorphism between learning and teaching on the one hand and between conditioning and indoctrination on the other. Furthermore, such an understanding of the relationship between conditioning and indoctrination does give us an interpretation of both that enables us to escape a cultural and historical relativism in our treatment of each subject in educational discussion. To have taught Newtonian physics as containing an irreformable framework before Einstein or to have taught Ptolemaic astronomy as certain before Galileo would seem, at least according to one view of indoctrination, to have done no wrong. Likewise, to have taught biblical fundamentalism before Darwin would not have been indoctrination. But now, in the light of new knowledge, to teach such things must *ipso facto* be to indoctrinate. People in the past cannot surely, it could be argued, be blamed for teaching what they felt there was overwhelming evidence for believing to be true. But such an account would make what is or is not indoctrination relative to time and place and, for that matter, relative to cultural or sub-cultural groups and to the access of such groups to evidence. What the foregoing account suggests, however, is that the charge of indoctrination can still be laid against the fundamentalists even before Darwin and against the Ptolemaians even before Galileo. The grounds for such a charge are that both the formulations of such doctrines and the methods of their transmission involved fundamental distortions to that basic form of human experience to which the structure of natural languages attests. Certain kinds of common-sense experience to which natural languages attest and which were coherent in their linguistic expression were used with appropriate logical deductions and reductions to rule out other kinds of common-sense experience equally linguistically attestable. The operation of open-class concepts in natural languages, moreover, permitting new discoveries to be incorporated within known schemes in a basic continuity of judgement, was rendered disfunctional by the indoctrinator's exhaustively quantificational strategy, which never missed an opportunity of trying to close and bound such classes. The Ptolemaians and the fundamentalists in this regard are not being judged for not having evidence that is now open to us. They are, however, being judged because they were violating formal logical principles implicit in their language as well as ours, and for reducing distinctions between different categories of common-sense experience to which their language as well as ours testifies (Brent, 1978, pp. 104–6, 121–5, 197–207). It is on such grounds as these that we can charge them with indoctrination, and with this our case rests.

We have in our analysis and criticism of Bloom and his heirs thus been brought back once again, as we were earlier with Skinner, to our notion of rule-following defined in such terms as the transcendence of the particular and exemplified in the operations of open-classes in natural languages. There is, however, one further issue of which we must finally dispose before we conclude our discussion in this chapter.

4.9 AFFECTIVE AND COGNITIVE STATES: CONCLUDING REMARKS

Far from concepts for emotions being reducible to the natural history of the organism along with cognitive concepts, as the Quine/Skinner hypothesis requires, it is arguable that such a reduction takes us in the wrong direction. Emotion-concepts have at the core of their meaning cognitive appraisals, and as such, without the rule-following notion implied by 'cognitive appraisal', our language of emotions could not make sense. As such, they could not in turn function as part of a theoretical model that reduced both 'cognitions' and 'emotions' to rule-conformities. What we must therefore seriously ask is whether descriptions of emotions are simply descriptions of behavioural or biochemical things, or a mixture of both, that simply just happen to us. Such is, after all, the question that the Skinner/Quine hypothesis must answer affirmatively at the very outset if the hypothesis which involves the reduction of cognitive performances to 'things that just happen to us' is even to begin to make sense. Yet, as has often been pointed out, very few if any of our emotion-words can be understood simply as redescriptions of endocrine activity in the human blood-stream. It might be argued, for example, that 'joy' and 'sorrow' might be shown to be equivalent to separate sets of biochemical events. One can feel happy or sad without knowing why, even though, even here, the putative equivalence is belied when tears are sometimes interpreted by the weeper and others to be tears of joy. It might also be that 'joy' and 'sorrow' can also be either biochemically or behaviourally correlated with the activity of rats running around in mazes. But when one then goes on to describe other equally basic emotions, then problems begin for such a correlationist point of view. On what grounds, for example, are we entitled to say: 'He is afraid'? On grounds of supposed endocrine activity being quantified algebraically as the biochemistry of fear? But something like the same endocrine activity can be going on in the person described as 'sorrowful' as the person described as 'fearful', and, moreover, different kinds of endocrine activity depending on the particular frightened or sad individual. What enables us to distinguish the sorrowful from the fearful person is that, in the one case, we judge that he whom we call 'afraid' is behaving like this because he has rationally appraised his situation as one of danger, whereas the one that we call 'sad' we judge to have appraised his situation as one of loss of his own or his loved ones' desired objectives. Without the assumption of such cognitive appraisals, therefore, there would be no distinction that biochemistry could possibly give us between fear and sorrow. It is hence arguable that, far from 'reason' being the 'slave of passion' in that the former is some kind of shadowy after-image of the latter, our emotion-words would have no clear meaning unless the concept of following a rule, appraising a situation as being of one kind rather than another or whatever, had a clear and distinct meaning from that of 'things that just happen to us'. In the last analysis, passion may be the slave of reason in the sense that even talk of emotions cannot be reduced to the model of rule-conformity and so be adequately explained (Bedford, 1956/7, pp. 256 ff.).

We saw that one critical example of the 'transcendence of the particular' was the ability of users of natural languages to form open-class concepts in the formation of which some features of some particular things were intentionally ignored and different features or different things depending on the open-class concept in question. We saw also that this ability, presupposed by the existence of open-class concepts in natural languages, was to be understood also with reference to what the later Wittgenstein had to say about the detection of universals in terms of the family-resemblances of their particulars. We found, moreover, that another exemplification of that ability was seen in the ability of human languages to express what Bennett described as 'tensed denials in past time' (above, pp. 28-31). We now, as a result of our discussion, have a new example of a further form that this ability takes to add to our list of other examples of other of its linguistic manifestations. The way in which even descriptions of emotional states cannot be reduced to quantified equations of causal, biochemical reactions and explained wholly in terms of them points to the way in which human beings are not even in their emotional activities to be regarded as simply conforming to rules or laws.

At the conclusion of this chapter, therefore, we witness the final failure to spell out a programme of curricular objectives and the means for their transmission in a way that is comprehensible in terms of a behaviourist understanding of knowledge and its acquisition. We have exposed the mistakes of such a curricular programme in terms of the failure of the viability of underlying theoretical models whose form we discussed and criticised in our previous chapters. We shall now, having shown that rule-following models cannot be dispensed with as instruments of curriculum planning, go on to explore some rule-following models, or at least some attempts to formulate such models, and their application to curriculum decision-making. In doing so we shall have to develop our analysis of the various forms of transcendence and rule-following so as to demonstrate how such notions, while enabling us to explicate the concept of 'creativity', nevertheless sets some bounds to curriculum development which prevents lapses into subjectivism.

Chapter 5

Marxist Alternatives

So far our discussion has had principally a negative conclusion, namely, that rule-following explanations cannot be reduced to rule-conforming ones and still give rise to a model that can adequately cope with the relationship between specialised and ordinary forms of discourse. The intractability of such a relationship within a rule-conforming model we exemplified in scientific discourse in the light of the quantum revolution in biology (Chapter 3). We saw, moreover, the effects of this negative conclusion upon a particular model for curriculum construction, namely, Bloom's taxonomy, that we held thereby to have failed (Chapter 4). We shall therefore, in this chapter and the next three be considering various versions of rule-following models for curriculum planning as these, too, have arisen as reactions to inadequate, rule-conforming models. In this chapter, we shall be considering fundamental models underlying contemporary critiques of the curriculum by classical and phenomenological Marxists.

In Chapter 1 we were able to begin with what we called a 'typical characterisation' of the traditional classroom drawn in terms of a dialogue between a teacher named Mr Callaghan and a student teacher named Julia. It is particularly difficult to draw a typical characterisation of Marxist proposals for curricular reform since such reforms are, as we shall see, to be regarded in the context of such a theory as 'transformations' with all the problems that spelling out what is termed 'praxis' presents. But before we commence our theoretical discussion, we shall try to tell the story of Julia's second teaching practice in a 'free school', trying not to win any critical points that we make too cheaply by basing our story closely upon the account given of the Islington White Lion Free School in an important part of the phenomenological Marxist literature (Whitty and Young, 1976, pp. 179–87).

5.1 A TYPICAL CHARACTERISATION OF A MARXIST ALTERNATIVE TO THE TRADITIONAL SCHOOL

Julia arrived for her second teaching practice at the Black Owl Free School. Her lecturer in charge of teaching practice supervision had instructed her to make contact with the principal, Dr Edward

Maxton, but, having missed him several times and found him vague over the phone as to how to prepare, she decided it best simply to arrive early on the first day of the new year. Arriving at 8 a.m. she found five busy adults already on the premises, one or two writing and typing, three to four sweeping, dusting and emptying bins. 'Could you tell me where Dr Maxton's office is?' she asked nervously of a tall man wielding a mop. 'You're speaking to him and the name's Ted!' replied Dr Maxton fixing his mop in the bucket.

Ted and Julia walked to a small classroom and then sat down. Julia expressed concern that she did not know what she was to teach and was most anxious that she would have some opportunity to teach her main 'subject specialism'. Ted looked hurt at Julia's words and retorted that the philosophy of the school was against 'the whole notion of subject specialisms' since this reflected an 'elitist' frame of reference in which an 'illusion' of superior knowledge 'legitimated' the 'reality' of superior power. 'But how do you decide what to teach and how to teach it?' asked Julia. 'With reference to our children's needs as experienced in the social context, dynamic and changing, with which they interact,' Ted replied.

Julia looked bewildered and reflected on the differences between Ted and Mr Callaghan on her first teaching practice. Mr Callaghan was a bit of an old stick-in-the-mud, but at least you knew where you stood with him and precisely what you had to do. All this seemed rather vague and woolly and Julia began to feel depressed about teaching practice assessment and what would be required for it. Ted sensed her mood, gave her a smile and a friendly nudge, and said: 'Just wait ten minutes until the kids arrive and I will show you!'

At 9.15 the pupils began to arrive, some later than others, lessons not being compulsory, as Julia discovered. A class of fifty children of various ages assembled and Ted, joined by four other teachers, and Julia got the pupils to form their chairs and tables into a circle which the staff joined and Ted commenced: 'Now we begin a new year. I want you to tell us what you think that you will need to be able to do as a result of coming here. There's plenty of time, and in our school, yours as well as mine, it is *your* time since none of you have to come or have to say. I want you to just take your time, think about it, then contribute your ideas to the rest of ours.' The pupils looked nervously at one another as Ted clenched his teeth into what resembled a parody of a wry smile and stared resolutely down at the blank notepad in front of him. Two girls raised their hands and one, acting as spokesperson, said: 'We, me and her, don't wanna do maths and all that. We want to be hairdressers!' 'Great!' responded Ted, 'No one here is going to make you do anything you do not want to do. If you want to be hairdressers, then I suppose you want us to help you find out about different sorts of hair styles and fashions, different methods of setting hair with different kinds of preparations? We'll show you some films, arrange some visits to places where they run courses when you are old enough . . . O.K.?' The two girls looked nervously at one another and then began after a time to nod vigorously.

'Now!' said Ted cheerfully. 'Two happy – forty-eight to go!' A similar arrangement was made for a boy who wished to become a taxidermist. Another boy said that he was only interested in skateboards, and for a living intended going 'on the labour', and he too was similarly accommodated. The remainder looked nervously at one another, shuffling their feet while a large, aggressive-looking minority looked intentionally bored and quite fed-up. Ted allowed this to go on for more than an hour, taking ribaldry and banter in good part. Then he began prodding, assisted by the four other staff, and grudging and sometimes half-serious suggestions began to be made. 'I'm interested in bodies!' said one boy, trying hard not to choke upon his giggles. 'Good,' replied Ted, 'we could do all sorts of things about bodies, involving human, animal and plant, biology as well as health, sex, food and dieting and whatnot' – writing furiously as he said these words what ideas the pupils had 'suggested' to him. 'How about getting jobs?' asked another fifteen-year-old with self-conscious aggression. 'Yes,' replied Ted, 'that's right. Society and how it works or fails to work to provide our needs. Any other suggestions?' 'How to handle salesmen!' suggested a frail-looking fourteen-year-old to whose stature the instant advice of, 'Smash their faces in!' from three or four boys seemed inappropriate. The fourteen-year-old had had with his parents a painful experience with a shop that had sold them a dud record player. 'Great!' said another teacher, 'we could do something on psychology, on what it is that makes some people con men and others suckers for what they are trying to sell. This might include studying different kinds of families . . . ' 'We could also,' said a second teacher, 'do something on the law and how one gets one's rights without putting oneself in the wrong by just hitting out!'

The pupils gradually drifted away (attendance was not compulsory) by 4.30 p.m., but the staff continued their first day's planning session well into the evening. Julia expressed the comment that the pupil-teacher ratio (8 : 50) was very favourable, but Ted was quick to point out that 'we can share the children out *because we share out the other tasks*: cooking, cleaning, admin., "youth work" (because the school is open evenings and weekends), accounting, handling and raising money, public relations and so on; there are no more trained workers in our school than in the average LEA school, and we cost slightly less than it does' (Whitty and Young, 1976, p. 184). The curriculum planning session now focused on topic areas (a) the body, (b) employment and (c) thinking and decision-making along the lines discussed with the pupils, and the staff began preparing such materials as work cards, audio-visual aids, books. Julia's disquiet now began to subside, despite firm warnings from the staff that she could not afford to be 'too academic'. She felt that she could use suitably simplified parts of her degree course-work in human biology to contribute to the programme on the body. As the discussion continued, it now became clear how matters were to be organised. Between two and three teachers took one of the three areas to fill two periods a week for two to six weeks. Each area was to be offered once a week to two separate groups of children, older and younger.

Julia's teaching practice proceeded and began to get into full swing. In the course of time the prospective taxidermist and hairdressers were set off on their individual projects, though they did show up to other topics sometimes. The teachers themselves advertised their courses by wall-poster campaigns (after all, pupils did not have to come), and Julia's contribution to 'The Body' was a large fat lady throwing away calorific food items. As time went on, meetings with both parents and pupils took place during the evenings, but the parents, much to the distress of the staff, were very self-conscious and made only the vaguest of suggestions. The pupils tended to dominate the discussions with expressions of self-guilt about having done so little during the previous week. But Julia then observed that, because of parental concern, teaching basic skills of literacy and numeracy were introduced and she remarked to Ted that the graded programmes in reading, writing and maths worked through by almost all the pupils represented a very traditional approach reminiscent of Mr Callaghan's on her first teaching practice. Ted replied that this was part of the 'local consensus curriculum' (Whitty and Young, 1976, p. 183), and academic theory, even Marxist academic theory, had no right to override working-class concerns with essentially patronising middle-class attitudes.

5.2 THE MARXIST PERSPECTIVE: GENERAL PRINCIPLES

Such, however, can be claimed as a 'typical characterisation' of a Marxist classroom only with some important reservations. To ask a Marxist critic for a 'typical characterisation' of his views on education is, of course, rather like asking a Marxist for a carefully worked-out blueprint for his version of a just society. He must respond rather with his notion of *praxis*, namely, that what is educative can, like what is just, only be realised in the process of acting upon the world and not simply realised in our abstract ideas alone. Thus 'to be realised (that is, "made real") in ideas' but not 'to be realised in the concrete flux of events' are, from a Marxist standpoint, two contradictory expressions, and so to ask in advance of praxis questions about solutions to problems of education or society is to behave incoherently and irrationally. Praxis arises therefore from the engagement of people in the real events of history and from their critical responses that men make as potentially free agents against forces that oppress them. Perhaps a typical characterisation of the underlying assumptions of Marxist pedagogy therefore ought to be set out in summary in negative terms as follows:

(*a*) The classroom is to be ordered without the use of the kind of competition that encourages some children to be successful at the expense of the subsequent *alienation* of other children who are declared to have failed.

(*b*) Workcards should be used on a group and not on an individual basis in order to foster *equality* and not *elitism*.

(*c*) There should not be in the classroom any imposition of values emanating from one social group by the teacher either in language or in schemes of assessment that made the teacher a vehicle of class *oppression*.

(*d*) Knowledge should not be partitioned into subjects and otherwise hierarchically organised, because such hierarchies and partitions are but reflections of the teacher's frame of reference that licences (*legitimates*) some questions rather than others thus *distorting* reality through *false-consciousness*.

(Whitty and Young, 1976, pp. 133–60)

What is held to be generally wrong with all four assumptions ((*a*), (*b*), (*c*) and (*d*)) here contradicted are that each reinforces by *reification* a particular form of social organisation: that of capitalism, whose social relations are held to require *transformation* for reasons that we must now discuss in detail.

In the above summary we have italicised such key concepts as 'false-consciousness', 'oppression', 'liberation', 'power', 'powerlessness', 'equality', 'elitism', 'legitimation' and 'reality'. Such concepts and their interrelations form the Marxist perspective within which both Dr Ted Maxton's account to Julia of the principles of a 'free school' and our more formal and summary statement find their putative justification. In such a context, their use in criticism of the organisation and practice of educational institutions would be but a specialised application of a more general critique of capitalist society. As such, the Marxist provides us with a theoretical model which functions with a formal similarity to that of Skinner as described in

Chapter 1. He begins with more or less isolated and disparate common-sense observations such as a frustrated and unemployed teenager, undisciplined and unmotivated secondary-school classes, the failure of trades' union shop stewards to argue a safety case because of lack of expertise, industrial anarchy, the drift away from science and so forth. Then the Marxist social scientist, like the Newtonian physicist, tries to construct an overall model of explanation that brings together observations that are disparate at the level of common sense. Finally, he goes on to explain their interconnection in the light of a general, overall theory that continues to grow more complex as it incorporates within it more and more items drawn from more and more areas of common-sense experience.

The principle problem, as we shall see in discussing Marxist proposals for curriculum planning, is that the model assumes two forms, derivable from classical Marxism and phenomenological Marxism respectively, and that the two are too frequently not distinguished in framing such curricular proposals. Let us therefore by means of a protracted discussion seek to clarify the nature of these two forms. Basically, Marxism in its classical form considers, as did classical empiricism, that it makes sense to postulate a natural order of things beyond language and society which determines the development of human understanding and social relations. Where classical Marxism differs from classical empiricism is in the process by which such an order of nature is disclosed to human beings. Phenomenological Marxism, however, seeks to dispense with reference to any natural order beyond language and beyond society. Like phenomenologists generally, it finds such reference too problematic and its object too ambiguous. Let us then begin with a brief account of classical Marxism.

5.3 CLASSICAL MARXISM AND THE NATURE OF REALITY

Classical Marxism insisted that it makes sense to speak of a reality unfolding itself in the flux of history beyond appearance and change and that a theory grounded upon such a presupposition could provide great explanatory power. The explicit form that the presupposition about extra-linguistic and extra-social reality frequently took was of a goal of historical development towards which human beings and their societies were moving and which itself was the dynamic of that development. As such, the model of explanation was highly biological, as we shall see also was the pattern of reasoning that it generated. Just as seeds or foetuses can be regarded, through genetic programming, to be potential plants or animals, and this potentiality becomes actualised when they so develop, so history is regarded as so developing by actualising what is already potentially there in its developmental process. Such arguments are called 'teleological' arguments since they are arguments about the nature of development from the outcome or 'goal' (= *telos*) of such development regarded as what powers and determines the development. This fundamental reality, potentially present in nature and in history but actually unfolding towards its final form, was for Hegel, Marx's philosophical antecedent, spiritual. For Marx, however, spirit must be excluded and the process of natural and historical development be regarded purely as a material one. Like the empiricists, therefore, Marx held that there was a reality beyond language and society accessible to men through direct experience and in the light of which some common-sense assertions could be confirmed and others discarded. But Marx differed from the empiricists regarding the means by which the fundamental, empirical reality was disclosed. The empiricists understood the disclosure in the way in which they believed objects in the physical world and their relationships were disclosed to the Newtonian physicist. The early Marxists paralleled their contemporary evolutionary theorists in biology by understanding the disclosure instead in terms of observations and deductions from the study of organisms.

As we saw earlier with both Locke and the early Wittgenstein, classical empiricism regarded certain simple ideas, produced causally by primary qualities of objects, or certain logical particles or 'names' in language mirroring basic objects in the world, as infallibly given and unable to be altered. False pictures of empirical reality were the results of incorrect logical formulas applied to infallible sense-data. Mermaids and ghosts were the result of simple ideas (Locke) or logical atoms (Wittgenstein) infallibly received in sensation but incorrectly put together in reflection (Locke) or on the basis of an incorrectly constructed logical scaffolding (Wittgenstein). But how were these logical formulas to be defined? The answer of both Locke and the early Wittgenstein was that such formulas were to be found in Aristotelian logic, though, in the case of the latter, this was to be supplemented and extended by means of the sentential calculus of modern symbolic logic. The result was a highly static and passive view of how a picture of the world was built up. The simple ideas presented to the mind in sensation, or the logical atoms encapsulated in names strung together to form propositions, were in themselves unproblematic. The problem of rationality was the problem of how the individual was to be brought to terms with what was unalterably given.

Marx, on the other hand, on the basis of his Hegelian antecedent, took an alternative route. Hegel rejected the notion that Aristotelian logic could provide an unalterable and infallible guide by means of which what was unalterably given in the world could become what was unalterably given in both language and mind. The process whereby the structure of reality becomes known is by means of an evolutionary, dynamic process. 'The is', said Hegel, 'is prior to existence.' The evolutionary and dynamic nature of the objects that make up our universe marks them out in stark contrast to the static and passive simples of the epistemology of both Locke and the early Wittgenstein. At the basis of Aristotle's logic stood Aristotle's three so-called 'laws' (or 'general principles') of logic. These are:

1 The law of identity (if x is A, then x is A).
2 The law of non-contradiction (x cannot be both x and not-x).
3 The law of the excluded middle (either x or not-x but not both).

Such general principles implied, as did Locke's simple ideas or Wittgenstein's 'names', that it was possible to be clear and determinate at least in principle about what should occupy the space filled by the x's in turning such schemas into real sentences. Such, after all, is implied by the capacity of the various kinds of valid syllogistic argument to unfailingly yield true conclusions once the truth of the premises were established, however much it may be possible to have true conclusions from false premises validly put together and true and false mixtures and so on. For Hegel, however, the structure of reality is to be regarded as in process of coming into being, so that such determinate deductions cannot be made about what is real. It is possible when observing the development of a biological organism to form some idea of the basic structure from which genesis is derived, yet one cannot precisely predict the final form of the development in any strictly deductive way. If you apply such a biological paradigm to explain how any kind of development takes place, be it of inorganic or organic matter, or be it of human thinking, of history or of the history of ideas, then in all these spheres you will regard anything that seems fixed or given as an illusion. What appears as a fixed, passively received, object infallibly given to the senses will always, in the light of further developments, be seen to be wrong, partial, one-sided and so on. But how, then, was it possible in epistemological theory to characterise the dynamic, evolutionary nature of objects, events and ideas and to justify descriptions in such terms as true knowledge?

We must, claimed Hegel, understand both the evolutionary dynamism of objects and the psychological process by which the mind grasps them as a dialectical process. A dialectical process is a process that develops by analogy with the way in which a human argument develops. We begin by stating our thesis, and about such a statement or thesis we might assume with Aristotle's law of identity that what it says it is, it says it is, that it cannot be both affirmed and denied (non-contradiction), and that it must either be so or not be so (excluded middle). But to make such a claim in the real world of human experience (outside Aristotle's idealisation not only of the form of arguments but the basic form of a proposition that makes up their premises) does not yield knowledge that conforms to such fixed structures. Any such initial statement (thesis) will be contradicted (antithesis) and in the actuality of such plausible contradictions undermines the credibility of an epistemology in terms of infallible sense-data, fixed and determinate like that of Locke. Any such Lockean account of epistemology is undermined by the way therefore that any thesis is contradicted by its antithesis and no such contradiction is itself ever final. As such, Hegel's concept of emerging truth breaks Aristotle's law of the excluded middle and claims that in so doing the inadequacy of that law to explain the facts of how the epistemic subject acquires true knowledge. For these syntheses that arise in both the development of the world and in the development of man's understanding of it, show that neither thesis nor antithesis is finally true, but rather that both are in a certain way true. The 'middle' that Aristotle wished to 'exclude' is seen to be the essential core of reality itself.

Marx and the early Marxists undoubtedly considered therefore that, in the dialectic, they had discovered the principle of development behind not only the development of human ideas and social organisation but also the principle by which both physical and biological entities developed. In fact, Marxist dialectics stress the material nature of any development since Marx denied the presence of any spiritual element in the unfolding of what is real and true. Thus Marxist philosophy is, when viewed from its dialectic aspect, described as 'dialectical materialism'. Some general examples will help us here as some specific educational examples are to be discussed and analysed later.

Example 1   The most familiar example of dialectical method is the Marxist theoretical understanding of the nature of conflict in our present social and economic order and the prediction of the outcome of such conflict. The present thesis that we see is capitalism: the *status quo* with which the forces of the working-class movement, alienated from the means of production, are in conflict and represent the antithesis. In the thesis, it is the few who rule, but in the antithesis, this state of affairs is contradicted and it is the many who rule. The dictatorship of the few is being replaced by the dictatorship of the many, the 'dictatorship of the proletariat'. What, however, according to a dialectical analysis is going to be the necessary outcome of this development? A state of affairs in which neither the thesis nor the antithesis will be seen to constitute reality's final form but a synthesis where neither the few nor the many rule but where in a classless society the coercive power of the state has withered away. Note how, in such dialectical critiques of 'capitalism', development takes place through the dynamic produced by 'contradictions within the system'. Thus a boss argues that his profits justifiably belong to him because he bears the capital risk, but when there are no profits, that workers should accept decline in wages in order to bail him out. The present writer is, however, unable to understand strictly in terms of the logic of the Marxist position why schemes for profit-sharing should not be regarded as 'socialist' and a valid dialectical development.

Example 2   A second not so familiar example of the application of the dialectic to an understanding of physical reality reflects the influence of the pre-Socratic philosophers on the early Hegelians (Burnett, 1914, pp. 57–68). The conflict between the primary elements, earth, air, fire and water in Anaximander, for example, suggests crudely what was later to become an admittedly far more sophisticated understanding of the behaviour and development of matter. When, for example, 'earth' or 'matter' (literally 'wood') as the thesis meets its opposite, fire, that is the antithesis, then the result is neither matter nor fire but ashes (synthesis). Likewise, when water as thesis meets fire as its antithesis, the resultant synthesis, steam, is neither fire nor water.

Example 3   To exemplify thirdly the application of dialectical analysis in the history of ideas, we might focus on the development of the doctrine of the trinity in early church history. The thesis here is constituted by Patripassianism or the doctrine that the Father suffered. That the Father suffered necessarily followed from Jesus' equality with God described in terms of the Greek word *homousios* (= 'of one substance'). The antithesis, equally rational and as such unable in itself to be ruled out, was that Christ, who really suffered, could not be of one substance with the Father because that would mean that God suffered. It is, after all, arguable that the semantic rules for the concept of 'God' in any natural language precludes the identity with matter implied by a description 'God suffers'. The Greeks may have spoken of 'Pan dying', but even with the Greeks, reflection on the meaning of their terms ruled out the identification of divinity with matter even there. So the Arians were able to argue, tied to beautiful Aristotelian syllogisms, that: 'The Son, who is tempted, suffers and dies, however exalted he may be, cannot be equal with the immutable Father beyond pain and death. If he is not equal, then he is inferior' (Chadwick, 1967, p. 124). The Son therefore cannot be *homousios* as the thesis states, but must rather be *homiousio* (= 'of like substance') as its antithesis states. A dialectical argument, it might be claimed, can resolve the problem in a way in which an Aristotelian argument cannot. Moreover, it can establish the problem's resolution by a general and formal procedure for judging what is true that makes the solution more than a subjective one. We have a thesis that states that the Son is equal to the Father and that the Father suffers. We have an antithesis that directly contradicts it and that states that the Father cannot suffer. According to Aristotle's law of the excluded middle, both cannot be affirmed as true. But according to dialectical argument, the resultant trinitarian synthesis is confirmed as true. Both thesis and antithesis are combined into a new and harmonious whole in which both were seen to be in some way true. The Son is of one substance (*homousios*) with the eternal Father, and yet the Father does not suffer because he is of a different essence, a different Person.

Thus we see by means of three examples how the growth of scientific knowledge about both the social and natural world and of the history of ideas can be understood as developing in accordance with a dialectical model. Yet, it may be objected, 'can' does not imply 'ought'. Simply because development *can* be understood in such a way, it does not necessarily follow that we are justified in so understanding development. Simply because some items of knowledge or moral precepts have been grasped by a kind of dialectical process of inquiry, that they were so grasped does not in itself demonstrate their truth or rightness. All that such accounts can at most be held to demonstrate is the psychological or social-psychological processes by means of which what is true or right comes to be grasped by human beings. We cannot simply justify the truth of a statement with reference to its origins. The Marxist answer to such an objection would be to attack the overall Aristotelian context from which its force is derivable. To pose questions of truth and morality in such a form, the Marxist will protest, is to show that our thinking has remained within the confines of an Aristotelian and empiricist tradition. We cannot detach thought from action in the way that the distinction between 'criteria for truth and falsehood' and 'criteria for describing the processes by which they are acquired' implies. It is only as a result of involvement in a developing, non-static, dynamic natural and social order that we can anchor ourselves, our actions and our destiny in what is real, true or good. A static, Aristotelian world-view could be otherwise apprehended, but it is precisely such a world view that the Marxist has held to be contrary to experience. This involvement, through which understanding is both affirmed and justified, is known by the technical Marxist term 'praxis'. Only in solidarity with the oppressed, for example, can true knowledge of their predicament and the justification for their acts against their oppressors be understood.

In contrast, therefore, with Aristotelian thinking, dialectic thinking may be regarded as proceeding by analogy with the paradigm of development taken from biological rather than physical sciences. Hence, if we wish, as I do, to claim that in the last analysis the dialectical model is defective, it will not do simply to restate the counter-claims of Aristotelian logicians and their contemporary heirs. We must look at the adequacy of the model in overall terms. The dialectic model is an organicist model. Within the development of an embryo, for example, there are stages where different organs appear to be in competitive conflict for food or nourishment which the embryo is absorbing. A point is reached in an organism's successful (in evolutionary terms) development where new and higher-order functions are achieved where organs previously in conflict begin to interact and achieve mutual interdependence. Furthermore, man's evolutionary development, resulting in the formation of human societies, can be understood in an analogous fashion. First of all, in a Hobbesian 'state of nature', man's survival needs are satisfied by the individual's struggle against his fellows for limited resources, but, with the formation of human societies, man's survival needs are satisfied by co-operation rather than by conflict. But note what the juxtaposition of these two examples enables the dialectician to appear to achieve – and only 'appear', because he assumes rather than argues that they are connected. Because human struggles are accompanied by claims (theses), counter-claims (antitheses) and final agreements (syntheses), and because biological development can be understood as analogous to such a process, it is assumed that a biological process literally can be understood in terms of a human argument. But arguments by analogy only establish that, at most, some things *can be* understood in terms of others, not that they *ought to* be so. To establish that what can be so understood ought to be so understood requires an independent, non-analogous argument or description. Yet this is precisely what the dialectician has not simply failed to give us but has even failed to realise that he needs to give us since he regards both biological development in terms of history, and historical development in terms of biological, both 'analogical' and 'literal', quite indiscriminately (Brent, 1978, Chapter 2).

We might, however, explore some further grounds upon which a biological paradigm might be held to service a dialectical model that will provide a non-analogical framework uniting biological and physical understandings of the world with a materialist understanding of mind. We saw in an earlier chapter (Chapter 3) that the precursors of the kinds of methodological principles to be found in modern quantum physics were to be found also in evolutionary theory in biology. Whereas the universe of Newtonian physics, with its causal principle that defined the fundamental relationship between a limited number of basic objects, called for a clear and determinate, Aristotelian account of the world, biological universes represented expanding universes that were at no one point in time capable of being described exhaustively and determinately. Furthermore, once the random principle of evolutionary theory had been combined with the infinite possibility of the species to reproduce themselves, then the clear determination of the outcomes of courses of events and their causes became impossible. Methods of investigation therefore in quantum mechanics might be argued to portray the same logical form as those in biology, with the result that a biological model could be applied to physical events in a non-analogical sense in a way that dialectical arguments in part imply. Recurrence of particular events, like particular members of species, could not be predicted always with accuracy so that descriptions of such particulars only became also capable of prediction and therefore important when the focus of such descriptions was in terms of classes of events. The presence or absence of one particular event or species member was indeterminate since the recurrence of such classes, being random, was at most probable. Some such account, therefore, might conceivably be held to support the non-analogous application of biological models of development to physical matter as dialectical understanding requires. Furthermore, a non-analogous pattern of the same logical form as a human argument can arguably be said to be present in such probablistic and statistical quanta-descriptions. Behaviour of contradictory particulars which occur in one pattern as the thesis and which do not occur in another as the antithesis are seen to be increasingly irrelevant as patterns of recurrences are established and with them general tendencies that constitute syntheses of earlier observations. We see here, presumably, why both dialectical arguments and quantum physics are both able to dispense with Aristotle's law of the excluded middle.

There are, however, a number of problems with such an account if it is to succeed in incorporating historical development within a dialectical frame of reference. Yet, without such an incorporation, the real point of Marxism as a social theory founded on a dialectical model is lost. The real point of showing that historical and natural developments possessed similar logical forms was to show how prediction of historical events could proceed in a way similar to the prediction of biological-cum-physical events. Yet the predictive value of the dialectic in social theory is only apparent because there are no non-analogical connections and because, at a critical point, the analogy breaks down. We cannot, it is true, predict clearly and determinately the precise form of society that will succeed capitalism, but, the Marxist will claim, this is surely no more damaging than the inability of biologists to predict in exhaustive detail what will be the outcome of the development of what he is examining at an embryonic stage. Yet we can chart the likely outcome in terms of some general form, and to this extent it makes sense to talk about 'prediction'. But note why it is that we can proceed thus with biological developments, but why we cannot with historical developments, so that at this point the analogy breaks down. We can observe features present in the developing embryo and make inferences from such observations of the developments' final form because we have previously observed similar developments in plants or animals of the same kind or type. It is, moreover, only because of such previous observations, however indeterminate particular outcomes might be, that the end of an embryonic development in terms of general tendencies could be predicted. But in the case of historical developments from one stage to another, there is no past experience from which to generalise. Each stage must constitute a unique transformation since mankind has only one history and not a series of different ones. The predictive use of dialectic methods in Marxist theory in the realm of social history rests upon a far more shaky and intuitive basis than its supporting biological analogy suggests.

There is, moreover, a further objection to dialectical interpretations of historical development, and one that is related fundamentally to the central thesis pursued in this book. We saw at the beginning of this chapter that Marxist educational theorists could be regarded as sharing with us in our quest for a rule-following paradigm of human behaviour in the wake of Skinner's failure to produce a logically coherent rule-conforming one. Yet the Marxist paradigm, as it now begins to emerge, is only deceptively a rule-following one. It appears to be rule-following because, if rule-following is linked conceptually with rationality and rationality is linked conceptually with patterns of argument, then it may look as if dialectically based action (praxis) is genuinely rule-following behaviour. But, on careful scrutiny, such an account will be seen in the final analysis to be a version of a causal, rule-conforming model of human behaviour. The reason why we follow the pre-determined way that both matter and society develops is not because these conform or can be brought into conformity with our choices, intentions, decisions or whatever. The reasons exposed by the dialectic are not *our* reasons, so that we follow them not autonomously but heteronomously. If nature or history develops by a process analogous to a human argument, then it is nature or history's dialogue, its reasons, choices and decisions, that we are compelled to follow and not our own. There is, moreover, an at least questionable anthropomorphism that is shown here ultimately to be present in dialectical reasoning, namely, the reading into the behaviour of both nature and social development a kind of rational and argumentative process properly applicable to individuals in discussion. How far it is legitimate to do this in the case of inanimate matter we have tried to show to be at best questionable and at worst incongruous. Further-more, the incongruity was compounded for the classical Marx, since for him, unlike Hegel, the dialectic was a materialist dialectic. At least Hegel's dialectic achieved a measure of coherence in that the rational rule-following to which the evolution of matter and history conformed was spiritual and implied a divine mind, thus following those early, pre-Socratic dialecticians who affirmed that: 'The All is alive and has God in it.' Conformity with the dialectic, although it may appear to be rule-following, is thus still a rule-conformity. If behaviour exhibited in 'praxis' is 'rational', then it is only so because the laws of nature are rational, not because any exercise of human autonomy was involved, any transcendence of the particular, or real choice of one course of action in preference to another. 'Rational' behaviour exhibited in praxis is thus a disguised form of causal determination. In the final analysis, therefore, the dialectical model of understanding obliterates the rule-following/rule-conforming distinction and thus violates the basic criteria of intelligibility that we have argued to be required as axiomatic for any intelligible account of human psychological or social-psychological actions.

From such objections to the epistemological viability of dialectical explanations, there follow also ethical problems of the sort that we saw earlier (Chapter 3) to have been raised by the use of evolutionary theories to make ethical judgements. Such ethical problems are not 'problems' in the sense that moral obligations are difficult to unravel or justify, but in the sense that moral questions cannot coherently be asked within naturalistic systems of ethics. If a natural organism develops in a genetically determined way, then it makes no sense to ask questions that presuppose an ethical 'ought'. The only sense that 'ought' can have is whether a certain development was or was not pathological judged in comparison with generalisations from observations that have established normal, healthy types. When we ask whether someone 'ought' to have developed a hunched back or a limp, we are using 'ought' in this non-moral sense. We cannot blame or impute moral responsibility to the person because of his hunched back or his limp, unless, of course, it was because he had some choice over the course of action which lead to the hunched back or limp, and some knowledge of the outcome of such an action (for example, smoking, hang-gliding or other hazards). Likewise, when such a biological model, invested with a dialectical interpretation of rationality, is imposed upon an understanding of man in terms of a social science, similar problems of value arise. How can a capitalist be held morally culpable if it is historically determined that he should play the role that he does? Moreover, when the proletariat arises, since they are but a part of an inevitable antithetical tide that turns against the capitalist thesis, there is really no point in telling them that they 'ought to' rise. That we may choose or decide to become revolutionaries is really, on the model of classical Marxism, an illusion. Rule-following behaviour is, in the end, as much an illusion that conceals underlying rule-conformities according to classical Marxism as it was also according to both classical and operant behaviourism.

We have, moreover, already exposed the basically Newtonian and empiricist caste of thinking at the heart of rule-conforming models of the social sciences, and we have seen here in classical Marxism the reappearance of such key concepts as 'cause', 'causally determined', 'rule-conformity' in our preceding account. It was, indeed, Lenin's great boast that Marxism was 'scientific'. We can now see that all those arguments that we applied against both empiricism and the versions of behaviourism that it fathered apply equally well to classical Marxism. In view, therefore, of these problems about classical Marxism, we are now in a position to see both the need for and to discuss the reformulation of the classical model by pheno-menological Marxists who try to take into account at least some of the criticisms levelled here.

5.4 THE PHENOMENOLOGICAL ALTERNATIVE TO CLASSICAL MARXISM

Although there are some distinctions to be drawn between a phenomenological and a sociology of knowledge reinterpretation of classical models in the social sciences, such distinctions will not affect our discussion in this section. The two terms will therefore be used interchangeably. Basically, both phenomenological and sociology of knowledge reinterpretations start with a rule-following model of human action. Human beings in community both construct and reconstruct their pictures of both their social and their natural worlds in a fashion that can only be conceptualised in accordance with an irreducible rule-following model. In fact, to use the word 'pictures' in our commencing description of their point of view is probably erroneous. To incorporate the notion of a 'picture' into the discussion implies that human beings have access to some reality beyond language of which they construct approximate pictures together in language. For the sociologist of knowledge it is better to leave out the word 'picture' from our account of epistemology and to say, rather, that all reality is socially constructed, that the way that men conceive of both nature and society is through the socially constructed concepts and categories of their speech communities (Berger and Luckman, 1967, and Whorf, 1956). 'Reality' cannot be understood apart from the concepts and categories of particular social groups since, by definition, according to the sociologists of knowledge, 'real' means that which is so socially constructed. Some support might arguably be gained for such a position from the failure of Wittgenstein's highly articulated 'picture theory of the proposition' already discussed (Chapter 2).

How, then, in accordance with the phenomenological perspective, is the classical Marxist model to be reformulated? As we have been mainly concerned so far with the dialectical foundations of classical Marxism, let us first briefly sketch the specific concepts and their interrelations which constitute, on such dialectical foundations, the classical Marxist critique of capitalist society. The thesis in contemporary historical development is constituted by a system in which a few own the means of production on the basis of which is founded their power as the ruling class. The antithesis is constituted by the working-class movement which is drawn into conflict with the ruling-class because their 'alienation' from the means of production results in a disequilibrium which can otherwise be termed 'inequality'. The workers have ceased to own the means of production with the result that they are 'alienated'. Their experience of powerlessness or alienation thus provides the revolutionary and antithetical dynamic that causes them both to act in conflict with the thesis and leads to the resulting transformation of both thesis and antithesis into a new synthesis. There are, however, thetical forces developed in the course of the evolution of the system which react against and try to impede antithetical forces and hence the subsequent transformation. Upon the foundations of the sub-structure of dialectically competing economic forces, there has been generated a super-structure that serves to inhibit the forces of trans-formation. The function of the super-structure is to conceal from men the underlying, sub-structural economic reality and so prevent its change and transformation. The superstructure therefore generates false-consciousness in terms of which the workers are deceived into thinking that their conditions are unalterable and that their treatment is just. The law courts, parliamentary institutions, the churches and educational institutes, as superstructural components, generate a number of myths about the impartiality of laws that protect owners of the means of production, the necessity of free enterprise and competition to secure political democracy, the providence of God that assigns men to their station and its duties, the fixity of intelligence and its unalterability and so forth. There is, therefore, in the classical Marxist model an implicit sociology of knowledge, that is to say, an implicit theory about how putatively objective bodies of knowledge are used to order and sustain certain forms of society. But it is important to note precisely how classical Marxism differs from its phenomenological reinterpretation that we are about to discuss. According to the classical model, for all the emphasis on powerful and socially generated illusions in ordering social relations, there is the possibility of some final reference to an underlying reality 'out there' beyond language, economic and material in character, which is both the basis of objectivity in language and the dynamic of all change. To grasp this underlying reality, and in the light of such understanding to see by contrast the superstructural myths for what they are, is to have achieved 'true' as opposed to 'false' consciousness. As such, classical Marxism can be regarded as a particular instance of general theories that oppose epistemological relativism on the grounds that not everything can be based upon falsity or illusions since the concepts 'false' and 'illusion' are parasitic on those of 'truth' and 'reality' (Brent, 1978, pp. 186–90 ff.).

Within the classical Marxist perspective, therefore, the notion of a reality 'out there' as the anchorage of objectivity is intelligible. Such a reality emerges through the twists and turns of superstructural illusions. It can, moreover, be expressed in language, however much its dialectical character will make for difficulties of description in contrast to the static and unchanging reality presupposed by Aristotle and the empiricists. What the phenomenological reinterpretation of the Marxist model now tries to do is to dispense with any concept of a material, underlying reality. Rather it rests its case upon the notion of Marxist reality, being like, it is argued, any other social reality, namely, socially constructed. The justification for trying to dispense with the notion of some extra-linguistic, non-socially constructed reality can be documented with reference to the kinds of problems raised earlier in this book in connection with philosophy of language and philosophy of science. In both Wittgenstein's and Quine's work, there emerged a complex set of problems about the origins of human descriptions and analyses of the universe and man's place within it that were accentuated by philosophical interpretations of quantum physics. Meaning and truth could no longer be characterised in terms of language encapsulating or depicting structures comprehensible apart from language. Moreover, the classical Marxist perspective was causal and deterministic, and we have shown good grounds for the abandonment of such models in the social sciences, quite apart from the abandonment of the concept of cause in some kinds of physical explanation, in particular that of quantum physics. Furthermore, a Kuhnian view of science, whatever we shall have to say about its limitations in subsequent chapters, with the problem of paradigm clash and the resultant attempted replacement of an evolutionary by a revolutionary understanding of scientific progress, was to increase reformist pressures upon the classical Marxist model of explanation. A dialectical account of the way in which language, mind and society were informed by a reality beyond language, mind and society at least recognised as problematic what empiricism grossly over-simplified. But nevertheless, classical Marxism was seen by its phenomeno-logical reinterpreters as still too wedded to fundamentally empiricist ways of conceptualising problems of epistemology. The phenomeno-logical Marxist appears to be saying that the classical Marxist's revision of an empiricism founded upon an Aristotelian logic was not radical enough.

Let us see then in what the phenomenologist's reinterpretative strategy now consists. 'Phenomenological' means 'reasoning about appearances', and in view of the problematic character that we have exposed – not merely about observations of reality but about the concept of 'reality' itself – it is arguable that we ought to be satisfied simply with the scrutiny of the contents of our experiences that represent things as they appear to us. Here the perspective of the new sociology of knowledge and that of phenomenology will be seen to at least considerably overlap. The phenomenological Marxist's problem is therefore how to reformulate his classical model without reference to any putative extra-linguistic or extra-social reality. 'Objectivity' becomes equivalent logically to 'that which arises on the basis of intersubjective agreement'. Such an agreement can be about colour words or words for snow in the language of physical objects. Or it can be about the 'right' political party or Church, or the 'right' syllabus or scheme of educational assessment. Whorf in a famous quote once said: 'We cut up reality in the way that we do as a result of the absolutely obligatory patterns imposed by language on thinking' (Whorf, 1967, p. 21); and such writers as Wright Mills (1963) were to write similar sentiments into a programme of cultural relativism that extended even to logic.

The resolution of the phenomenological Marxist's dilemma about how to erase from his account any reference to an extra-social or linguistic reality thus proceeds as follows: human beings objectify their wholly subjective experiences by agreeing to describe experiences (and thus make them shared) according to mutually agreed standards, rules, criteria and so on. But a construction of reality resting on such intersubjective agreement can be notoriously unstable. Since such different sets of intersubjective agreements, interlocking with one another in a wider network, determine more or less the basic forms and conditions of social life, such linguistic and conceptual instability can give rise also to social instability. To create therefore the conditions for social stability, various strategies and devices are adopted in order to 'reify' (= 'to make concrete or a thing of') this shifting and intersubjective consensus that constitutes the real, social roots of what we think that we see 'out there'. We try to stabilise our social construction by taking it, as it were, out of human hands by anchoring it into some putative natural or supernatural order of things. Indeed, on this analysis, quite apart from those examples which we discussed in an earlier work (Brent, 1978, pp. 169–84), one form that such reification might take is the demonstrably false view of definition in terms of exhaustive quantification that we have already frequently exposed throughout this present work. Logical imperialism, characterised by such quantification with corresponding inductivist notions, proved to be the strategy that sustained classical empiricism and that constrained and constricted other kinds of thinking to that containable within inductivist definitions.

This view of the way in which nascent social constructions of reality are stabilised by means of reification or anchoring into some extra-linguistic or extra-social reality leads to a new and quite radical reformulation of 'false-consciousness'. On the classical view, 'false' consciousness derived its meaning from the contrast with 'true' consciousness in which the fundamental dialectically understood material and economic causes for why men behave as they do were grasped. According to the phenomenological reinterpretation, *any* consciousness of reality that pretends to be grounded in *any* extra-linguist or extra-social entities becomes now 'false' consciousness. In this respect, as we have seen, empiricist views on how language refers would be held to be an example of 'false-consciousness'. More dramatically in this respect for the phenomenological Marxist, classical Marxism represents false-consciousness just as much as did Aristotle and his empiricist successors. The original material character of the reality that, according to classical Marxism, unfolded dialectically and pushed the course of history towards its pre-determined end was quite independent of how human beings conceived it. Classical Marxist descriptions rested on the intelligibility of reference to extra-social and extra-linguistic entities, and analysis has shown how highly problematic presuppositions about the existence of such entities describable in a-social categories are. Initially, therefore, there is some plausibility in the phenomenologist's reformulation of the classical Marxist paradigm. Its plausibility is derived from the ability of such a reformulation to deal with problems intractable within the classical Marxist framework. One such fundamental problem we saw to be the imposition of patterns of human argument in the dialectic (thesis–antithesis–synthesis) whose function it is to remove psychological barriers which prevent the human mind from grasping what is real or true on to the production in nature of what is true itself. If, however, we make the quantum leap from an understanding of reality as externally given to an understanding of all reality as socially constructed, then the problems with the original understanding of the dialectic appear to recede. If, when we look at our descriptions of nature and society, what is being observed is not some external reality produced by some external nature but a social production created by human beings interacting in community, then it is by no means remarkable that our descriptions of 'natural' or 'historical' realities bear the impress of the movements of a human argument.

There are, however, new problems that the new, reformulated and phenomenological model must now face. The problems are those general problems that are inevitable in any subjectivist and socially relative account of knowledge. The sociology of knowledge, in itself a non-Marxist perspective, can to some extent deflect objections that its subjectivism and cultural relativism undermines its viability as an interpretative model. The sociologist of knowledge can claim that he makes no judgement whatsoever on a particular social group's conception of reality since it is generated by processes of reification, nihilation and so forth. His only concern is to uncover in formal terms the mechanisms and strategies adopted by individuals in order in community to create and sustain social reality and thereby to create and sustain also social orders, without making any judgement about the greater value or truth of one particular social construction as against another. There are, however, problems with such a perspective which, since I have discussed them in detail elsewhere (Brent, 1978, pp. 158–61), need not detain us very long here. Suffice it to say that there are severe logical problems to do with the internal coherence and self-sufficiency of the statement of the theory that make it impossible to hold. It is not possible in the logical sense of 'possible' to hold a theory that cannot be coherently stated. If I claim that a certain social group knows that *x*, then I am committed not simply to a description of their beliefs that *x*, but also to the truth of their beliefs. It is impossible to escape that commitment in using the concept of knowledge, yet the sociologist of knowledge claims that he *can* do so in his non-committed, value-free descriptions. A sociologist can, of course, espouse a 'sociology of belief'. When I describe someone's belief, I am simply committed to a description of someone's state of mind and not to whether that belief is true. But, of course, the phenomenologist's case rests upon his theory being a sociology of *knowledge*, and it is at this point that he fails to be able to use the term 'knowledge' coherently. 'Knowledge' is conceptually related to what is 'real' and 'true'. Our commitment to one belief system as constituting what is real or true rules out the reality and truth of other belief systems that are inconsistent with it. Likewise, the thesis requires that there are no exceptions to the proposition that, 'All bodies of knowledge, being socially constructed, are culturally relative.' But there must be one exception, and that is the proposition itself, which must represent the one cultural invariant. Furthermore, the conceptual structure that defines reality construction and maintenance, such as reification, false-consciousness, nihilation, legitimation, must also be culturally invariant, and it must make sense for them to be described as 'known' to be such.

The general problems which, for a sociologist of knowledge, might be explained away in terms of a paradox with which we simply have to live in our quest for frameworks with which to define our own and others' social structures are, however, compounded for the phenomenological Marxist in his reformulation of his classical model. The Marxist cannot rest content as can the sociologist of knowledge with the simple description of different forms of the creation and sustentation of social reality. Rather, he is conscious of being in the business of judging one social construction of reality both morally and epistemically in contrast with another. He is self-consciously judging capitalist constructions of social reality in contrast with Marxist ones. He needs the objectivity of a dialectically conceived extra-linguistic and extra-social reality. But the phenomenological Marxist, in declining to make reference to such an entity, has deprived himself of the means of supporting his case. There are, however, two ways in which he can answer the charge of relativism, both of which we shall see in due course to be only apparently satisfactory. One is to appeal to the rationality of the dialectic and to claim an increasing reasonableness in human social constructions of reality as one construction gives way to another as social organisations progress. The other is to appeal to a psychological view of human nature, particularly the psychoanalytic view of Freud. By such an appeal, he can try to show that some constructions of social reality are better than others, not because of reference to any putative extra-social or extra-linguistic reality that they may record better, but because in holding one construction of reality rather than another individuals are made less neurotic and more mentally healthy. But in that case and on either view, a view of human nature is being appealed to with an implied cultural invariance, and such implications will require spelling out. Furthermore, the Marxist's reformulated theory now gives a considerable number of hostages to the adequacy of Freud's psychoanalytic model which, at all events, he needs to synthesise with his own, sociological model. Any conceptual inadequacies, such as, in particular, those rule-following/rule-conforming distinctions that we have argued to be necessary for the adequacy of any model of explanation in the human sciences and that infect the Freudian model, will also infect the phenomenologist reformulation of Marxist explanation through its incorporation into the Marxist model. Let us therefore now briefly look at Freudian explanation in psychology and at its sociological use by phenomenological Marxists.

5.5 FREUDIAN PSYCHOANALYSIS AND PHENOMENOLOGICAL MARXISM

Freud's original psychoanalytic explanation of normal and neurotic behaviour was formulated on the basis of a number of cases of hysteria and their therapy (Freud and Breuer, 1974). He began his study into clinical hysteria as a disciple of Breuer. Examples of such cases were people who had suddenly developed physical symptoms of, for example, severe walking or eyesight difficulties without there being any physiological evidence for the causes of such disabilities. Now there were a number of different options available to the medical community for solving how such illnesses could have arisen. One was to argue that because there were no discernable *physiological* causes for such hysterical illnesses, there simply was no cause at all – the alleged 'patients' were simply 'malingerers'. Another alternative, more plausible in an era in which Newtonian physics as the paradigm of all science reigned supreme, was to insist that such cases nevertheless must have some physiological cause. In the light of that article of the Newtonian scientist's faith, that was the causal principle the practitioner of medicine must simply persist in trying to discover what was so far undiscovered. There was, however, a third possibility which was the one that Freud followed Breuer in adopting.

This was to claim that physiological explanations were inapplicable because the real cause of the hysterical illness was a traumatic experience rising not from the organism's interaction with inorganic and other organic entities, but rather from interactions with persons. Though the traumatic experience would ultimately be shown to possess a physiological base, the real cause of the physiological reaction would be irreducibly psychological, that is to say, would require for logical adequacy a description both in physiological *and* in psychological terms, and would require to be conceptualised as such. There is here at stake, of course, the principle of homogeneity of cause and effect. If what causes a physiological state is not itself definable physiologically, then there is not the required homogeneity necessary for a viable causal explanation. I think, however, that there is a possible Freudian reply, and one amenable to a dialectical argument about the nature of progress such as Marcuse would support. It is that as a result of the development of psychoanalytic theory, physiological and psychological concepts each in their own way would be found inadequate and transformed in synthesis in a new structure for explaining human behaviour and action. Thus Freud might escape the charge that, as a thoroughgoing materialist, having begun by ruling out physiological causes, he ends up asserting them. That I find such a reply inadequate will be clear from my fundamental thesis, namely, the inapplicability of rule-conforming models with their causal basis in adequate explanation of human action.

Let us, however, for a moment allow the Freudian case to continue, and let us look at one example on grounds of which Freud rejected purely physiological explanations of psychological action in terms of concepts devised at least in the current state of physiology. The example comes from Breuer's work with a case of a lady with a hysterical limp:

A young married woman was for some time very much worried about her younger sister's future. As a result of this her period, normally regular, lasted for two weeks; she was tender in the left hypogastrium, and twice she found herself lying stiff on the floor, coming out of a 'faint'. There followed an ovarian neuralgia on the left side, with signs of severe peritonitis. The absence of fever, and a contracture of the left leg (and of her back), showed that the illness was a *pseudo*-peritonitis; and when, a few years later, the patient died and an autopsy was performed, all that was found was a 'microcystic degeneration' of *both* ovaries without any traces of an old peritonitis. The severe symptoms disappeared by degrees and left behind an ovarian neuralgia, a contracture of the muscles of the back, so that her trunk was as stiff as a board, and a contracture of the left leg. The latter was got rid of under hypnosis by direct suggestion. The contracture of her back was unaffected by this . . . But after the patient had been compelled under hypnosis to tell the whole story up to the time when she had fallen ill of 'peritonitis' . . . she immediately sat up in bed and the contracture of her back disappeared for ever. (Freud and Breuer, 1974, pp. 304–5)

Now, note how the evidence presented in this example serves to refute the simplistic notion held still by many and in particular by medical sceptics of psychoanalytic theory today. Such a simplistic notion regards the Freud/Breuer thesis as in some sense pre-scientific in which psychological concepts are advanced simply to fill the gaps in physiological theory until such times as allegedly more adequate physiological concepts became available. Such would indeed represent the empiricist faith of the Newtonian scientist and the alternative explanation to problems of hysteria that Freud and Breuer consciously rejected. It is not the case in this example of a hysterical case that the failure to explain the cause of the contracture of the lady's left leg and back was due to gaps in a particular physiological theory. Rather does the case of the lady in question reduce the whole framework of physiological explanation when applied to her illness into chaos. Symptoms of peritonitis were inconsistent with the absence of fever and the particular contractures in question. The autopsy conducted following her death only two years after her cure revealed no traces of peritonitis. *Both* ovaries had been inflamed, and yet she had had difficulties with only *one* leg. Had the stiff back and the limp resulted from one or from a series of related *physiological* causes, then they would have either disappeared together when the physiological cause or causes disappeared, or remained together when they failed to disappear. The interrelationship between disease and symptom, the regularity of cause and effect and so forth in physiological theories, is thus thrown into confusion. What therefore both Freud and Breuer proposed was something that today would be termed a new 'paradigm' of inquiry which imposes a new and intelligible order upon what, under an old paradigm, had been an unintelligible and disordered chaos. It provides us therefore with yet another example of the failure of what we have called logical imperialism to solve the problem of knowledge in that it marks, yet again, empiricism's failure to impose its particular formal framework upon an account of human understanding to the exclusion of all others.

Let us therefore pursue in greater detail Freud's development of a new paradigm of explanation that was irreducibly psychological in character. As we saw, Freud began by locating the origins of his theory in the notion of a traumatic experience, namely, a specifically psychological experience that had afflicted a 'trauma' or 'wound' upon someone. The trauma assumed the form of a physical illness, but was substantially the result of the patient's repression of the traumatic experience which was so emotionally overwhelming that the subject could not come to terms with it. As a result of the repression, a neurotic illness occurred with physical features that were in reality misleading masks of mental repression. One example that suggests how such concepts arose in the theory can be seen in the famous case of 'Anna O.' in Freud's case-histories. Anna, among other things, in her most complex case suffered from a severe squint. There appeared to be no physiological causes of the squint with which she was observed to have particular difficulties at a particular hour of the day. Breuer tried to piece together the events surrounding the time when Anna's squint occurred for the first time in order to establish the distinctly psychological origins of the squint. He found that no eyewitnesses were available at the critical date when the squint had begun, but this, by this time, had ceased to be a barrier since he had found that first by the use of drugs and then later simply by hypnotism patients were able to recall what when fully conscious they appeared unable to recall. To quote Breuer's account which appeared in their joint work:

In July 1880, while he was in the country, her father fell seriously ill of a sub-pleural abscess. Anna shared the duties of nursing him with her mother. She once woke up during the night in great anxiety about the patient, who was in a high fever; and she was under the strain of expecting the arrival of a surgeon from Vienna who was to operate. Her mother had gone away for a short time and Anna was sitting at the bedside with her right arm over the back of her chair. She fell into a waking dream and saw a black snake coming towards the sick man from the wall to bite him . . . we were able to trace back all of her different disturbances of vision to different, more or less clearly determining causes. For instance, on one occasion, when she was sitting by her father's bedside with tears in her eyes, he suddenly asked her what time it was. She could not see clearly; she made a great effort, and brought her watch near to her eyes. The face of the watch now seemed very big – thus accounting for her macropsia and convergent squint. Or again, she tried hard to suppress her tears so that the sick man should not see them. (Freud and Breuer, 1974, pp. 92–4)

Thus, under hypnosis, Anna proceeded to relive the circumstances of her father's death at the time when she had been left nursing him alone. She had tried desperately to pull herself together and to compose herself in her father's presence, even though she was weeping tears that flooded her eyelids during his last, lingering hours. Trying to force back the tears and read the time, she had twisted her eyelids into a squint and at that particular time each day the squint reached its most difficult intensity. What had happened, claimed Freud, was that an overwhelming emotion and psychological experience had been repressed in a way that was analogous to the damming of some mighty torrent. Just as a torrent when dammed at one point has to find some outlet at another unless it is to burst its banks completely, so neurotic illness represents a sick outlet in the form of a physiological experience for a mental experience that has been repressed. What must take place if the neurotic illness is to be cured is that the repressed emotion be relived and re-experienced, this time allowing its full force to spend itself without being repressed. As a result, the neurotic illness that marked the presence of psychological repression would be healed since that of which it was a function would no longer be operative.

Now, what was for Freud critical for examples such as those which I have quoted was that in them it is not simply the case that patients conceal the traumatic experience responsible for the neurotic illness from other people, as when people say that they 'would rather not talk about' some deeply personal experience. It was not simply that they concealed such experiences from others, but that in some sense they had concealed such experiences from themselves. Anna was unable to recall squinting through the tears at her watch until she was semi-conscious and under hypnosis, and in Breuer's words such recollections of patients were,

> ideas which were intense enough not merely to cause powerful somatic phenomena but also to call out the appropriate affect and to influence the course of association by bringing allied ideas into prominence – but which, in spite of all this, remained outside consciousness themselves. In order to bring them into consciousness hypnosis was necessary . . . or . . . a laborious search had to be made with strenuous help from the physician. (Freud and Breuer, 1974, pp. 303–4)

On the basis of such instances, therefore, Freud and Breuer postulated that the mind is divided so that it becomes possible for one part of the mind to conceal from another part what had really taken place. Freud claimed that both the conscious part of the mind, the ego, and the subconscious part of the mind, the id, were both equally active and in their divided functions represented the division of the mind. In neurosis, the interaction between the id and the ego was in a state of at least partial breakdown with a corresponding distortion of reality. The id was the active repository of every experience that a person had ever had, and as such a kind of store of every fear, hope, wish, passion or anxiety. Such descriptions ('fear', 'hope' and so forth) were, moreover, but descriptions of different aspects or dimensions of a single, continuously active drive that eminated from the id. This drive was called the 'libido' and was ultimately sexual in character and demanding sometimes consciously and sometimes subconsciously satisfaction from the ego. As such, the metaphors 'repository' or 'store' are perhaps misleading, since they are too passive metaphors. Yet consider what would happen if a person was suddenly overwhelmed by every fear, hope, wish, anxiety or passion that he had ever had suddenly and in one moment. He would tremble, laugh, cry, become aggressive, self-humiliating and so on all at the same time. In other words, the whole structure of a more or less ordered rationality would collapse and break down in front of us. The explanation of why therefore in fact, given the nature of the libido, normal people do not exhibit such chaotic and disorganised patterns of behaviour is the role of the ego which is able to delay gratification of some libidinous demands while fulfilling others and yet sublimating some others. Thus, with the mentally healthy, by the mechanism of sublimation, namely, that of finding both an acceptable personal and social outlet for the libidinous drive, the ego orders the libidinous demands of the id, providing thus a coherent organisation of a healthy personality. The lover who desires his beloved but finds that she does not return his love cannot in a civilised society allow his libidinous torrents to impell him to rape. He therefore composes great or not so great poems in which his feelings achieve an acceptable and civilised outlet in a sublimated form, and he is thus spared the neurosis that arises from repression. As such, sublimation in a healthy person is the counterpart to repression in someone who is suffering from a neurotic illness.

Freud was to develop psychoanalytic theory further. The division of the mind into the id and ego, conceived by Freud in terms of interacting and, in the case of neurotics, conflicting mechanisms, was modified by the introduction into the scheme of a third division, namely, the super-ego. Basically, the super-ego is a mechanism fully developed by about the age of seven and is formed from an internalisation and de-individualisation of the father's voice into a general 'voice of conscience'. It represents a primitive moral system, but one that is infantile and irrational and as such unreflective and dogmatic. As such it is at variance with the conscious, rational and reflective morality of the ego in the final, adolescent stage of its development when it has ceased to be guided by the pleasure principle and is guided instead by the reality principle. There is, moreover, a close connection between Freud's concept of the super-ego and his formulation of the features of the Oedipus and Electra complexes. Oedipus was the hero of classical mythology who was brought up by a shepherd in ignorance of being in fact of royal birth and heir to the throne of Thebes. His father the king became demented and roamed as a beggar and the boy on a chance meeting mistook his intentions and killed him. Subsequently he married the widowed queen of Thebes without knowing that she was his mother. Thus Oedipus unconsciously killed his own father and made love to his own mother. Electra, at least in Euripides' version of her story (Euripides, 1954), was the heroine who saw her beloved father murdered by her mother and her mother's lover. She longed for vengeance in the form of her returning brother Orestes. At the close of the play she stands thus avenged, but her final speech reveals that her lust for venegeance has left her a thoroughly distorted personality.

Freud was to find in the Oedipus and Electra myths useful analogies of the way in which he believed sexuality developed in a social context. As the libido was ultimately sexual in character, sexuality began in infancy and the object of the baby's first desire was the maternal breast (with girls normally a transference took place in the direction of the father). But as the male child began to grow, he became conscious of a rival for the maternal breast in the form of the figure of the father. The child's socialisation, however, taught him that he must love and respect his father who loves him, who has protected and done so much for him. Thus there is built up a conflict between the love of social obligation and the hatred of sexual rivalry. When from about seven years of age the admonition of the father's voice is internalised as the super-ego or voice of conscience, the love, fear, guilt about hatred and jealousy of the father is projected upon the super-ego, which can be, and in history most often has been, associated with the voice of God. When the child fails to achieve some degree of healthy sublimation and thus fails to achieve equilibrium between the various conflicting mechanisms, he acquires that complex known as the Oedipus complex which is constituted by an unconscious desire to kill one's own father and make love to one's own mother. But the form in which sublimation takes place is frequently and perhaps always a religious one. Subconscious desires to make love to one's mother are projected upon mother goddesses with language that is contrived sub-consciously to conceal the sexual character of the emotions expressed. Christianity, for example, in its Catholic form venerates

Mary Mother of God ever Virgin, who 'prays for us sinners at the hour of our death'. In some of its extreme Protestant forms, moreover, Christianity tells the story of the cruel Father-god who allowed his own righteous and innocent son to be slain, by whose death our guilt about our hatred of the Father and his demands is assuaged.

We saw earlier (Section 5.4 above) in connection with the phenomenologist reinterpretation of the Marxist mode that the key concepts for reformulation were such concepts as 'liberation', 'legitimation', 'false-consciousness', 'alienation'. We promised there, moreover, that our discussion of Freud would reveal some new insights that might be argued to be capable of overcoming the standard of objections to classical Marxism. It is possible to argue *prima facie* that we can deploy psychoanalytic theory in support of the phenomenological reformulation. Let us briefly recap what the problem was. If we make the fundamental phenomenological shift in defining reality not in terms of some kind of intelligible bedrock beyond socially constructed linguistic categories, then all social constructions of reality must be equally valid and phenomenological Marxists' directives to adopt one rather than another can have no logical force. But with the aid of psychoanalytic theory, it is arguable that we can now say that, although there is no reality beyond socially generated linguistic categories that licenses one construction of reality against another, nevertheless some constructions of reality are more mentally healthy than others. In the psychoanalytic definitions of mental health and sickness, therefore, we have, it might be argued, an objective framework for judging rival constructions of reality. 'Liberation' can be at least in part understood in terms of what is experienced when repression ceases as the trauma is removed. The neurotic who claims that the reason why he cannot form satisfactory relationships with women is that no woman would find him attractive, is, in a sense, legitimating his behaviour – he is covering his tracks by means of a quite spurious justification, whereas the real reason is maternal rejection in the context of the Oedipus complex. The consciousness of being unable to walk as a result of an abdominal pain, moreover, was a 'false' consciousness since the real reason was because of being worried about a sister's future. 'Alienation', moreover, can, like these other concepts, be at least partially understood in terms of an overwhelming emotional experience produced by an economic order that cannot be come to terms with and which results in destructive and aimless behaviour. Although, moreover, Freud was dealing with individual psychology, and although in the reformulated Marxist model psychoanalysis must address itself to what it must hold to be the fundamental social causes of neurosis and distortion of reality, nevertheless it might be held that social applications of the thesis were at least implicit in, for example, Freud's location of Oedipus and Electra complexes in social relations between members of families.

There are, however, a number of problems, both conceptual, epistemological and methodological, raised by Freud's thesis, some of which we will be dealing with in our later more general discussion. But there is a specific epistemological issue that we shall deal with here because it directly affects the whole purpose of resorting to a Freudian explanation of social repression in reformulating a Marxist model in phenomenological terms. We have pointed to the use of Freud to avoid the problem of knowledge in the form of a problem about how to make objectivity judgements which are not socially relative when there is no extra-linguistic reality on which we can anchor such judgements. But we must now point to how the Freudian perspective that apparently enables socially generated world views to be judged, when in conflict, on a kind of neurotic/healthy continuum, is itself dependent on making certain objectivity-judgements, the justification of which is by no means clear from the way in which the thesis is stated. The Freudian neurotic/healthy distinction requires the notion of the possibility of objectivity arrived at by means of the ego's adoption of the reality principle, with the result that some objectivist (or 'transcendental') (Brent, 1978, pp. 166–8) basis is still required, and the question therefore of reality definition cannot be avoided by the Freudian thesis. There is a danger, and one of which I believe Marcuse to be at least implicitly aware, that the problems of how claims to objectivity can be rationally established cannot be avoided by recourse to the Freudian model. The problems that such a recourse was intended to avoid will be seen to be as critical for that model as they were for the model of the sociologists of knowledge. Let us now focus in greater detail on the problem of objectivity in its Freudian form.

The problem of objectivity for Freud is raised by his distinction between normal, sublimatory activity and abnormal, neurotic repressive activity. Sometimes Freud speaks as though there was no qualitative difference between sublimation and repression. On one occasion he described the artist thus:

He is one who is urged on by instinctual needs which are too clamorous; he longs to attain honour, power, riches, fame, and the love of women; but he lacks the means of achieving these gratifications. So . . . he turns away from reality and turns . . . all his libido . . . on to the creation of his wishes in the life of phantasy, from which the way might readily lead to neurosis. There must be many factors in combination to prevent this becoming the whole outcome of his development; it is well known how often artists in particular suffer from partial inhibition of their capacities through neurosis. Probably their constitution is endowed with a powerful capacity for sublimation and with a certain flexibility in the repressions determining the conflict. (Freud, 1974, p. 423)

Here, then, is an ambiguity in the role of sublimation and repression in psychoanalytic theory. If it is a 'powerful capacity for sublimation' that explains how artistic fantasy does not 'readily lead to neurosis', why is it necessary to employ the notion of 'flexibility of repression' also as its explanation? It would appear that he is not clear in passages such as this that his account requires a clear distinction to be made between repression and sublimation. Unless he can make this distinction, his account first will lack conceptual clarity because what it is for an experience to be an instance of sublimation can only be understood by contrast with what it is for an experience to be an instance of repression and *vice versa*. Secondly, unless the distinction is clear, his account will lack coherence. If 'riches', 'fame' and the 'love of women' (plural), if not 'power' and 'honour' are normal aspirations that can by their nature be attained only by a few, then it is a matter of necessity for any human society to cope with them in the organisation of its affairs. Since Freud does not subscribe to the notion of the nobility of pre-societal savagery, then sublimation must refer to that necessary organisation of societal affairs which, because it is normal, must be part of the definition of mental health. Freud's ambiguity about the distinction therefore vitiates his theory. Yet, if he maintains the kind of ambiguity that asserts no qualitative difference between sublimation and repression, the price of conceptual confusion and incoherence of statement is to leave his claim to a therapeutic role without adequate justification. On what grounds can he maintain that he has produced a cure if, in getting his patients to sublimate rather than repress, he is not doing anything qualitatively dissimilar? This dilemma is, moreover, considerably sharpened when sublimation and repression are analysed and distinguished partially by reference to them as functions of an ego that, in its final and developed form, is committed to the reality principle. Ultimately, therefore, both sublimation, repression and therapy must be tied in Freud to an unexplicated concept of reality and unexplicated rational means by which such reality is grasped. In therapy, repressions and corresponding traumatic illnesses are removed as a result of their 'real' origins being exposed and with the patient's coming to terms with the 'real' situation that has been disclosed.

Perhaps Freud's unargued ontological assumptions can be shown in starkest relief by following our earlier strategy with empiricism and by showing how Freud ran into difficulties regarding religious experience. In view of Freud's account of the Oedipus and Electra complexes and the formation of the super-ego, an important question emerges which Freud never appears to have answered either unambiguously or satisfactorily. Are there healthy *and* neurotic forms of religious belief, or is all religion a form of neurosis? There is, moreover, a prior problem that has contributed to Freud's ambiguity. We saw that, given the social conditions which produce reverence for the father as lawgiver and given the libidinous desire for the mother figure, guilt feelings are necessarily associated with the internalised paternal voice following the formation of the super-ego. Now, the problem for Freud is: are these given social conditions either culturally invariant or to be regarded at least as culturally normal? If they are not invariant or at least normal, the notion of 'conscience' (or 'internalisation of society's value-system' or what have you), indispensible for understanding social order in any society that lacks a one-to-one ratio between policemen and citizens, will be inexplicable within psychoanalytic theory for, for example, matriarchal and polygamous societies. If, however, they are or at least ought to be considered to be 'invariants' and therefore 'normal', there appears to be some necessary connection between at least some form of religious belief and any social order that constitutes the kind of problem for atheism with which Freud's *Future of an Illusion* (1934) is concerned. There are, therefore, undistinguished and therefore unargued problems about objectivity ('cultural invariance', 'normal' and so on) that vitiate the coherence of psychoanalytic theory.

This point can, moreover, be pushed home further with reference to the problem of distinguishing neurotic from healthy forms of religious belief, given that Freud's theory has now been shown to require the justification of such a distinction. The distinction as a justification for therapy rests upon the justification of commitments concerning what is real about the world. In the case of religious experience, therefore, sublimation rather than repression must rest on a healthy rather than a sick mode of coping with the facts of human experience. Certain facts of human experience are representable when coped with by the ego's reality principle in such a sublimated form as assertions, say, about 'God our heavenly father', But, in that case, healthy (sublimated) and neurotic (repressed) religious beliefs, produced by healthy or traumatic family relationships, will only be capable of being described as such with reference to a view of reality. Unless we are, in fact, committed to the existence of God as our heavenly Father, we cannot make the sublimation/repression distinction. Such beliefs or relationships will only be classifiable as such in proportion to the extent to which they bring people to terms with such a reality or cause them to exhibit a number of distorted repressions of it. If the universe and man's condition within it both in nature and in society were so horrifying and unintelligible that man finds the explanation for his existence so impossible without recourse to the idea of God, then that very recourse and its preconditions might constitute proper grounds for asserting God's necessary existence (Berger, 1971). Such proper grounds might be that matter itself reveals its own unintelligibility and disorder when isolated from a divine order, that individual human families reveal a distortion and an inadequacy in comparison with ideal relationships whose needed actualisation the human condition requires. Augustine's cry perhaps gives some rhetorical expression of such an argument when he said: 'Lord Thou art our resting place and our hearts are restless till they find their rest in Thee.' But clearly, once one spells out that kind of conception of reality that will, I have argued, give grounds to justify psycho-analysis as therapy and to clarify fundamental ambiguities and inconsistencies, then we are far from classical Freudian ontological commitments. But without such a conception, the sublimation/repression distinction simply cannot be made.

We have seen, therefore, that the justification of some overall view of reality was as problematic for Freud's use in reformulating classical Marxism as was the use of phenomenologist perspectives. Freud's understanding of what was real and what the ego could grasp in the nineteenth and early twentieth century undoubtedly rested on an empiricist view of truth which we have shown good grounds for discarding. We have certainly shown notwithstanding that, without an epistemological theory, Freud is left claiming that all religion, art or even science (space exploration, for example, being basically a sublimated libidinous drive to stick pointed things in round holes) are forms of neurosis because, without some justifiable ontological commitment, there can be no qualitative difference between sublimation and repression. But if such a qualitative distinction is denied, the conceptual collapse of psychoanalytic theory, particularly in application to a reformulated Marxist model of explanation, is precipitated.

Because I believe Marcuse's theoretical significance is to have grasped the inadequacy of Freud's ontological commitment for Freud's use in reformulating the classical Marxist model, we now turn to Marcuse's attempt to remedy such an inadequacy by means of a dialectical understanding of reality.

5.6 FREUDIAN REINTERPRETATIONS OF CLASSICAL MARXISM: DIALECTICAL SOLUTIONS

Freud did not relate his theory to any social theory, let alone a social theory supported by dialectical arguments. In the light of the relationship that Marcuse and others (Marcuse, 1954, 1964 and 1968) were to postulate between Freud's psychology of individual repression and conflict and Marx's social philosophy of class repression and conflict, we would do well at this juncture to try to argue on what basis their two distinct models could be brought into closer alignment. To begin with, there is the possibility of regarding the interaction between the id and the ego that produced (healthy) sublimation in the light of the logical interchange between thesis and antithesis that creates a synthesis. Take, for example, a man who is driven by his libidinous drive towards making love to a beautiful woman who does not wish to indulge him. His problem is that he cannot make love to her against her will and retain his own self-esteem and social approval. The thesis is therefore constituted by the proposition that he cannot both make love to her and retain social and self-esteem. The antithesis which negates directly the thesis is the proposition that he makes love to her and has no self-esteem nor social approval. If he now represses his antithetical solution, his repression will simply enable the thesis to remain untransformed. There will be no change in the situation and conflicts and tensions within it will remain unresolved. The only true synthesis will be a sublimatory solution in which the man, say, sublimates his desires, his remorse over unrequited love, in perhaps writing beautiful poems in which his tensions and frustrations are worked out creatively. Furthermore, the poems, because they reveal his true predicament, might lead the lady to see the situation in a new light and to return his love, with the result that sublimation has genuinely transformed a situation of conflict into a new, synthetical harmony.

Marcuse seeks to incorporate a Freudian analysis of mental conflict into his reformulated Marxist model. He argues that the ability of a modern technology to increase productivity has perpetuated the domination of the capitalist system and secured it from transformation. This is because contemporary capitalism, though replacing labour with machines, has blocked the creative, antithetical and sublimatory use of surplus energy by providing the means of immediate gratification to the libido. Furthermore, by the development of positive strategies of de-sublimation with corresponding immediate gratification, increased consumption has paradoxically increased domination and oppression. As Marcuse says:

The mere quantitative decline in needed human labor power militates against the maintenance of the capitalist mode of production (as of all other exploitive modes of production). The system reacts by stepping up the production of goods and services that either do not enlarge individual consumption at all, or enlarge it with luxuries – luxuries in the face of persistent poverty, but luxuries which are necessities for occupying a labor force sufficient to reproduce the established economic and political institutions. To the degree to which this sort of work appears as superfluous . . . whilst necessary for earning a living, frustration is built into the very productivity of this society and aggressiveness is activated. And to the degree in which the society in its very structure becomes aggressive, the mental structure of its citizens adjusts itself: The individual becomes at one and the same time more aggressive and more pliable and submissive, for he submits to a society which, by virtue of its affluence and power, satisfies his deepest (and other-wise greatly repressed) instinctual needs. (Marcuse, 1968, p. 262)

We see, then, in this passage Marcuse's view that aggressiveness cannot under present socio-economic conditions be sublimated into a humanising and genuinely civilised form because, in the over-production of goods (goods that 'enlarge human consumption with luxuries'), libidinous energy has been gratified directly so that no synthetical transformation of 'instinctual needs' can take place. Opposites such as being 'more aggressive' and 'more pliable and submissive' are, because of the dominative strategy of de-sublimation, held together as frozen contraries without any synthetical transformation taking place.

It is thus important to grasp how Marcuse sees the incorporation of a Freudian perspective into classical Marxist theory that is beginning to emerge in our discussion as answering certain problems intractible within Marxist theory taken by itself. Opponents of classical Marxism can appeal to some features of contemporary socio-economic conditions in order to support their claim that the predictions of classical Marxists have been falsified. Take, for example, the classical Marxist claims about the inevitability of revolution. Classical Marx argues that profitability was axiomatic to the capitalist system since, without profits, capital would not be attracted or reinvested. But unless companies show growth in profits, they cease to attract capital in a competitive market so that they fail to survive. The consequences for the individual worker employed within such a system is that his boss, having made, say, five dollars an hour from his labour this year, must make ten the next, twenty the next, thirty the next and so on. Now the individual worker might be prepared, to keep the company solvent and retain his job, to work twice as hard next year, three times as hard the year after and so on. But somewhere along the line, as the spring is wound up more tightly and more tightly, the worker will be unable to bear his exploitation further and the spring will recoil. The ensuing revolution, which is on this analysis both predictable and inevitable, will by the very nature of its historical causes accomplish a fundamental transformation in the relations of production. What has, however, falsified this Marxist prediction, according to its critics, is that productivity resulting from automation has both increased the capitalist's profits without increasing worker exploitation in the form of physical labour and longer hours, but rather an increase in worker leisure time and affluence. But for Marcuse this is a far from satisfactory reply to his particular form of a Marxist theory. Marcuse can, in the light of his Freudian incorporations into his Marxist model, argue that though the revolution has been thwarted, it ought not to have been thwarted. The 'ought', moreover, is not the 'ought' of a person who finds that the machinery of a theory has failed inexplicably to produce what seemed to be only one possible outcome. Rather it is a moral 'ought' that Marcuse seeks to ground in certain facts of human nature, namely, those about the conditions of mental health and ill-health as established (he thinks) by psychoanalytic theory. The way in which, paradoxically, an increase in leisure time and raised standards of living have proved part of the organised repression of capitalist society is that, instead of the forces of production satisfying basic needs so that residual libidinous drive could be sublimated, their over-production and waste creation, on which the workers' new-found 'freedom' is based, leads to immediate gratification of the libidinous residue.

For over-production and over-consumption to continue, the immediate gratification that is sublimation must be increasingly reduced by a process of de-sublimation. In the so-called 'sexual revolution', it is often claimed that freedom within society has been increased so that we are now more 'liberated'. How can, therefore, what appear to be liberating tendencies be held to be but perpetuations of domination? The reason for Marcuse is that so-called sexual liberation is part of the general phenomenon of 'sweeping de-sublimation'. Freud is often hailed quite falsely as the prophet of the permissive society. But Freud, in his less ambivalent moods about the sublimation/repression distinction as the criterion of mental health, proves to be a defender of some, for him, critical aspects of Victorian puritanism. For Freud a totally permissive society of immediate libidinous gratification would be a culturally impoverished society. In sublimation lay the perhaps mentally healthy key to the achievement of civilised forms of life and rationality. For Marcuse, moreover, as we have begun to see, there is no ambiguity about the healthy and progressive character of sublimation. Marcuse furthermore emphasises Freud's distinction between sexuality as a specialised, partial drive and eros as constituting the drive of the whole organism. Thus the 'localization and contraction of the libido, the reduction of erotic to sexual experience and satisfaction' Marcuse sees as marking the permissive society in de-sublimating experience so as to prevent its transformation. As Marcuse says:

> The Pleasure Principle absorbs the Reality Principle; sexuality is liberated (or rather liberalised) in socially constructive forms. This notion implies that there are repressive modes of de-sublimation, compared with which the sublimated drives and objectives contain more deviation, more freedom, and more refusal to heed to social taboos . . . a whole dimension of human activity and passivity has been de-eroticised . . . Thus diminishing erotic and intensifying sexual energy, the technological reality *limits the scope of sublimation* . . . Inasmuch as the greater liberty involves a contraction rather than extension and development of instinctual needs, it works *for* rather than *against* the status quo of general repression – one might speak of 'institutionalised de-sublimation'. (Marcuse, 1964, p. 69)

Marcuse has one individual and one social example which will help us in our general exposition of this passage. In exemplification of how 'a whole dimension of human activity and passivity has been de-eroticised', he contrasts (*a*) making love in a country meadow and (*b*) making love in the back of an automobile in a city park. Eros is converted through de-sublimation into a specifically sexual drive. The total environment in the case of (*a*) contributes to a general erotic experience, and yet in the case of (*b*) the environment is hostile to it and forces libidinous pleasure to be confined to the excitement of the erotogenic zones. Thus far Marcuse's Freudianism is purely individualistic. But, claims Marcuse, the basic and formal features of the individualist example (*b*) can be carried over into an analysis of patterns of social control. Note that satisfaction in the automobile environment was controlled and limited by the man-made social context. Likewise, the exhibition of sexual attractiveness has become integrated into the work situation. As Marcuse says:

> Without ceasing to be an instrument of labor, the body is allowed to exhibit its sexual features in the everyday work world and in work

relations . . . The sexy office and sales girls, the handsome, virile junior executive and floor walker are highly marketable commodities. (Marcuse, 1964, p. 71)

Thus the total work environment is not contributory to general erotic experience. The libido is managed and circumscribed to expressions of passing glances and feelings while the 'real business' of work goes on:

> This mobilisation and administration of libido may account for much of the voluntary compliance, the absence of terror, the pre-established harmony between individual needs and socially required desires . . . The technological and political conquest of the transcending factors in human existence, so characteristic of advanced industrial civilisation, here assets itself in the instinctual sphere: satisfaction in a way which generates submission and weakens the rationality of protest. (Marcuse, 1964, p. 71)

But the 'pre-established harmony between individual needs and socially acquired drives' is a false harmony and the grounds of its falsity is to be seen by analogy with the harmony that 'Anna O.' achieved between her overwhelming sorrow and her desire to tell her dying father the time. It is the neurotic and pathological harmony of the squint. Nowhere is such a process more clearly seen for Marcuse than in what he regards modern technological society as having done to art as one of the 'transcending factors in human existence'.

Whereas in Freud we saw there to be, with reference to the artist, a fundamental ambiguity regarding the sublimation/repression distinction, Marcuse maintains his lack of ambiguity in this respect and is convinced that true art is sublimation and as such qualitatively different from its repressive forms. Sublimation works through art as a means of transcendence because, through art, sublimation produces an alternative to existing reality, a creative antithesis to the present thesis. But he sees a distinction here between contemporary mass culture and the high culture of yesteryear. Plays such as *Romeo and Juliet* or *Don Juan* reflected not the life-styles of the contemporary feudal culture in which they emerged, but alternatives to that culture in the negation of its materialism and misuse of individuals. Such alternatives are wrongly nihilated by describing them derogatorily as examples of 'romanticism'. In Thomas Mann, as in nineteenth-century English novels, moreover, although there is represented contemporary bourgeois order, 'it remained an order which was over-shadowed, broken, refuted by another dimension which was irreconcilably antagonistic to the order of business, indicting it and denying it' (Marcuse, 1964, pp. 59–60). Art therefore represents 'alienated sublimation' (Marcuse, 1964, p. 69). It creates alternative possibilities from which men are alienated but whose alienation drives them to make actual. But what enables Marcuse to dispense with Freud's ambiguity is once again the dialectical backcloth to his use of the concept of 'sublimation'. The sublimated projection of a possibility is unambiguously *not* neurotic because, although stressful, it is creative, and creative because the antithetical movement against the thesis that it constitutes also generates conflict so that the creative possibilities in the situation can be actualised. 'One-dimensional man' is therefore, for Marcuse, the product of 'one-dimensional society' in which antithetical negations as representatives of alternative possibilities have been neutralised.

The way in which thought is held in one dimension, with opposites harmonised rather than transcended, is exemplified by Marcuse with reference to the universe of discourse employed by the mass media and in advertising:

The universe of discourse in which opposites are reconciled has a firm basis for such unification – its beneficial destructiveness. Total commercialisation joins formerly antagonistic spheres of life, and this union expresses itself in the smooth linguistic conjunction of conflicting parts of speech ... Captions such as 'Labour is Seeking Missile Harmony' and advertisements such as 'Luxury Fall-Out Shelter' may still evoke the naive reaction that 'Labour', 'Missile', and 'Harmony' are irreconcilable contradictions ... However the logic and language become perfectly rational when we learn that a 'nuclear-powered, ballistic-missile-firing submarine' 'carries a price tag of $120,000,000' and that 'carpeting, scrabble and TV' are provided in the $1,000 model of the shelter. (Marcuse, 1964, p. 81)

It is by means of the unification of opposites thus exemplified that ruling-classes have maintained their position in society's structure unchanged according to Marcuse's reformulated Marxist model, which defines false-consciousness in both a dialectical and a psychoanalytic form. By unifying opposites in this way, reality is distorted. Moreover, such advertising slogans and the process that underlies them helps both to exemplify and explain how what Marcuse describes as a 'happy consciousness', so central to Freudian psychoanalysis in the Oedipus complex, revokes real conscience in one-dimensional man. We saw at the conclusion of our exposition of Freud in the previous section that, in what Freud regards as normal cases of mental health, consciousness is produced through sublimation so that the Oedipus complex is avoided. In sublimation, which for Marcuse is unambiguously healthy and by which the super-ego is created, one is aware of the social barrier to instinctual gratification and so there may be the tension of an unhappy consciousness. However, this social barrier is transgressed or rather overcome by a free and rational agent genuinely solving the problem of that barrier and thus resolving the tension therapeutically. As Marcuse says:

> The Superego, in censoring the unconscious and in implanting conscience, also censors the censor because the developed conscience registers the forbidden evil act not only in the individual but also in his society. Conversely, loss of conscience due to the satisfactory liberties granted by an unfree society makes for a *happy consciousness* which facilitates acceptance of the misdeeds of this society. It is the token of declining autonomy and comprehension. Sublimation demands a high degree of autonomy and comprehension. (Marcuse, 1964, p. 72)

The happy-consciousness of a person whose instinctual drives are immediately gratified is therefore a person who, contrary to what he may feel, is not really free. Freedom demands autonomy and autonomy presupposes being able to choose rationally, yet in immediate gratification there is no room for the sublimatory function of the ego with its rational principles and therefore no true freedom.

We thus conclude our account of Marcuse's incorporation of Freud into his Marxist framework. We have argued that the development by Marcuse of a new model which is different from that of classical Marxism was required by the failure of classical Marxism in its original conception of the dialectic to produce a genuinely rule-following model of human action. Our purpose, moreover, was also to address Julia's very practical problem of understanding the philosophy and practice of Dr Edward Maxton's 'free' school. The kind of Marxist model required to explicate such demands for radical curricular change, we argued to be a reformulated Marxist model. How can children be alienated and affected with false-consciousness by competition, the imposition of teacher-values and so on? How, moreover and more pertinently, can the teaching of academic subjects in traditional forms lead to the domination by one group in society of another? Our discussion of the psychological mechanisms by which this takes place according to Marcuse will help to demonstrate the radical case, namely, that learning is not merely an individual psychological process. It will soon be time to make such general statements of the applicability of the new Marxist model to account for the generation of radical curriculum proposals more specific by means of a specific analysis of specific curricular proposals. But, for the moment, let us show grounds for our argument that Marcuse's reformulation of the classical Marxist model, however articulate, is in the final analysis unsuccessful and that in subtle ways basic rule-following/rule-conforming conflations maintain their hidden and debilitating influences, as well as the problem of social relativity and reality definition.

5.7 MARXISM AND THE PSYCHOANALYTIC MODEL: PERSISTENT INCOHERENCIES

We have seen, therefore, that Marcuse may be represented and in our opinion may best be represented as trying by the use of psycho-analytic theory to resolve fundamental problems associated with the classical Marxist model of social explanation. We have furthermore argued such problems to be concerned with a dialectical under-standing of the role of an unfolding reality in classical Marxism which the individual can come to terms with as a free, rule-conforming agent. Our argument, among other things, established that the classical, dialectical understanding of reality, though grounded in what was intended to be an alternative to Aristotelian logic that serviced an empiricist epistemology, nevertheless shared common assumptions with classical empiricism about the exclusively extra-social and extra-linguistic character upon which were founded true propositions. Those common assumptions were what the new sociology of knowledge, as well as Quinean pragmatism, argued to be questionable both in the light of social and anthropological studies, and in the light of Einstein's revolution in contemporary physics. Both Aristotelian and Hegelian dialectical logic assumed the notion of what was real existing 'out there' beyond language that either syllogistically or dialectically became encapsulated in true concepts joined accurately together as true propositions. But such a way of stating what as the problem of knowledge had to be solved was rejected by the sociologists of knowledge. Furthermore, we have tried to show how both the failure of classical empiricism as well as the behaviourist theories that replaced it *and* the dialectic in the tradition of classical materialism were supportive of the sociology of knowledge's phenomenological case. There are, of course, rationalist and to some degree later Wittgensteinian alternatives which, we would argue, are more satisfactory than those preferred by sociologists of knowledge as answering to the defect of their social relativism. Such alternatives will occupy us for the remaining chapters of this book. But the alternatives at which we are now looking, namely, that suggested by Marcuse's work, unlike these other two, can be seen as a genuine attempt to meet the phenomenologist case within its own terms. We have interpreted the significance of Marcuse's work to be a reinterpretation of the classical Marxist model that takes into account critical phenomenological objections to it but that seeks to redeem such a model from cultural relativism that would otherwise destroy it by incorporation of a psychoanalytic dimension.

Marcuse, however, to judge from some of his statements, would not be prepared to accept the role that we have assigned him. At one point, for example, he says:

A historical project realises given possibilities – not formal possibilities but those involving the modes of human existence. Such realisation is actually under way in any historical situation. Every established society *is* such a realisation; moreover, it tends to prejudge the rationality of *possible* projects, to keep them within its framework. (Marcuse, 1964, p. 174)

Here we see the re-emergence in Marcuse's account of the classical conception of the dialectic in accordance with which what is real is materially present 'out there' and unfolds according to a process that is a curious hybrid of the development of an argument and the development of a biological organism. The historical process is one in which 'given possibilities' experience 'realisation' in a way that conforms to 'rationality', just as with the developmental process of a biological organism whose final form is in some sense already potentially present in its embryonic development. We have, however, already given our grounds for the rejection of a dialectical understanding of reality in such terms. To the extent, therefore, that classical notions of dialectical materialism intrude into Marcuse's argument – to that extent at least – we have already shown its invalidity. Remember briefly some of our grounds for the rejection of such classical notions. The appropriateness of an analogical inference from both biological development and an argument among humans to the development of matter (and history, whose conditions are according to the theory material) was shown to be at least questionable. The inadequacy of such an analogical inference was further reinforced by the inability of the classical Marxist model, despite both appearances and the intentions of its framers, to satisfy our conditions for a rule-following as opposed to a rule-conforming model of human action, which we argued in our earlier chapters to be indispensable for an adequate psychological or sociological account. If, therefore, Marcuse's classical Marxist assumptions are in any way integral to his account, we have already shown grounds for its rejection. But we have in the way in which we have interpreted Marcuse's relevance conceded that he might have been more subtle than we have implied.

Society and its interrelations together with knowledge (all knowledge, that is, according to phenomenologists) that sustains such relationships exists only in the minds of its individual members. Thus, to use phenomenology's partial correspondence with Kant, social institutions that generate bodies of 'truths' and 'falsehoods' are constituted not by 'things in themselves' but 'things as they appear to us'. Classical Marxism's assumptions about extra-linguistic and extra-social reality are therefore illusory. But Marxism cannot exist on the basis of the social relativity of all bodies of knowledge because of its normative character that legislates programmes of radical change. But Marcuse has, we have tried to show, posed the possibility of using psychoanalysis as a way out of this phenomenological and relativistic impasse. At first sight, such a move has both plausibility and cogency. If even in our Marxian quest for what is real and true we are limited to 'things as they appear' to human beings within particular communities of societal judgements, then it would appear that both the human-argument and biological-developmental structure of the dialectical case are far less of a weakness. If our accounts of both the development of the natural and social worlds bear the impress of the development of a human argument, then this feature will be in no way remarkable if such accounts describe 'things as they appear' to us. Such accounts will be infused with our socially acquired categories of thought, logics and so forth, which in turn will bear the impress of all our social arguments, conflicts and disagreements about them. Furthermore, the synthesis between the form of a human argument and the form of a biological development will become possible in that bodies of knowledge creative of social structure are generated by individuals in interaction with their social environment. As Berger and Luckman say:

... it is possible to say that the foetal period in the human being extends through about the first year after birth. Important organismic developments, which in the animal are completed in the mother's body, take place in the human infant after its separation from the womb ... The human organism is thus still developing biologically while already standing in relationship to its environment. In other words, the process of becoming man takes place in an interrelationship with an environment. (Berger and Luckman, 1967, p. 46)

Ideas and observations are thus records that bear both the individual biological form and the societal argumentative form in the context in which they are produced.

The problem for the Marxist is, however, as we have seen, that such an epistemologically relativistic position is destructive of his case since it would leave everything as it is and yield no argument for change. Relativism is what Berger and Luckman's position in the previous quotation at least must amount to, since, not allowing as does Chomsky, correctly in our view, some pre-existing cognitive structure, the very plasticity of the human organism must make bodies of knowledge subject to the vagaries and contingencies of different social institutions at different times and places. Marcuse's solution to this problem, as we have interpreted it, is to present the possibility of accepting all knowledge as the product of the social construction of reality and yet to escape from relativism. He does so by deploying, as the absolute criterion by which rival constructions of reality are assessed, the Freudian mental health criteria as embodied in the sublimation/repression distinction. As such, Marcuse appears to assert an empirical claim against the phenomenologist position in that he rejects relativism on the grounds that the mind is not as pliable as this form of relativism suggests, but has some kind of normal and universal mechanisms such as the id, ego and so on. The problems, however, with this Freudian, psychoanalytic escape route from the horns of the dilemma created by the notion of non-relative 'things as they appear' are two-fold. One is a logical problem to do with the statement of the thesis. Having accepted the requirement that what is real can only be what appears to be real to us, the thesis then requires that it itself is beyond mere appearances. The statement, 'All reality is socially constructed', cannot itself be regarded as just another social construction. The second is a logical problem to do with the coherence of Freud with a phenomenological thesis such as is required if Freud is to be used as a means to rehabilitate Marxism while admitting the justified eclipse of classical theory. The use of Freud to reformulate the Marxist model in the light of phenomeno-logical criticism accepted as valid presupposes that Freud's theory itself requires for its coherence no reference to extra-linguistic, extra-social reality. Yet clearly from what we have shown that the theory states about the ego and the 'reality principle', it does require the making of such references. What made 'Anna O.'s' cure a *cure* was that she was assisted by the analyst to unravel and relive the *real* traumatic experience that lay behind both her squint and her hallucinations about snakes. Only reliving the real experience and not some happy, hallucinatory alternative could produce the real cure. The claim, therefore, that Freud can produce criteria for judging between rival social construction of reality without producing a coherent view of some extra-social reality into which a construction of reality ought to be anchored fails. Either a Freudian must take for granted an empiricist view of extra-social nature, or he must take a dialectical view of nature that is equally extra-social. But if he does either, his enterprise will founder on the case against both empiricism and classical dialectical definitions of reality made in this book. Our own solution, to which we have frequently made reference, is a Chomskyan solution (above, pp. 15–17, 65–8, 119–25). We see the objectivity of human judgements as 'things as they appear' as the product of a basic framework of judgement testified to by what is clearly expressible in all human languages and reducible to certain fundamental categories of common sense. In such an interpersonal agreement in a human form-of-life, we find the touchstone of what is real and true. We began our argument for such a view of objectivity in a previous book (Brent, 1978, pp. 190–211), and we shall be continuing it in a new form in our remaining chapters. Here, in a moment, we shall be concerned to show the need for such an argument by showing that, quite apart from containing an inarticulated notion of objectivity, Freud has failed to produce a genuinely rule-following model of how such objectivity is grasped and asserted by human beings.

For the moment, however, at this point let us pursue our critique of Marcuse to its final conclusion. Could not, it may be objected, the real point of Marcuse's work be that he redefines reality dialectically in order to preserve the validity of a theory that he requires in order to reinterpret Marx? We could allow this point, of course, and still claim that he was unsuccessful in view of our objections to classical dialectical arguments. But we cannot even grant his entitlement to do this. If we were to so grant, we would be licensing a vicious circularity that would ultimately undermine what we regarded as the real significance of what Marcuse was attempting. Remember that because we found dialectical understandings of extra-social, extra-linguistic reality as problematic as empiricist ones, for this reason we licensed a phenomenological move the subjective character of which could be ameliorated by the appeal to an objectivity conceived in terms of a Freudian understanding of mental health. At least such amelioration was the promise that made us look seriously at Marcuse's account in the first place. If now we are, after due examination, to declare such psychoanalytic foundations themselves inadequate, we can scarcely use, as it were, the walls and roof that they were intended to support to support them in turn. It is unfortunate therefore that one can scan the works of Marcuse in vain for any critical discussion of the Freudian framework, which is simply accepted and its validity assumed. As a result, Freudian assumptions that are themselves questionable are incorporated into the classical Marxist model in place of questionable assumptions there without discussing, analysing or further supporting their claims. Were Marcuse to have so questioned his Freudian assumptions even to the extent that we have so far done here, he would have had some chance of detecting the fundamental incoherence of:

(*a*) Resorting to psychoanalytic redefinitions of Marxist concepts in order to preserve objectivity in the light of an established phenomenological case against such concepts.

(*b*) Using the rejected definition of reality which provided grounds for employing the original redefinition to shore up the objectivity of the psychoanalytic basis for the redefinition when that objectivity under analysis has in turn been undermined.

In (*a*) and (*b*) we find the formal expression of the fundamental incoherence which vitiates Marxist theory in the last analysis when we examine it in its final and apparently most defensible form. We shall find those specific educational and curricular proposals that we will shortly examine to be similarly vitiated by a reproduction of the same deep incoherence perpetuated by their underlying theoretical models.

There are, moreover, additional grounds on which Marcuse's underlying Freudian assumptions are questionable, at least in the form in which they are found in his argument. Yet a more adequate reformulation of Freud's case will undermine its use for the purpose that Marcuse intends. There is, as we shall now see, a case to be made that in its present form Freudian assumptions do not satisfy the fundamental conditions that, we have argued, are required for an adequate, rule-following model of human action. Yet it was our break with behaviouristic rule-conformities that was the point of departure for our present quest, since an adequate rule-following model was precisely what we were lead to believe to be on offer, first in a classical and then in a phenomenological Marxist account. We saw that classical Marxism in the dialectic only appeared to be offering a rule-following account. Human action appeared rational, but in fact was determined by a heteronomous rationality embodied in the development of both physical and social matter, which paradoxically made more sense in Hegel where the dialectic was conceived of as spiritual rather than as material. But far from Freud's model providing any real remedy for this inadequacy, he merely perpetuates it. It has often been pointed out in the literature that

Freud represents a putatively causal and mechanistic account which is nevertheless vitiated by a deep-seated anthropomorphism (Nagel, 1974). The id, ego and super-ego are supposed to be mechanisms that interact, check each other, achieve equilibrium among other things, but which are then quite inconsistently described as behaving as if they were persons. The id 'demands satisfaction' from the ego, it seeks to 'overwhelm' the ego with its libidinous 'desires'. The ego acts like a person acts when its actions are described by such verbs as 'restrains', 'represses', 'sublimates'. Although quite frequently 'sublimation' is described as a 'mechanism', its functions are characterised in terms of rule-following activity such as 'coming to terms with', 'seeking a socially acceptable channel'. Now, if Freud regards such concepts as logically necessary to his thesis, that is to say, devoid of what he intends his thesis to mean if its mentalistic terms are rewritten in physicalistic ones, then it is his language of mechanisms that requires writing out. Such seems to have been his position by contrast with an earlier view from 1895 onwards (Freud and Breuer, 1974, p. 302). But if we regard rather his mentalistic language as a poor substitute for some future physicalistic retranslation, then we find ourselves retreating back once again to behaviourism. Freud therefore did well to abandon his earlier view, which saw rule-following language as conceptually inferior to rule-conforming language, but finds its use an unfortunate necessity given the present state of the theory. He would far better have sought an adequate rule-following, mentalistic model devoid of physicalist elements that render such an account incoherent. Thus we return to the very criticism of Freud first mooted at the beginning of our discussion (Section 5.5 above), that his faithfulness to his ultimate materialism reduces him to the inconsistent position of both needing and not needing to reduce rule-conforming aspects of his account to rule-following ones. We shall subsequently see precisely what must be preserved if his account is rewritten in consistently rule-following terms by considering a second problem raised by his thesis.

A further problem is raised by the notion of unconscious ideas, reasons, items of knowledge and so forth, the unconscious nature of which is fundamental to the Freudian framework. Now, at first sight, these notions too raise conceptual problems. To what extent does it make sense to speak of having a reason for doing something of which I am not conscious? If I have a reason for doing something, I must be conscious of the reason otherwise I cannot be said to do it *for* that reason. Furthermore, if I do something because I want or desire it, surely I must be conscious of wanting or desiring it. I may try to disguise the fact from you, but I must surely be myself conscious of why I am so acting. Without being conscious of wanting or desiring something, I would not exhibit the actions that flow from that consciousness. Sometimes such conceptual problems are argued as a pretext for the acceptance of a behaviourist reduction of unconscious ideas or knowledge in the following way. It is argued that it makes far more sense interpreting conscious knowledge as knowledge-that performances, while other kinds of so-called 'unconscious' knowledge are rather dispositions to behave in certain ways that are activated under the right stimulating conditions. Sometimes, moreover, this denial of unconscious ideas of knowledge assumes the principle that we shall be criticising in far more detail in Chapter 8, namely, the principle of Harman's Fork, which states that all knowledge was either conscious knowledge-that or knowledge-how which involved no rule-following activity at all. Thus in the light of such conceptual problems it is assumed that descriptions of unconscious reasons, desires, knowledge and so on are but obscure ways of describing the causes of behaviour in terms of physiological or behaviourist psychological events such as drives, dispositions, propensities to respond to stimuli. Thus we would be forced by such conceptual problems to take the road to a complete reduction of Freudian perspectives to behaviourist ones. Breuer's description sometimes lends itself to such a reinterpretation, as when he says:

Thus there seems to be no theoretical difficulty in also recognizing unconscious ideas as causes of pathological phenomena. But if we go into the matter more closely we come upon other difficulties. As a rule, when the intensity of an unconscious idea increases it enters consciousness *ipso facto*. Only when its intensity is slight does it remain unconscious. What seems hard to understand is how an idea can be sufficiently intense to provoke a lively motor act, for instance, and at the same time not intense enough to become conscious. (Freud and Breuer, 1974, p. 302)

In distinguishing in this passage conscious from unconscious ideas purely in terms of degrees of intensity than can be causally increased or decreased ('to provoke a lively motor act'), Breuer has paved the way for a behaviourist reduction. If, however, the behaviourist reduction is carried out purely on the grounds of the conceptual difficulties of qualifying 'idea', 'knowledge', 'desire' with the adjective 'unconscious', then the resulting account is subject to all those difficulties which we have demonstrated beset behaviourist accounts in general. Conceptual inadequacy in one area is not remedied by adopting conceptual inadequacies in others. Moreover, it denies Freud's contribution to an understanding of human action in rule-following terms for which we shall argue in Chapter 8, namely, a conceptually viable account of unconscious rule-following, knowledge-that claims as a category quite distinct from conscious knowledge-that and knowledge-how that is unconscious of any underlying rule-structure.

Suppose, then, we were to take the alternative route and, instead of reducing the rule-following features of Freud's account to rule-conformities, we were rather to endeavour to write out the rule-conformities with rule-following features. Suppose that, instead of trying to redescribe the functions of the id, ego and super-ego in causal and mechanical terms, we were to emphasise their rule-following aspects to the extent that we ceased to regard them as mechanisms at all. How would such an account read? Though the answer to this question will be more fully set out and argued in Chapter 8, to conclude this section on a positive note, our account briefly and in summary form might read as follows. What Freud describes as 'traumatic experiences' are really fundamental pieces of mislearning. Such pieces of mislearning are fundamental since they occur early in life and are deeply embedded in a person's overall conceptual structure so that their effect is to distort that structure overall. Learning as opposed to conditioning we have argued (Chapter 4) to be irreducibly rule-following. That learning is of a piece with human action in general we have thus argued to be attested to by a profound analysis of what is implied both syntactically and semantically by truth-assertive languages which we have shown to be inexplicable in terms of rule-conformities. But because the concept of being able to follow a rule also, as we argued, implies being able either consciously to break it or mistakenly to apply it, people do come to wrong conclusions, form incoherent concepts and so forth. Freud, while trying to construct, we believe, a consistent rule-following model, could not accept that such an account of mistakes constituted a genuine explanation. But this was because, as we have also seen, his fundamental assumptions were constituted by an empiricist philosophy of science abstracted from a Newtonian, causal paradigm, as they were also on either a Marxist or a neo-Marxist view of social science. But, as we saw (Chapter 3), such mistakes, slips or aberrances are admissible within an Einsteinian universe, and are even able to be quantified in terms of statistical probability which, founded on randomness, by definition imply the acceptance of exceptions to general tendencies. We have further argued against Quine that, in terms of descriptions of categories of human action, such statistical quantifications are mere redescriptions of people making mistakes, slips, aberrances masquerading as explanations. Their proper explanation is rather of a piece with the detailed analysis of the concept of rule-following irreducible to causal categories. That is why we have argued that the language of choice, intention, necessity and so on is not only far richer in descriptive terms but also points through its analysis to those far richer explanations, such as those proposed by Chomsky on the one hand and modal logicians on the other (Katz, 1979). Mistakes, therefore, on a consistently rule-following reformulation of the Freudian model would not be admissable as items for causal explanation.

When people consciously break a rule or mistakenly apply it on the outer edges of their conceptual structure, no great harm is necessarily done since either self-correction or correction by others is relatively straightforward. But when such mistakes or failures to apply rules occur in more central cases to a person's overall developing conceptual structure, then distortions permeate the structure as a whole and reality is distorted. Hence the appropriate rule-following version of Anna's squint, where her squinting at a particular hour in response to her dying father's question about the time might be construed as a continued misapplication of rules of meaning and action in which what is appropriate to one situation or context has been generalised over a series of situations or contexts. Another example is of an adolescent who displays hostility towards all women because one particular woman, his mother, battered him as a child. It does not follow, however, that because one particular woman battered him, therefore all women wished to do so. Thus the breaking of rules of inference at a fundamental level in his conceptual structure has lead to a distorted view of reality. Such a distorted view is, moreover, affectively charged and appropriate emotional responses have been redirected at inappropriate persons (Wilson, 1970). The correction of such fundamental as opposed to peripheral pieces of mislearning requires unpacking a large number of false premises, inferences and deductions made from combinations of them, but such is how the role of the dialogue between the patient and his analyst is to be understood.

But, it may be objected, how can such an account do justice to Freud's appeal to the phenomenon of mental blockage, which surely requires a causal and mechanistic explanation if Freud's account is to make any original contribution to explaining human action? After all, 'Anna O.' or our teenager with a history of battering as a baby were both unable to recall the deductions, implications and applications of the rules that, on this restatement of the theory, they must have mistakenly made. In this respect we have so far perhaps misleadingly talked of rule-following as implying that people '*consciously* break a rule or mistakenly apply it'. In answer to this objection, we may say that a rule-following model of human action requires a concept of tacit or implicit knowledge of fundamental applications, deductions and inferences, since the span of memory in human beings is both severely limited and one-dimensional. The rule-following counterpart of causal repression in our reformulated Freudian model will be the logical fact that we cannot think of two or more statements together and at the same time. Note that this is a logical and not simply an empirical impossibility. Were we to try to devise empirical counter-examples in terms of surgery which divided the brain in two, with corresponding examples of double vision and double thinking, our attempt would founder on the concept of a person and personal identity (Bennett, 1974, pp. 85–92). The logical, rule-following counterpart to causal forgetting is, therefore, the logical fact that we cannot think of the premises of an argument at the same time as we think of the conclusion. In a deductive argument, thinking a major premise at t_1 and a minor premise at t_2 logically entails us thinking the conclusion at t_3. But we are not thinking of all three propositions (major, minor, conclusion) at the same time. If we did so, then it would be impossible to 'think' at all since we could not move forwards from premises to conclusions and back again, when we so desired, to check the premises and so forth.

Knowledge of the premises, their logical relations supporting inferences and deductions and so on may therefore be said to be 'implicit', 'tacit' or 'unconscious' when all that is conscious, explicit or open is knowledge of the conclusions. To deny that we have unconscious knowledge in this sense would be *ipso facto* to deny that our conscious knowledge of the conclusion is 'knowledge' at all, since what would count as evidence justifying such knowledge would not be consciously available. Now, a further point follows from this. We are not able to recall consciously all the conclusions and their premises at one and the same time out of which our world view is constructed and which, by acting as new premises yielding new conclusions, condition the growth and development further of that world view. Were we to begin suddenly to try to question every conclusion by working back to every premise, find that the premise itself was the conclusion to some further argument, work back to its premises and so on, then our inquiry about the world and ourselves would come to a full stop. A project of pure inquiry, like that of Descartes, or an investigation of linguistic universals, like that of Chomsky, is a once-in-a-lifetime's affair executed to ensure that what ourselves or others know and say is founded upon justifiable foundations. But so, too, is the work of the analyst as therapist hopefully a once-in-a-lifetime's affair as far as the individual patient is concerned. 'Anna O.'s' and the teenage woman-hater's distorted reasons for action, once consciously applied but now unconscious, are not therefore such because they are the result of a causally defined repression. They are to be described as unconscious but not forgotten as distant premises are unconscious but influential in producing the latest propositions in our inquiry both about the world and ourselves, and the correction of such distortions at a fundamental level are no less painful.

Thus we see in general terms where the positive reconstruction of the Freudian model will lead us in our subsequent chapters. We must now break off from this argument to demonstrate how these two general Marxist models and their associated fallacies have generated specific curriculum proposals.

Chapter 6

Classical and Phenomenologist Marxist Pedagogy

In our last chapter we had begun to preview the positive, rule-following model that we shall be discussing in further detail in our subsequent chapters. We must, however, at this point break off to turn our attention to the way in which both the classical and phenomenological Marxian models that we have discussed and criticised have generated radical proposals for educational reform. Our argument is that those defects that we have exposed both in the classical and phenomenological Marxist models will also be present in such educational proposals generated by such models. Thus we shall find Freudian reformulations of the concept of oppression that ought not, given the theory's point of departure, to require reference to some extra-social, dialectically unfolding reality, and yet such proposals have finally and inconsistently to make reference to such a reality in order to support their case. We shall find, moreover, phenomenological reinterpretations of the classical Marxist critique of education executed under pressure of argument for a rational, rule-following version of the 'liberated' curriculum placed inconsistently within a framework of causal, rule-conforming statements presupposing the inescapable determination of historical development. To this task, therefore, we must now turn.

6.1 GENERAL FEATURES OF A MARXIST CRITIQUE OF SCHOOLING

At the close of Section 5.1 we looked briefly at four general features of the radical, Marxist critique of the contemporary curriculum. These may be summarised as (*a*) no alienating competition in the classroom; (*b*) group work that produces equality and not individual work that produces elitism; (*c*) teachers should not impose values critically related to a class view or interest unreflectively adopted by them so that they become agents of class oppression; and (*d*) knowledge partitioned into subjects reflects social hierarchies and thus reinforces oppression. In the light of our detailed discussion of general theoretical models of explanation, it will be our purpose here to discuss more formally and in detail than we did in Chapter 5 the general pedagogical approach of Marxist critics of school curricula.

We shall follow up our general description and criticism in this section with three specific areas which exemplify Marxist approaches: namely, language teaching (6.2), science curricula (6.3) and English teaching (6.4).

Regarding, therefore, our four features (a), (b), (c) and (d), it will be seen from our discussion of general theoretical Marxist frameworks that these specifically educational features are not in fact generated by a unified model. Rather (a) and (b) are generated by the classical model, (d) by the phenomenological model, with (c) being ambiguous as between the two and for reasons with which we are now to deal. Let us reflect for a moment as to why it is the case that these four educational statements reflect their theoretical parentage's fundamental incoherence. Features (a) and (b) were the demands for the reduction of individual competition and emphasis upon the success of a group learning unit to which each individual child's different contribution was seen by the children themselves to be of importance. The emphasis on such group work, therefore, was designed to prevent, on the one hand, alienation in the form of individuals who, because they were categorised as below average, reacted in frustration against the system from which such acts of categorisation had alienated them. Accordingly, they began to fail tests deliberately and refused to fulfil their maximum potential on the grounds that this was a race that they could never win, with the result that the actions of the categorisers became not true predictions but prophecies that were self-fulfilling. On the other hand, the class organised on the basis of group learning units became the albeit embryonic foreshadowing of a new society based upon co-operation and mutual respect rather than upon conflict. As such, of course, criticisms embodied in (a) and (b) are not exclusively Marxist and could equally well be generated on the basis of a liberal-democratic, consensus model of society. Indeed, they were part of the general, social-democratic programme of comprehensive reorganisation of British secondary reorganisation in the late 1950s and early 1960s. It was not so much according to this view that competition per se was wrong, but a particular pathological ('alienating') form of competition reflected specifically in such practices as the 11+ and competence and attainment testing at that age. After all, countries with a variety of social systems have sporting competitions and all human groups appear to include among their social practices less formal but none the less ritual performances whose outcome is indeterminate. Now, sport can be argued to be a paradigm of healthy competition, with an intrinsic value for all participants. Even if, for example, we play squash and we find ourselves forever at the bottom of the ladder and playing reserve in the lowest grade, nevertheless we benefit since we keep ourselves exercised and healthy. Furthermore, in sports, competition stimulates us to try harder, to practise more diligently, to run harder, to return shots from more difficult balls, even though we lose. To that extent competition makes us physically more healthy. Moreover, the team effort reduces alienation since, in a tight-fought match, even a single game won by a poor player who will otherwise lose can make the difference between the team's victory or defeat. Unfortunately, however, the sporting analogy, although frequently pressed over a long history of its use in educational debate, does not transfer accurately to performance in academic subjects. The effect of self-fulfilling prophecies evidenced both in the old 11+ and its effects of streaming demonstrated that competition at least of an individual kind had not helped the academically weaker to grow stronger or even keep what they had achieved up to par but rather the reverse. Either what was supposed to be genetically determined I.Q. scores fixed for life showed more divergence between grammar and secondary-modern pupils at the age of 16 than at the age of 11; or instead, 'A'-stream secondary-modern pupils performed greatly in excess of 'C'-stream grammar-school pupils even though they had begun by being ranked below them.

However, as we have said, the prescription to set rather than stream and to favour group rather than individual competition in the classroom are not prescriptions necessarily generated only by Marxist models and no others. In fact, liberal democrats can and did share with the Marxists moral qualms about the debilitating (or 'alienating') effect of setting or streaming. But on classical Marxist presuppositions, the difference with the liberal democrat was over the ability of one kind of social structure rather than another to tolerate without being overthrown the changes that would remedy the situation. The aims and objectives of education were not considered problematic by the classical Marxist, but simply the social structure that hindered or promoted their realisation. Goals in the form of certain academic subjects to be pursued by students with various psychometrically quantifiable abilities that determined which group of subjects and at what level they ought to pursue them were unquestioned. The key to a student's educational success was seen to be the total reconstruction of the societal context of education, which enhanced the achievement of educational objectives for a few while holding back the many. Thus the problem stated in (*d*), namely, the creation of bodies of knowledge as a nomic or ordering force shaping a certain kind of society, was not a problem for classical Marxists. Nor, moreover, were the value-implicates so deeply entrenched within the structuring of school subjects as (*c*) suggests. For classical Marxism, it was simply a case of dispensing with religious instruction and removing capitalist propaganda from school history texts that good historians would wish to do anyway. False-consciousness would be removed simply by giving the working class the education denied to but a few.

Indeed, in a very recent work, Harris refers to the work of Bowles and Gintis in the following way, which reveals the continuance of the non-problematic acceptance of concepts of knowledge and evaluation of ability that phenomenologists would question:

> Bowles and Gintis demonstrate ... that education's role in increasing mental performance does not explain why people with higher education receive higher income. Now this is not to deny that education ... is not closely associated statistically with cognitive attainments; nor is it to deny that the more education one has, the better one's chance of economic success. What Bowles and Gintis challenge, however, is the *causal* relationship between the higher cognitive attainments of the more educated people and their better economic chances ... *only a very minor portion* of the substantial association between education and economic success can be accounted for by the school's role in producing or screening cognitive skills ... while increased income is related to years of education, it is related only tenuously ... to ability as indicated by I.Q.; and education really rewards children according to race, sex, personality characteristics, and especially social background. (Harris, 1979, pp. 145–6)

Here 'intelligence', 'ability', 'mental performance', 'cognitive styles' are taken to be what psychometric measurement says they are. If they are not true indicators of ability, then the moral protest of this quotation ('education really rewards children ... according to social background') loses its force, since one reason for advancement is just as badly founded as another. Thus, too, subjects such as maths, science or English (with the possible exception of history and religion) were what the experts in them defined them to be, and the notion of such 'experts' and 'definitions' was unproblematic. The intractable problem for capitalist society (but not for its Marxist alternative) was the problem of securing greater access to them for people whose measurable ability entitled them to such access. Such people were entitled to replace those mediocre people who were there at the top purely on the basis of 'social background' and on access to education disproportionate to their measurable ability. The problem was one of securing a society in which private ownership of capital was abolished and, as a result, the power to rig the system nepotistically so as to secure the promotion of the less able. The problem of alienation was therefore the problem of the 'bright' working-class child who was bound to be unrewarded commensurate with his ability under a capitalist system which maintained and would not give up without violent conflict the barriers of privilege. In a socialist society, just as in Eastern Europe today, there would exist a society as hierarchically organised as capitalism, but, in such a society, the most 'able', following the abolition of class interest based on the ownership of capital, would rule in the place of privileged mediocrity, psychometrically defined, as at present. Only the abolition of private capital would produce such a change, particularly in education, where private schools with direct and discrete links with prestigious universities make money the key to acquiring jobs to which such an education is a passport. With the abolition of private capital would therefore come genuine equality of opportunity, and only in such a social setting would 'bright' working-class children and children of minorities be motivated to rise commensurate with their true ability.

The classical Marxist model therefore leaves definitions of bodies of knowledge and the abilities needed to acquire them and to what level as unproblematic givens. So much is, on the classical model, the problem one of structural barriers of class and wealth that cannot be broken without conflict that, in a socialist society like the DDR (East Germany) today, quite rigid streaming and selection from the age of 7 can go on and still be consistent with standards of equality. As such, the practices as opposed to the theories of classical Marxist educators were far more reconcilable with those of their social-democratic opponents than are the educational practices of phenomenological Marxists in the free-school movement. The educational ends of both classical Marxists and social democrats were identical, and what they differed over were the means by which these ends were to be achieved. The social democrat, believing in the possibility of rational change through parliamentary and general societal consensus, disagreed that only both a violent overthrow of established society and the illiberal apparatus of a totalitarian state were required to achieve educational ends as part of general political ends. But with the breakdown of the classical and the rise of the phenomenological model, the possibility of a *modus vivendi* based upon a practical consensus between mutually exclusive philosophies has come to an end, and for reasons that we must now make clear.

Where the phenomenological Marxist in education would take issue with his classical colleague is over features (*c*) and (*d*) of his practical approach. The classical Marxist considered that teacher-values (*c*), except those emanating from what was almost self-evidently capitalist propaganda, were accepted as unalterably given, as was the subject organisation of school subjects (*d*). However, the phenomenological Marxist argues that, to the contrary, both reflect deep-seated, ideological (= 'reality-distorting') structures that perpetuate and reinforce oppression. Remember what we said earlier about the phenomenological approach. The phenomenologist regards the significance of bodies of knowledge, standards and values as in every case socially constructed, the real purpose of which is to sustain social orders and by implication the interest groups that these favour. To regard these as unalterably given, as did the classical Marxist, was to fall victim to the illusions created by mechanisms of reification and false-consciousness that reference was being made to some extra-social natural or supernatural order of things as the anchor of objectivity. As Esland says:

> Thus, the naming which confirms the separation between zones of knowledge in a curriculum – called 'subjects' or 'projects' – is thought to represent certain ontologies, essences of human experience ... which can be considered to have meaning other than in the minds of the individuals in which they are constituted, irrespective of their human realisation ... The individual consciousness recognises objects as being 'out there', as coercive, external realities ... Knowledge is thereby detached from the human subjectivity in which it is constituted, maintained, and transformed. (Esland, 1971, p. 75)

Now we should note carefully what it is that Esland is arguing here. There is a distinction to be made between the meaning of a proposition and its truth, however much we might agree that the empiricists over-simplified the basis of this distinction. There is therefore a sense in which a proposition can be 'considered to have meaning' 'in the minds of individuals', but which is nevertheless untrue. Since 'knowledge', albeit 'knowledge in a curriculum – called "subjects" or "projects"', is conceptually tied to 'truth' (to 'know' x when x is untrue as opposed to knowing that x is untrue is self-contradictory), one cannot claim to know a proposition and also to know that it is false. For example, the proposition, 'Jimmy Carter won the 1980 Presidential Election', has meaning but is false, so that although it has meaning it cannot constitute knowledge. Yet Esland in this passage denies this distinction. Esland denies that knowledge of what is true is about recognition of 'objects as being "out-there" as coercive, external realities'. He then makes from what we admit arguably to be the case the false conclusion that knowledge exists only 'in the minds of individuals ... in the human subjectivity in which it is constituted'. There is, after all, at least a case to be answered that, although external reality is not directly accessible to us, there are nevertheless invariant and formal categories pertaining cross-culturally over human languages in terms of which any human construction of reality will process data about the world and man's activities within it. The rule-following nature of the processing admits and requires that some errors can be made, for reasons that we have already argued, and such errors may account for what has meaning for some groups of individuals but which nevertheless is untrue since rules have been only partially followed. But Esland does not consider such an alternative to empiricism and, in this passage, espouses relativism as the only alternative. Esland is thus in this passage adopting an extreme relativist position. Now, an extreme relativist might argue that we are deceived if we claim that the set of meanings comprised in the proposition, 'Reagan won the 1980 Presidential Election', were superior to the set of meanings comprised in the proposition, 'Carter won the 1980 Presidential Election'. But such a superiority could not rest upon a correspondence between the first sets of meanings (about Reagan) on the grounds that there corresponded to them, unlike the second set (about Carter), 'objects as being "out-there" as coercive, external realities'. As we have seen, such a view represented, among other things, a naïve, empiricist view of perception that foundered upon examples of cross-cultural differences over colour words and snow words (Chapter 2). Now, an extreme relativist might argue, as Esland appears to do in this passage, that, in the light of such considerations, 'Reagan won the 1980 Presidential Election' is a set of meanings existing 'in the minds of individuals' with no more claim to be superior to its negation existing in the minds of other individuals. It is conceivable that there could be a group of individuals with other and contradictory sets of meanings in accordance with which Carter was victorious, that those who assert Reagan to have won have been deceived by a massive media conspiracy, and who would be able to dispose of the significance of contradictory sets of meanings in the light of their own presuppositions. The strength of our belief in our own set of shared meanings about Reagan's victory would originate, on such a view, purely from massive and 'coercive' group pressure rather than from any external reality the conformity of our propositions with which shows us to be right. Group pressure might equally well have confirmed that Carter was the victor, especially if he had had the personal charisma of a film-star such as James Dean and had perhaps met his death.

But we have already argued that such an extreme relativism is destructive to any form of a Marxist case, just as we argued it to have been to Quine's version of empiricism (Chapter 3). This being the case, Esland's relativism, exemplified in this passage, would destroy the thrust of his attack on the subject-centred curriculum and contemporary methods of testing ability and evaluating achievement. If all bodies of knowledge are relative to social relations that fortuitously spring up and disintegrate as a result of historical and environmental accidents, then there are no permanent epistemological norms and values. Esland quotes Wright Mills with approval as supporting his position that 'norms of truth change' when Mills said:

'Criteria, or observational and verificatory models are not transcendental. There have been, and are, diverse canons and criteria of validity and truth, and these criteria, upon which determination of the truthfulness of propositions at any time depend, are themselves, in their persistence and change, open to socio-historical relativization.' (Quoted in Esland, 1971, p. 77)

But if all bodies of knowledge – whose real purpose, according to the theory, is to order social relationships – are socially relative, then, as Esland's argument so far stands, one framework of judgement becomes as good as another since there is no common framework in the light of which rival frameworks can be judged in such a way that those committed to any alternative framework would find plausible. Teachers could therefore, in strict consistency with such an argument, argue that it did not matter that their particular frame of reference with its in-built values and so forth was imposed by them upon children since any social order requires structure and such structuring requires reification.

Esland might, however, at this point protest:

Through the procedures of psychological testing and school evaluation, the pupil and the curriculum have been reified. 'Bodies of knowledge' are presented for the child to learn and reproduce according to specified objective criteria. (Esland, 1971, p. 75)

But it might be objected that, according to phenomenologist sociology, this is how any social enterprise, even a Marxist one, must proceed. We cannot on such a view judge one socially created reality against another, since this would simply involve us in leaving one social reality and inhabiting another as a result of a conversion experience for which no reasons could be given other than such as would appeal to the already committed. Granted, therefore, that any social enterprise, whether of society at large or the sum total of institutionalised educational activities within it, requires some kind of order, authority or structure, by what right can Esland claim that the existing structure ought to be relativised and questioned? By what right can he claim that children *ought not* to be 'introduced to the "mapped-out" theoretical zones of knowledge called "subjects"'. If 'nomizing' and 'stabilizing' nascent social constructions of reality are what 'reification', 'false-consciousness', 'nihilation' etc. are concerned with, without such strategies it might be argued the alternative would be chaos and anarchy (Brent, 1978, pp. 186–90 ff.). Chaos and anarchy, moreover, in the classroom are, according to opponents of radical curriculum reformulation, precisely what the outcome of 'relativising' and 'de-reification' of the curriculum will be. Any order is better than one, as a cynic might have wryly concluded about the White Lion Free School which formed the basis for our 'typical characterisation' (in Section 5.1), where an examination of what was finally actually done revealed some very traditional curriculum materials, methods and procedures of evaluation. As a result, we are left with the question that, if such traditional organisations of knowledge and evaluation are wrong because they sustain one kind of social order, what kinds of knowledge and processes of transmission and evaluation would be right because they reflected what kind of alternative social order?

Esland, in order to answer these questions, needs, like any other Marxist, to incorporate, define and justify a dialectical theory of historical development. Only if we can be guaranteed that our antithetical opposition to the thesis that is the established curriculum will, by a developmental process that is rational, lead to a new and creative synthesis can the possibility of chaos be disregarded. If historical development does not possess such a character, then the Marxist critique and proposals lack a satisfactory basis. Certainly Esland is aware of the dialectical dimensions of Marxist theory in such passages as:

> The epistemological sufficiency of objectivism is directly challenged by the sociology of knowledge, which insists that man is seen as existentially related to his social structure. The essential feature of this tradition, which derives from Hegel's *Phenomenology of Spirit*, and the *Economic and Philosophic Manuscripts* of 1844 by Marx, is that human sociation is a dialectic phenomenon. (Esland, 1971, p. 77)

But unlike Marcuse, of whose work Esland shows no evidence of making use, he seems unaware of the very great difference that a phenomenological approach must make for the classical Marxian understanding of the dialectic, as we sought to bring out in our discussion of Marcuse. 'Human sociation' was for classical Marx a 'dialectical phenomenon' because it involved an interchange between men in society and an external reality beyond society determining historical change and unfolding dialectically. But Esland has not grasped that, once he adopts a phenomenological position, that dialectic becomes problematic and cannot simply be reintroduced without further discussion with such words as: 'The tensions of consciousness are not autonomous, but react dialectically with each other' (Esland, 1971, p. 83). It must, however, be admitted that although a Freudian interpretation of oppression in Marx might have made his account far more sophisticated, the Marcusan road would finally have lead him into a final and unnegotiable impasse. Without reference to certain invariant and categorical norms (which Esland has already denied in his quote from Mills to be possible), even Marcuse's reformulated Freudian account of the dialectic collapses into incoherence. The difference between what is true and how men may sometimes construct accounts of that truth once more intervenes. Esland, while happy most of the time to speak of the 'creation' rather than of the 'discovery' of knowledge, nevertheless lapses into occasional acknowledgements of extra-linguistic reality, presumably from his classical Marxist heritage. For example, at one point he says:

> It will be argued that occupational perspectives derive *much of* their cognitive support from institutionalized world views reinforced by the rituals of membership and orthodoxy, and the strategies of loyalty maintenance. (Esland, 1971, p. 73)

Had he been true to his phenomenological assumptions, he would have had to say that 'occupational perspectives derive *all of* their cognitive support' from such sources.

Finally, when discussing the hereditary *versus* environment debate over IQ, Esland relapses, as we saw that Marcuse did, into a causal and deterministic account of an unfolding reality, out-there, determining albeit mysteriously and in a way that is apparently beyond definition the course of human history beyond the control of individuals. Both teachers who argue that children fail because they lack inherited genetically IQ and those who argue that intelligence fails to surface purely because of social background are, according to Esland, influenced by the same erroneous paradigm that sees IQ there in the nature of human beings. Both are under the erroneous influence of an ideology of the employing interest group whose criteria for intelligence is piecemeal problem-solving in the workplace and obedience and application of previously laid-down rules.

But the questioning of such a framework, the discovery of its failure to answer all the problems of why children fail, are according to Esland to be explained as follows:

> It could be argued that we are witnessing the anomie, that is, the denomization, or conceptual dismantling, which accompanies the break-up of a paradigm. One of the features of this process, Kuhn has argued, is that certainties become opaque and are seen as relative socio-cultural productions. Reifications are dereified, and alienation gives way to anomie. (Esland, 1971, p. 93)

Note that the 'conceptual dismantling' '*accompanies* the break-up of a paradigm', rather than, as a phenomenologist thesis clearly requires, 'constitutes' such a break-up. To say that conceptual dismantling would constitute the break-up clearly implies that paradigms can be put together or taken apart according to human choice or decision. Yet, true to the classical Marxism that we have seen to be in this critical respect clearly irreformable by a Marcuse, yet alone an Esland, historical development must be, like natural development, irreversible and causal. And as such an extra-linguistic natural order of things, in the last analysis, clearly protrudes despite all obfuscations to the contrary.

We thus see that, in a general Marxist phenomenological approach to the curriculum such as that we have exemplified in Esland's work, the deep-seated problems destructive of the classical Marxist model, when reformulated in phenomenological terms that are intended to rehabilitate them, recur once again in new forms which vitiate both the consistency of the new reformulation as well as its adequacy. Yet we saw that on the success of that phenomenological reformulation hinged the possibility that the proponents of radical curricular reorganisation might be able to give us a genuine rule-following model for making curriculum decisions which would nevertheless still justify the use of such mechanical and causal expressions as 'reify', 'oppress', 'conflict', 'break-up', 'alienate' or 'repress'. It is, however, on the basis of the justification of such expressions that the justifiability rests both of the Marxist moral protest and the morality of his remedy. Let us, however, pursue our critique into a more circumscribed area, namely, that of the radical attack on the science curriculum and its teaching, to see whether and in what form our criticisms would apply there also.

6.2 YOUNG'S CRITIQUE OF THE SCHOOLING OF SCIENCE

The drift away from science has been well-documented, and its effects are alarming not only to capitalist society but also to M. F. D. Young (1976, p. 47). One explanation could be that teachers are failing with a subject that is difficult in comparison with others to be sufficiently strict about indiscipline and sufficiently demanding over what their pupils could attain were such pupils to overcome their laziness. Young, however, rejects such a moralistic account of the origins of the drift away from science. The real origins of such a drift Young locates in the character of a capitalist society that, as part of its dominative process, has to deprive ('alienate') the mass of the population of power over their lives and conditions. In this particular instance, the 'power' is that of scientific knowledge to transform both conditions and social relations in their place of work. Young cites as an example a PVC factory where workers were exposed to a carcinogenous substance:

> The health of the PVC workers has in this case become a trades union issue . . . However, the unions face certain problems which take us back to the failure of science education for all but the specialist few. Lacking knowledge of the physiological processes involved, of the technology of a plant they had no part in designing, and in particular, the technology of very accurate detectors no one had yet designed, they remained largely dependent on experts. (Young, 1976, p. 52)

As it happens, the unions concerned in Young's example did achieve access to the scientific information required to make their case via a specialist group of radical scientists with a mission to expose what they saw as the evils of capitalism. Young, however, apparently finds a society which makes room for such individual groups of experts opposed to predominant economic thinking that disregards workers' health to whom the unions can turn as nevertheless not really satisfactory. Such a solution perpetuates, he would argue, the predominant elitism, and is reminiscent of theoretical Eastern European solutions that may not, in fact, pertain in practice. Any form of elitism involves the domination of the workers and their failure to achieve liberation. And it is at this point that Young's phenomenological as opposed to classical Marxist assumptions begin to emerge. If the workers have access to rival expert groups that share their distrust of their employers and are able to thwart their wishes with their aid, why cannot this be regarded as a process of liberation? Looked at from a structural and mechanical perspective such as that of classical Marxism, when forces that normally oppress workers have failed to be effective, then *ipso facto* liberation must be taking place. That Young denies this reveals an implicit rejection of the causal and mechanical classical Marxist model. Young's focus when employing the concept of 'liberation' is a phenomenological focus in terms of 'things as they appear and therefore are' to those who are to be liberated. As such, 'liberation' is primarily a mental and social psychological phenomenon and cannot result while the workers still feel powerless because they are conscious of not having access to certain knowledge and of therefore still being dependent upon experts, however sympathetic to their cause. Thus, at the heart of Young's critique of schooling, there will be an almost Marcusan, mental-health interpretation of liberation.

Young's charge, which thus carries over into an educational context, is that science teaching is removed ('alienated') from pupils' problems because it is taught as a body of facts detached from those problems and not as a set of specifically social practices. Young therefore endeavours to analyse the social structure of schooling in which such an alleged distortion of the real nature of science takes place. Young sees this distortion as arising out of the hierarchical organisation of the practice of science with ever-increasing levels of experts and expertise as one ascends to the pinnacle of the hierarchy. The 'good' scientist becomes the 'pure' scientist, whose excellence in the disinterested pursuit of truth is evidenced by his ability to get research papers published in successive journals referenced internationally by esteemed workers in his field. Servicing this hierarchy and legitimating its structure is the science curriculum in which pupils are selected and re-selected by means of competitive examinations. Thus the impression is created that science should be and can only really be practised by elite groups. As Young says:

> It is only in the academy that so called 'pure' science is practised, and even there the claim of 'pure' science as disinterested has little foundation as university departments compete for a more generous allocation of government or business funds. (Young, 1976, p. 50)

Moreover, the organisation of science in the academy reflects historical attitudes and traditions emanating from the nineteenth century and not corresponding to anything implicit in the nature of scientific inquiry itself.

Moreover, such a historical tradition is exposed by Layton, whom Young quotes with approval in the words:

> The purpose of introducing science into the secondary schools was never in doubt to such leading advocates as H. E. Roscoe, the first president of the Association of Public School Science Masters (the precursor of our Association for Science Education); school

science was, for Roscoe, as Layton quotes him, to be 'the means of sifting out from the great mass of the people those golden grains of genius which now are too often lost amongst the sands of mediocrity'. (Young, 1976, p. 48)

But in this process of 'sifting the golden grains of genius', the mass of the pupils, charges Young, are 'alienated' from learning science when they begin to see that they are by slow degrees being excluded from that select group of sufficiently small numbers of academic paper writers to sustain the economic organisation of paper publishing. It is, after all, only possible to have so many writers when to publish profitably you require, say, 3,000 readers. But what is critical for Young's charge is that this process is wrong, is, in other words, 'alienating', as opposed to the way in which a healthy society becomes more functionally differentiated on the basis of the division of labour. Perhaps, for example, 'golden grains of genius' was but a perverse way of describing such a division of labour with its implication that only those at the top were truly valuable. What Young means by 'alienation' therefore becomes critical for his case. Young uses 'alienation' in two senses, namely:

(*a*) 'Prevented from using the power that science gives people to influence or control their working conditions.'
(*b*) 'Being made psychologically adverse to pursuing a subject in which one's failure seems to have been largely predetermined.'

And in these two senses we find present, once again, the unsynthesised elements of two distinct versions of a Marxist model that we detected in our analysis of Esland's work.

We shall return to this critical theme in a moment. Let us, however, pursue for a moment a little further the substance of Young's elitist charge against the organisation of science education. Suppose that someone were to object that 'sifting out the golden grains of genius among the sands of mass-mediocrity' was simply a realistic reflection of the way things are and that bright paper readers were, in fact, our best scientists so that their publications justified their power and prestige in the hierarchy. There are a number of ways in which Young could reply to this retort, though not all of them are mutually consistent, namely:

(*a*) An elitist policy for science education is socially disfunctional. Where society increasingly requires at all levels men and women who can understand and apply science to social and economic problems, a system that 'turns-off' the majority from pursuing scientific knowledge is leading to a failure to attain important social and economic goals.

But Young's thesis is stronger than (*a*), which is simply an appeal to find ways of involving more people in scientific knowledge since any good capitalist would, for obvious reasons, wish for this. But neither is Young's protest simply one that demands an answer to 'for whose benefit ought science to be more widely understood and used?' Rather Young's argument is:

(*b*)   An elitist policy for science education is wrong because it distorts the character of scientific inquiry by making it consist of a fixed number of determinate categories and truths the degrees of possession of which determines which of the fixed and determinate places in the hierarchy a given scientist is to occupy.

As such, our critique of Skinner in our opening chapters (1–3) and the empiricist philosophy of science implied by the quest of an exhaustive quantification of curriculum objectives would be to some extent supportive of Young's critique. We would further agree that having come to the conclusion that, in the light of Einstein's revolution in theoretical physics, such a view of science rests upon a distortion of the nature of science. Young is therefore entitled to ask why such a distortion has come about. The distortion for Young is part of the false-consciousness generated by the ruling scientific establishment in order to maintain the hierarchy on top of which they are so commandingly placed. Exhaustive quantification of rules of scientific methodology and fundamental categories in science will prevent new creative thinking which challenges the original members of the elite because of the shortness of life and proneness to fatigue. If the target of Young's attack is an empiricist philosophy of science with its reality-distorting passion for exhaustive quantification and causal determinism which we have also demonstrated in the case of Bloom's taxonomy to have distorted the planning of curriculum objectives, then we should agree that:

The particular way in which science was established . . . was more concerned with the protection of a particular social order than opening up ways in which the natural world might be understood and transformed. (Young, 1976, p. 49)

But where, of course, we take issue with Young is over why 'the protection of a particular social order' is wrong. We accept, unlike

White and Cooper (below Chapter 10), that the particular social order is wrong on primarily epistemological grounds (such an order rests on a lie – a distortion of reality), and not on such ethical grounds as arguments over distributative justice. We do not regard the basis of the wrong as being on grounds of an infringement of canons of a dialectically understood transformation of reality, which, we are arguing, is an incoherent Marxist notion, whether in a classical or in a phenomenological form. Our argument is that it is reality-distorting because it violates what is continuous with a basic human community of judgement, reflected in the semantic structure common to all human languages, in terms of which, we believe, a basic and culturally transcendent form of human consciousness can be established. This is an argument that we have mooted in our earlier chapters (Chapters 2 and 3) as well as in an earlier book (Brent, 1978, pp. 196–202 ff.), and which we are to develop later in Chapter 8. For now, however, let us continue, so as to give detailed substantiation of our charge.

Young's argument about the way in which a 'particular social order' distorts reality is both dialectical and ambiguous. Sometimes he talks as if 'change' is part of the natural order of things, so that really 'change' can be equated with 'development' conceived in quasi-biological terms and applied to society. As he says:

A quite different notion of relevance might involve the project of discovering pupil relevancies, their theories of the natural world, which are ... potentially available. This is quite different from accepting pupils' 'theories' uncritically or assuming that all pupils are potential Einsteins, but it would involve transforming typical conceptions of a lesson and of teaching, and accepting an inbuilt unpredictability of outcomes through the following of pupil initiatives rather than attempting to guide pupils to fit in to the teacher's prior plan of the lesson. (Young, 1976, pp. 55–6)

Here both pupils and teachers are viewed as theory builders about the natural world so that they conjointly discover the nature of reality 'out there'. 'Outcomes' may be 'unpredictable', but they are discoveries beyond nature and beyond society. Yet such a view seems too close to that of a 'culture of positivism' which Young wishes to oppose. And so a classical Marxist dialectic element now finds its way into Young's argument. While theses and antitheses are separated and fail to interact, no true 'transformation' (by which Young appears to mean 'change' which is 'development' and therefore approved) can take place. So, too, individualistic, empiricist notions of science keep people apart, creative historical developments thus being retarded:

> School science, reflecting the individualism that is often seen as an inescapable part of scientific discovery, separates pupils from each other and any sense of link with others who have engaged in similar problems. Newton's laws of motion, for example, are learnt as disembodied 'facts' separated from their relation to Newton as a man who like ourselves lived at a specific time with all its conflicts and troubles. (Young, 1976, p. 56)

We see here once again that the Marxist can, because of his faith in the classical dialectic, be undisturbed by conflicting theory building in the classroom with unpredictable outcomes. Amid all conflict and chaos, a creative synthesis must be working itself out, and so such conflict and chaos can be welcomed. Scientific truth, moreover, is still, according to this passage, 'out there', for the quest for such truth can be still described as 'discover' as opposed to 'invention' or 'creation', although that process of discovery, being located in the material facts of man's nature, has the same dialectical form as any other development in the natural world.

At other times, however, as we have previously charged, Young eschews such an objectivist and classical model in statements that bear the contrary, relativist and phenomenological impress. According to such a thesis, what is wrong with traditional school science is not that it distorts the true nature of inquiry into an extra-social, extra-linguistic world. Rather does school science, as at present constituted, distort reality because it perpetuates that false-consciousness that there is some order of reality beyond the social construction of it by human beings in community. Commenting on a class that he had 'sat-in' on of which he found many things to praise, Young says:

> In a less rigidly authoritarian school structure, the teachers too would doubtless have been engaged in projects of their own. But then, to put it crudely, teachers are supposed to transmit the knowledge created elsewhere, not actually to *create* knowledge themselves. (Young, 1976, p. 58)

Moreover, that false-consciousness is to be understood in a phenomenological and not in a classical manner in Young's work, the following quotation appears to stress:

> What constitutes school science would, I suggest, be very different

if teachers were to see themselves *and* pupils as scientific theorists. It would be, if you like, an attempt to de-alienate scientific knowledge, to recognise that knowledge is inextricably linked to its production by people, in a political context, not only in the school, which is dominated by a 'culture of positivism' which locates knowing in methods, not persons. (Young, 1976, p. 56)

'Alienation' here has one of the severally mutually inconsistent senses with which Young uses it. Here it appears to mean 'making scientific knowledge *something other than it actually is*' through the mechanism of a phenomenological Marxist interpretation of false-consciousness which regards knowledge *created* by the social group as somehow *discovered* outside of it. But, at other times, Young, just as in the opening sentence of this passage, reverts to the classical Marxist notion that reality unfolding dialectically is 'out there', to be 'discovered' rather than 'created'. With the following sentence, Young makes a serious attempt to clarify and overcome the disjunction between two distinct sets of presuppositions:

This is not to deny the discoveries that have been made, but to state that the purposes that have given meaning to the scientists' pursuit of truth have been success in the sustaining of the scientific establishment. (Young, 1976, p. 59)

Thus it appears that Young is not critical about the epistemological basis of scientific knowledge itself, but simply the *use* to which such knowledge has been put in order to sustain social and political orders. Yet Young does not appear to have grasped how fundamentally inconsistent such a statement of his view is with the phenomenological strands of his argument. We began this section by showing that he was initially concerned to propound a far stronger thesis, namely, that it was not simply the use to which scientific knowledge was put that was suspect, but prevailing accounts of the epistemological structure of such knowledge itself, reflected as this is in proposals for school subjects. Ideology for Young was not simply the classic Marxist notion that made it descriptive of certain extra-scientific stories that had been told in order to legitimate the inequitable distribution of such knowledge. Rather, 'ideology' referred to the way in which understanding of the underlying structure of scientific knowledge itself was false and distorted reality. Certainly we saw that Young's original example of workers in a PVC factory implied as much, since such an example implicitly rejected an Eastern European solution in which, after the revolution, new groups of

Marxist experts will replace the capitalist ones on the pinnacle of some new, allegedly more justifiable hierarchy that could be said, in some meaningful sense, to 'liberate' the workers. 'Liberation', as with 'false-consciousness', was originally intended therefore to bear the weight of a consistently phenomenological reinterpretation.

We have mentioned, moreover, that Young's use of the concept of 'alienation' also reflects his adoption in an unsynthesised form of conflicting Marxist models. Alienation (*a*) was the claim that the teaching of science, in its present form, 'alienates' the majority of students because it deprives them of the power that science gives over nature that would enable them to control their own working practices and hence their own lives. We have interpreted Young as supporting such a view of alienation with a classical, objectivist dialectical argument. What produces this deprivation of power is the social organisation that separates 'pure' science and its practice from technology, thus preventing a creative and transforming synthesis. Whether they are subjectively conscious of this alienation or not, objectively it robs those who apply science at a technical level of the theoretical perspectives to transform their practice. We saw, however, that there was an alternative, subjectivist view of alienation. Alienation (*b*) makes 'alienation' refer essentially to the psychologically debilitating effect that the present hierarchical and elitist organisation of scientific knowledge has upon the majority of children in our schools. Furthermore, such a view of alienation in subjectivist terms is also supported in Young by means of a phenomenological critique of the reality-distorting character of such an organisation of scientific knowledge. Such a view makes the solution to psychological debilitation far more radical than that of a cosmetic operation that will leave the organisation of science intact while not making the majority feel so inferior with respect to it. There is, however, a problem of coherence between views of alienation (*a*) and (*b*) that might be reconciled in the following way, but which cannot, on Young's argument, in the final analysis be so reconciled, as we shall now show.

It might be thought that there is a simple solution to the problem of incoherence between the classical and phenomenological critique, which might be expressed as follows:

(*a*) and (*b*) are really equivalent views. There is sense in talking of a reality beyond linguistic criteria that express it in a social context. However, the character of that reality is so complex and dynamic that any system of human thinking about it will always be partial and provisional. If curriculum subjects transmit illusions of permanency about such systems of human thinking, then they both

distort human understanding *and* the reality that such understanding seeks to grasp.

On such a view, (*a*) and (*b*) might be reconciled on the grounds that
students' resentment against science is justifiable (that is, that it is
'alienation' rather than just plain jealousy which, if pursued, will rock
the boat for everyone, themselves included). They psychologically
feel alienation because their actual knowledge of reality makes reality
other than it actually is and is thus really 'alienated'. Because such
knowledge has been thus distorted, it becomes inaccessible for both
intellectual and psychological reasons, so that students become
powerless to control both their natural and social environments. If we
are not content, as is Young, simply to assert *that* school subjects such
as science represent a distortion of reality but wish to describe *how*, in
the case of science in particular, reality is distorted, our analysis in
our first three chapters will help, albeit at a price that we shall finally
argue that Young would be unprepared to pay. What is wrong
with rigidly hierarchical societies with clearly determinate classes of
individuals, exhaustively quantifiable, is what was wrong with a
description of the logic of classes as bound by a limited number of
particulars, whether in technical or scientific or in ordinary
languages. What is wrong, moreover, with an elitist view of scientific
knowledge is that it reflects a false, empiricist view of science. Science
is cut off from ordinary language and certain common-sense
experiencing of the world with which our non-empiricist interpretation of Einstein's revolution in physics has shown us to be in
reality continuous in a sense defined by Wittgenstein as family-
resemblance. In empiricist philosophy, and the structuring of both
school science and behaviourist psychology in accordance with its
paradigm, a distortion of the nature of human understanding of the
world has taken place with epistemological as well as traumatic and
psychological implications. After all, one of the distinctively rule-
following features of Freud's account that we wished to preserve
was one that pointed to the role of reality distortion is neurotic
illness.

If this were to have been the substance of Young's charge,
uncluttered by recourse to dialectical arguments that obscure rather
than further it, then it will be clear from the argument of our first
three chapters that we would have fully supported it on grounds of
strictly logical as opposed to Young's sociological analysis. But had
this been Young's case, then all that Young and others sometimes
wish to derive from it regarding the justifiability of any kind of
academic assessment simply cannot be made to follow. Suppose that
Young admits that man's natural and social worlds have forms that

are, in principle, objectively specifiable (albeit in terms not simply of raw observations but also of the forms given to such observations by basic categories of human experience). Suppose that he were to further admit that bodies of knowledge, socially constructed, only appear to constitute a state of permanent and fortuitous change over time because of psychological difficulties in comprehending every facet of reality. Suppose further he were to finally add that some bodies of knowledge are useful in leading to the control over nature in contrast to others in proportion to their representation of that reality in less distorted forms as opposed to simply being described as 'real' because they were more useful. In the light of such admissions as these, it follows that individual students can be categorised, graded and assessed to the degree in which they handle and process various kinds of data about the world and their place in it. Some kind of assessment can, given such admissions, be justified, though we would agree that the kind of assessment in Bloom's taxonomy would be ruled out, as would be the sort that finally came to be practised at the White Lion Free School, on which our typical characterisation (in Section 5.1) was based. Because fundamental classes in terms of which assessment categories are defined are open-class categories into which possible instances enter through identification by family-resemblance, it follows that categorisation of individual students into categories that register attainment of degrees of excellence can never be final. Academic structures must be open-ended and their member-ship open to continuous revision on a multi-faceted view of human competences, abilities, 'intelligence' and so on. But on such a view, far from such an analysis implying the degeneracy of our present, so-called 'capitalist' society, it certainly reveals a far more favourable comparison with Eastern European Marxist society, based upon so-called 'scientific' Leninism, which is not adverse to an educational system founded upon strongly behaviourist principles.

There are, however, indications that Young would not wish to accept such conclusions. Even though he does not make such a case clearly and consistently, at heart Young is more committed to the relativistic thesis (*b*) and would not wish to accept the price that must be paid for a genuine synthesis with the objectivist thesis (*a*). By refusing such a synthesis, he can reduce assessment and planning to that sufficient level of chaos and anarchy to allow the mysterious forces of the underlying dialectic, in which he (but not I) believes, to go to work. We have already seen in the paper that we have here extensively analysed that knowledge is frequently described as 'created' and not 'discovered', as though reality definition could be understood as relative to particular cultures and historical circum-stances. Certainly such a relativisitic thesis is espoused by such contributions to collections under Young's editorship as those of Esland and Blum. Blum typically says:

> If objective knowledge is taken to mean knowledge of a reality independent of language, or presuppositionless knowledge, or knowledge of the world which is independent of the observer's procedures for finding and producing the knowledge, then there is no such thing as objective knowledge. (Blum, 1971, p. 128)

What counts as knowledge is what is comprehensible within systems that human beings create in particular communities of judgement as a result of accidental historical circumstances. Where cultures conflict, there is no independent means of resolving the conflict between them. Once it has been admitted, as we will happily admit, that there is no knowledge of reality 'independent of language' or 'independent of the observer's procedures for finding and producing the knowledge', but that there is nevertheless objective knowledge because there are some features common to all human languages and some presuppositions common to all communities of judgement, then the notion of dialectical development becomes redundant. But it is quite the opposite of such a notion that must be clung on to by the Marxist at all costs, since without it either curriculum or social chaos will lack justification, as will the hope of the automatic development of a new and better order beyond it. So we have an incoherent argument in the form that Young must therefore propound it.

Only, therefore, on such a relativistic thesis can an attack upon any kind of assessment be sustained, as it must if the mysterious dialectical forces can be allowed to work. Once positivistic elements intrude, as we show that they had begun to do in Young's thesis, then one is forced to the conclusion that we are being asked to reject one type of assessment in favour of another epistemologically superior type which Young has failed to spell out. Is Young and the radical group that he leads in favour of subjects, but taught and learned differently? Is he, alternatively, as we have tried to show, advocating that the structure of the subject matter of the curriculum itself needs reformulation? If so, will knowledge thus reconstituted still resemble, if not subjects, at least what Hirst describes as distinct 'forms' of knowledge? It is the conviction of the present writer that epistemological reconstruction of curricular foundations will uncover basic continuities in human judgement, transcultural in kind, that bears resemblance to Hirst's forms of knowledge thesis but which, incidentally, propounded in such a form, is likely to raise some more than mild protests from Hirst himself (Hirst, 1974*a*, pp. 84–104 1979).

Certainly Young and his followers, from their attacks upon Hirst, suggest that knowledge, whether described in terms of forms or distinct subjects, is the product of the processes of reification and false-consciousness (Young, 1971, p. 23), so that they are unhappy about any kind of curriculum reorganisation that preserves distinct kinds of knowledge. But the ability of epistemological relativism to sustain such an argument for curriculum change is more apparent than real. If all bodies of knowledge, schemes and categories of assessment and so forth are socially relative, then the replacement of one scheme of assessment by another cannot even be *argued*. Such replacements are neither justifiable nor unjustifiable, they just happen and the clandestine causes of why they happen are all that need spelling out. So we thus return, in the final analysis, to the obliteration of the rule-following model to a rule-conforming distinction that a phenomenological account, as we have shown, originally set out to preserve. The retention or non-retention of a scheme for curriculum organisation or assessment, however, on a rule-conforming understanding of change, simply cannot be advocated, since this would involve using categories in the language of advocacy that we have seen to be ruled out on a rule-conforming model such as 'choice', 'decision' and so on. In the final analysis, we see that the radical advocating curriculum change on relativistic grounds cannot justify his advocacy. The very criticism of cultural relativism that he levels at the status quo must also apply to his own alternative. There can be no 'reasons' for change, only 'causes'. Yet the advocacy of cause itself denies phenomenological denials of objectivity in terms of an intelligible extra-social and extra-linguistic 'nature'. Thus the phenomenological Marxist argument for curriculum reconstruction collapses for similar reasons to why both classical and Marcusan formulations of an argument for social reconstruction collapsed.

Young and his followers are, of course, ambiguous over whether subject areas which ought, as we have seen, on a relativistic basis, to have been ruled out are in fact to be so treated. One collection of papers under Young's editorship does seem to preserve subjects like science, English, music, where writers are content to produce a Marxist critique of subject matter and the way that it can be constructed differently and taught differently (Young, 1976). They ought logically, as we have seen, to be ruled out, since they must according to the argument represent the imposition of the frame of reference generated by one social construction of reality (the group to which the teacher/subject specialist) belongs on another group (namely, the pupils), which does not initially share that frame of reference. Yet, as we saw, if all knowledge is socially relative, those who impose as well as those who oppose the imposition have no basis on which either to justify their own practices or to reject those of their opponents. We have, moreover, seen why at this juncture it will not do to invoke the criterion of power *versus* powerlessness. To insist that the subjects to be selected are those structured and taught in a way that increases their takers because there is experienced through them an increased control over their social and natural environments, is to admit that reality has a structure beyond any socially generated definitions. But, as we saw, if this is the case, once again we meet with the problem about the objective possibility of assessment and grading that Young and his co-authors appear to want to deny, but for reasons which we have just seen, they cannot consistently deny. There is, nevertheless, a strictly phenomenological alternative, such as that which we have argued Marcuse tried to take and which Young and his associates could have tried to follow. We saw that sometimes 'alienation' was interpreted in a psychological way, and the way in which the existing academic communities organised themselves as elites was held to be wrong because of the way in which it debilitated the majority psychologically. Young might therefore have argued that *some* subjects taught in some forms in contrast to others, or the same subjects taught in different forms, could be distinguished from one another by reference to a purely psychological definition of power-reducing 'alienation'. The 'liberation' experienced in learning such subjects in such forms would therefore resemble the liberating experience of a course of psychotherapy that has broken traumatic fixations whose social origins are in the repressive creations of capitalist societies. We have, alas, already shown in our discussion of Marcuse that a consistent phenomenology cannot function in defence of a Marxist case by the strategy of integrating a Freudian perspective. In the final analysis, Freud was too dependent on a concept of reality that was culturally invariant and without which his procedures could not be justified as 'therapy'. Once again, we return to the need to define how reality is processed if the 'reality principle' cannot be defined in empiricist terms but cannot on the other hand be interpreted in terms of epistemological relativism.

But with our mention of 'liberation' in Marcusian terms, we can best now pursue our analysis of a fallacious argument by looking at our promised second example of the Marxist critique of schooling, this time a critique of both the teaching of literature and its social role. We shall see, once again, a reproduction of the basic incoherence between underlying theoretical frameworks and the perpetuation of the inadequacies of such frameworks.

6.3 HAND'S CRITIQUE OF THE SCHOOLING OF ENGLISH

Nigel Hand (1976) begins his critique by stressing the value of the 'wholeness' of experience which it is the ideal of many English teachers to achieve, but contrasting such an ideal with existing English syllabuses where: 'Each fragmented version of English offers a compartmentalised view of language, or literature, or both' (Hand, 1976, p. 9). Hand thus from the outset shows that he takes the dialectic seriously and accepts the universalised principle of value that the whole is more value that its component parts. Alternatively, in accord with the biological analogy on which we saw that dialectical arguments trade, in healthy development thesis and antithesis, inconsistent with each other and operating in a way disfunctional to an organism's development, achieve a higher level of operation or synthesis where they come to function properly as part of some larger whole. On the foundations of such a dialectical argument of what is valuable, Hand is now to ground his critique of the contemporary English curriculum.

We saw that Young opposed science teaching as presently constituted on the grounds that it stratified society hierarchically into a number of closed elites with rigid rules on how the small number within each closed class at the pinnacle of the social hierarchy was to be constituted. Such a view of the science curriculum he believed thus to have been the historical creation of nineteenth-century capitalism. Hand similarly sees literary criticism in the form in which it is taught in schools and assessed in examinations as produced in a similar historical milieu with a similar social function. The thesis is constituted by a concentration on content and the ignoring of the form that the novel takes, 'form' thus constituting the antithesis. The Victorian novel required no consideration of the literary form in which it was expressed, since the world that it portrays is required to be continuous with the real world, a reproduction of 'real' characters in 'credible' relationships in that they are congruous with things as they are. Thus the 'characters' can be isolated from the texts and discussed in examination questions as though they were real people with meaning and purpose outside the literary form in which they are created. Perhaps two examples of this kind of literary criticism may serve to make Hand's point. The first is the ending of Dicken's novel *Great Expectations*, which is frequently criticised as lacking in realism. Neither Pip nor Estella were the kinds of characters suited to such a 'phoney' happy ending, and so, such a type of literary criticism goes, the ending should have been tragic. Judged in terms of literary criteria that Dickens might himself have accepted, perhaps such a criticism is valid because the characters ought to have, on such criteria, an independence of the form of the novel, what they become and how they will behave becoming independently predictable. But supposing that we were to apply such principles of criticism, say, to Sophocles' *Electra* or to novels such as Grahame Greene's *The End of the Affair*? Both writers (at least regarding Greene's earlier period) believed in divine transcendence, and Greene incorporated miracles into his text, and thus they can be regarded as 'unrealistic' and discontinuous with the everyday world of the given. But the presence of miracle and divine transcendence in both Sophocles and Greene, while not allowed to detract from both tragedy and a sensitivity to human predicaments, are there to record against the mystery and aimlessness of the chaos of human affairs the writers' ultimate faith that the world adds up and has meaning. To fail to grasp the character of the writers' literary form therefore leads to a failure to grasp the true nature of their work.

But we need now to ask Hand, as we did Young, as to why it should be considered so wrong to have criticised one set of works by literary standards immanent in another? Surely artistic standards are culturally relative, so that if one group chooses to adopt certain standards, then that is simply a manifestation of their creativity as human beings? All that follows from a cultural relativistic view of literature is surely that one ought not to use standards derivable from one literary school in order to criticise another, all choices *beyond* that being arbitrary and a question of individual tastes. On what grounds, therefore, is Hand in a position to say that one kind of curriculum for literary appreciation is wrong and another right? Surely, on a relativistic argument, the curriculum in a subject like English is (or ought to be) purely a question of taste too? Hand's reply from his paper would consist of two answers which might be summarised as follows. Teaching literature in terms of content to the exclusion of form is wrong because:

(a) Such a view of literature leads to a distortion of reality so that it blinds us to a writer's true view of the world.

(b) Such a view of literature fragments literary criticism. It separates content (thesis) from form (antithesis) and thus prevents 'wholeness' of view (synthesis) in which both form and content are blended together into a far more valuable perspective.

Let us discuss (a) first. Hand argues that the treatment of *Animal Farm* as a text in the curriculum as a piece of anti-socialist propaganda distorts Orwell's true intention. As Hand says:

> *Animal Farm* enacts the perversion of a revolution, but the *form* of

the book – the medium in which the story moves – is a critical irony embodying not a sense that revolutions are wrong and should not take place, but a sense of what, by comparison, a true revolution would be like. However, in the course of its mediation through the educational and social system . . . true irony embodied in the form of the book is eliminated . . . How is the elimination achieved? By the demand for, say, a description of the 'character' of Napoleon, or Squealer, or Boxer . . . – as if they were real people (!) . . . so that the form . . . is sidestepped – the critical and liberating consciousness of the book is denied. (Hand, 1976, p. 10)

Thus, because the characters of Napoleon, Squealer and Boxer are isolated from the text and are hypothesised about as if they had an independent existence free from the literary form in which they occur, the true and significant message conveyed by the form is obliterated. Hence Hand's first answer would appear to be that teaching literature in the form of character studies with evaluation in terms of realism, plausibility and so forth is wrong because it perpetuates a wrong understanding of the essential message of a writer. As such, the character of this first criticism seems very close to measuring truth in terms of an external reality that, in some of their moods, our radical curriculum theorists would, as we have seen, seek to deny.

Hand's second answer (*b*) in terms of the dialectical development of literary criticism seems, however more, consistent with a Marxist case. Let us pursue this second answer, therefore, by asking what would constitute for him literary criticism that emphasises form as an antithesis to content as thesis. Hand's models for emphasis upon form rather than content are Joyce and Eliot. The mark of their literature is their 'reflexivity' in which the writer gets his characters to 'soliloquize' as in Shakespeare. Here we see that the works themselves 'enact their creation' because the writers 'write the act of creation *into* their work'. As a result for the curriculum:

Fundamentally, this gives us a model for the humanities in which the child is enabled to see, and experience, active relationships between society and its works and between himself and those works. (Hand, 1976, p. 11)

As such, literature is not seen as simply reproducing reality as given, with characters and situations plausible within and continuous with the existing societal givens. Rather, though Hand does not refer to him by name, Marcuse's notion of the purpose of literature is being maintained, namely, literature as the negation of the given, as the means of providing images of alternatives to the given. As Marcuse says:

> Whether ritualised or not, art contains the rationality of negation. In its advanced positions, it is the Great Refusal – the protest against that which is . . . The neo-conservative critics of leftist critics . . . insist . . . that the classics have . . . come to life again, that people are just so much more educated. True, but coming to life as classics, they come to life as other than themselves; they are deprived of their antagonistic force, of the estrangement which was the very dimension of their truth. (Marcuse, 1964, pp. 63–4)

The understanding of Joyce and Eliot in terms of form is nevertheless not to be allowed to license English teaching as helping children in their inner growth. Hand protests that 'children's inner growing up' does not take place in a social vacuum and that the social context which generates the literary form must be evaluated. Hand's resultant synthesis between content without form (thesis) and form without content (antithesis) is one in which both are consistent with a dialectically developing reality constitutive of social progress.

With these two answers to how we can find what sort of approaches to literature satisfy a curriculum that is 'liberating', we return to the basic disjunction that we noted in both Young and Esland between classical Marxist and phenomenological Marxist dialectical definitions of reality. Such a disjunction is perpetuated in Hand also without an adequate synthesis of the conflict of model that it represents. These two distinct ways of answering the questions posed in (*a*) and (*b*) we will now show to be incoherent when we press the analysis of underlying models. Why should not Hand's advocacy of a 'correct' interpretation of Orwell (*a*) as socialist but against both Eastern European communism and Western capitalism be regarded as an 'adjustment to the given' which is condemned as a strategy of false-consciousness and reification? Surely, according to answer (*b*), Orwell's writing is part of the 'society and its works' with which the child ought to have 'an active relationship'. If, therefore, we in interaction with that social given that is Orwell's message in *Animal Farm* or *1984* create a new transformed meaning and purpose for what Orwell writes, then surely we are merely doing what the phenomenological thesis licenses us to do? The trouble with such a concession, however, is that at first sight it robs Hand of the means of refuting the following interpretation of Orwell's significance, however bizarre he might find it. Such an interpretation might run as follows: Orwell may have considered himself a Tribunite socialist (whatever that may mean), but what his work did was to sensitise people to the totalitarian tendencies of post-revolutionary events endemic in any socialist revolution. Orwell, or at least part of him, may have remained committed to some notion of a socialist revolution that would not necessarily (he would argue) have had such a totalitarian outcome. But we need not be bound by such an Orwellian hope that we might find, in the worst sense of that word, pious. Surely our understanding of Orwell's message does not have to reproduce slavishly the Orwellian given, but can result from a creative but critical interaction with his thinking?

Hand might, of course, have argued that capitalism disregards fundamental moral values and that children are, by being given an interpretation of Orwell that defends capitalist democracy, being lead to acquiesce in an immoral system. We may express some perverse pleasure that neither Hand nor the other contributors to Young's various collections ever get involved in such arguments. At all events, the name of the game in such arguments invariably becomes a swapping of horror stories between so-called 'capitalist' and so-called 'socialist' societies, with corresponding horror stories about how, say, talented working-class youth is oppressed by the contemporary curriculum or deprived in a free school. Rather than the support of 'bourgeoise' morality, therefore, Hand's argument instead rests upon the principles of dialectical change. Hand's argument must therefore be that anything that prevents change is *ipso facto* irrational and uncreative. Thus, because our interpretation of Orwell as anti-socialist reinforces the status quo, protecting it from change or transformation, for that reason it is both irrational, uncreative and wrong. Our interpretation is not 'wrong', therefore, because it misrepresents Orwell's true opinion, but because, in other words, it rests on a lie. Only a casual reading of the radical Marxist case would convince us that, because this was their argument, we ought to accept what Marxists propose. Nor is our interpretation 'irrational' because it represents an unintelligible point of view founded upon, among other things, mutually inconsistent presuppositions. Our interpretation is therefore 'irrational' and 'wrong' on a restricted, dialectical definition of reality in which change takes place according to the movements of a human argument in which anything that prevents an antithesis rising in opposition to a thesis prevents reasoning and is therefore wrong. Moreover, for Hand's argument to work, that 'argument' of which we have just been speaking and the way in which it progresses and is retarded cannot take place purely within human minds that agree and disagree about phenomenological appearances. If so, our interpretation of Orwell would have been as good as Hand's, so long as it could achieve a similar consensus of subjective human assents. For Hand's argument to work, therefore, the 'argument' must be mysteriously 'out there', correcting our individual points of view and determining what is right and wrong as it determines the development of nature and of human societies as a part of nature. So, once again, as we did with Young and Esland so we also establish with Hand, a basic ambivalence produced by a failure to retranslate a causal, rule-conforming model of historical development consistently in terms of a rule-following one. As far as the curriculum is concerned, moreover, it represents a strategy of reducing each curriculum subject or activity to the amorphousness of the melting pot, relying once again on the mysterious, 'argumentative' or 'dialectical' forces of history to develop new orders of curricula out of chaos. And at this point there emerges the very dialectical view of reality clearly at the heart of Hand's proposals, whose adequacy and basic intuitionism we have queried through extensive criticism both here (Sections 5.2 and 5.3) and in our earlier book (Brent, 1978, Chapter 2).

Hand saw in drama his hope of fulfilling the English teacher's valued aim of 'wholeness'. Drama, after all, was not rigidly assessable through the reality-distorting examination system, as were other subjects. For Hand, however, as we have seen, 'wholeness' is only achievable by relating both form and content in drama to the historical and social context that he claims unifies or synthesises them. Thus literature must play its role in dialectically conceived historical and social progress. We should like then, in conclusion, having exposed what we believe to be inadequate, dialectical assumptions implicit in such a view, to relate Hand's desire for 'wholeness', however fine it might sound, to a further, earlier criticism of certain invalid epistemological strategies. Earlier, particularly in criticism of the philosophy of science held by classical empiricists, we referred to what we described as 'logical imperialism'. Here we referred to the way in which, in the history of forms of inquiry with totalising claims, certain items of common-sense experience are taken and a general theoretical perspective is developed on the basis of these in the light of which other items of common-sense experience and their derivatives are declared to be invalid. We argued with reference to Kant (Chapter 3) how, in the history of inquiry, what were thought to be invalid sub-sets of common-sense experience reassert their validity, as in the case of 'chance' (if not of 'fate' and 'destiny') in the sub-set that Kant believed to be invalid. There we foreshadowed, as an explanation of this phenomenon witnessed in the history of inquiry, a thesis about the irreducibility of certain fundamental common-sense categories to one another and their role in constituting a basic framework of human understanding. We claimed, furthermore, that such a framework could be understood as extending throughout all human languages in a way similar to Katz's version of Chomskyan semantic structures (Katz, 1979). In view of Hand's reductionist strategy, therefore, in which the significance of literature must be a social and political significance, we can regard the form of Hand's argument as reflecting the more general reductionist fallacy of logical imperialism. We are particularly entitled to argue the fallaciousness of his reductionism since we have demonstrated that his dialectical defence of such a reduction (in the name of higher-order, developmental syntheses and so on) has failed. It was therefore a fallacious argument that generated Hand's view that literature cannot be studied in its own right and for its own sake, as formalists like Eliot assume, because, as we have argued and will argue further, schemes for literary appreciation derive their validity from their continuity with basic, common-sense aesthetic categories of understanding, irreducible to other such common-sense forms underlying, say, science or morality. Literature, like science, according to the Marxist dialectician, must be reduced to historical and social forms of understanding whose true nature is intuitively discerned by the Marxist behind the allegedly mystifying and falsifying flux of ordinary language and common-sense experience. We shall be pursuing in Chapter 8 our argument as to why the history of inquiry itself should continuously instance the failure of one kind of inquiry, continuous with one sub-set of common-sense categories, to dominate other kinds of inquiry continuous with other sub-sets. Thus our analysis brings us back once again to the pursuance of our major thesis: namely, our quest for a framework of human understanding that can be established as common to all natural languages and which represents as the touchstone of truth a common agreement in a human form of life. Such a framework, satisfying the conditions of a rule-following model for human action, will lead us to a genuinely rule-following model for making curriculum decisions. To such a task we shall turn in Chapter 8.

6.4 MODELS, REALITY AND CURRICULUM DECISIONS: SOME CONCLUSIONS

In conclusion, therefore, let us summarise where the argument of this chapter has taken us. We have in our search for an alternative to a Skinnerian model for determining curriculum objectives and their means of assessment looked at a Marxist model, or, more properly, two versions of a Marxist model. Such a model, *prima facie*, seemed attractive. Its proponents shared with us a self-conscious opposition to Skinnerian behaviourism in seeking a rule-following model that left room for the exercise of human freedom as opposed to a causal, rule-conforming model that excluded this. In our pursuit of such model, moreover, we were fortified, as were the Marxists, by a collapse of the deterministic philosophy of science that underpinned Skinnerian behaviourism in the light of the quantum revolution in physics. But when we analysed the two versions of a proposed Marxist model, we uncovered the true extent of the failure to expunge from such a model rule-conforming, deterministic categories, even in the version that involved phenomenological reformulation. We saw that Young and his associates, when making specifically curricular proposals, perpetuated that failure in their critique of schooling. They were found to have employed indiscriminately both causal and classical as well as phenomenological and psychological Marxist models which were, in the last analysis, shown to be in any case incapable of synthesis. Our argument was that any attempted synthesis of a phenomenological with a Marxist perspective was ultimately bound to fail. Any consistently rule-following reformulation of a Marxist model will necessarily undermine such key Marxist notions as 'oppression' and 'historical determinism' that are rule-conforming categories which must inform any recognisably Marxist model.

We found, furthermore, that phenomenological subjectivism should not enable a Marxist case to be coherently made. Since we share with the Marxist a view that subjectivism is an incoherent notion, albeit for our own non-Marxist reasons, for which our frequently expressed indebtedness to Chomsky will soon be apparent, we agree that processes of reality definition and their justification are important. Yet we found dialectical justification and definitions of such processes unsatisfactory, both in their classical and phenomenological forms. The unsatisfactory character of theoretical dialectical understanding was, moreover, reflected in an ambiguity about educational practice. Young, Esland and Hand were all ambiguous regarding whether subjects in any recognisable form were to be ruled out, or only subjects in some specific form. Likewise with assessment, where it was unclear whether *any* kind of assessment, grading of work and so on was wrong, or only a particular kind of grading and assessment, presumably the one which reflected capitalist values. We saw that once what was real was regarded as external to language and independent of social categories of thought, imposing, albeit dialectically, order and meaning upon the development of social forms, then assessment in principle was possible, however much one might wish to dispense with it as it was shaped by a capitalist social order. On this classical Marxist view some kind of organisation of knowledge into curriculum subjects was also possible, but one which reflected rather than distorted reality into false-consciousness. Reference to reality and to ways in which it was objectively processed was therefore inescapable on a classical Marxist view, as was the objectivity of some representations of it in contrast to others, and of some means of acquiring such representations of it in contrast to others. We could not, however, escape from such implications for curricular subject matter and assessment by retreating from such ontological commitments and by resting a Marxist case upon mental health criteria in order to distinguish one subjective set of propositions and practices for acquiring them from another. We saw that the use by Marcuse of Freudian mental health criteria of what were good and bad formulations of what is real and the processes by which we make such formulations could not help the phenomenologist, who also wished to be a Marxist and yet remain consistent. The Freudian criteria of mental health involved reference to the 'reality principle' and thus itself presupposed the objectivity of ways of defining and processing reality.

We have seen, moreover, that our fundamental disagreement with Young and his associates is not that we do not believe that a distortion of reality has taken place regarding the nature of curriculum subject matter, nor that Skinner and the empiricist/behaviourist tradition has been guilty of such distortions. Our point at issue with Young has rather been over whether a dialectical understanding of reality either makes sense or produces clarity over the way in which distortions of reality take place. We do not believe that the only alternatives to the naïve realism of empiricism that we have exposed is a socially relativistic view of either knowledge or dialecticism. Our alternative is to regard judgements about what is real and true as the product of certain fundamental categories of human understanding in terms of which sensory data are processed and which become therefore constitutive of human experience. Such categories can only be examined in a social context, since they are closely related to human speech-acts, but this does not imply that they are relative to particular communities of human social judgements. We will argue in Chapter 8 that such categories, definable, not exhaustively but in terms of what we saw in Chapter 2 Wittgenstein called 'family-resemblance', are constitutive of basic forms of human understanding. Such forms of understanding persist in an observable chain of family-resemblances both across human languages and with an immunity to change that survives the historical forms of their truth-assertions. Such a basic form of human understanding can be distorted and the development of its testimony to what is real retarded if, for instance, categories are treated as closed or if some categories are treated as if they were properly others in some invalid reductionism. We saw such to be the case with Bloom's curricular taxonomy and its empiricist and behaviourist assumptions. If that is what Young had meant by his attacks upon subject organisation and assessment, then we would have been in agreement with him. But it was not, since his account is vitiated by incoherent dialectical notions that spawn an incoherent political and educational philosophy. Such incoherent notions, committed as they are to a rejection of notions of necessity and invariance, must lead Young and his associates to dissent from the way in which our argument must now proceed. Notions of continuities in human judgements will be seen to imply transcendent, invariant categories implicit in all human thinking, whose existence is demonstrable from an analysis of structures basic, according to Chomskyans, to all human languages. With such notions, the proponents of a Marxist model, with their commitment to dialectically progressing conflicts that sweep away all possible continuities, can have no sympathy. Yet we have demonstrated that their lack of sympathy is unfounded. Their alternative, according to what we have argued, is an incoherent one based upon an incoherent concept of reality that is therefore a distortion of reality.

A dialectical understanding of human conflicts and their resolution having therefore failed, we must now pursue further a properly rule-following account of human action. Such a rule-following account, as we have shown from our criticism in this chapter, must explore among other things what makes possible agreements and disagreements between human beings in terms of a basic continuity in judgement witnessed across varieties of socially located speech-acts.

Chapter 7

Bernstein, Hirst and Rule-Following Models

We have traced so far the failure of two distinct models of inquiry to explain human action in both a general societal and a specifically curricular form. Both models were formally comparable in that both assumed classical as well as revisionist forms. In the first place, there was the model of classical empiricism that underwent, first, a causal behavioural and then a non-causal 'operant' reformulation. In the second place, there was the model constituted first by classical Marxism and subsequently undergoing phenomenological revision. In the final analysis, our quest for an irreducibly rule-following explanation of human understanding and its issue in speech-acts has to do with reality-defining processes that are constitutive of man's mind. We have not yet here fully extended the thesis of our previous book, that reality-defining processes assume a limited number of distinct forms, in a way which we hope to do later in Chapter 8. But what we have so far established is the dependence of a rule-following model on some account of reality processing in which propositions in language come to be true or false. We saw this in particular when we analysed in detail the two forms taken by a Marxist model of explanation. The epistemological foundations of both forms we saw to be unstable because of a defective epistemology that had produced deep-seated errors. How the notion of subconscious or 'implicit' knowledge of the rules for processing reality is to be justified we shall try to answer when we develop the theoretical strands of our argument further later in this work.

But first let us turn to the more practical concerns to do with educational foundations that constitute the major focus of the theoretical argument of this book. Let us tell, as our third and final 'typical characterisation', the story of Julia's third teaching practice.

7.1 A TYPICAL CHARACTERISATION OF THE 'CONSENSUS CURRICULUM'

Julia was pleased to learn of her allocation for her final teaching practice. It was to be the grammar school that she had attended herself a few years previously. The school had begun to go comprehensive when she had just entered the sixth form and she was about to witness what it had become now that it was a comprehensive right through.

As she drove through the gates for her preliminary discussion with heads of departments and class teachers, she noticed the additions to the Georgian architecture in the form of a modern, plate-glass three-storey block which, she was later to discover, housed science and language laboratories and a new assembly hall. She took the opportunity to wander around the classrooms after her discussions, two of them happening to be empty because of the absence of pupils at games, and noticed a certain unevenness in the rows of desks. This Julia found surprising, since she always remembered how immovable those desks once were, bolted as they had been firmly to the floor. Their bolts had been removed so that now they could simply be pushed around. She passed the old assembly hall, giving it some passing glances, and then walked through that part of the old building that opened out on to the path which lead to the new. She wanted to see the new assembly hall which had been built to replace the old in view of the increased numbers following comprehensive reorganisation. When she arrived there, the difference between them struck her forcibly and seemed to go beyond the requirements simply of increases in numbers. The old hall had still showed, prominently displayed, the old house shields and cups. The rolls of honour for sporting and academic achievement could still be seen written upon the polished dark wood on the balcony written in faded gold-leaf, and at either side of the doors through which they had filed in and out to morning assembly. In the new, larger assembly hall, such boards were tucked away in alcoves and the stone and polished wooden décor, with microphones and lights strategically placed, were left by themselves to create their own, strictly aesthetic effect.

As she began her teaching practice proper, Julia soon began to notice further differences. Classrooms in her day had simply carried the number of the year followed by the letter (A, B or C) of the stream that the particular class housed. Instead, the doors now simply displayed after the year number the initials of the form teacher. Julia mentioned to her teacher/supervisor the change, and he explained that for several years they had dispensed with streaming and gone in for a degree of setting instead. Some lessons were taught to pupils in forms of mixed ability, and others in sets reflecting attainment in specific subjects. Moreover, setting and mixed-ability teaching in forms was not organised on the somewhat careless and intuitive basis that some subjects, such as maths, physics or languages, were highly structured, whereas others, such as English, history or music, were not, so that the former required setting according to specific abilities in that subject, whereas the latter could be taught to mixed-ability groups. Rather was the setting/mixed-ability differentiation on the basis of 'skills' subjects that became, for later years, 'disciplines'. These were taught in sets, such as sets for 'reading', 'literature', 'writing', 'maths' and 'physics', whereas the mixed-ability forms were engaged in project or topic work organised into distinct areas such as 'Man the creator', 'Man and his environment', 'Man and society' (Pring, 1973, p. 133). The skills or disciplines thus learned in sets were therefore, in mixed-ability forms, applied in a problem-solving way, and each area could furnish tasks which provided for the kind of team effort in which, say, one young person good at writing but bad at maths or vice versa could join with others who had weaknesses where he had strengths and vice versa. Thus every student, irrespective of the level of his performance in sets, could thus see that he had something to offer to a group learning project, even though he might later go on to specialise in some specific part or parts of his setted skills or disciplines.

Teaching of such project or topic learning in forms was team-teaching. A team of teachers with different subject specialisms showed students how to apply what they had learned in sets to the specific problems of their topic and project areas. Julia soon saw why it was necessary to be able to shift desks around, forming sometimes discussion circles, sometimes loci for individual groups and sometimes audience rows. Julia noticed how, in plenary session, the besweatered, jacketless teachers readily showed their disagreement to their students, thus demonstrating the value of criticism and the possibility of a variety of points of view. The 'Old Guard' on the staff, some of whom had taught Julia many years before, made in the quietness of the staff-room many muted complaints about the new regime. They remembered when they all used to wear not only jackets and ties but gowns as well, when classes stood up from their fixed desks when a teacher entered the room, when each individual teacher could be relied upon to furnish incontrovertably all the answers and to teach not only intellectual but moral standards. Now they just contradicted each other in front of the pupils, adding to the moral confusion and lack of authority without jackets and without ties!

Julia thought wistfully, too, of the 'old days', of the traditional emphasis there had been on sports and games in inter-house rivalry, in which it was the duty of everyone to run for the house in the cross-country, to play in one of the teams: hockey, cricket, football or basketball or whatever. She was, however, honest with herself that there had been some unpleasant aspects. There were always a few great individualists who had just simply not wanted to run or play cricket or what have you, and there were often private scenes in the playground when there were no teachers around when those who had refused got beaten around if they were boys, with the prefects turning a blind eye. There were also other more subtle ways of making life unpleasant, like messing up desks, leaving threatening notes or simply calling 'wet' at such non-conformists. But there was a more positive and enthusiastic side to the old regime. There had been enthusiasm in the houses and a sense of belonging with everyone pulling together. Such enthusiasm had been reinforced by house chants, songs and slogans as part of the established tradition through the years. Each house had their individual chants, song and slogans, which were deployed against rival houses on the sports field with considerable gusto. Moreover, the houses gathered regularly before such events as sporting fixtures, when housemasters and house-mistresses specified with pride in their exhortatory speeches the lists of specific and desirable characteristics to be exhibited by members of 'their' house. But despite her nostalgia, Julia also reflected on what she had read and heard in her undergraduate course in educational studies about 'curriculum integration', the 'core' curriculum, 'forms of knowledge' and so on, and wondered whether a curriculum that was team-taught within such a framework did not represent a 'plus' for the new regime and a hard-won progress.

7.2 BERNSTEIN'S DURKHEIMIAN MODEL OF EDUCATIONAL CHANGE

For a theoretical model of social explanation and change that might explain what Julia observed in our third 'typical characterisation', we turn to the use of Durkheim's social theory made by Bernstein and translated into a more practically worked-out version in the shape of the 'consensus' curriculum by Lawton (Lawton, 1968, 1973). Bernstein regards changes within the school, such as those witnessed by Julia, as explicable in terms of changes within a social structure from one where social cohesion or 'solidarity' was mechanical to one where it was organic. Basically, Durkheim considered that the way in which pre-industrial societies achieved social cohesion and stability was radically different from the way in which industrial societies achieved the same. 'Mechanical solidarity' described a cohesiveness in social structure constituted by every member behaving to a very high degree in approximately similar ways. People wore the same clothes, followed similar, basically agrarian or hunting occupations, shared very similar moral and religious values, adopted similar routines. In such a society, the importance of a very large and diverse number of 'collective representations' or ritual or symbolic assertions, both in speech or in action, of collective agreement and unity cannot be too highly stressed. Such representations were the social mechanism for the imposition of similarity of behaviour and were thus *ipso facto* the expression of mechanical solidarity. There are, of course, no extant traces that would evidence the existence of any society in so primitive a form. What we do have evidence for is the existence of that form of mechanical solidarity that occurs in what Durkheim termed 'segmented' societies. Societies organised on the basis of clans are segmented societies in which, within each clan, the solidarity is mechanical, with the relations between the clans that unite them into a social whole being both loose and merely additive.

With the rise of industrial societies, we witness a change in the nature of social solidarity that, in fact, made such industrialisation possible. Organic social structures are characterised by the division of labour in terms of which a differentiation of social functions takes place that requires individuals to behave in dissimilar ways. An economic organisation based upon the division of labour is thus symptomatic of social differentiation rather than its cause. As a result, under organic solidarity, the concept of the person as individual becomes important, since organic societies cannot afford to lose even a small number of individual members in the way that mechanical societies can do and still hope to survive. If hunters or warriors lose a number of members through war, disease or famine, then it is comparatively easy for, say, the farmers to replace such lost members from their own numbers. But if organic society loses, for whatever reason, the services, say, of even a small number of medical practitioners, miners or engineers, then a serious societal breakdown is threatened. Their skills are not the common repertoire of all similarly behaving members, but rather of one section of highly differently behaving members (Durkheim, 1964).

Now, Durkheim considered the role of the central value system (or 'collective consciousness', as he called it) as marking important contrasts between the two kinds of solidarity. Under mechanical solidarity, whether the society was unicellular or segmental, the collective consciousness could extend in minutest detail over all aspects of the life of the collectivity. Collective representations that expressed the collective consciousness also expressed the regulation of approximately similar patterns of behaviour down to the minutest detail. After all, if the principle of social cohesion or solidarity was one that involved all members of the society behaving similarly, then, without such similarity of behaviour, the cohesion of the group was threatened so that coercive pressures to conformity with group norms was legitimated. Any deviance or oddity had to be ruthlessly obliterated if social cohesion were to survive. With the development of the division of labour, however, and its correlative organic solidarity, the ability of the collective consciousness to achieve this degree of specificity of control on every substantive item of behaviour was diminished. This last sentence is, moreover, to some extent misleading, since it makes it seem as though it were a purely contingent matter that, under organic solidarity, such a diminution simply happens. In fact, it is part of what it means for solidarity to be 'organic' that the collective consciousness so contracts from specificity of control, otherwise differentiation of individual social functions cannot take place. Organic solidarity is not dependent causally and therefore contingently on the division of labour, since the division of labour presupposes organic solidarity. Under organic solidarity, therefore, the collective consciousness is transformed into a number of formal, general norms and moral principles. Legislation in organic societies is typically consensual rather than coercive, as is the distinction between both the civil and criminal law and between morality and law. Consensual legislation is legislation that makes it possible for men to form associations, make agreements and contracts, go to arbitration and so forth, if they so choose to do so, or otherwise not. In fact we can perhaps grasp the character of organic collective consciousness by reflecting on the strangeness that we feel about what we read in such literature as the Book of Proverbs in the Bible or in Virgil's *Georgics* (1964). Such literature captures the character of a mechanical collective consciousness, by contrast with which the character of organic solidarity can readily be seen. In such literature, religious and moral maxims are mixed indiscriminately together with rules for etiquette such as table manners when at a ruler's table, instructions on when to plant what crops at what season of the year, and tips on the characteristics of a good wife. Under collective consciousness in organic solidarity, such specific regulation of all aspects of life without discrimination is no longer functional (Durkheim, 1915).

There is, however, a threat to social stability under organic solidarity which barely existed under mechanical solidarity, and this is *anomia* or 'normlessness'. Because the very organic structure of social relations is characterised by *difference* in patterns of behaviour, because, in turn, this requires a collective consciousness contracted to a formal and general small number of norms and values, there is a real danger that men may apply and follow such norms and values so ambiguously and erratically that breakdown in social cohesion takes place. What is important, correct, valuable in pursuance of an occupational, professional or vocational end is still specific, clear and definable in great detail. We 'know', within limits and in specific terms, what makes a 'good' builder, miner, doctor, nurse, shop-assistant, teacher. Criteria can be laid down that command general agreement in the form of codes of practice or articles of professional associations. But what happens when a 'good' miner, doctor or teacher asks what it is to be a 'good' citizen? The miner, who knows in great detail the processes for getting coal safely out of the ground, faces a genuine dilemma when he goes on to ask in what circum-stances should he push strike action for the good of his occupation against an incomes policy of a social democratic government. A doctor may know what are the means to be taken to prevent conception, but he may face a dilemma when he asks himself whether he should divulge to the parents of an under-sixteen-year-old that she has requested the pill. There are no longer any pithy, proverb-like prescriptions that can specifically lay down the precise pattern of substantive behaviour for such cases involving general social relations.

Now, Bernstein applies this basic Durkheimian model to changes within the school, such as those witnessed by the fictional Julia in our third 'typical characterisation'. He regards the changes that took place in terms of a shift from mechanical to organic solidarity. The traditional, selective school, with its cups and house-chants, was like a segmented society whose segments hung together by the individual, undifferentiated cells of which each house or unit was composed behaving similarly to one another. Such house-chants, cups and so on are the collective representations in terms of which the collective conscious is constituted. In such songs, the specificity with which each value is spelled out points to the mechanical nature of collective consciousness. Mechanical solidarity is, moreover, also evidenced in the speeches of the teachers who were able to spell out for their houses over large areas of activities in substantive detail what makes a 'good' house member. Moreover, obedience to group norms was coercively imposed, as Julia remembered with some abhorrence, as she recalled the beatings she had witnessed of some boys by others behind the gym when some boy, for example, wished not to conform to that norm to be fulfilled by every 'good' house member that he play cricket for his house. Thus the situation in the traditional school had corresponded to the conditions of mechanical solidarity in which legislation was coercive and not consensual.

Similarly Bernstein claimed that the distinction between setting rather than streaming represented the distinction between organic and mechanical solidarity. As Bernstein says:

If the basis for ordering relationships among the pupils is not a fixed attribute, then the school structure ceases to be stratified and becomes differentiated. This is the case where cognitive ability is seen as a process rather than a substance, a process which does not develop in a uniform way in all subjects, but a process which can be shaped and modified by the social context. (Bernstein, 1971a, p. 163)

Streaming represented ordering relationships in terms of a fixed attribute such as IQ that would enable some pupils to outstrip others in all cognitive performances. Thus children were grouped on the basis of similar performances and rigid stratification took place. 'Streams' thus insulated from one another took on the mechanical features of segmented societies. It was not simply a uniformity of excellence (or mediocrity) in specific subjects such as maths or English that one could 'expect' from an A-stream (or C-stream) boy or girl, but uniformity of moral performance as well. As with the collective consciousness under mechanical solidarity, in which no distinction was made between moral and other attributes, so, too, with the form teacher who would charge wayward pupils with the censure: 'This is not the kind of behaviour that we expect from the A-stream!' Setting, however, is concordant with the conditions of organic solidarity. In the set, it is recognised that performances will not 'develop in a uniform way in all subjects'. A school organised in terms of sets represents, therefore, a social organisation in terms of cohesion on the basis of social differentiation. The solidarity in this case is therefore clearly organic.

With the acceptance of the principle of team-teaching, too, we see shifts from mechanical to organic solidarity. The traditional teacher was regarded as the fount of all knowledge and of all moral values, and as such was the agent of a collective consciousness decidedly mechanical in character. In his activity, no distinction was made between what was legal and what was moral, what was a fact to be accepted or a value that could at least be questioned. The traditional teacher claimed the right to impose facts, values, laws and morals, all equally coercively and equally unquestioningly. But, in team-teaching, organic as opposed to mechanical social relations are in evidence. As Bernstein says:

The subject is no longer dominant, but subordinate to the idea which governs a particular form of integration. If the subject is no longer dominant, then this could affect the position of teacher as specialist ... His allegiance ... may tend to switch ... to the bearing his subject has upon the idea which is relating him to other teachers. (Bernstein, 1971a, p. 167)

The teacher therefore plays a role in the organisation of the school which is not justified in terms of his being *like* other teachers in that, like them, he is a subject specialist. Rather is it his ability to illuminate *different* aspects of what is under consideration on a common theme or topic that marks his function in the team. As Bernstein continues:

> Under these conditions of co-operative, shared teaching roles, the loss of a teacher can be most damaging to the staff because of the interdependence of roles. Here we can begin to see the essence of organic solidarity as it affects the crucial role of teacher. The act of teaching itself expresses the organic articulation between subjects, teachers, and taught. The form of social integration, in the central area of the school's function, is organic rather than mechanical. (Bernstein, 1971a, p. 168)

In team-teaching, too, Bernstein argues that differences of contributions by the teachers alters also the character of the learning experience. Instead of learning experiences being insulated from one another, he claims, in the case of teaching in terms of separate subjects, one kind of learning experience can be related to another. Team-teaching thus affects the organisation of subject matter too, since strong boundaries can no longer be maintained. 'Integration', by which Bernstein appears to mean the removal of (illegitimate) strong boundaries between subjects (Bernstein, 1973, pp. 68–9), becomes the watchword for curricular organisation. Among such all-pervasive collective representations constitutive of mechanical solidarity that went into our typical characterisation were such symbols as the gowns which the staff wore. Along with house-chants and so on, these were the very reductions required by the Durkheimian model which predicted a contraction and generalisation of the hitherto all-pervasive collective consciousness under organic solidarity. The general moral principles that remain are, because they are general, more prone to ambiguity and thus more prone to generate *anomia*. Thus substantive symbols that carry their own, verbally unarticulated but often repeated message are disfunctional under organic solidarity. More frequent discussion of how general rules are to be applied to specific instances are required if *anomia* is to be avoided, and thus schools councils with *genuine* possibilities for *real* dialogue become important.

Bernstein developed his basic Durkheimian model in application to explaining educational change in new ways subsequent to the earlier articles to which we have here so far made reference. He went on to relate his model to problems of working-class ineducability in his famous theory of speech codes, which he has more recently quite radically reformulated further (Bernstein, 1973). There is not space here to do justice to the socio-linguistic controversy that has surrounded the theory of speech codes. We shall rather therefore concentrate on that aspect of the theory that impinges most closely on the central argument of this book. Basically, Bernstein argued that it was possible in speech communities to find two distinct codes: namely, restricted codes and elaborated codes. The restricted code is related to mechanical solidarity as the elaborated code is related to organic solidarity. As Bernstein says:

> Ritual involves a highly redundant form of communication in the sense that, given the social context, the messages are highly predictable. The messages themselves contain meanings which are highly condensed. Thus the major meanings in ritual are extra-verbal or indirect; for they are not made verbally explicit. Ritual is a form of restricted code. (Bernstein, 1971a, p. 163)

We have already noted how rituals such as house-chants or the wearing of gowns are expressive, according to Bernstein, of the collective consciousness under mechanical solidarity. The restricted code, like such non-verbal symbols, is a language of implicit meanings and particularistic in character. The elaborated code, on the other hand, is a language of explicit meanings and universalistic in character. As a result, descriptions in the latter can be understood whether in written or aural form at a spatial or temporal distance from the states of affairs that they describe.

Bernstein and his associates have attempted over the years to define the features of the codes in various publications, the vagaries and details of which will not concern us here. Suffice it to say that Bernstein's argument briefly is as follows. Someone whose socialisation through the family – itself reflecting the wider social structure – had given him access only to the restricted code, would be less successful at high-grade cognitive performances than someone who had access to an elaborated code as well. This was because the syntactical and semantical structure of the codes themselves, the way in which sentences within them could or could not be related to one another (Bernstein, 1973b), either retarded (restricted) or enhanced (elaborated) the possibility of such performances. Although Bernstein's semantic and syntactical descriptions have been either varied or changed completely in the development of his thesis, we will retain here for simplicity his earlier descriptions in terms of classical grammar. The elaborated code, for example, was described as containing the preference for the passive rather than the active voice, as well as the use of impersonal pronouns. As a result, it was claimed, the elaborated code encouraged an emotional detachment from what was being described or evaluated, and such detachment was an essential prerequisite for high-grade cognitive performance. The use of prepositions, moreover, that are indicative of logical as well as spatial and temporal relationships reinforce the elaborated code as an index of high-grade cognitive performance.

The restricted code, however, in failing to produce general meanings and in being tied to the particular, is indicative of a restricted rationality. We might here call upon our own earlier argument in support of Bernstein's definition, at least of rationality. According to this argument, if it can be shown empirically that there are members of a speech community whose communications are expressed purely in terms of a restricted code, then those communications would be indicative of a restricted rationality. It would represent the non-attainment of what we earlier (Chapter 1) described as the 'transcendence of the particular' as one of the criteria for applying the concept of rationality. There are, moreover, further features of the restricted code which would be indicative rule-following, with which we saw the concept of rationality to be critically connected. One such feature was described by Bernstein as follows:

> A statement of fact is often used as both a reason and a conclusion, or more accurately, the reason and conclusion are confounded to produce a categoric statement, e.g. 'Do as I tell you', 'Hold on tight', 'You're not going out', 'Lay off that'. (Bernstein, 1971b, p. 42)

Let us briefly explicate Bernstein's point with reference to 'Hold on tight'. The restricted code, being 'a language of implicit meanings', will thus leave implicit the argument that gives this command its true cogency. Written out explicitly, it might read:

> All people both want to and ought to avoid danger
> (Major premise)
> The bus is lurching dangerously to the right
> (Minor premise)
> There is a handle to be held in such conditions
> (Minor premise)
> _____
> Therefore hold on tightly to the handle (Conclusion)

What Bernstein appears to be arguing, therefore, is that the failure of the restricted code to make such arguments explicit leads the restricted code-user to fail to grasp the distinction between the grounds for an argument (its premises) and the conclusion to which such grounds give rise. Lack of clarity between grounds (premises) and conclusions are clearly indicative of a failure to achieve high-level cognitive performance. Nor need we, in the light of our earlier argument regarding the character of induction and open-class universal terms, pay heed to the criticism that 'high-grade cognitive performance' is simply a subjective and intuitive judgement on Bernstein's part. We argued that human ability to produce general cases could not be explained in terms of a large number of particular observations (Chapter 3). We argued, too, that the empiricist error that sought to explain induction in terms of particular observations and nothing else (such as pre-existent mental structures) was paralleled by the fallacy that regarded natural languages as defective because their universal terms could not be defined in terms of an exhaustive list of particulars, the full enumeration of which would close the class (Chapter 2). A particularistic language in which patterns of reasoning were left implicit would not, therefore, on such an argument be sufficient for producing sophisticated accounts of the world or encouraging the kind of thinking that would lead to their production. At least, left to itself, the kind of thinking represented by the restricted code with its fixation upon the particular could not do so any more than could a mind which, according to the classical empiricist model, was a *tabula rasa* that passively received sensory impressions from particular objects. We see, therefore, in the light of our own account, that it is not simply the result of a kind of carelessness that, in the restricted code, premises – one of which is the major (universalised) premise – are left implicit. It is not simply the case that, by a kind of slip, important distinctions are made ambiguous so that error consequently takes place. Rather it is the structure of the restricted code itself that, to use a Chomskyan expression, fails to 'trigger' the realisation of a basic human competence to universalise various kinds of data in various ways so that a person under the influence of such a code fails, for this reason, to perform his competence in making such premises explicit.

There is, however, a further feature of the restricted code that will be worthwhile mentioning in order to establish Bernstein's thesis about rationality and rule-following before we launch into a critique of that thesis and its underlying Durkheimian model. Bernstein, in earlier statements of the theory of codes, described what he regarded as the phenomenon of 'sympathetic circularity', redescribed later as 'sociocentric sequences' (Bernstein, 1973, pp. 74–94). Examples of this feature of the restricted code were such statements as 'Just fancy!' or 'It's only natural, isn't it!' Such statements have the function of bringing a line of argument or inquiry prematurely to an end before discrete and non-obvious aspects of the case or problem can be unravelled and made explicit. Consider what happens in an inquiry that follows an announcement such as: 'The Russians have landed a rocket on the moon.' We then ask how the person who made the announcement knew, and we hear in reply that it was read in a newspaper or heard on the nine o'clock news. Supposing then we are so affectively aroused by the news that we exclaim 'Just fancy!' and simply rest content with the experience of warm joy or cold horror depending on our point of view. In such a state, we ask no further questions. Yet there are many further questions that we ought to ask and which this explanation and concommitant emotional state is preventing us from asking: questions such as by what methods they have achieved the feat, whether there has been a change of policy in the Kremlin about manned space flight and so forth. Such further and more penetrating questions have been effectively blocked by the form of the statement in the restricted code. Likewise, in moral questioning and inquiry, 'It's only natural, isn't it!' is frequently used to prevent further questioning and to conceal effectively what is at stake in a given moral issue. Such statements ought to be questions followed by question marks, but that we intuitively place exclamation marks beside them instead shows our awareness at that level of their true function.

We have thus seen that a Durkheimian model has generated both a general theory of socialisation within the school community and also a specific theory about the structure of the family within general social structure and the transmission of speech-codes. We have also seen how Bernstein's thesis claims both to be consistent with such an underlying model and also, in some of its aspects, appears to require a rule-following model of inquiry characterised by a definition of rationality such as that discussed earlier in this work (Chapter 1). Organic solidarity, as characterising social structure in general, generates an elaborated code in speech communities both consistent with that structure and high-grade cognitive performances. The practical, educational import of the thesis appears both widely diverse and open to conflicting interpretations, such as those instanced in programmes of verbal enrichment characteristic of such projects as operation Headstart, which derived theoretical support, however inaccurately, from the theory of codes (Lawton, 1968). More generally, the model seeks not simply to explain and predict but also implicitly to justify change. On the one hand, it predicts change from a closed school with a rigidly defined subject-centred curriculum to an 'open' school with an 'integrated' and 'problem-solving' curriculum. It informs us that we need not fear that certain changes (at least) imply breakdown of social authority (like not wearing gowns, not having pupils stand up when staff come in, open disagreement among staff in front of pupils). It does, however, seek to sensitise us to the potential for chaos (*anomia*) in a contracted and generalised central value system. He calls those subjects or curriculum areas that transmit shared values and norms as the 'expressive' as opposed to the 'instrumental' part of the curriculum (that is, that part of the curriculum devoted to entry into the occupational structure of wider society). Thus both he and Lawton stress the need for some form of 'core' or 'common culture' curriculum that will strengthen the individual's grasp on those values that make him part of a shared collective enterprise, despite the social differentiation that accompanies the division of labour. The model, moreover, as we have noted, seeks to justify at least certain changes that have taken place as well as to explain and predict them. If the elaborated code is a feature of a social structure that is characterised by organic solidarity, then an organic society will foster rationality in the form of high-grade cognitive performances more than mechanical societies that encourage a restricted code. Whether the Durkheimian presuppositions that underly Bernstein's theory will license such a justification is something that we have yet to consider. Such a consideration, moreover, is made doubly important because our argument so far appears only partially supportive of Bernstein's account of elaborated codes and rationality. Our differences with him, particularly with reference to the causal character of his model with its own particular biological analogy, must now be clearly delineated. Let us turn, therefore, to some criticisms of Bernstein's thesis, taking first those with which we disagree and then those with which we agree, in the light of which we would seek to modify his account.

7.3 THE DURKHEIMIAN MODEL: SOME CRITICISMS

Let us begin, then, with some objections associated with the names of such writers as Labov and the Baratzes (Labov, 1973, pp. 198–212; Baratz and Baratz, 1972, pp. 188–97). Although empirically based, these do have important epistemological implications in their basic assumptions which bring them within the scope of our present study. These writers have denounced Bernstein's thesis in such terms as 'institutionalised racism' and have claimed the thesis represents an ideological legitimation of working-class educational failure whose true origins are in the class character of an unjust capitalist society.

Labov interpreted Bernstein as meaning by 'restricted code' 'non-standard English', and Bernstein's concern for working-class ineducability was transferred in a North American setting not unnaturally to concern for minority groups such as blacks living in urban ghettos. Many American researchers, moreover, had interpreted Bernstein's thesis as a demand for programmes of verbal enrichment, as in operation Headstart. Headstart, however, broke up as an acknowledged failure with mutual recriminations all round. Labov did some research in which he analysed the non-standard English of the products of New York ghettos, one example of whom was Larry H., a fifteen-year-old ringleader of a gang called the Jets who had recently been downgraded from grade 11 to grade 9 and was threatened with further action by the school authorities. After much trial and error, Labov, in an interview, finally got Larry talking about what God must be like if God exists. On analysis, Larry H.'s reply is shown by Labov to reveal the logical form of a highly complex argument when stripped of the ghetto slang and expletives with which it is accompanied. The argument involves the use of counterfactual conditionals (Larry H. says that he does not believe in God, but *if* God were to exist . . .) that are hardly indicative of a restricted code fixation on particulars in the immediate perceptual field or of the conflation of grounds (premises) or arguments with what follows from them (their conclusions).

Now, it should be noted that there appears to be no disagreement over what is to count as rational or high-grade cognitive performances between Bernstein and Labov. Labov does not take issue with Bernstein over what is a good or a bad argument. Rather the disagreement is over whether there is any empirical basis to Bernstein's claim that there is a series of linguistic entities that make up distinct speech-codes that enhance or retard the attainment of sophisticated patterns of reasoning. The Baratzes and others, however, would propound, as I understand them, a far stronger epistemological thesis that would deny the right of a member of one sub-culture to pass judgement in this way on the forms of reasoning of a member of another. The argument of the Baratzes is that disaffection in the classroom, failure to learn and so on is in fact generated by the action of the ruling class in their imposition of their own dominant minority culture upon the majority who do not share it. Of course, so the argument runs, middle-class children are going to succeed in a school the culture of which is continuous with the culture of their homes and whose learning strategies are consistent with the practices in which they were reared. But the values and goals of the white, middle-class school are not prized because of any transcendental or intrinsic worth that they may have, but simply because they are the values of the dominant economic group. As such, Bernstein's elaborated code simply serves, by its claims to higher rationality, to legitimate the imposition of one culture upon another by obscuring the real social determinants of working-class educational failure. Such failure is no accident, but rather a product of an oppressive social structure that in fact engineers it. The minority dominant culture has, they argue, laid down goals and defined cognitive strategies and abilities for attaining them on grounds most advantageous to themselves and their offspring, namely, in terms of the subjective cultural products and ways of their own group. As the Baratzes say:

> Remediation or enrichment gradually broadens the scope of concern from the fostering of language competence to a broad-based restructuring of the entire cultural system. The end result of this line of argument occurs when investigators such as Deutsch and Deutsch (1968) postulate that 'some environments are better than others.' (Baratz and Baratz, 1972, pp. 190–91)

Clearly in this quotation the Baratzes regard any statement that contravenes their cultural relativistic thesis as the *reductio ad absurdum* of any line of inquiry.

If, however, such an argument succeeds, then the use of Labov's work in support of their thesis becomes illegitimate. If it could never be the case that 'some environments are better than others', irrespective of whether a particular environment or language (such as the ghetto environment and non-standard English) were better or worse than others, then there would appear to be no justification for any kind of organised, community programme for education. There therefore emerge here two epistemological positions conflated incoherently into one in a manner reminiscent of those radical Marxist theorists with whom we dealt in the preceding chapter. There are two quite different criticisms:

(a) Either Bernstein is right that some forms of argument, strategies for understanding the world and so forth are superior to others, but wrong in locating such superiorities in family-structure and speech-codes characteristic of middle-class groups.

(b) Or Bernstein is wrong because there are no transcendental criteria such that one cultural product or cognitive strategy could be objectively judged to be superior to another.

We saw in the previous chapter that there was a failure to distinguish similar questions on the part of Young and his associates over the radical, free-school curriculum. According to (a), we can objectively distinguish between a good and a bad argument as well as a sophisticated from a naïve one, and we can detect patterns of linguistic organisations that mark their achievement. But such patterns do not, according to a critic like Labov, neatly occur or fail to occur in fixed products of clearly definable social groups like standard and non-standard English which he correlated with elaborated and restrictive codes respectively. As such, Cooper supports Labov's thesis. He argues that, in some respects, the grammatical form of what Labov calls NNE (non-standard Negro English) is identical with its logical form in a way in which standard English is not, whereas in other respects this situation is reversed. For example, one feature of NNE is that 'is' (or variants), when used copulatively in standard English, is omitted. As a result, 'is' as a copula cannot in NNE, as it can in standard English, be confused with 'is' when used to express the relation of logical equivalence ('=') where in NNE 'is' is always retained. For example, when we say in standard English 'we are at Jane's house', the word 'are' simply joins 'we' and 'at Jane's house', performing a different logical function from 'we are the Body of Christ', since here identity or equivalence is being asserted. Thus here NNE is arguably logically superior to standard English in making clear logical distinctions which standard English, by using the same term for two logically distinct functions, obscures. On the other hand, NNE obscures distinctions that standard English makes clear, because it has no very clearly developed devices for coping with reported speech. As Cooper says:

> The hearer is entitled to draw quite different implications about the attitudes of the person being spoken about, depending on whether he is given an *obliqua* or *recta* report. If I am told 'John asked "Is the old bag coming to tea?" ' I shall form a lower opinion of John's attitude towards his aunt than I should be entitled to form if I am told 'John asked if the old bag is coming to tea'. (In the latter case, it is the reporter's attitude towards the aunt which I am entitled to infer.) (Cooper, 1978, p. 120)

Thus we see that Bernstein as well as Labov and Cooper are all agreed that there are criteria which make some speech utterances logically superior to others. What divides them is where precisely such speech utterances are to be found and in what categories are they to be grouped. But as such they deny (*b*), to which we have shown the Baratzes to be committed.

In the light of this distinction, and in view of the Marxist character of the criticism of Bernstein, we shall do well to note the extent to which Bernstein's work can be used, notwithstanding its claimed

Durkheimian basis, to support a Marxist case, and the extent to which it cannot. Perhaps either Labov's (or, for that matter, Young's) argument is that there are sophisticated and rational strategies for analysing the world as a prerequisite for changing it. Perhaps part of the dominative character of capitalist society is that, in subtle and discrete ways, the structure of society and of the family has been so distorted as to deprive large sections of the population of the ability to use such higher-order rationality. To that extent, both they and Bernstein will be found to share possible assumptions in common. Where they will part company is over the precise mechanism that prevents access to such a higher-order rationality, with Bernstein locating such a mechanism in speech-codes. Nor would I have anything to say for or against, the case which I would find both logically and epistemologically viable on both sides. All that is lacking would be empirical evidence such as would show that either higher-order rationality was clearly connected to prior learning of a speech-code; or that it was not but was clearly connected with more general and structural social factors; or that it was not but, say, was a question of the somewhat discredited notion of innate intelligence. Either alternative might be true or they might not, and whether they were true or false would be established by empirical research beyond the concern of a work in philosophy. But if the argument against Bernstein is the socially relativistic argument that, when cultures clash, one culture's method of assessing truth, falsehood, meaning and validity is as good as another's, at that point I cannot admit that there is even a viable and testable thesis for reasons that I articulated against phenomenological Marxism in my previous chapter (above, pp. 207–11) and in my previous book (Brent, 1978, pp. 157–61).

Now, it is interesting in pursuing the philosophical pre-suppositions of Bernstein's thesis to observe that Bernstein himself rejects Labov's criticisms in that they ignore Chomsky's competence/performance distinction which Bernstein seeks to uphold (Bernstein, 1973). Chomsky's view of competence, as we shall see, involves the notion of innate mental structures which are reflected in all human languages, the full potentialities of which are only realised partially in actual performance. Bernstein insists that he has never doubted that the cognitive endowment of all human beings is approximately similar. What he was concerned with is how human beings whose competence is approximately similar actually perform that competence so divergently. His original work in the 1950s began by showing that in IQ tests having a verbal form there was a strongly verbal cultural loading (Lee, 1973, pp. 13–20). Non-verbal tests for intelligence on the products of direct-grant grammar schools and on City of London messenger boys from secondary-modern schools showed a far greater degree of positive correlations between scores than did the verbal tests. Reformulate the IQ scores as performances that is some cases mask or retard basic competence, and we have Bernstein's present position. If, therefore, Labov was able to find in Larry H. evidence of a high order of rationality, then, claims Bernstein, he has made no discovery that his original theory did not predict. If, as in other experiments (Lawton, 1968, pp. 103–43), Larry H., when brought under a certain kind of face-to-face questioning, was shown to be capable of a high degree of rationality, this is therefore in agreement with Bernstein's thesis about competence. It was the differential in performance of such competence when such extraordinary pressure was removed that Bernstein was concerned to locate in speech-codes as a function of class/familial structure.

While accepting the validity of Bernstein's reply as well as the thesis of the possibility of trans-cultural criteria of truth, meaning and validity, it must be asked to what extent he has really grasped the way in which what is presupposed by the Chomskyan notion of 'competence' is incoherent with what is presupposed by his Durkheimian model. Durkheim's model was fundamentally a causal model in that different kinds and qualities of human thinking were determined by those *sui generis* social causes that lead to change from mechanical to organic solidarity. Yet, with reference to competence in a Chomskyan, psycholinguistic sense, Bernstein is appealing to mental processes that, we shall see, are to be regarded as in some sense prior to the social. Durkheim might well have said of the notion of competence what he said about the Kantian *a priori*: 'it is no explanation to say that it is inherent in the nature of the human intellect' (Durkheim, 1915, p. 14). He continues:

... what philosophers since Aristotle have called the categories of the understanding: ideas of time, space, class, number, cause, substance, personality, etc ... depend upon the way in which the group is founded and organized, upon its morphology, upon its religious, moral, and economic institutions, etc. (Durkheim, 1915, pp. 12–13, 15–16)

But even accepting the view about the form of social institutions determining the form of thinking (which we do not), and even ignoring the incoherence of the presence of Chomskyan competence with such a model, Bernstein's theory in other respects cannot be squared with such an underlying model. Bernstein's thesis is not that of Whorf's, namely, that language determines thinking, in that it imposes 'absolutely obligatory' patterns (Whorf, 1956, pp. 60–61). Rather his thesis maintains that, although thinking without language can take place, it would be of a rudimentary and unstructured kind in that language shapes and sharpens thinking without determining it absolutely. Yet for Durkheim, as we see from this quotation, fundamental concepts like space, time, cause, number or class are determined by the shape and structure of social institutions. We see, therefore, that there are unresolved problems with the underlying Durkheimian model that must be resolved by a more logically adequate reformulation of its basic concepts if such a model is to incorporate adequately Bernstein's acceptance both of competence and his rejection of causal determinism. Let us now discuss how this is to be done.

In the light of our general objections to causal explanations of human action, particularly linguistic action, we can see some reasons as to why the causal framework, in terms of which Durkheim's model is structured, is inadequate (Chapters 2 and 5). Like dialectical arguments about historical development, Durkheim's theory relies heavily on societal development being understood by analogy with biological development. Societies are either segmented and like simply unicellular organisms such as amoeba or polyps where collections of cells hang loosely together without much differentiation; or societies are organic, like highly organised life-forms with differentiated cell structures with high levels of interaction and integration of function and so forth. As such, the objections that we raised (above, pp. 249–52) to the assimilation of social to biological explanation in the case of dialectical understanding of historical development will apply here too, and we need not rehearse them further. We can also see how such a causal account in the social sciences is as incapable of producing the kind of ethical argument about the rightness of change that we saw (Chapter 3) to be the case with the theory of evolution in biology. Yet Bernstein's theory, propounded on the basis of a Durkheimian model, we saw to be one that not only claimed to be able to explain and predict but also to justify change. Implicit in the statement of the theory was the assumption not only that the change from mechanical to organic society was reflected in a change in institutional and curricular organisation within schools, but also that such changes *ought to* take place. Yet a causal model, violating as it does the fact/value distinction in ethics, cannot yield such a justification of an ethical assumption (Brent, 1978, pp. 118–21).

But our objections to the Durkheimian causal framework are not simply that it fails to yield an adequate ethical justification which it plainly requires. We must give grounds also why such a causal account of the origins in social structure of categories of thinking also fails, because it is at this point that Durkheim's thesis came into fundamental conflict with our own. Let us look therefore more closely at what he believed to be the cause of the change from mechanical to organic solidarity, with a corresponding change in categories of thinking. The cause he argued to be that of population growth, accompanied by a growth in what he termed 'moral density'. By moral density he meant not simply an increase in population numbers *per se*, but a numerical increase accompanied by increased interaction between members in the form of increased communication, transport or general mobility. This, his 'law of gravitation of the social world' (Durkheim, 1964, p. 262), was further explained with reference to the theory of evolution. As Lukes says:

> Appealing to Darwin's theory that the more alike two organisms are, if resources are scarce, the more severe is the competition between them, he reasoned that, given scarce resources, increased contact between undifferentiated individuals would entail heightened competition between them – which is resolved by the division of labour. (Lukes, 1973, p. 170)

Thus it is not, he claimed, that individuals created in rule-following ways solutions to problems and thus self-consciously moved from one set of social relations to another. Logic, classes, categories and so on were, as we saw in an earlier quotation, the effects and not the causes of social change. As he says:

> Cosmic space was primitively constructed on the model of social space, that is, on the territory occupied by society and as society conceives it; time expresses the rhythm of collective life; the notion of class was at first no more than another aspect of the notion of a human group; collective force and its power over men's minds served as prototypes for the notion of force and causality, etc. (Quoted in Lukes, 1973, p. 442)

Hence spatial relations, classes and so on are, in any given type of society, a function of tribal groups, clans, territorial relations or whatever. On this view, our argument in this book regarding understanding universals as open-class concepts, substituting family resemblance for exhaustive definition of bound classes and so on is but the effect of a change from a closed society with fixed class boundaries of a social kind to an open society where class structure is more fluid and less precise.

Thus we find that the basic assumptions of the Durkheimian model conflict both with our basic argument as well as with Bernstein's introduction into it of the notion of competence. Now, against such an argument regarding the social determination of thinking, there are a number of objections to be made, falling under roughly three headings.

First, we have shown grounds already why causal accounts about the determination either of thinking or of behaviour or of thinking *as* behaviour cannot be supported by appeals to evolutionary biology. Such accounts themselves, by resting on the sufficiency of descriptions of natural events in terms of statistically recurring probabilities, call into question the principle of individual causal determination. We have already charged, with reference to theories both of Skinner and of Quine, that such accounts are statistical redescriptions of problems masquerading as explanations.

Secondly, there is the kind of objection expressed by Lukes as follows:

> No account of relations between features of a society and the ideas and beliefs of its members could ever explain the faculty, or ability, of the latter to think spatially and temporally, to classify material objects and to individuate persons, to think causally and, in general, to reason; nor could it ever show that the necessity, or indispensibility, of doing all these things was simply an aspect of social authority. For, in the first place, the very relations established must always presuppose the prior existence of these very abilities; the aboriginal must have the concept of class in order even to recognise the classifications of his society let alone extend them to the universe . . . In the second place, the very necessity of these conditions of thought makes the hypothesis of their causal determination unstatable. (Lukes, 1973, p. 447)

The thesis is 'unstable' because, for the thesis to be valid empirically, we must be able to state how social conditions could so change that men were not caused to think in any possible category of space, time, logic, classification or whatever. Yet we have to use these very categories to think the possibility of their non-existence, so that we find ourselves postulating what is logically impossible. What Durkheim's thesis on this showing demands is some notion of competence, such as that which Bernstein clearly has sought to give it. Such a notion of competence would perform the critical theoretical function of showing what it was about human beings that made it possible for them in the first place to construct the social orders that they did. Far, therefore, from such a rationalist explanation warranting the charge that: 'it is no explanation to say that it is inherent in the nature of the human intellect' (Durkheim, 1964, p. 14), rather, in the final analysis, is it precisely this kind of explanation that the logic of the argument demands. We shall be arguing too (below, pp. 330–42) that, in the final analysis, the logic of a later Wittgensteinian argument also demands a particular kind of account of what makes possible an agreement in a human form of life (Brent, 1978, pp. 154–7 ff.).

Thirdly, we may deploy an argument derivable from my central thesis in this work which will represent in some ways a development of these first two objections. My thesis has been that any rule-conforming model of human action is bound to collapse on the sound Kuhnian principle of the inadequacy of any paradigm that finds critical phenomena intractable in terms of its central features. When we analyse the character of human languages, we find that such a causal, rule-conforming model cannot apply. Irrespective of the specifically Chomskyan examples yet to be discussed, such phenomena as tensed denials in past time or open-class concepts make linguistic ability indicative of an ability to transcend the particular, to process sensory data by ignoring certain features of some particulars in order to propound a general case (above, pp. 114–25). Moreover, we demonstrated in connection with an empiricist strategy (exemplifying what we described as 'logical imperialism') that an ideal language in which general terms consisted simply of closed concatenations of particulars, far from improving linguistic communication, would make language incapable of functioning as a system of communication. If general terms, if language did not have an open-ended character, we argued, then any human language would be reduced to chaos every time some new particular and possible instance of the class was discovered (above, pp. 77–86). Unless, for example, we were able not simply to classify actual tables in the general term 'table' but new possible instances of tables too, then language would be unable to function. It would be overwhelmed with new expressions, with members of the speech-community absent from the immediate perceptual experience that gave rise to the new term, unable to grasp its meaning. The ideal language of the empiricists' dream, where every concept was a sign indicating the unique and exhaustive list of features of that to which it referred, was a logical impossibility. What might have made such a language just about possible was a universe with a fixed number of objects. But we saw that Einstein's universe was an expanding universe in which possibilities were infinite (above, pp. 112–19). Human understanding reflected in ordinary language was therefore isomorphic with the structure of Einstein's universe. If, however, human understanding of the world did not come about as a result of a causal process, and if statistical redescriptions of such a process were no real explanations of what it is to follow as opposed to conform to a rule, then rules for understanding in human languages were normative in character. To follow a rule implied being able to break the rule. It is arguable, therefore, that human communication systems are, for this reason, to be regarded as normative. It is possible to break certain rules in some instances and for some purposes, such as the logical rule of non-contradiction in some parts of quantum physics; or, say, to produce some exhaustive definitions of universal terms for some purposes. To do this, however, in general would mean that a human system of communication collapsed in general under weight of a total contravention of a normative order.

Now, we must see how from this, my general thesis, a third objection arises to the Durkheimian account in far more detail than the general objection to social determinism. If we accept Bernstein's additions to the account, as we have argued that we must, and accept the pressures to reformulate it in rule-following terms, the account itself becomes drastically altered. It is arguably far from the phenomenon that the Durkheim/Bernstein thesis describes as mechanical solidarity, with a restricted code representing a state of affairs logically prior to organic solidarity (or perhaps 'embryonically prior' would be better in view of the biological analogy), our understanding of such a social organisation rather being parasitic upon our understanding of organic solidarity with an elaborated code as representing a genuinely normative linguistic order. If the restricted code that is the linguistic index of mechanical solidarity exemplifies a breakdown in certain rules normative for human communication systems (meaning that if they were not generally applied they would become chaotic), then there is implied the *a priori* presence of such rules implicit in those systems (such as rules for identification of members of open-classes through family-resemblance) even when they have restricted code types of feature. Moreover, it is further arguable that, in the light of our central thesis, the change from mechanical to organic solidarity when indicated by the change from restricted to elaborated code represents a *reversion* to a normative order implicit in language. The restricted code itself represents a fixation on particulars, a failure to generalise, a tendency to close classes because of a preoccupation with actual rather than possible instances and so forth. As such, it represents the violation of a normative order that, if generalised and no longer limited to a few exceptions, would cease to function as a communication system at all. It is interesting to note to what extent empiricist accounts almost represent a self-conscious reversion to the principles (or rather violating principles) of a restricted code. The example is the self-conscious fixation on particulars in the claim that a sentence can neither have meaning nor truth unless it is anchored, either itself or through a regress of propositions, in certain experiences of particulars beyond language ('sense-data'), given infallibly in sensation. Simple descriptions of such sensations are defined ostensively (that is, by pointing to them without the use of words). Likewise, in the restricted code, all is particularistic and descriptions can be understood, not from the passages in which they occur by themselves, but only if one has direct access to that beyond language to which such descriptions refer. Another example is the early Wittgenstein's desire for an ideal language in which each 'sign' would picture the particular that it described, rather like the restricted code user who, when asked how the ride on the train was, places his hand on his backside and says 'Ouch, hard!' (above, pp. 70–5). We see how then in the light of our general argument for a rule-following model the Durkheimian model, in the light of this third objection, undergoes critical reformulation. The existence of a social order developed mechanically in that it is indicated by a restricted code, presupposes a normative linguistic order that is elaborated, characterised by open categories and so on, however much that order may be implicit in human speech acts, like Chomsky's notion of competence. Unless such a normative order exists implicit in language, there cannot be a restricted code that we have argued to be necessarily understood in terms of a violation of or departure from such an order. Restricted and mechanical features cannot totally inform a linguistic communication system, any more than can exhaustively defined closed-classes overall, without semantic collapse.

Thus with mention of an implicit, universal and normative semantic order characteristic of human languages, such as that for which we have argued in our previous book as well as in this, we find ourselves very much with Bernstein's use of 'competence' on Chomskyan ground. The implicit or tacit character of such an order locates it within the general thesis of Chomsky that has recourse, as we have already mentioned (above, pp. 215–18), to the notion of 'tacit', or 'unconscious', or 'implicit' rule-following. As such, moreover, we have seen that we share similar ground with Bernstein, since, although Bernstein never brings this point out, evocation of the competence/performance distinction locates his thesis in rule-following, linguistic models that require such notions as innate ideas and implicit or tacit knowledge of rules, with social situations acting as triggering mechanisms. Furthermore, we see that a Durkheimian model, with its essentially causal presuppositions, requires reformulation if it is to service Bernstein's case.

In aid of such rule-following reformulation, let us begin by recalling the thesis of our previous book. The point of dialogue and its effects when genuine was, we argued, to make explicit the framework of judgement in human assertions about themselves and the world. Such a framework was normative and included not simply logical but semantic rules as well, among which were rules for making and distinguishing between empirical/mathematical/moral/religious/aesthetic/historical-sociological sets of meanings and truths. We said:

> ... when men try to talk about reality as though it were construct-able in terms of only one form ... they find that they cannot state their case. The judgement that they are trying to make becomes unsayable. When men talk about their reality, for example, as though it were constructable in totally aesthetic terms, the forms of knowledge implicit along with the general principles of logic in their language as in ours, necessarily become explicit. Distinctions come necessarily to be made between moral and non-moral aesthetic descriptions, empirical and non-empirical aesthetic descriptions, mathematical and non-mathematical aesthetic descriptions, religious and non-religious aesthetic descriptions, historical-sociological and non-historical/non-sociological aesthetic descriptions ... Discussion therefore becomes ... the means of unravelling and making explicit that universal framework of judgement with which particular judgements are confronted when men engage in public discourse. (Brent, 1978, p. 216)

Katz's Chomskyan thesis of semantic universals does not yet include rules for making specifically empirical, mathematic, moral, religious, aesthetic and historical-sociological judgements in a way that would explain how what Hirst describes as these 'forms of knowledge' are present in human languages. We will outline in Chapter 8 both the need and the means of working out their inclusion in terms of semantic rules of a Katz type of semantic theory (see below, pp. 326–32). We will also be looking at a defence of the logical coherence of talk of 'implicit knowledge of rules', so critical if we adopt such a semantic model.

For the moment, however, in the light of this statement of our earlier thesis, let us conclude with a rule-following interpretation of Durkheim's causal notion of 'moral density' as responsible for the shift from mechanical to organic solidarity. In the light of such a rule-following reformulation, we can understand what he is saying in a new way. We can understand 'moral density' in terms not simply of communication, but in terms of an increased intensity of dialogue in which the drift from the implicit normative framework witnessed in a restricted code is reversed by the explicit reassertion of a logically prior framework of judgement. In the restricted code, men contravene the normative rule-structure implicit in their communication systems by strategies that we have described as logical imperialism (reducing one form of understanding to another, exhaustive quantification and so on). So long as they proceed to do so gradually and partially throughout the system, the logically invalid character of the strategy as normative infringement my go unnoticed as also the threatened collapse of the communication system. Men may not, because of the kind of social organisation – namely, mechanical solidarity – that surrounds use of the restricted code and encourages it, notice how they are distorting and violating the rule-structure implicit in their language. They might not recognise the blind alley into which the development of a restricted code might lead them, particularly when, like the empiricists, they are deploying exhaustive quantified analyses and definitions in order to say what they think to be precisely true or false. Thus, in mechanical societies, contraventions of the normative, semantic order implicit in speech-acts may tend to go unnoticed and be perpetuated for long periods of time, even as may sometimes happen self-consciously in organic societies, as we noticed in the case of our analysis of empiricism as an example of logical imperialism. But, with the increase in 'moral density', that is to say, increased interaction and community made possible by new discoveries, the intensity of dialogue is increased. With such an increase, the detection of false moves in man's quest to impose meaning and order upon the world is more likely to take place and the implicit and tacit normative order of language made explicit and extended in the form of new and more valid accounts of the world and of man's place within it.

With the mention both of Hirst's theory and the forms of knowledge, and of our previous interpretation of it as a possible part of a theory of semantic universals, we reach the point in our present discussion in which, in the light of our present thesis, we can extend such an interpretation. Hirst's theory and its further discussion, moreover, falls naturally into the present context, since, while presupposing, as we shall show, a rule-following model, it can be understood also in some ways in terms of Bernstein's general theory of changes within the school. In fact, there can be an interpretation of Hirst's thesis that makes it precisely what a strictly Durkheimian model would predict, though its rule-following aspirations are better satisfied if we understand it in the light of the reformulated Durkheimian model that we have proposed. Although we have extensively described and discussed Hirst's theory in our first book, nevertheless, for the benefit of new readers, let us briefly summarise what Hirst's theory states (Brent, 1978, Chapters 3 and 4).

7.4 HIRST'S THEORY AND THE DURKHEIMIAN PERSPECTIVE

Hirst's argument is that the contents of a curriculum of liberal education are able to be established objectively in that the choice of objectives is not arbitrary. By 'objectively' he therefore appears to mean that reasons can be given for some forms of curriculum subjects and activities rather than others that will be mutually binding on both sides in warring curriculum factions. As such, Hirst's thesis claims to be able to settle certain controversies over the nature of education, such as (*a*) the subject-centred *versus* the project or topic-centred approach, or (*b*) the debate over whether education should be 'liberal' rather than 'vocational' or vice versa. As the thesis requires reference to certain constructs called 'forms of knowledge' that are postulated as defining the basis of the ground shared by both sides, for this reason presumably the thesis is also called a 'theory' (Hirst, 1974*a*, p. 47 and pp. 30–53).

Hirst's thesis is that if you take any kind of serious human activity in which claims about 'knowledge' or 'truth' are made, and ask what kinds of statements and procedures for testing their truth these can be reduced to in analysis, you will find that they reduce to six or so different kinds of statements with corresponding different tests for truth. Thus, if we take any one of the limitless number of subjects either on offer in the various curricula of schools, colleges, technical institutes or universities or, for that matter, practised in industrial technology or design, we can see that such subjects or practices presuppose one or more of these limited number of forms of knowledge. Engineering presupposes empirical and mathematical forms with also economics that in turn presupposes the historical-sociological form. Design technology may not require the historical-sociological form in addition to the first two, but in its place must be put the aesthetic form. Subjects like physics and chemistry, too, though substantively different from one another, share formally the distinct empirical and mathematical forms to which must be added the moral, since without respect for truth as respect for evidence such kinds of inquiry could not get very far. Social work or law, on the other hand, presupposes the moral and the historical-sociological or whatever. When, however, we come to the forms themselves, once we have arrived at them through such reductive analysis, we find that they do not reduce to one another or to some third form. Each form remains a logically distinct kind of inquiry with logically distinct kinds of tests for truth. That this is so is not for Hirst a mere assertion. We can try a kind of language experiment to see what we can and cannot logically make our language assert with meaning. The logical sense of 'can' in the previous sentence does, of course, need stressing.

In one sense, people 'can' and do make the following statements, but only to produce the partial collapse of the normative, semantic order of their language:

(*a*) Someone who was so beautiful as her could not but be good (reduction of a moral to an aesthetic statement).

(*b*) For me the drug problem is simply how to find the stuff and acquire the money to pay for it (reduction of moral to an empirical statement).

(*c*) God could not in view of the theory of evolution have created the world (reduction of religious to empirical statement).

(*d*) The beauty that I see in nature is all that talk of God really amounts to (reduction of religious to an aesthetic statement).

(*e*) Two plus two must equal four because, look, here are two amoeba and over there are another two and all together they make four (reduction of a mathematical to an empirical statement).

(*f*) The French Revolution was inevitable just as a chemical reaction must occur when given chemicals are united in a specified solution (reduction of historical-sociological to an empirical statement).

In each of these statements, and in countless others that could be produced, we have an assumed reducibility of one kind of inquiry or form of knowledge to another. Yet the reduction of one statement to the other produces no new synthesis or order of meaning, but rather a misunderstanding or misrepresentation, often intentional, or both of the statement that is so reduced. (For a fuller discussion of reducibility and irreducibility and their epistemological implications for Hirst's thesis, see Brent, 1978, pp. 94–138 ff.)

From such a thesis, certain solutions follow for certain current controversies in educational debate. The debate over whether the curriculum should be taught in a subject-centred or in a topic- or project-centred way is resolved by saying that either is valid so long as subjects or projects or topics introduce students to the forms of knowledge. Likewise, the dispute over whether education shall be liberal or vocational is shown equally to have involved an argument at cross-purposes. The forms of knowledge, definitive of what it is to have a rational mind, are definitive therefore of what it is to be liberally educated (Hirst, 1974*a*, p. 39). But technical and vocational activities, as we saw with engineering and law, draw upon them and rise out of them. As such, liberal education, consisting of the initiation of the student by the teacher into the forms of knowledge, is not necessarily inconsistent with a vocational or technical education.

Rather we should see general education liberally defined as leading from a general introduction to the forms of knowledge into some particular and substantive application of a group of 'forms' in technical or vocational education (Brent, 1978, pp. 130–34).

Now, in the light of an unreformulated Durkheimian model, Hirst's approach to curriculum planning appears to some extent to represent a social-therapy approach in a society which, because it is organic in nature, has anomic tendencies that require remedy. Reactions to the concept of 'liberal' or 'general' studies by many hardened practitioners of trades, crafts, technical, and technological subjects in colleges of Further Education in the United Kingdom (Technical and Further Education (TAFE) colleges in Australia) present, on this view, examples of the need for social therapy. Students and very often staff claim, for instance, that they 'know' their subjects and skills, that they can 'see' the vocational and occupational point of doing them. But talk in liberal studies of human appreciation of the aesthetic or moral rights and duties of good citizenship are considered 'vague' or 'woolly'. Thus the FE (or TAFE) curriculum and the attitudes that it generates are precisely those predicted by Durkheim in relation to conditions of organic solidarity. We know how and can spell out what makes a good engineer, builder, hairdresser or plumber, say, in terms of the division of labour, but in terms of a contracted and generalised collective consciousness, we cannot rival such precision in our definitions of the 'good' life or the 'good' man or woman. Hirst's theory of liberal education therefore postulates that technical knowledge is the extension in particular, chosen occupational spheres of forms of knowledge transmitted in a programme of liberal, general education from society's shared values regardless of particular occupational pursuits. As such, in Durkheimian terms, it represents the passing on of valued knowledge constitutive of the consensus represented by the collective consciousness (or central value system) in contrast to the individual and often conflicting occupational values of given individuals. The theory may thus be represented as one of strengthening, under conditions of organic solidarity, the central value system whose general and abstract character is likely to generate an anomia that pulls society apart. The irreducibility, moreover, of these six or so distinct categories is, on such a reading of the theory, an index of the social pluralism in values generated by conditions of organic solidarity (see also Brent, 1978, pp. 171–3, 182–3).

We have, however, already seen why Durkheim's, like any other causal, rule-conforming explanation such as that of the emergence of a theory such as Hirst's, requires rule-following reformulation. In such a reformulation, we have already appealed to the notion of implicit or tacit knowledge in Chomskyan theory as postulating the implicit presence of the rules for an elaborated code in speech-acts characterised explicitly as restricted code, and that correlate with conditions of organic and mechanical solidarity respectively. As such, if we made Hirst's theory part of a theory of linguistic competence implicitly present in a restricted code so that the forms were transcultural and in some sense survived and persisted over changes in social structure, then we shall have incorporated the theory into a theory of semantic universals. But since Hirst would reject the incorporation of his theory into such a model, we will do well to draw our general consideration of Chomskyan themes in our argument into a specific description and discussion of the theory of linguistic universals in the next chapter, with particular reference to the philosophical issues raised. Such an incorporation, as we shall see, will lead to as radically great a change of understanding of Hirst's thesis as the explication of the competence performance distinction and its incorporation into Bernstein's thesis did there also. To this task, begun in an earlier work (Brent, 1978) and continued here, we now turn.

Chapter 8

Forms of Knowledge, Categorial Concepts and Linguistic Universals

In the previous chapter we discussed Hirst's thesis of the forms of knowledge as being the kind of account required by Bernstein's application of the Durkheimian principle of organic solidarity to required changes in the organisation of the curriculum. Such a model of curriculum change, as a causal model, we argued to be invalid as an account of the reasons for human action. Pressure for reformulation in rule-following terms we saw, however, had come from within the model itself, which was found to require the Chomskyan competence/performance distinction. In this chapter, therefore, we shall be considering Chomsky's rule-following model and some philosophical objections to it. In particular, as a model for understanding curriculum, we shall be considering what both Hirst and Hamlyn regard as a more satisfactory, later Wittgensteinian alternative to Chomsky's work as a framework for curriculum judgements. Then, finally, we shall conclude our account with our grounds for why Chomsky and the later Wittgenstein are not the representatives of such conflicting theses as Hirst and Hamlyn assume. In the course of this concluding argument, we shall, through a particular analysis of particular substantive and categorial concepts, be making a far more detailed application of family-resemblance analysis to the forms of knowledge as semantic universals than the general account of such an analysis already given (above, pp. 77–87).

8.1 CHOMSKY AND THE THEORY OF LINGUISTIC UNIVERSALS

Although there are important philosophical implications in Chomsky's theory, it is considered by Chomsky himself to be an empirically testable theory. The critical question for him is whether linguistic data presented by human languages could be adequately explained within a behaviourist framework of assumptions. Chomsky invites us to understand investigations into language-acquisition in terms of feeding data into a black box and examining the resultant output. If the behaviourists were right about language-acquisition through a stimulus–response–associationist process, then the output would be very similar in form to the input. But if the output is far richer, more articulate, and represents a structured reorganisation of the input data, then we are entitled to make an inductive inference that within the black box there is a complex processing mechanism to account for this changed form. Let us call this mechanism a language-acquisition device (LA) and describe in Chomsky's words the empirical character of the resultant research programme:

> To study the substantive issue, we first attempt to determine the nature of the output in many cases, and then to determine the character of the function relating input to output. Notice that this is an entirely empirical matter; there is no place for any dogmatic or arbitrary assumptions about the intrinsic, innate structure of the device LA. (Chomsky, 1975, p. 122)

We ourselves earlier in this work might appear to have pursued a similar empirical method, in that in criticising what either an empiricist or behaviourist could or could not do with language (that is, make language mirror each particular object in the universe clear and determinately), we appeared to be basing our criticism on the factual basis of what human languages were like, though they might have been otherwise (above, pp. 85–7). My own view is that such an argument is better classified as *a priori*, since it is about the basic form of human linguistic experience and what necessarily follows from this. Against the view that what could possibly have been other cannot be necessary, or *a priori*, I would maintain that only what could have been other in something less than evolutionary time scale warrants the description empirical as opposed to necessary. There is not space here to pursue my argument in greater detail (but see Kitcher, 1980, with which cf. Brent, 1978, pp. 214–22). Suffice it to say, however, that whether 'empirical' or '*a priori*' is a more adequate description of a thesis postulating an innate language-acquisition device, the methodological issue is here more complex than Chomsky suggests. Let me exemplify my problem with reference to the philosophy of logic, in which the question is often posed as to whether the laws of logic (like generative grammars) represent the laws of thought (substitute 'principle' if you do not like 'law', but it amounts to the same). If they do, the question can then be raised as to whether the statement: 'Because human thought (equivalent to laws of logic) proceeds in a certain way, then it logically follows that x implies y', is an empirical statement. But if it is, then any *a priori* or analytic statement, being about what the structure of language allows or does not allow us to say, is an inductive inference from a fact about the world, namely, the fact of human language. If, however, we grant this, the decision as to whether Chomsky's thesis is empirical or *a priori* becomes impossible to make because the distinction itself cannot be made (though see Kitcher, 1980). If, however, Chomsky has stated his methodological position somewhat misleadingly, a critic such as Cooper has done so even more when he claims that Chomsky cannot be a genuine heir to classical rationalism's theses. His grounds are that Chomsky's thesis, being self-confessedly (but misleadingly, I have claimed) an empirical thesis about innate ideas, is not in accordance with Leibniz's claims about the *a priori* necessity of the foundations of human thought (Cooper, 1972, pp. 468–76 ff.). Moreover, Cooper's criticisms appear more markedly strange since in other of his writings, he supports Quine's attack on the synthetic/ analytic distinction (Cooper, 1980, pp. 97–104).

Let us, however, begin by pursuing the thesis as though it were primarily an empirical thesis, like a scientific theory conceived in terms of a Kuhnian paradigm. Accordingly, we might claim that Chomsky was right and the behaviourists were wrong because Chomsky's theory accounted for and explained data intractable within the latter's theory. Now, Chomsky would admit that simple correlations of words with objects, such as a child correlating the word 'horse' with an animal seen grazing in a field at a parent's instigation, could be explained in terms of a stimulus-response process in a way that I have already described (above, pp. 21–5). In view of what we have described about the nature of learning an open-class universal (like 'table'), Chomsky perhaps ought not to have even admitted that (above, pp. 77–80). But even granted that admission, a human language could not be acquired solely by means of a stimulus-response learning process (Chomsky, 1959). One reason why this is so is because a stimulus-response theory implies that children cannot acquire language without something closely approximating to how it regards a process of formal instruction. It implies that, since children from about the age of four onwards articulate grammatically well-formed sentences with novel associations made between other sentences and other words, it must be because somewhere in their social environments complex schedules of reinforcement exist. The more complex and articulate the form of the behavioural performance, therefore, the more complex and articulate the stimulating schedule of reinforcement and vice versa. Thus behaviourism presupposes that something analogous to learning a second language has gone on in learning a first. Take any standard, written introductory course for learning a foreign language, for example, German. We are systematically introduced to the grammar and syntax through carefully graded, step-by-step explanations and exercises. At the same time, we are systematically and in a planned way introduced to the various contexts in which communication in the language will go on. Under the titles of such contexts, we learn words, phrases, styles of address and so on. Under such titles as 'Im Flughaffen', 'Im Bahnhof', 'In der Klasse', 'Im Garten', we are taken in an orderly progression from the home to the wider culture and taught to describe all that we need to describe, ask what typically we may need to ask. Yet children are not taught their first language in this manner. They pick up isolated fragments of what adults are saying to each other and to which they are exposed in no order of complexity or in any systematic way. Moreover, the linguistic data themselves are often degenerate forms of the grammar and syntax which is incomplete and the expressions of which are only partially formed. Yet before going to school, as a result, apparently, of exposure to such arbitrarily occurring experiences with no clear form, the child is speaking grammatically. Therefore, Chomsky argues:

> The problem is, precisely, to determine how the child determines that the structure of his language has the specific characteristics that empirical investigation of language leads us to postulate, given the meagre evidence available to him. Thus the child learns the principles of sentence formation and sentence interpretation on the basis of a corpus of data that consists, in large measure, of sentences that deviate in form from the idealized structures defined by the grammar that he develops. (Chomsky, 1975, p. 127)

Yet children from about the age of four impose logical regularity upon the illogical irregularity of adult speech. Chomsky's solution is to postulate an innate rule-structure with which the child is born, in the light of whose order it comprehends the data, finishing off by itself the malformations and deviations by means of such an innate endowment. Some empirical support for this thesis, moreover, can be found in such writers as McNeill, who argued on the basis of investigations that children did not repeat syntactical patterns in proportion to the number of times that they hear these from adults, but are rather highly selective about what they repeat. Thus it is arguable on the basis of the empirical evidence that the child is operating with a pre-existent syntactic structure that leads him to process some data before others (McNeill, 1972).

There are, moreover, other features of the data of language with which a behaviourist model cannot cope because as a method it is badly flawed, in addition to those that we have already described (above, pp. 115–25). Chomsky's main argument is that a method which restricts itself to looking at actual linguistic performances by individuals or groups cannot hope to be able to explain the creativity of language. From an early age, children are able to produce sentences with new combinations of words and ideas, often, as with the phenomenon of family-resemblance, adaptable to apply to new and unusual situations and objects. But if this is the case, and our ability to do this is never exhausted, we must only ever perform a small part of what the rules of our language enable us or make us competent to perform. It is technically possible, for example, to produce a sentence which goes on for ever, as in the case of the nursery rhyme, 'The House that Jack Built' ('This is the priest all shaven and shorn that married . . . that . . .' and so on). We have, of course, pointed to certain metaphysical implications of the structure of ordinary language, which, as such, is isomorphic with the structure of an expanding universe (above, pp. 117–19). But what we regard as the implications of such a view of language we have already spelled out so that they need not detain us here. Whether, then, it be a consequence of the shortness of life or of the nature of human experience indicated by a language that is isomorphic with a post-Newtonian world, our competence can never be fully performed, for the reason that only non-linguistic causes will end the never-ending sentence (for example, boredom, exhaustion, my death or some such event).

What, therefore, syntactic and related semantic theory must be able to do is to describe the rule-system definitive of that basic linguistic competence to some extent independently of descriptions of performances (Chomsky, 1972, pp. 115–20). In a phrase that we have coined, we must give some account of the semantic and normative order that, while it may be broken as an exception to the rule in degenerate forms of speech, must nevertheless be postulated if the existence of a characteristically human, rule-following communication system is to be explained at all. The problem here is that in observable performances only the surface structure of a sentence is available to us. Yet, if all there was required for understanding the sentence was the form of its surface structure, as behaviourists insist, that surface structure would have to be clear and determinate, just like the clear and determinate grooves that produce the articulate sound of a well-playing record disc (above, pp. 286–7). But, in the case of the surface structure of natural languages, that we have argued in this respect (above, pp. 287–8) to be irreformable, there are not merely degenerate and ill-formed features, but also ambiguities. The hearer therefore is required actively to select which interpretation applies. Therefore, in return, there is implied the availability of semantic rules applied by the hearer to such surface structures.

Take, for example, the *double entendre*: 'I like her cooking.' From a single surface structure, several sets of distinct meanings can be derived, and one set of rules rather than another be acted upon. Its meaning cannot be understood as either a stimulus that elicits a given response or as a series of sounds which become meaningful (morphemes) because they picture objects or situations that they describe. This sentence can mean: 'I like the way she cooks' (that is, I am a male chauvenist pig that thinks she looks pretty in an apron'). Alternatively, it can mean: 'I like what she cooks', or 'I like to see her cooked' (that is, I am a cannibal). Take, as a second example, a sentence which, although not a *double entendre*, exemplifies sentences whose surface structures exhibit formal similarity but whose semantic functions are divergent. Compare, for example, the sentence (*a*) 'John is easy to please' with the sentence (*b*) 'John is eager to please' (Chomsky, 1972, pp. 103–6 ff.). If what these sentences meant was conveyed by their surface structure, it would be impossible for us to deduce that (*a*) has a passive meaning ('easy' is what John is to be pleased) whereas (*b*) is active (his eagerness is directed to others to please them). Implicit rule-following must be taking place, Chomsky argues, below the surface at the level of the deep structure of the sentence. It must, moreover, be 'implicit' because, unless we are generative grammarians, we are not conscious of the rules that we are applying nor of our selection of different rules in order to derive different meanings.

Now this 'deep-structure' of implicit rules applied to a sentence is definitive of human linguistic competence. The spelling out of its terms will be found in the writing out of transformational rules by means of which meaning can be derived from the surface structure. In fact, this is perhaps a too inductivist way of characterising semantic processes since there are few reliable cues in the surface structure to 'derive' anything so that it really becomes a problem of how deep-structural meanings are 'transformed' into surface-structural statements. This spelling out of the terms of linguistic competence is what those lists of tranformational rules and tree diagrams are which form the mechanics of the theory, but with the details as opposed to the philosophical implications of which we cannot be concerned here (see, for example, Chomsky, 1972; Katz, 1972; Lyons, 1977). Thus, in such terms, Chomsky argues his case that, since what we are exposed to in experience are ambiguous and indeterminate surface-structural performances, we could not make the articulate sense that we do of data that are basically inarticulate. Moreover, when we say 'without deep-structural rules', as in the last sentence, it is important to note that Chomsky is arguing that there must be, in some real sense, albeit unconscious, *knowledge* of deep-structural rules.

Exception, however, has been taken to this notion by many writers who seek to apply to it the principle of Harman's Fork (Harman, 1967, and, for example, Hamlyn, 1978, p. 33). This is the principle that knowledge is either knowledge-that, in which case it is rule-following and conscious, or it is knowledge-how, in which case it is rule-conforming (that is, conditioned, albeit self-conditioned) and the processes are unconscious. You can know how to ride a bicycle, so the argument runs, without being conscious of how you are able to ride it and without knowing that the rules of cycling are such and such. Why should we not adopt, for the sake of economy of description, a dispositional account of language acquisition, namely, that under certain conditions organisms with the physical and physiological characteristics of human beings will tend to respond in certain ways without having to postulate unconscious knowledge that the rules are such and such? There will undoubtedly be complex physiological mechanisms whose physiological structures in, say, the brain have not been unravelled yet, but there is no necessity to quantify their operations in terms of the obscure category of unconscious rule-following. In the sense of innate dispositions, like the innate brittleness of glass, which, if knocked, breaks (Cooper, 1975, p. 124), we recall part of our earlier quotation from Quine (above, pp. 52–3) when he said: 'For . . . the behaviourist is knowing and cheerfully up to his neck in innate mechanisms of learning-readiness . . . Innate biases and dispositions are the corner stone of behaviourism.' There may, therefore, be 'innate mechanisms' in the sense of 'innate biases and dispositions'. The glass's breakability may be regarded as implicit in the structure of the glass, leading to cracks of one sort rather than another. So, too, may linguistic performances be regarded as innate possibilities more economically than what is required by Chomsky's elaborate transformational algebra (Cooper, 1975, pp. 31-8 ff.). Why, then, is Chomsky's particular account not to be regarded as unnecessary scholasticism?

The reason why Chomsky argues that the characteristics of the data of human languages requires the introduction into a rule-following model of a third category, namely, that of unconscious knowledge-that between the two prongs of Harman's Fork, should nevertheless by now be clear. The stimuli that would, on a behaviourist model, activate such a variety of articulate and rich sets and series of dispositions, are too weak and degenerate to make possible their activation in such a form. Such stimuli would, after all, be the kind of ambiguous and degenerate surface-structural phenomena described. Thus Chomsky is claiming that a radically different framework is required to that of a dispositional framework that would demand that we be able to make sense of non-acquired, innate dispositions to use language by analogy with acquired skills such as cycling. (We know how to cycle because, when presented with a bike, we just cycle, quite unconscious of peddling and balancing in co-ordination and so on.) Whether, given the conceptual inadequacy of Harman's Fork and the illegitimacy of the analogy from conscious learning-how to unlearned features of language performance, Chomsky's conceptualisation of unconscious knowledge-that by analogy with conscious knowledge-that is any more adequate is a question that we shall be dealing with further in Section 8.6. For the moment, let us, in conclusion, briefly show how Chomsky's definition of competence as distinct from performance has lead him further in postulating a theory of linguistic universals applicable to all natural human languages. We have seen, moreover, why a more than dispositional data-processing capacity is implied by scientific descriptions and explanations in, say, quantum physics (above, pp. 114–17).

If the surface structure of the sentences of our own, native language would be unintelligible without a basic linguistic competence by which their deep-structure could be unravelled, it is arguable that second languages – for all the artificial devices, such as classical grammars, phrase-books or dictionaries, consisting of performances that are also surface-structural – must likewise require the learner to have a basic competence in them too. Here Chomsky's case rests upon a controversial but, we believe, arguable case that, in the final analysis, all human languages are translatable. We shall be considering further Katz's thesis of the 'effability' of human languages, namely, that thoughts communicable in one language are communicable in others, in Section 8.12. In order, therefore, to explain the phenomenon of 'effability', Chomsky postulates that our innate, unconscious knowledge of a rule-structure consists of a class containing all natural languages that is itself a sub-set of the class of all possible languages. Presumably, therefore, Chomsky would exclude from innate endowment artificial, computer languages. Language acquisition is then to be understood as a child actively and intentionally (albeit unconsciously) selecting from the total sub-set of natural languages those rules which best interpret the linguistic data of the particular speech community into which he is born. Thus he is to be regarded as applying inductively to the degenerate and ill-formed snatches of adult conversation to which he is exposed the total sub-set in order to discover which particular rule-system is the best hypothesis for explaining and predicting the actual syntactical and semantical performances of his social group.

Undoubtedly Chomsky's argument implies what we saw in our first book that Nagel once described as a 'normative psychology' (Brent, 1978, pp. 129, 206–7, 218–22). It is not that there could not be other kinds of communication systems or other ways of establishing what is true or false about the world, just as there are artificial languages. Because, however, human minds are constructed in one way rather than another, human thinking has to follow one course rather than another if understanding is to be achieved. The 'if' in the last sentence is what makes it necessary to qualify 'psychology' by the adjective 'normative'. Human beings are, of course, psychologically capable of misunderstanding either accidentally or deliberately, they are capable of avoiding issues, misinterpreting data and so forth, and for such capabilities there must be psychological descriptions and explanations as well. We argued that Hirst's forms of knowledge too could be argued to be part of a normative psychology. There might be kinds of descriptions of the world in which, say, complex physical descriptions could find expression without reference to systems of mathematical quantification whose function is to reduce complex phenomena to forms sufficiently simple as to make the human mind capable of grasping them. There might be creatures capable of understanding such descriptions without a mathematical form of knowledge, yet such understanding could not be human understanding nor could we grasp it without transformations into mathematical terms. For human beings, description and understanding is therefore arguably of a restricted kind. We cannot understand religious propositions, however irreducible they may be, without reference, say, to moral and aesthetic propositions. It is therefore normative that, if we are going to engage in religious discourse, we adopt aesthetic and moral modes of thinking in a certain, non-reductionist kind of way.

With the mention of Hirst's thesis in connection with the theory of semantic universals, we come now logically to Hirst's objections to locating his thesis in such a context. We shall see that such objections are founded upon a reading of the rule-following, epistemological account of the later Wittgenstein, particularly reinforced as these are by Hamlyn's more recent characterisation of Wittgenstein's and Chomsky's theses as mutually exclusive. In the course of our defence of a Chomskyan thesis, we shall be returning to a full and final consideration of the connection between creativity and identification by family-resemblance as well as to a defence of the viability of the notion of unconscious rule-following understood by analogy with conscious rule-following. Let us therefore now turn to this our final task.

8.2 HIRST'S THESIS AND WITTGENSTEIN'S LANGUAGE-GAMES

We saw that, for Hirst, forms of knowledge could be isolated and their approximate number delineated by a kind of language experiment. Trying to break down in logical analysis subjects or fields of knowledge into distinct forms of knowledge more general than themselves, we found that we could not do so. The 'could', moreover, was a logical and normative 'could', since we 'could' talk gibberish if we so chose, but not if we wished to preserve a meaningful structure to our language. Try to analyse the forms further into some more general underlying form, and we find that we cannot in a logical and normative sense in language do this and have a meaningful description left over at the end. Now, Hirst accepts my way of characterising the way that he sees us tracking down the anchorage of meaning in language in terms of reducibility and irreducibility. In fact, it is about the only feature of my account that he accepts in any way favourably (Hirst, 1979a, p. 104). But, as such, I cannot see that his strategy of analysis is very different from that of Chomsky, who has his own versions of reducibility and irreducibility. Chomsky conceived the problem of explaining a truth-assertive (that is, any human language with subject-predicate sentences) as one of producing a reductio-analytic explanation as exemplified by a tree diagram (Lyons, 1977, pp. 66–82) with corresponding transformational rules. Here the surface structure of the sentences is broken down by way of noun phrases, verb phrases, and further noun phrases to the phonemes (basic units of sound) or morphemes (basic units of meaning, not simply basic words like 'pass' but also 'ed' that means 'past tense'). Such phonemes and morphemes, however, are not further reducible, since further to reduce them in analysis would result in no further new component of sound or meaning, but in simply the meaningless letters of the alphabet, or their meaningless sounds.

Now, Hirst has something corresponding to certain kinds of morphemes in a Chomskyan sense such as could, we are going to argue, when spelled out with their appropriate semantic rules, play their part in a Chomskyan theory of semantic universals. What Hirst calls 'categorial' concepts are central to a form of knowledge as a whole and determine its tests for truth in a way that other, 'substantive' concepts do not. In other words, our understanding of the logically distinct categorial concepts explicates what it means for the forms to be irreducible. I have exemplified and discussed previously the nature of such concepts (Brent, 1978, pp. 101–30). Suffice it to say here that Hirst's thesis requires us to hold that, although we can change substantive concepts in a piecemeal way, we cannot change categorial concepts without changing thinking in the form of knowledge as a whole. If, then, we ask Hirst why categorial concepts are regarded as liable to change – why, in other words, they cannot be regarded as semantic universals transcultural and trans-historical – he has open to him three kinds of answers, some of which find support from Hamlyn's (1970, 1978) understanding of the later Wittgenstein. Since in the three answers both Hirst's and Hamlyn's arguments are mutually supportive, we shall regard such arguments as the Hirst/Hamlyn thesis and seek to answer them in tandem. The three types of answers, then, are roughly as follows. Hirst's first answer is that categorial concepts as the basis for objectivity claims can be shown with reference to the history of the different forms of inquiry in fact to have changed. Secondly, following Hamlyn, he would insist that it is not surprising that change has taken place since what constitutes 'meaning', 'truth', 'objectivity' and so forth is what has been publicly tested by means of interpersonal criteria. As such, a social context must exist and have reference made to it. We have here no contingent, but rather a strictly logical claim, namely, objectivity concepts only mean what they do when there is such an interpersonal backcloth already present. Thirdly, there is a far more economical way of understanding the requirement of a deep-structure and that is the existence of a pre-linguistic 'form of life'. Not only is such an explanation more economical but is superior to the Chomskyan alternative in that it does not require an allegedly unintelligible notion of tacit or implicit knowledge of rules.

Let us therefore consider in greater detail these three objections, related as they are to each other in various ways.

8.3 THE BASIS FOR OBJECTIVITY AND THE FACT OF CHANGE

Let us take the first objection to our proposals about categorial concepts as semantic universals that misleadingly appears at first sight to be a purely factual objection. According to this objection, it looks as if Hirst would concede that objectivity could, logically, have been a question of a normative order binding upon all men in a commitment presupposed by any human language but that, as a matter of fact, objectivity judgements are dependent on interpersonal criteria that differ from one society to another and from one time and place to another. Let us see, therefore, how Hirst's appeal to the later Wittgenstein could have given rise to such a misunderstanding of the thesis as an empirical thesis so that we can bring out more clearly why it is a misunderstanding.

Hirst insists that we can understand his justification for the theory of the forms of knowledge strictly in terms of what the later Wittgenstein meant by language-games (Hirst, 1974a, pp. 92-5 ff.). To be able to have disagreements in opinion, we must have achieved a prior agreement in a form of life as constitutive of the ground-rules of the particular language-game that is being played. Valid or invalid moves in a language-game arise from this fundamental agreement on rules, without which there is no 'game' and therefore neither validity nor invalidity. What we do in our social and historical context when planning a curriculum therefore is to look at the language-games which are being played, empirical, mathematical, moral, aesthetic or whatever, and deduce from how the players agree or disagree about particular judgements what ground-rules they are using in common. These ground-rules, unlike Chomsky's linguistic universals, cannot be held to be the unalterable 'givens' holding transculturally, but are themselves subject to change. As Hirst says:

> How different social contexts make possible the expression of fundamentally different forms of agreement in judgement cannot be prejudged. It may also be the case that in different contexts identical types of agreement are expressed in different conceptual constructions and . . . it must not be presumed that the 'given' anchorage of objectivity is not in the end itself subject to change. (Hirst, 1979a, p. 105)

What Hirst therefore describes as 'categorial' concepts may thus express agreement in a form of life, whereas the 'substantive' concepts are about agreements in opinion. Since, however, changes in the substantive concepts are a daily occurrence, whereas changes in categorial concepts occur relatively infrequently, it is tempting to conclude that the latter are permanent. Categorial concepts are nevertheless, as the '"given" anchorage of objectivity', subject to change. But references to the history of the inquiry, as, for example, the quantum revolution in physics, will show that, as a matter of fact, change has taken place (above, pp. 94-8).

We saw that, if categorial concepts change, then the form of knowledge both as a form of thought and a set of characteristic methods of investigation undergoes total change. It is not difficult in view of this to see why, because of this feature of Hirst's account, some writers should have sought to interpret the later Wittgensteinian thesis on which the account rests in terms of Kuhn's paradigms. Categorial change implies the revolutionary displacement of one conceptual organisation (or Kuhnian paradigm) by another as an exemplification of 'social constructions within a form of life whose given elements, even those of a non-social kind, are subject to change' (Hirst, 1979a, p. 105). More than one commentator has interpreted Hirst as implying in changes in the basis of objectivity the kind of conceptual shift which appears in

Kuhn's description of paradigm revolutions in science. Dearden, for example, says:

> There are ... epistemological arguments for asserting such a necessity for a teacher of some kind. The first ground for the assertion is the degree of discontinuity between theoretical and 'commonsense' perceptual or practical concepts. Theoretical concepts are interconnected in elaborate and carefully constructed systems, and even where the same labels are used there is a shift in concept from the commonsensical to the theoretical. (Dearden, 1968, p. 123)

Thus scientific descriptions are regarded as representing specialised, Wittgensteinian language-games, and between the conceptual and logical structures of such languages (or forms of knowledge) and ordinary language there exists a logical disjunction ('shift'). Furthermore, between one kind of version of knowledge paradigm and another a similar logical and conceptual disjunction is claimed to hold, to be detected in that which, for example, allegedly pertains between classical and quantum physics.

It is important to grasp what such a point of view implies. It is not simply that there are differences between common-sense and theoretical languages and between different versions of a given theoretical language but which are logically related. There is a logical disjunction which necessitates the revolutionary displacement of one type of language by another. So, too, different versions of forms of knowledge are similarly to be understood as subject to revolutionary displacement. This, when linked with the theory of language-games, can be likened to men beginning by playing one kind of language-game but, as time goes on, they devise new sorts of language-games which replace the originals. But note what this presupposes about the nature of language and universal terms. We can exhaustively define one sort of language-game or scientific, aesthetic, moral or other type of paradigm exhaustively, compare with an exhaustive definition of another, and on the basis of our finding non-equivalence declare that a linguistic or paradigm revolution has taken place. But, as we have seen, Wittgenstein denies that such a view of definition is tenable, so that between different versions of forms of knowledge we ought, on the basis of family-resemblance and the open-ended character of language-games, see that there is a basic continuity between such apparently different versions. Differing versions of forms of knowledge, like games, form a family with 'a complicated network of similarities, overlapping and criss-crossing' (above, pp. 78–81). When we learn to use a general term like 'table' by referring to a finite number of actual objects to which the word applies, we become able to classify an infinite number of possible tables and to make an infinite number of possible statements about them. So, too, Hirst ought to have argued, if his thesis is to be truly founded on one aspect of the epistemology of the later Wittgenstein in the case of conceptual and propositional organisations which are forms of knowledge. Here, too, we learn references to a finite number of instances of actual concepts and actual propositions (empirical, mathematical, aesthetic or whatever), but as a result are able to classify an infinite number of possible concepts and propositions. This is because of their open-ended character understood in terms of family-resemblance. Language-games and family-resemblance therefore dispense with any need to understand language in terms of shifts in 'the "given" anchorage of objectivity'.

With, however, these references to our own objections to the association of language-games with Kuhnian paradigms, the argument has begun to change rapidly from an apparently empirical one to one about a kind of logical necessity. We are no longer talking about a matter of fact that could possibly have been otherwise, but rather of a necessary feature of any human communication system that is to succeed in communicating. It is therefore to a consideration of Hirst's and Hamlyn's view of Wittgenstein's thesis as a logical thesis that we must now turn, namely, that objectivity implies a social backcloth so that semantic rules cannot be understood as an individual, human endowment.

8.4 'TRUTH' OR 'OBJECTIVITY' AS MEANING 'WHAT IS TESTABLE AGAINST A GIVEN SOCIAL BACKCLOTH?'

At all events, representing the difference between Hirst and Chomsky (or, for that matter, between Chomsky and Hamlyn or the later Wittgenstein) as a difference over the way to read empirically the history of types of human inquiry always was a misleading way of putting the case between them. If we wish to refrain from using 'empirical' loosely and to escape the charge of winning the argument by trading on that looseness, we would do well to accept Popper's criterion that, for a thesis to be genuinely empirical, it must be falsifiable. Thus we would have to be able to specify what conditions would have to pertain if a given thesis were false, granted that such conditions might never be realised. But with either Chomsky's or the later Wittgenstein's thesis, this is not possible. What Hamlyn says about Wittgenstein's language-games would, I believe, equally apply to Chomsky's thesis, namely:

Talk of a view of the world in this connection may suggest that we might have had other views, that we might have developed a conceptual structure different from that which we have developed in fact. In a certain sense this is true; things might have seemed otherwise if we had been different creatures, if we had had, to use Kant's phrase, a different form of sensibility or, in Wittgenstein's terminology, had shared in a different form of life. But it is no use pretending that we could have any conception of what this might have been like . . . (Hamlyn, 1970, pp. 71–2)

I have, moreover, already argued (above, pp. 292–3) how the same objection to the empirical character of Chomsky's thesis applies. We cannot specify under what conditions the thesis would be false since we could have 'no conception of what this might have been like'. Both theses represent deductions from the structure of human languages as basically given. They concern what necessarily is to be deduced or presupposed about the basic conditions for human communication systems when we consider what kinds of claims men can or cannot validly make in human languages. We cannot hypothesise what a human language would have to be like not to be a human language since, without a human language, there would be no language in which to express the hypothesis. One cannot, using a human language resting upon certain rules, describe a human language that operates by different rules. Both Chomsky and Wittgenstein are, contrary to what the former would admit, like logicians rather than scientists, teasing out the logical form of arguments, propositions, concepts and meanings.

Our objection to the cultural relativism implied by Kuhn's paradigm thesis (and Wittgenstein's language-games interpreted in such a light) is that human languages could not function communicatively if its operations could create the kinds of disjunctions that are postulated between different conceptual structures. We saw that, unless languages were able through family-resemblance to incorporate new discoveries within known schemes even at the mundane level of concepts like 'table', then a permanent and incommunicable chaos would necessarily result, particularly in a universe with no fixed numbers of objects (above, pp. 83–7, with which cf. above, pp. 115–19). It is not, therefore, simply as a matter of fact that 'the followers of Newton and Einstein remained on speaking terms' (Pring, 1972, p. 9) refutes Kuhnian relativism. Sometimes as a matter of fact people choose not to speak to one another for wrong reasons or because of psychological incapacity. It was logically the structure of their language in enabling new discoveries to be comprised within known schemes that enabled the dialogue to go on and determined that it could not be halted. Kuhnian relativism arguably therefore fails for reasons similar to those for which, we argued earlier, Quine's thesis about radical translation failed (above, pp. 64–70).

However, our thesis about family-resemblance and the logical form of human languages is not that adopted by Hirst or Hamlyn in rejecting the status of the theory of language-games or forms of knowledge as an empirical status. In fact, my use of what, after all, is a thoroughly Wittgensteinian notion in my previous book produced from Hirst the somewhat startled retort: 'On the significance of . . . reconciling Newtonian and Einsteinian physics I fail to see what he is after' (Hirst, 1979a, p. 104). But both Hamlyn and Hirst would consider their thesis to be a logical thesis on other grounds that would rule out an account of objectivity in terms of a logically possible thesis about semantic universals. Their objection to such a thesis is that it misconceives the meaning of concepts like 'truth', 'objective', 'right' or 'correct', albeit in terms of an error produced by an individualistic epistemology deep-seated in philosophical tradition and stretching back to the sixteenth century. It is not that such concepts could have meanings derivable from the judgements that individuals make by means of an internal and innate rule-structure, but that, as a matter of fact, they get the rules instead from that social backcloth or objectivity judgements which is agreement in a form of life. What such concepts rather *mean* is what is publicly testable so that they therefore logically imply such a backcloth. Without such a public and interpersonal backcloth, objectivity concepts are not simply possible but different, but rather meaningless. As Hamlyn says:

> Innate knowledge would imply having the concept of truth or something like it without the possibility of being a party to that agreement without which the concept of truth could get no purchase . . . Whatever the correct analysis of the concept of knowledge, the knower must be capable of getting things right, and this must not be just a happy accident. Moreover, getting things right means getting them right by public, inter-subjective and objective standards. (Hamlyn, 1978, p. 90)

Hamlyn therefore argues that, on the subject of how objectivity judgements are logically possible in language, Chomsky and the later Wittgenstein radically diverge. Chomsky claims that objectivity judgements are built up and creatively extended because, as the rationalist argued in one form or another, there are innate mechanisms which determine what forms of inquiry are possible and what forms are not. For Chomsky, the requirement for human communication systems to function in the way that they do is that there are certain morphemes or basic units of meaning that all languages share in common and which, collectively with the rules by which they operate, constitute a theory of semantic universals. Such universals are grounded in a natural language capacity. Thus the problem of knowledge is seen in part to be the problem of constructing an adequate natural history of human inquiry. Hamlyn, however, wishes to deny that there is a logical relationship between criteria of objectivity and the psychology of making objectivity judgements as Chomsky presupposes. What Wittgenstein is claiming, he thinks, is that all that is logically necessary for men to make statements about what is true or false is the existence of an inter-personal backcloth against which such claims are made and judged. As a matter of contingent fact, it may be that there are innate categories, or that the mind is a *tabula rasa* and simply sensitive to sensory stimulations. But Wittgenstein is held to argue that neither of these contingencies, that are simply part of man's natural, psychological history, are of philosophical importance, nor do they affect the epistemological issue as Chomsky thinks. All that is necessary, contrary to Chomsky, for 'true' or 'false' to make sense, is that agreement in a form of life that makes agreement and disagree-ment in opinion possible in a given community of judgement. What further biological basis makes this possible is held to be, according to Wittgenstein, philosophically irrelevant (Hamlyn, 1970, pp. 136–42).

Now, it must be fairly recognised that, to some extent, Hamlyn has the backing of ordinary usage on this point, related as it is to the claim that the description of the theory of language-games as a culturally relative theory of truth rests upon a logical absurdity. If what 'true' and 'false' *means* is 'that which is testable against an interpersonal backcloth of agreed criteria for judgements', then questions about 'cultural relativism', foreign in any case to ordinary usage, become meaningless. After all, in normal usage 'subjective' is used in the sense of 'peculiar to an individual', in contrast to 'objective', which is the negation of 'subjective' in this sense. The introduction of the definition of 'subjective' as 'culturally relative' may therefore be held to contravene ordinary usage in that it rests upon a conflation of the subjective/objective distinction in terms of:

$$\left\{ \begin{array}{l} \{\text{not peculiar to an individual } (= \text{objective})\} \text{ but} \\ \{\text{peculiar to } \{\text{a group of}\} \text{ individuals } (= \text{subjective})\} \\ \text{who constitute a social group.} \end{array} \right\}$$

But it may be objected that, also in some circumstances using ordinary language as our guide, it does make sense to ask in some conflicts between communities of judgement which is right and which is wrong. I say 'some' because I take Hirst's point that, since there are different kinds of evaluations of different kinds of statement – empirical, mathematical, aesthetic, moral, religious and so forth – then it makes no sense to ask for some absolute judgement as to which kind of evaluation represents the real or true in contrast to the others. But when rival communities of judgement clash over similar kinds of evaluations – for example, Einsteinians, Newtonians and witch-doctors; Euclideans, Lobachevskyans and astrologers; Buddhists, Catholics and Protestants – then it does make sense to ask which is true or false, valid and invalid. Moreover, what makes it possible to speak of 'similar kinds of evaluation', namely, 'family-resemblance', is also that which enables new agreements in judgement to come about between such rival communities of judgement. Ordinary usage is, furthermore, supportive of the quest for what makes the achievement of new communities of judgement continuous with the old possible, since the logic of ordinary language commits us to asserting that what is 'true for me' is also both 'true for us' and 'true for everyone'. Hamlyn's thesis to this extent violates common-sense intuitions. It is significant that followers of the later Wittgenstein have never generally been able to bring themselves to agree with the sociologists of knowledge in their claim that ordinary language is, in this respect, sustained by an illusion (cf. Brent, 1978, Chapter 4).

I believe, moreover, that at this point Hirst makes an important contribution to one puzzling aspect of the work of the later Wittgenstein regarding the character of objectivity judgements. Consider a man who asserts that the earth came into existence 150 years ago. Of such a case, Wittgenstein argues as follows:

185. It would strike me as ridiculous to want to doubt the existence of Napoleon; but if someone doubted the existence of the earth 150 years ago, perhaps I should be more willing to listen, for now he is doubting our whole system of evidence. It does not strike me as if this system were more certain than a certainty within it. (Wittgenstein, 1969, p. 190)

Wittgenstein's point is that, when confronted by the man's assertion that the universe is 150 years old, there is no question of our being right and he wrong or vice versa. There could be no rights nor wrongs in such a conflict since neither side would have an agreed community of judgement on the basis of which to argue. 'Our whole system of evidence' is in doubt. We should, claims Wittgenstein, simply not know how to answer such an assertion. Now, I find this Wittgensteinian example puzzling, not only because it violates common-sense intuitions, but also because there are formally identical examples when, in common practice, we do claim to know how to answer such an assertion. There is no formal difference, after all, whether we claim that the world is 150 years old or that its age rather stretches to 4004 BC as did Philip Goss (see above, pp. 159–62). But in real-life contexts in which such claims are made, we neither terminate the dialogue nor are we willing to listen beyond a certain point. If the person is judged by us neither to be a charlatan nor unwell, what we claim to the person in question is that he cannot be making an empirical, scientific claim, but that it must be some kind of religious or aesthetic claim. The procedures by which we deny his claim as it stands are not anything within our whole system of empirical evidence. Rather they are the semantic procedures by which we declare fundamental forms of knowledge irreducible to one another, irrespective of any particular system of evidence within such forms. As such I submit that Hirst, however unwillingly, is explicating the rational basis of an intuitive way of dealing with such assertions over which Wittgenstein is riding roughshod. Our action in real-life circumstances implies intuitive recognition of a shared semantic system as a human form of life behind the social forms of life in conflict with our own. Our appeal behind those features of claims noted in our last section, in which what is true is not equivalent to either true-for-me or any collection of me's, is therefore an appeal to a common framework of judgement in which irreducible categories cannot with meaning be conflated. Our retort, implying that he has no right to conflate the categories, implies our recognition that he has access to them. Moreover, our retort would have no basis, therefore, if that framework were purely a creation of our particular, social community of judgement (Brent, 1978, pp. 169–211). Hence, if Hamlyn follows the later Wittgenstein down this particular road, he must disregard some parts of the logic of ordinary language claims about objectivity on which his argument appears to be founded.

Quite apart from such general objections to such an account of objectivity as logically implied by ordinary usage, it is to be doubted whether the Hamlyn/Hirst thesis on a further and more specific ground meets Chomsky's case adequately. Remember that feature of Chomsky's case that we considered to have been argued somewhat misleadingly, namely, that it is an empirical case. We considered that rather it was not strictly an empirical case, since necessarily we cannot specify how a language could be both a human language and other than its logic requires, however much we might concede the possibility of an alternative evolutionary development. Chomsky's point is that a theory explaining truth-assertive languages (that is, human languages basically of the subject-predicate form) cannot be neutral over what particular account of the natural history (psychological, sociological) of the inquiry is true. The logical *form* in which various kinds of assertion are made and assigned inter-subjective meaning implies, logically, the superiority of an account of the origins of such assertions in rule-following terms that is more than dispositional. The linguistic form in which such assertions are made, in other words, cannot be independent of what can and cannot be asserted as Hamlyn's Wittgensteinian interpretation considers it must. Thus we are brought back to what we have argued to be the logical requirement that there must necessarily be a deep-structure of semantic rule-following derivations if we are to make sense of how the often degenerate and ill-formed surface structure of sentences come to be understood. Thus Hamlyn's fundamental position that what objectivity means is what is testable against a public backcloth of judgements is considerably weakened by the argument that what makes possible for human beings to reach agreement in a form of life is a kind of individual, species-specific rule structure which gives human assertions their peculiar form.

At this point, therefore, we come to Hirst's third objection to forms of knowledge as part of a theory of semantic universals. He needs at this juncture a proposal like Hamlyn's that will provide a viable alternative to Chomsky's postulation of a deep-structural innate endowment as an explanation of how the child comes to interpret the linguistic data of his speech-community. Let us therefore look at the Hirst/Hamlyn proposal for a more economical alternative in the form of a pre-linguistic form of life as a more detailed explication of Hirst's third objection to what we have been proposing.

8.5   A PRE-LINGUISTIC FORM OF LIFE AS AN ALTERNATIVE TO DEEP-STRUCTURE

Hamlyn contends with Hirst's concurrence that, in the first place, there is an alternative way of interpreting the phenomenon of deep-structures and surface-structures that is consistent with his demands for a strictly social definition of the meaning of objectivity. Secondly, he would support such an alternative, as we shall see, with a dispositional account of language acquisition supported by the argument that any claim to knowledge must be a claim to conscious knowledge, otherwise it is meaningless to regard it as other than knowledge-how. Let us now briefly consider this alternative account, which attacks the notion of deep-structure because of the requirement that we understand propositional knowledge in such a case as tacit or unconscious.

We turn, therefore, to Hamlyn's alternative. Hamlyn's objection is that there is a more economical explanation of the child's ability to understand and communicate linguistically which does not require the elaborate theory of unconscious rule-following selections from different sets of innate semantic rules. Hamlyn agrees that the child could not understand degenerate and ill-formed utterances heard at random by means of the kind of stimulus-response process advocated by the behaviourists. The child does have to be able to make reference to standards and criteria that must be logically, though not necessarily, temporally prior to his understanding of what is asserted in language. But actual speech is only, he claims, at all events in evidence from about the age of 2 years and upwards. What is prior (logically if not temporally) according to Hamlyn is the social form of life, not entirely or necessarily linguistic in character, into which the child has been initiated in physical and emotional interaction, in signs, symbols, gestures and so forth, from birth. Here he learns prelinguistically, according to Hamlyn, what it is to be corrected, how one object (subject) is related to another object (predicate) by pointing and so on. Such a form of life can, being social in form, perform more convincingly, or so he claims, the functions of Chomsky's deep-structure and so more economically explain how the surface-structure of sentences comes post-linguistically to be interpreted. As Hamlyn says:

> Parents communicate with pre-linguistic children by gestures, actions and expressions, as well as by talking to them; they show them things, direct their movements and correct what they do. Above all perhaps, in the earliest days, they express and thereby communicate feelings by their responses to the child. It is in the context of this sort of thing that we must see the understanding of language eventually emerging. The grammatical notions of subject and predicate correspond in their use to those of drawing attention to something (perhaps by an indicative device or an expression the conventional use of which has this function at least) and of expressing something about it. (Hamlyn, 1978, p. 104)

Thus Hamlyn replaces the concept of unconscious knowledge of a semantic rule structure (the deep-structure) with the concept of a pre-linguistic form of life in which, by learning non-verbal signs, symbols, gestures, conventions and so on, the child is later to deal with the malformed surface-structure of linguistic utterances. Thus language comes to be learned and its meaning interpreted on the basis of a prior form of life consisting of pre-verbal symbols, gestures and so on in terms of which truth-assertions (subject-predicate statements) arise in language, either later or even at the same time by analogy with such pre-verbal actions.

It is important, however, to note that, as a proposed empirical thesis, Hamlyn's proposal seems vague ('this sort of thing', *'perhaps by an indicative device'* and so on). Nevertheless, as by now it should be clear, he is not primarily concerned with examining any specific empirical thesis as such, but rather the conditions that any empirical thesis must satisfy in order to be logically viable. The validity therefore of this suggested alternative to Chomsky's theory of deep-structure as primarily an *individual* endowment is dependent on Hamlyn's prior claim that objectivity judgements are, rather, logically dependent on rules, standards and criteria furnished by a *social* backcloth. We saw that Hamlyn's claim was that we need not go further than that social backcloth to the conditions of its natural origins in order to make sense of concepts such as truth or objectivity. We have argued for our part the Chomskyan case that the linguistic form of truth assertions (the subject-predicate form) logically entails a further account of a human form of life underlying all particular social forms of life in terms of implicit, semantic rule-following structures. (The ability to transcend the particular, to propound general cases in the light of a small number of data, to classify in terms of genuinely open-classes and so forth were all exemplified in characteristic subject-predicate expressions (above, pp. 48–53)). From the outset, therefore, the logical starting-point from which such an alternative to Chomsky's postulate of deep-structure is pursued is shown to be at least questionable. Let us, however, develop our criticism further with particular reference to Hamlyn's postulated alternative to the deep-structure, even though we have argued that his general case for pursuing such an alternative is misconceived.

Our specific criticism of Hamlyn's alternative to semantic deep-structure takes us back to the very beginning of our argument in this book (above, pp. 26–30). What is questionable about Hamlyn's proposed alternative is the extent to which such a thesis requires the assimilation of linguistic acts to such non-linguistic symbols as gestures or (facial) expressions among others. To what extent can Hamlyn sustain his argument in our preceding quotation that 'grammatical notions of subject and predicate *correspond in their use* to those of drawing attention to something'? In Chapter 1, we deployed Bennett's argument that linguistic symbolic systems could not, in a human sense, be continuous with non-linguistic symbolic systems (above, pp. 26–30). We retold Bennett's fable of the bees to show how actual communication systems, behavioural in kind, in insect communities would have to develop in order to be comparable with a human communication system of a linguistic kind. Remember that part of what such a system would have to be able to express was tensed denials in remote past time, which, as such, is one kind of subject-predicate statement that Hamlyn is arguing to be derivable from ('correspond in their use to') a non-linguistic symbolic system. The bees might be able to dance a pattern of dance in the presence of pollen traces that might correspond with, 'There was pollen here'. But once the pollen traces had faded, they could not in a pattern of dance express the existence in remote past time of the pollen. To be able to do so would presuppose the ability to understand and express the some-time existence of past things generally, that involves in turn the ability to identify and then re-identify particulars over time. Only language in a human sense appears to be able to construct general terms of that kind, and only a human language therefore expresses that ability central to a rule-following model which is the transcendence of the particular.

Now, then, we must ask of Hamlyn's pre-linguistic account of acquisition of criteria of objectivity, rules for classification and so forth how the transcendence of the particular could take place as the prerequisite for making general classifications on the basis of gestures, signs, symbols that indicate particular things. We have seen that those universals which stand as the predicate of subject-predicate sentences simply cannot be understood in terms of stringing together of particulars, as Hamlyn's pre-linguistic account must presuppose if it can explain the origins of human language. Imagine a parent pointing to a small quantity of sugar in order to express the subject-predicate statement: 'This is sugar'. He might point to the child's mouth and to his own mouth to indicate another quantity of sugar that perhaps was of a different colour and that had just been eaten. But, even granted that this adequately represented the present-tense propositions, how with purely non-verbal signs does the father indicate that, 'There used to be sugar here'? What pre-linguistic sets of signs and gestures could have provided the deep-structural foundations for interpreting such a tensed denial? What is at stake here is what possible non-linguistic form could express the human ability to identify and reidentify the same particular (the sugar) over time in the absence of present stimuli (pollen or sugar traces or whatever) so as to express a general case. In fact, if non-linguistic symbols like gestures, signs and so forth, constitutive of a pre-linguistic form of life, are understood by the child as precursors to language, on this argument they will be seen simply to reproduce the problem of how the child understands the surface-structure of sentences rather than to solve it. We must regard the child as, in some sense, interpreting such non-linguistic gestures linguistically, albeit prior to actual linguistic performance. Without a distinctively human and prior data-processing ability whose biological programme is linguistic in form, general tensed classes (the predicates of subject-predicate sentences) could not be constructed from individual and particular present-tense pointings, gestures and so on. Moreover, general terms which are family-resemblances could not be grasped simply from perceptions of strings of particulars.

Hamlyn would now have to emphasise strongly the second strand of his argument, namely, that though there must be some kind of human ability to follow rules, interpret non-linguistic gestures, signs and so on as the foundations of language, nevertheless such abilities are merely dispositions to respond, and require no descriptions in terms of unconscious knowledge of rules. Such dispositions, moreover, however well-formed they may be, cannot be called 'knowledge' until they have undergone public testing (Hamlyn, 1978, p. 90). Hirst would concur with the Hirst/Hamlyn thesis in the following words:

> If ... we must hang on to the essentially dispositional, non-experiential character of knowledge we must also hang on to the necessity for there to be public tests on agreed criteria that govern all cases of knowledge ... there are publicly agreed criteria which govern all cases of knowledge ... Remove these criteria and the claim that there can be knowledge loses its point and application. (Hirst, 1979b, pp. 103–4)

Such a view, moreover, although clearly indebted to Ryle (1949), is nevertheless distinguished by both Hamlyn and Hirst from behaviourism. The dispositions are dispositions to a knowledge-that which is irreducible to knowledge-how. But until such dispositions are cashed in terms of actual performances, they cannot be termed 'knowledge' at all. Thus, in the final analysis, our argument for reinterpreting Hirst's forms of knowledge thesis as a thesis about semantic universals rests upon being able to justify the concept of unconscious or implicit or tacit knowledge of semantic rules. Their thesis must finally rest on their claim that unconscious rule-following is a meaningless notion, as is the defence of that claim, since they have failed to make their case logically or empirically in terms of the social reference of objectivity concepts.

Certainly Hamlyn frequently expresses his perplexity over by what right Chomsky can argue that the child, in acquiring language, is to be understood as acting by analogy with a scientist. He tests the linguistic data with which he is presented and selects by inference the particular sub-set of rules from his innate universal grammar that best interpret such data. As Hamlyn says:

> As applied to the growth of knowledge in the individual, however, the idea has the consequence of making the child into something like a little scientist. This is evident in Chomsky's way of setting out the issue, when he speaks of the child as having to discover the grammar of the language and of his putting forward hypotheses about the rules that have to be followed. (Hamlyn, 1978, p. 36)

The answer, of course, to Hamlyn's perplexity is that Chomsky does not mean that the child literally behaves like a little scientist, but only by analogy with what a scientist does. The scientist has conscious knowledge of the rules and procedures, whereas the child's knowledge is unconscious, tacit or implicit. Let us therefore examine the nature of this analogy in the context of the justification of analogies in constructing models of explanation.

8.6 ANALOGICAL INFERENCE, EXTENSION AND IMPLICIT KNOWLEDGE OF RULES

Quite frequently we have introduced the standard objection to Chomsky's account of tacit or implicit knowledge of semantic and syntactic rules in terms of the principle of Harman's Fork (see, for example, above, pp. 290–1). We saw, moreover, earlier that it was not only for a linguistic model such as Chomsky's that the application of such a Fork was intended to leave no room as a meaningful model of explanation. Psychoanalytic theory too, since it relied upon unconscious acts of rule-following (characterised in terms of willing, choosing, deciding, wishing subconsciously), was also ruled out as providing an adequate model on this principle. We saw also that the Freudian model itself, particularly as described by Breuer (above, p. 214), was clearly subjected to pressure for rule-conforming reformulation that would result also in unconscious knowledge-that being reformulated in dispositional terms. Our contrary argument was that, as we had argued the necessity for a model of explanation to be irreducibly rule-following, the Freudian model should be reformulated rather in a rule-following connection. But if we did so, as with Chomsky, the indispensibility of a category of knowledge-that which was irreducibly both rule-following and unconscious soon became evident. Having been lead, therefore, both by Freudian and Chomskyan phenomena irresistibly, as we maintain, to the necessity of postulating a third category of knowledge between conscious knowledge-that, let us now look at the way in which such a category is to be both articulated and justified. We shall argue such a justification particularly with reference to Cooper's counter-arguments (1975).

Cooper accepts that the pressures to postulate such an unconscious propositional type of knowledge in the case of psychoanalytic theory are irresistible, but argues that there are no grounds for yielding to such pressures in regard to Chomskyan linguistic theory. Harman was wrong to believe that the categories of knowing-that and knowing-how are exhaustive of possible kinds of knowledge, but nevertheless, Chomsky was wrong to think that children could be said to 'know' a universal grammar in this third, implicit or unconscious, sense. Cooper claims, following to some extent Nagel (1969), that 'implicit knowledge' can be understood in terms of Freudian psychoanalysis by means of drawing an analogical inference with explicit and conscious, standard propositional examples, but that there is no such inference possible in Chomsky's cases. All that is possible in such cases is an analogical extension which will not provide the kind of justification which Chomsky's use of the concept of 'tacit knowledge' requires. Let us begin, therefore, with an explanation of the terms 'analogical inference' and 'analogical extension', and see why the distinction should discriminate so critically against the viability of Chomsky's thesis.

An example of an analogical inference might be the description of the movement of electricity in terms of currents or waves in which certain criteria which define exhaustively the behaviour of the one have analogous counterparts in certain criteria which define exhaustively the other. An example of analogical extension is when we sometimes talk of dogs being 'neurotic', in which case there is only some non-exhaustive list of analogous counterparts that neurotic humans and neurotic dogs have in common. Chomsky speaks by analogy of the child behaving like a little scientist who makes inferences from the data of his particular speech-community which enable him to select the appropriate grammar that is a sub-set of the universal, innate grammar with which every child is born. But this requires him to be able to make an analogical inference from what learners of second languages do when they consciously acquire knowledge of such languages. All, however, that the actual behaviour of children entitles us to admit is that there is an analogical extension between what they do and what conscious, rule-referring speakers of propositions in second languages do. Freudian examples of unconscious knowledge do admit of understanding in terms of analogical inference, since the knowledge which exercises unconscious influence upon behaviour was once conscious. There is no such temporally prior experience now forgotten in the case of the child's implicit or tacit knowledge of universal grammar which makes analogical inference impossible in such Chomskyan cases.

I now propose to question Cooper's claim by means of three different strategies. First and briefly I will query whether, in the light of what the later Wittgenstein has to say about fundamental concepts in science and mathematics which are creative because they are open-ended (defined by family-resemblance rather than exhaustively), an analogical extension would necessarily vitiate the viability of tacit knowledge in the new linguistics. Secondly, I will take it for granted (despite my first objection) that analogical inference is still a requirement for viability, but I will notwithstanding demonstrate that a reformulation of a Freudian example in terms of rule-following as opposed to causal explanation will turn examples of tacit knowledge in Freudian psychoanalysis into strictly inferential bridges between Chomskyan examples and explicit propositional knowledge-claims. Thirdly, I will relate such an account to the Neo-Cartesian theory of innate ideas which I will show, even in its classical form, to require a logical rather than a causal account of forgetting. Here, finally, will be demonstrated Cooper's unexamined and unarticulated empiricist assumptions which take for granted the temporal priority of experience to knowledge but treat such temporal priority as equivalent to logical priority.

8.7 THE ANALOGICAL INFERENCE/EXTENSION DISTINCTION

First, then, I would like to query the rigidity of the distinction presumed by Cooper's criticism between analogical inference and analogical extension. The distinction between inference and extension appears to rely heavily on a sharp disjunction between, on the one hand, what is in principle exhaustively definable, and on the other what is purely metaphorical. Such a disjunction is implicitly attacked by Wittgenstein's doctrine of family-resemblance, to which frequent reference has already been made in this present work. Remember what Waisman, a mathematician heavily influenced by Wittgenstein's work in this respect, said of family-resemblance in application to the problem of defining mathematical concepts (above, pp. 83–5). There was no value in arguing about the correct definition of such categorial concepts as 'calculus', 'operation' or 'proof'. We simply point to particular examples and 'allow the concept to reach as far as the similarity reaches in these examples', as an expression of the way in which inquiry 'gives language the freedom to comprise new discoveries in a known scheme'. It is arguable, therefore, that analogies with conscious rule-following, marked by qualifications such as 'implicit', 'tacit', or 'unconscious' because they are extensions rather than inferences, are not vague metaphors, as Cooper implies. Points of the analogy drawn with the phenomenon on which it is based can overlap and criss-cross in many complex ways, even though the relationship is not a tightly deductive one, in a way that is more than metaphorical. In other words, an analogical extension can be more than the logical equivalent of extending the concept of a rose to my love in 'My love is like a red, red rose' while falling short of being tightly inferential.

Analogical extension, therefore, founded upon the principle of extension from actual to possible new classifications on the basis of family-resemblance, is a strength rather than a weakness of the role this might play in the theorising of the new linguists. Unless we were able to 'point to examples' of conscious rule-following that involve explicit knowledge of rules and 'allow the concept of knowledge' to reach as far as the similarity reaches in examples of unconscious and tacit knowledge, we would freeze inquiry into the nature of language and prevent new insights being achieved. We would be using a stipulative and exhaustive definition of propositional knowledge necessitating conscious and intentional rule-following. This freezing of the process of inquiry is precisely what a limitation to analogical inference would achieve, therefore, whether applied to concepts such as 'calculus', 'operation' or 'proof' in mathematics, or to concepts like 'knowledge', 'inference' or 'rule-following' in the new linguistics. This can be further exemplified in talk of electrical 'current' or radio 'waves', since the insistence that the analogies of 'current' and 'waves' be deployed strictly inferentially may be, in itself, the obstacle to the development of new understandings of electricity in science.

What, however, I now propose doing is to ignore what I believe to have been a damaging critique of Cooper's analytic methodology, and to accept his criticism within its own terms. As my second ground for rejecting Cooper's account, then, I will show that, even within the terms of his own analysis, Cooper's denial of understanding Chomsky's concept of implicit or tacit knowledge as an analogical inference is misconceived by a comparison with a version of a Freudian example where Cooper accepts that unconscious knowledge can be so understood.

8.8   FREUDIAN EXAMPLES AND UNCONSCIOUS KNOWLEDGE-THAT

Let me then secondly begin by reformulating the principle of Harman's Fork in such a way that will hopefully do justice to his original argument, but will also assist us in unravelling further difficulties with the Chomskyan case, which will be shown to have far more features in common with my reformulation.

Let us take two examples of knowledge-that and knowledge-how, such as those which Harman originally claimed that Chomsky's examples of implicit knowledge fell hopelessly between:

(*a*)   John knows that the battle of Hastings was fought in AD 1066.
(*b*)   John knows how to swim.

The first statement (*a*) involves knowledge of rules, at least some of which John must be able to articulate if we are to admit that he has knowledge. Though this point is controversial, I would suggest that its denial would run into the by now standard difficulties of such a denial posed by Gettier examples (see above, pp. 57–8). A parrot might squawk: 'The battle of Hastings was fought in 1066', but we should refuse to take this as evidence of his *knowledge* of this fact. Our reasons for our refusal is that we can ask John (but not the parrot) *how* he knows, what he *means* by 'battle', 'Hastings', 'fought' or 'AD 1066'. At this point, his behaviour involves a variety of rule-following activities such as pointing, looking, referring, analysing. He will, at very least, if our claim about him as knowing is in the weakest sense of propositional knowledge, refer to the teacher as a source of the information, implying some contrast with, say, a relative who is not in so strong a position as being likely to know. If our claim is in the strong sense of propositional knowledge, then John will do things like refer to a history book and to the way in which its writer refers in turn to documents written in turn by eye-witnesses whose descriptions referred to actual events. He does such things as pointing us to atlases and maps whose references are different in kind from those of history texts. These, in their pictorial representations, refer to aerial photographs which in turn depict the landscape where the town of Hastings is to be found. For his justification of '1066', on the other hand, he points to entirely different sets of criteria in the form of the conventions of historical computation, the convenience of dating and so on. Sometimes this description of a family of rule-governed, reference activities is picked out by the intention-criterion of claims to knowledge. Claims to knowledge are necessarily intentional. When I claim that I or someone else claims to know that p, I am claiming that his behaviour and mine are intentional. This is how the human articulator of the proposition can meaningfully be said to claim to know it but the parrot cannot.

It might be thought that know-how sentences (type 2: 'John knows how to swim') are also intentional, so that knowing-how and knowing-that cannot be distinguished by this criterion. Swimming, like speaking, is an act, and what distinguishes an act from other happenings like emotions, feelings or pains is that the agent intends that what happens should take place. But the intentions of the agent determine the character of claims to know-that in a manner different from the way in which they determine claims to know-how. In the case of asserting knowledge-that, what we have seen to be the intentional application of rules of reference, analysis and convention is necessarily conscious. In the case of knowledge-how, conscious reference to rules is not merely self-defeating but has no logical application to the examples. However much John may have intended to learn how to swim and then to swim, there is no distinction bètween his swimming behaviours which corresponds to the distinction between assertions about the battle of Hastings and parrot-squawks which bear phonemic similarity to such assertions. In this connection, it is misleading to present, as Harman and others have done, the inferference of rule-learning with acquisition of knowledge-how, as though this were merely an empirical probability. Were there to be creatures who learned to perform acts like swimming simply by learning rules, then we should simply describe their knowledge as knowledge-that and their swimming behaviour would be formally identical with what human beings do with their vocal chords when articulating propositions. It would then be a matter of empirical inquiry how the neurophysiological mechanisms of such creatures made this possible in precisely the same way as Chomsky regards it an empirical question to determine the essential character of human language in a similar way. In connection with such creatures, the concept of knowing-how to swim would have no application. It is perhaps unfortunate that human physiology has made it possible for human beings to swim as a result of only one kind of knowledge, knowledge-how, whereas human beings can articulate propositions involving rule references in accordance with the paradigm of knowledge-that, or simply squawk (if they are ignorant of German): 'Ich weiss dass die Schlacht von Hastings in AD 1066 stattgefunden war.' Had our neurophysiological apparatus made knowing-how to make such squawks without semantic rules to follow impossible, we would not have had behaviourist attempts to assimilate propositional knowledge to them.

Harman's mistake is not, however, that of the behaviourist. He would, I think, be sympathetic to my characterisation of propositional knowledge in terms of conscious rule-following. What he would, on the other hand, wish to deny is that there can be tacit, implicit or unconscious rule-following activity. When intentional acts are unconscious, no rules are applied, so that such unconscious intentional acts are intentional in the sense that learning how to swim is intentional. No propositional knowledge can be involved. The child does not learn his native language by consciously asking the meaning of words, looking up the rule for well-formed expressions in the language to which he is listening and so forth. The child's knowledge of language is simply knowledge-how. To what does there correspond in the child's acquisition of syntax that bears analogy with our questions to John after his statement about the battle of Hastings? John is able to make at least some of our rule-references within the family of procedures encompassed within our notion of propositional intentionality. But he is able, when making his first statements in his native language, to articulate none of the rules of transformational grammar which he is putatively applying. Harman's mistake is, however, according to both Nagel and Cooper, to think that the Fork (either propositional and therefore conscious, or dispositional and therefore unconscious) is sufficient to impale the Chomskyan thesis. Freudian examples can make sense of the notion of unconscious knowledge by strict analogical inference with our criteria for John's conscious knowledge about the battle of Hastings. Chomskyan examples, however, will still fail the test. This is because, Cooper thinks, in Freudian examples the knowledge was originally conscious but has been repressed by a traumatic experience. Although, while suffering from neurosis, the knowledge could not be recalled, when cured the person can recall the reasons for their odd behaviour. There is no counterpart to this process of explicit knowledge learned and then repressed so that it is describable as 'implicit' by an analogical inference in learning grammar.

There are two points to be made against Cooper here. The first briefly (I will develop this later) is that his comparison begs the question in a fundamental way. It assumes that an account of knowledge supported by empiricists is superior to Chomskyan innatism. Thus Freudian examples, which presuppose that all knowledge comes from sense-experience, learned explicitly and then forgotten through a causal process of repression, is coherent (whether ultimately provable), whereas an account of implicit knowledge of a universal grammar is not coherent because the innatist hypothesis is not so. But Cooper has failed to argue this in this context. Of course, if you make this empiricist assumption about the nature of knowledge, Freudian accounts which make them too will appear correct because we can make analogical inferences between them. My second point is that the Freudian examples themselves need a rule-following and not a causal reformulation if they are to be logically valid (see also above, pp. 196–9). If, as Cooper, claims, a dispositional account of language can be defended, then the general principle of Harman's Fork, as we have formulated it, falls to the ground, since all knowledge is knowledge-how. But if this is the case, then understanding Freudian examples by analogy with examples of conscious rule-following, knowledge-that claims will fall to the ground too. Their incoherence will rest upon the alleged incoherence of the rule-following/rule-conforming distinction. Freudian examples as analogical inferences are parasitic, therefore, on Chomskyan distinctions such as that identical overt behaviour like saying or squawking can be distinguished in terms of following of semantic rules or of having none to follow.

Let me elucidate first of all my second point in the light of my foregoing account of Harman's Fork. We saw that however intentional swimming might be in terms of the conscious activation of one pattern of behaviour in preference to another, there was not a distinction possible between two identical patterns of swimming behaviour, such as that present between making or simply squawking a statement about the battle of Hastings. There was, in other words, in cases of knowledge-how such as knowing how to swim, no counterpart to the distinction between rule-following and having no rules to follow in cases of knowledge-that, such as statements about the battle of Hastings. There is, in other words, no distinction between intending to swim and just swimming. Now, Freudian examples, I want to argue, are interesting because they presuppose ways of analysing putative knowledge-how which enable identical patterns of behaviour to be distinguished in a way analogous to the distinction between saying/squawking in putative examples of knowledge-that. Between identical sorts of overt behaviour, distinctions can be made in terms of the presence or absence of *unconscious* rule-following. Human non-propositional behaviour becomes, in effect, like standard examples of propositional behaviour, analysable in terms of rule-following, on the one hand, or having no rules which we can follow and achieve the desired result on the other.

Let us take as our example squinting-behaviour rather than swimming-behaviour, so as to align such an example with actual Freudian case-history (above, pp. 191–2). Consider the following two examples:

Example A

Miss Smith lives by herself and is never confident of the accuracy of her clocks. She passes each day on her way to the shops a window which is intensely and brightly lit. She knows that there is an accurate clock hanging in the shop, but she is unable to see this due to the brightness. But, by slow degrees, she learns how to squint so that she can see it.

Example B

Miss Jones is found to have a squint which occurred suddenly at one point in her life concerning which she has no clear recollections. There is no explanation available or convincing in physiological terms of what caused the squint. The psychoanalyst observes, however, that the girl has particular problems with the squint at 7.00 p.m. in the evening.

In Example A, no propositional knowledge was involved in Miss Smith's squint *per se*. In fact, if we taught her rules of squinting (like the rules of swimming), this might hinder or retard her performance or its learning in that it might damage her eyesight. But, in Example B, this is not the case according to the psychoanalysts. What has happened here is that the squint is a symptom of a trauma, a repressed memory that something took place, and, as such, reference is being made by the behaviour to unconscious knowledge-that. When the causal blockage which represses conscious recall of knowledge is removed, then the intentional rule-following is discovered. She recalls the night that her father died after she had nursed him over a long illness. As she realised that he was about to die, she had been weeping profusely, but when finally he was dead, she told herself that she must pull herself together, stop crying, be prepared to tell public officials the precise hour of her father's death and so forth. So, repressing her tears, she squinted through swollen eyelids to see with great difficulty the hour of 7.00 p.m. Although as a result of having repressed her feelings she could not remember the events, that she had unconscious knowledge of them is indicated by her squint and by the difficulties which she has with it around the hour of 7.00 p.m. (cf. above, pp. 191–2).

The squinting-behaviour in Example B cannot, as can that in Example A, be assimilated to the paradigm of knowing-how. Miss Jones, unlike Miss Smith, was not intentionally squinting in the same sense as that in which someone intentionally swims through water. Miss Jones's squinting can, according to the Freudians, only be explained, to put matters in my way, in terms of intentional rule-following. Her twisting and tightening of her eye muscles is a kind of propositional assertion about the hour of her father's death, what this required of her, and her unwillingness to give way to emotions about it. We have, therefore, as I said earlier, a distinction between different kinds of knowledge-how analogous to the knowledge-that distinction between asserting and squawking (he asserts-that, the parrot squawks-that). However, what Cooper has failed to grasp is that, for a valid analogical inference to be derived from this case, we require the distinction between asserting and squawking characterised in terms of rules-to-follow or no-rules-to-follow in the paradigm cases of conscious knowledge-that. Without such a distinction in the paradigm case, the distinction in cases of analogical inferences must also fail to be coherently made. In accepting a dispositional view of language, Cooper is not entitled to claim, therefore, that Freudian analogical inferences are valid from conscious knowledge-that to unconscious knowledge-that. Propositional knowledge without such a distinction is simply knowing how to make assertions, which is simply the ability to respond in a certain way if certain specifiable conditions obtain. For Cooper, therefore, the only viable reformulation of a Freudian explanation, which must, for him, be otherwise unviable, must be a reformulation which is in strictly causal terms. Example A would have therefore to be formally identified with Example B, since all that is necessary as an explanation is an account of the causal conditions for squinting, namely, either bright lights and the need to tell the time or a father's death, grief and an overwhelming need to read the hour of 7.00 p.m. For Cooper, Example B must simply involve a more complex set of stimuli for the elucidation of the response. What 'unconscious' knowledge in the final analysis must be is simply knowledge whose assertion is conditional on an unusual set of stimulating conditions.

This I take to be what is proposed when, at other points in his argument, Cooper sees the logical superiority of the Freudian model as an analogical inference by virtue of its causal aspects. Loss of memory through, for example, a blow in an accident (Cooper, 1975, pp. 29–31) represents a causal blockage of a disposition to recall an event. Chomsky's account cannot represent an analogical inference because it has no counterpart to such an event explaining how conscious knowledge has become unconscious. Let us now, however, in criticism of Cooper's position try to connect by analogical inference our normative model of generative grammar to the Freudian causal one, not by insisting that it be made more causal and dispositional, but by insisting rather that the Freudian causal model be restated in normative, rule-following terms. This procedure will bring both models into a valid relationship of analogical inference by analogy with both prongs of Harman's Fork. In doing so, we shall bring out a logical account of forgetting which can replace the causal account of forgetting in Freud's original paradigm, which will have a direct counterpart in Chomsky's innatist presuppositions in formulating rules which are tacitly or implicitly known.

8.9 RULE-FOLLOWING REFORMULATIONS OF FREUD AND THE
ROLE OF FORGETTING

It is arguable that Freudian examples do not require to be causal at all in order to make their case. In fact it might be said that the introduction of causal notions represents a conflation betwen two distinct categories, one of rule-following, and the other of rule-conforming (above, pp. 196–9), and that such a conflation is to be seen in a description of Miss Jones's squint as being *caused* by unconscious rule-following. Freudian unconscious rule-following could be better and more clearly expressed by ceasing to regard what has happened as causal at all. This is, I think, what was behind Wilson's (above, pp. 215–16) reformulation of Freudian explanations in terms of rule-following ones. Wilson's example, remember, was of a youth who, following a history of batterings from his mother as a child, continually expresses hatred and hostility towards all women. What has happened here, Wilson claimed, is that a fundamental piece of mislearning (as opposed to causal 'repression') has taken place. The youth is to be regarded in infancy as having formulated a syllogism falsely. His inductive rule-referencing has gone wrong. From the fact that one woman wished to batter him he has derived the universal statement:

All women wish to batter me (Major premise)

He then adds to his major premise:

x is a woman (Minor premise)

and logically there follows:

x wishes to batter me (Conclusion)

Psychotherapy becomes the process of correcting fundamental pieces of mislearning by uncovering mislearned rules of induction by teaching the proper ones. Psychotherapy, according to this reformulation, becomes the process in which we unpack the long chain of propositions threaded together by validly inductive or deductive processes until we reach the invalid inference or deduction which has distorted the structure of the youth's overall world view. This is why the Freudian cases that appear to be cases of knowing-how are correctable by pointing to rules to which reference ought to be made in a way that standard examples of knowledge-how are not.

Now, what I find interesting about such a reformulation is that it makes Freudian examples far more similar to Chomsky's much-derided examples of the child as a little scientist unconsciously testing inductively the data of linguistic performances in his linguistic environment and unconsciously deducing the sub-set of rules of the universal grammar which explain and predict such performances. But what if Cooper were now to object that such unconscious 'knowledge' by such a reformulation simply becomes an analogical extension from the paradigm cases of the concept of knowledge and ceases to be the required analogical inference? His grounds would be that, because there are no longer any causal descriptions explaining absence of recall, all that our rule-following reformulation represents is simply a version of conscious and not unconscious knowledge. This version simply falls within paradigm cases for knowledge-that and ceases to be an analogical inference.

Cooper would, however, be wrong. The rule-referring analogue of causal repression would be the logical principle that we cannot think of two or more things at the same time. Note that this is a logical and not simply an empirical impossibility. Were we to try to devise empirical counter-examples in terms of surgery which divided a brain in two, with corresponding examples of double vision and double thinking, our attempt would founder on what we meant by the concept of a person and personal identity. The logical, rule-following counterpart to causal forgetting is, therefore, our logical reasons for claiming that we cannot think of the premises of an argument at the same time as we think of the conclusion. In a deductive argument, thinking a major premise at t_1, a minor premise at t_2, logically entails us thinking the conclusion at t_3, if we are thinking logically. But we are not thinking of all three propositions (major, minor, conclusion) at the same time. If we did so, then it would be impossible to 'think' at all since we could not move forwards from premises to conclusions and back again, when we so desired, to check the premises and so on. Knowledge of the premises may therefore be said to be 'implicit', 'tacit' or 'unconscious' when all that is conscious, explicit or open is knowledge of the conclusions. To deny that we have unconscious or implicit knowledge in this sense would be *ipso facto* to deny that our conscious knowledge of the conclusion is describable as 'knowledge' at all. A further point follows from this. We are not able consciously to recall all the conclusions and their premises at one and the same time out of which our world view is constructed. Were we to begin suddenly to try to question every conclusion by working back to every premise, find that the premise itself was the conclusion to some further argument, work back to its premises and so on, then our inquiry about the world and ourselves would come to a full stop. A project of pure inquiry like that of Descartes, or an investigation of linguistic universals like that of Chomsky, is a once-in-a-lifetime's affair executed to ensure that what ourselves or others know and say is founded upon unshakeable foundations.

Let us now see how this characterising of causal repression in terms of logical forgetting enables us to reinterpret our Freudian example of squinting. We shall use standard tests for validity and invalidity as explained in any standard text on logic (for example, Hodges, 1977). Some sets of premises and conclusions at the foundations of Miss Jones's world view have been invalidly inferred or deduced, with the result that a distortion of her total cognitive perspective has arisen. These invalid inferences and deductions are unconscious in the sense that premises are no longer thought once their conclusion is asserted. Let us therefore analyse the case of Miss Jones (example B), placing invalid inferences between single asterices (*..........*) and invalid deductions between double asterices (**..........**). We break the web of belief at the point where Miss Jones argues:

A.1   *All nurses must record when a patient dies* (Major premise)
A.2   I am my father's nurse (Minor premise)

A.3   I must record the hour of my father's death (Conclusion)

From this conclusion (A.3) she reasons:

B.1   If I am to record the hour of his death (p), then I must stop crying (q) $(p \rightarrow q)$
B.2   I must (from A.3) record my father's death (p)

B.3   I must stop crying $(\therefore q)$

She conjoins A.3 (= p) and B.3 (= q) with a third (r) thus:

C.1   If I am to record his death (p), I must pull myself together (r) $p \rightarrow r)$
C.2   I must record his death (p)

C.3   I must pull myself together $(\therefore r)$

and then with a fourth (s) thus:

**D.1   Either I pull myself together (r) or I continue crying (s) $(r \lor s)$
   D.2   I must pull myself together (r)

   D.3   I must not continue crying $(\neg s)$** (INVALID form of disjunctive syllogism $r \lor s, \neg r, \therefore s$)

The final conclusion of argument A implying B and conjoining with C and D is E (((A→ B) . (C . D)) → E) thus:

E.1   If I am to stop crying (D.3** invalid) (¬s) then I must squint (t) (¬s → t)
E.2   I am to stop crying (¬s)

E.3   I must squint (∴ t)

My grounds for A.1 as an invalid inference and for D as an invalid deduction, quite apart from the latter's being an invalid form of the disjunctive syllogism, is as follows. The inductive process which established A.1 was faulty because it does not follow from the fact that something is a social convention that one has to follow it, and even if this were granted, it is not clear that the social convention in question is a rule for nurses *per se* and that when the patient is also her father it cannot be suspended. D is not simply invalid because ((r v s) . r) → ¬s when tested by writing a truth-table is non-tautologous. D is also invalid because an inclusive rather than an exclusive 'or' (v) was reasonably in her situation, since continuing crying could have been a means to pulling herself together so that she could have done both. We thus see that the psychoanalyst is correcting fundamental pieces of mislearning by a process which can be understood by analogical inference with a logician unpacking the premises (up to this point only tacitly known) of explicitly known conclusions.

Miss Jones, when she squints but cannot remember why, is therefore doing something inferentially analogous to a person who, in thinking a conclusion, cannot be at the same time logically thinking of the premises as well. Her other experiences serve also to make her actions analogous inferentially to someone who unpacks premises emotionally charged as her particular actions happen also to be. Our reformulation ties the analogical inference of Freudian examples more tightly, moreover, to their paradigm cases, as well as forming an inferentially analogical bridge between such paradigm cases and Chomskyan analogies. Our example of a paradigm case of knowledge-that was the statement about the battle of Hastings. What distinguished such examples, we argued, from a parrot's simply knowing-how to squawk the statement was that they involved conscious and intentional rule-references. However, we saw that we do make statements of knowledge-that without being conscious every day of our lives of all the rule-references which we should have to make in order to be described as consciously and intentionally claiming knowledge of the battle of Hastings. A child may only, in some minimal sense, be able to make appropriate rule-references to what might count as evidence (such as teacher said so). But this minimum is necessary for the example to instantiate knowledge-that in distinction from knowledge-how. As adults, moreover, we have passed the stage of exhaustively or almost exhaustively consciously pointing to rules supporting many of our elementary knowledge-that claims. We have proceeded past the premises which established them which are no longer conscious. What matters for us in such normal cases if we are to be described as knowing-that (as epistemic agents rather than as parrots) is that, if challenged on any particular proposition, we can work back and recall the sorts of grounds upon which the proposition was established without, hopefully, the painful experiences of non-normal neurotic sufferers in such circumstances. What, however, both our reformulated Freudian examples of unconscious knowledge, derivable by analogical inference from a conscious paradigm which also has its logically unconscious aspects, now have in common is that both rest upon formal logical thinking which becomes now conscious, now unconscious, in the process of building up a picture of the world. We are made aware of such unconscious knowledge when it is pointed out that we have breached a rule which we have hitherto (for example, non-contradiction) been following, when we re-examine past induction and deduction by unpacking premises. This is, moreover, what both the normal example or propositions about the battle of Hastings and the pathological example of squinting both have in common. Our entitlement to describe such knowledge or false belief by analogous inference with paradigm, conscious cases is that, when pointed to appropriate rules, the knower will become conscious of his knowledge, or, where he has failed to achieve this, his false belief. Moreover, there are direct parallels here with a person following or sometimes not following the rules of generative grammar all his life, and only becoming aware that he followed or broke (some) of them when this is pointed out to him.

At this point I am aware that Cooper might claim that, however closely the parallel with Freudian and normal examples has now been drawn, Chomskyan examples still fail to be valid analogical inferences because, with Chomsky (unlike with Freud), there is no prior consciousness of or acceptance of the rules in question. To this final objection we now turn with our third reply.

8.10 THE COHERENCE OF THE POSTULATE OF INNATE ENDOWMENT

Cooper might finally object that, granted we can interpret 'forgetting' in a logical as opposed to a causal way, there still has to be some first stage in the development of the conceptual or propositional web of a person's knowledge in which he was conscious of the propositions which form the foundational premises. Granted that we cannot test in a rule-following way every proposition at the same time in a coherent body of knowledge, and granted that, as our conceptual and propositional web develops with the growth of experience, some acts of rule-following can no longer be conscious in order that others might be so, nevertheless the premises which form the basis of the structure of our experience must have been consciously learned at some time. But here, of course, we reach the fundamental conflict between an empiricist such as Cooper (1972), on the one hand, and proponents of a rationalist theory of innate ideas like that of Chomsky and Katz (1972) on the other. An empiricist theory requires that foundational premises be ostensive references to either something or to some atomic experience of something, so that such premises must express conscious knowledge. But an innatist hypothesis would require a different interpretation of the nature of the foundational premises. Such a hypothesis requires that, once we work back through the systematically constructed propositional and conceptual structure of experience to the foundational premises, such premises will be found not to be inductively derivable from any basic set of facts about the world nor deductively derivable from any further proposition, but derivable instead from certain innate categories of consciousness. Such categories are necessarily unconscious until cashed in terms of experience.

But why, then, it may be asked, are such categories tacit and implicit rather than explicit and conscious? The innatist reply to this in terms of our reformulation of the problem must be in terms of our logical account of forgetting. We cannot think of the premises at the same time as we think of the conclusion, and our first items of experience are to be regarded as minor premises or as conclusions to fundamental major premises which are explicit formulations of implicit and innate ideas. Thus, when later we work back to the foundation of our logical and propositional web of knowledge, we reach the first items of experience and therefore the first items of conscious knowledge, but, accepting all the standard objections to sense-data and so on, we are forced to proceed one further step which involves making conscious and explicit knowledge that was originally tacit and implicit. It is important, moreover, following Hamlyn, who had his own alternative solution to this problem (above, pp. 297–300), to insist that such a hypothesis is a logical and not a psychological hypothesis. Innate ideas, representing unconscious knowledge, such as logical principles like non-contradiction or the principles of generative grammars, should not be regarded as temporally prior to experience, but are rather applied *pari pasu* with the stating (and therefore learning of) the propositions which logically presuppose them. (I am, of course, using 'stating' in the widest possible sense to include 'stating to oneself', 'thinking' and so on). Locke spoke as though Leibnitz and Descartes thought such ideas to be temporally prior, and so persistently misrepresented their position (Leibniz, 1968, pp. 167–71). But this in no way follows. Granted that the physiological conditions for the exercise of acts of knowing must be temporally antecedent to such acts (the physiological basis of innate ideas must be temporally prior), actualised innate physiological mechanising which can logically count as acts of knowing are involved in asserting the foundational premises. Such acts involve both conscious and unconscious rule-following. As such, they cannot be understood purely dispositionally. Once we claim with Descartes, therefore, that there are intuitions logically distinguishable from deductions (1911, pp. 7–8), and once we concede that such intuitions are applied *pari pasu* with records of sensory phenomena, then the problem created by empiricist dogma is removed.

We may observe that the child's reply, 'John hurted', to the question, 'Why are you crying?' logically presupposes the principle of identity. We may record this logical presupposition thus:

Something either is or is not the case
Either John hurt me or he did not (Mary or Philip or someone else did)

Therefore John is responsible for my crying and not Mary or Philip or someone else

But our claim for the priority of the opening premise is not a temporal one any more than our account of forgetting has been a causal one. To say that the child knows implicitly or tacitly the principle of identity when he asserts, 'John hurted', is not to imply that he thinks this first, but simply that he cannot both be conscious of 'John hurted' and conscious of the principle of identity at one and the same time. One cannot think the conclusion consciously at the same time as the premises. A stage of development is reached later when the child, like any other human being, will want to check a certain area of experience which may be discordant with some other area. At this point he will work back from conclusions to premises and back again to other premises to which the former premises stood as conclusions and so forth, till finally fundamental propositions are reached whose major premises are formulations of innate principles. The formulation of them represents the making conscious of unconscious knowledge, and can only be conscious after the application in experience of such innate ideas. The empiricist desire to understand this description in terms of experience registered on sense-organs, forgotten and then remembered as a result of environmental triggering of recall and so on is therefore simply a reflection of empiricist epistemological prejudices. And it is these prejudices which are reflected in Cooper's refusal to give what to him is the superior title of 'analogical inference' to the concept of tacit or implicit knowledge in the new linguistics.

We have shown, therefore, in this section that Chomsky's case for tacit or implicit knowledge cannot be ruled out as logically incoherent, using analysis in terms of analogical inference as Cooper tries to do. There is an inferential bridge linking both Chomskyan and Freudian analogies between conscious and unconscious knowledge and what is logically involved in 'forgetting' in both. Moreover, we saw that there were grounds for doubting that the analogical inference/extension distinction was as clear-cut and as stable as Cooper believes, as I mentioned (in section 8.7). My bridging of what is purportedly an example of such an inference (Freud) and an example of an extension (Chomsky) would have served to illustrate such a 'bridging'. As such, we have considered the last and perhaps most potent objection to the kind of theory of semantic universals into which we would seek to incorporate and within which we would seek to develop Hirst's theory of the forms of knowledge. In earlier sections, we considered what we described as a Hirst/Hamlyn thesis that sought to locate forms of knowledge within a particular inter-personal and social form of life without reference to any further human form of life. We found that such a thesis foundered on being unable convincingly to connect pre-linguistic forms of objectivity with post-linguistic ones. Let us now see in specific terms how what Hirst claims about categorial and substantive concepts can better be understood and developed within a theory of semantic universals.

Chapter 9

Categorial and Substantive Concepts, Morphemes and Family-Resemblance

We saw earlier (Chapter 8) that Hamlyn set the later Wittgenstein against Chomsky on the grounds that Wittgenstein's notion of language-games defines objectivity in terms of an interpersonal backcloth of human judgements that removes the necessity for postulating innate, universal semantic structures. Whether this is true to what the later Wittgenstein intended or not is a question for those concerned with the history of ideas. Although such an interpretation might appear to be supported by some of Wittgenstein's remarks (for example, 1969, p. 90, discussed above, pp. 301–2), we have argued that such an interpretation runs contrary to other of his insights, particularly those embodied in his doctrine of family-resemblance, which stresses the basic continuity of human judgements (above, pp. 73–85, 119–25, 277–82). Our use of this doctrine in connection with Wittgenstein's notion of objectivity is to claim that the doctrine points to certain irreformable characteristics of human languages and the fundamental key to their translatability. If our understanding of this basic insight has therefore been valid, Hamlyn's position in regarding Wittgenstein and Chomsky as necessarily at variance is without foundation.

As Nagel (1969, pp. 181–2) pointed out, there is no necessary final distinction between Chomsky's and the later Wittgenstein's position here. The theory of linguistic universals could be understood as outlining what it is about human beings that makes possible that agreement in a form of life which makes possible, in turn, their agreement and disagreement in opinion. Furthermore, my particular understanding of linguistic universals in terms of tacit assertion of universal premises (section 8.10) involving implicit rule-references suggests a reconciliation between Chomsky and Wittgenstein in another way which I believe to dispose effectively of another of Hamlyn's objections that either every idea is innate or no idea is (Hamlyn, 1978, p. 21). Hamlyn, like many other interpreters of the later Wittgenstein, then, consistently divorces his theory of objectivity in terms of intersubjective agreement from his view of universals in terms of family-resemblance. I have contended that

Hamlyn is wrong to do this, for reasons which are basically to do with the close connection between the notion of 'game', 'language-game' and 'family' in Wittgenstein's thinking. Now what, following Bambrough (pp. 77–80), I took Wittgenstein's view to be is one that is opposed to the view that universal or open-class concepts can be understood as simply the sum total of the particulars subsumed within them. When a child learns to call an object a 'table', he is not learning a picture constructed out of all adult observations of particular tables which enables him to make the identification. If he were to do so, coming back to his teacher every time that he finds a new possible object which might count as a table to ask whether it fits some putative picture or not, then we would doubt that he had learned (as *humans* learn) what a table is. This is because, in applying open-class concepts, he has to know rules which enable him not simply to identify what are actually tables within present human experience, but what could possibly count as tables. On this point I do not think that Chomsky and the later Wittgenstein are as far apart as Hamlyn implies. In using family-resemblance to understand the creativity of language, Wittgenstein is near to making a similar point to that embodied in Chomsky's competence/performance distinction. It is not an actual performance in naming tables that counts as human learning of such open-class concepts, but rather the ability to detect possible tables by application of the rules of definition in terms of family-resemblance. This ability is therefore directly comparable with what Chomsky means by 'competence'. What I have sought to do in this chapter is to understand the innatist hypothesis in general, and the theory of linguistic universals in particular, in terms of an analogical inference with major or universal premises implicitly or tacitly understood in the explicit or conscious articulation of minor premises or conclusions that go with them in syllogistic arguments. Because I do not believe that a universalised premise, any more than a universal or open-class concept, is simply formed from a con-catenation of particular instances, I do not have to believe that every particular instance of an idea is innate, as Hamlyn seems to think that I do. All that has to be unlearned and implicit knowledge in order that *human* learning can take place is knowledge of the structure of rules that enables family-resemblances to be detected so that we can pass from actual to possible instances with open-class concepts and thus order particular experiences.

Furthermore, we have argued that human languages in which objectivity-judgements are made by means of open-class categories involved in family-resemblances, logically imply one kind of account of the psychology of the human language-user as opposed to another. In other words, it is false on an account of language-games that makes 'family-resemblances' central to the understanding of objectivity judgements to claim, as Hamlyn does, that such an account is logically independent of the natural history of inquiry. The ability of the human language-user to classify on the basis of being shown a small number of actual tables new possible instances of tables whose features bear no one-for-one correlation with those original instances we saw to be inexplicable within empiricist or behaviourist accounts of mind (above, pp. 72–4). What is implied by family-resemblances analysis is a human ability to, in Peters' words, 'transcend the particular' (above, p. 30).

We argued earlier as well (above, pp. 112–19) the clear presupposition made by such an account of a particular kind of human ability. When our senses are bombarded with stimuli of particular features of objects, we have to be able to accept some stimuli but reject others if we are to be able to classify in the way that in languages we actually do. We have to disregard the fact that Table a has three legs and Table b four, because if we did not, we could not include them in the same class. Nor can we say some features leave stronger impressions or elicit stronger behavioural responses, since a and b may, as we saw, had no common features (above, p. 78). Rather a creative, rule-following ability is required that actively and at will ignores some features and selects others, linking those features so selected in a rule-following way. Furthermore, not simply open-class concepts in ordinary language presuppose the ability to transcend the particular, but also the post-Einsteinian description of the physical world in terms of statistical schemes of probable recurrence of particular events. Here, too, the indeterminacy of open-classes, the way in which we are not, as we are in the case of the causal principle, compelled to subsume any given particular within a general class, points to a data-processing ability without which human understanding of a merely probably natural order would be inevitably chaotic. A world of statistical probability, just like our ordinary-language ability to describe things generally in terms of family-resemblance, requires for its understanding the ability to transcend the particular, to break the hold that particulars would otherwise exercise upon a conceptual order. Without this, language would not be able to generate open-classes and would thus be thrown into the kind of chaos exhibited by an imaginary language that failed to be intelligible because it had to devise a new word for every particular new thing or new feature of an old thing (above, pp. 82–4).

It is therefore my general argument that it is possible to produce a synthesis between Chomsky and the later Wittgenstein which will produce an argument supportative of a theory of semantic universals within a form of life. I propose now arguing that what Hirst describes as categorical concepts in his forms-of-knowledge thesis can be understood in a way that Hirst himself would reject (Hirst, 1979a) in terms of family-resemblances that presuppose the kind of innate ability that Chomsky seeks to investigate in his search for common morphemic elements that all languages hold in common. If my analysis of the forms of knowledge in such a context carries through, we shall, in consequence, have a transcendental (in the sense of 'transcultural') argument for the curriculum that is properly philosophical. (See also Brent, 1978, Chapter 4.)

We will begin therefore by looking at those features of Hirst's forms of knowledge which do admit of exhaustive definition, namely, the substantive concepts. We should, after all, expect such concepts to be exhaustively definable, since their valid applications in interpreting experience is determined by methods which, by a clear and determinate reduction, go back to the categorial concepts as the foundations of inquiry. The categorial concepts themselves, following Waismann's suggestion regarding mathematical categorial concepts (above, pp. 84–5), will be shown to be subject to definition in terms of family-resemblance which renders them immune to displacement so that they are not subject to change. As Hirst himself would agree, however, categorial concepts are extremely difficult to elucidate, and at this stage of the discussion we must remain content with a few tentative examples to elucidate my thesis, taken from most though not all of the forms. Nevertheless, such a tentative arrangement will, for the moment, however, I hope extend the discussion significantly.

The substantive concepts, I submit, are not true universals, but rather what the early Wittgenstein had in mind as 'concatenations' of particulars. They represent closed classes. When, for example, 'water' in an ideal language is written H_2O, it has a clear and determinate sense because it now consists of a string of particulars, namely, two atoms of hydrogen and one of oxygen, no more and no less. Further classifications become impossible other than in terms of these determinate features. If a sample of what in ordinary language is called 'water' is now produced and analysis reveals more than the string of particulars H_2O, then ordinary language must be displaced. When to the particulars H_2O further particulars such as $MgCl_2$ are added, a new term is devised, namely, 'carbon tetrachloride'. So, too, with 'atom', 'electron' or 'photosynthesis'. 'Photosynthesis' may be redefined by adding or modifying particular items following a new understanding of what is involved in the process, but in principle the particulars which make it up can be enclosed within a determinate classification. As concatenations of particulars, the closed classes that are the substantive concepts can be broken up and reformulated in accordance with the needs and interests of the scientific community.

If we turn to substantive concepts of the moral form, we here too find closed-class concepts. What counts, for example, as 'theft' may change from one generation or sub-culture to another, but identification of instances takes place by looking to see whether a given instance represents one of the string of particulars that composes the class. If something is theft in one sub-culture but not in another, this is because the particular example of an instance has been added or subtracted from the way in which that sub-culture closes the string at one point rather than another. To claim for expenses which one has not had may be classed as theft by one man, while yet another may abstract this particular instance from the class on grounds that bureaucracy will not pay taxi fares even in dire necessity, but will pay hotel expenses. He therefore pays for taxi fares which he has had out of expenses for hotels for stays which he has not had, and rules his claim out as theft. Yet, for both men, the class is closed, clear and determinate. In fact, if the class were not closed, then legal decision-making would be inoperable. If, however, such moral substantive concepts, like empirical ones, could not be broken up and reformulated in accordance with the needs and interests of the community, then social change would be impossible. Of course, such decisions to redefine concepts by adding or subtracting from their exhaustively definable lists of particulars are not arbitrary. They are governed by rules which define categorial concepts such as causal rules in the empirical form or rules of universalisability or the utilitarian calculus which govern categorial concepts in the moral form. But the procedure for defining substantive concepts themselves are exhaustive ones, as we have seen, so that they must represent closed-classes and not genuine universals.

In the case of the religious form, 'sacrifice' may be taken as an example of the closed character of a substantive concept. The difference between what is and what is not a valid sacrifice is something that the religious believer 'needs to know' just as much as the scientist 'needs to know' where 'water' leaves off and carbon-tetrachloride begins; or, in ethics, we 'need to know' what is or is not 'theft' in some clear and determinate way. This we can see to be the case with priestly manuals such as the Book of Leviticus, in which are enumerated exhaustively each particular animal, kind of grain or vegetable, particular occasion and method of its being offered so as to constitute a 'sacrifice'. Nor is only the priestly expert able to determine the boundary between the sacred and profane so as to close the concatenation of particulars which define the class of all things that can be sacrificed. In ordinary language before what might be regarded as the artificial languages of priestly castes, the difference between what was and was not a sacrifice had to be exhaustively defined for the concept to be usable. It was something which men 'needed to know' clearly and determinately, and not in terms of family-resemblances. Without being able to close such classes, such concepts (as with 'theft' or H_2O) could not function in our communication system. True, the prophets did start talking about, 'The Sacrifices of the Lord are a broken spirit and a contrite heart', but such statements, rather than additions to an open-class by means of detecting family-resemblance, are really revolutionary displacements of one closed definition by another. Strings of particulars such as a broken spirit and a contrite heart were to be included, whereas animals and other objects of the Levitical paraphernalia were to be excluded as particulars bounded by a closed-class. Such revolutionary displacements were perhaps a response to the social conditions of the Jewish Exile, where, without the Jerusalem Temple, no valid sacrifice could be offered. Nevertheless we see that strings of particulars constituting a religious substantive concept could be added together and subtracted from, according to rules derivable from categorial concepts. These religious substantive concepts are also therefore closed-class concepts, representing strings of exhaustively definable particulars.

The substantive concepts of the historical/sociological form may be exemplified by the concept of social class, which, too, admits of exhaustive definition. The social scientist 'needs to know' how a given class structure is to be defined, whether it is on the basis of wealth, culture or education, power or simply registrar general's categories. Strings of particulars are formed, re-formed and so on by enumeration, addition, subtraction and displacement, in accordance with rules derivable from categorial concepts. Here, too, therefore, exhaustive definition rather than definition by family-resemblance is necessary for the operability of the categories. And so we conclude our discussion of some examples of the way in which substantive concepts are necessarily defined.

On turning from substantive to categorial concepts, it is easy to see at first sight why Kuhn should have thought that they ought similarly to be exhaustively definable. Because the substantive concepts are able to be broken down and remade according to changes in human beliefs about knowledge of the world, it is deceptively easy to conclude that categorial concepts can also be remade and unmade, albeit less frequently. Because revolutionary displacement occurs with 'water', 'theft', 'sacrifice' or 'social class', then the underlying agreement 'in form of life' behind such changing agreements and disagreements 'in opinion' may be thought also to be subject to revolutionary displacement. But what I wish now to develop is my earlier argument that such 'given' anchorage of objectivity is not, in this way, subject to change. The categorial concepts, because they are, as genuine universals, open-class concepts, cannot be said to 'change' in what I have termed the 'revolutionary displacement' sense of this term at all. My reasons for this general assertion I have already explored earlier in this book (above, pp. 80–7 and pp, 276–89). Open-class concepts, identifiable in terms not of exhaustive definition but of family-resemblance, possess an immunity to change because they are open to possible new admissions to their classes as well as actual existing inclusions. What we will now do is to examine some specific examples of Hirst's categorial concepts to see how they fare when subjected to a family-resemblance analysis.

Now, our original argument was based upon Bambrough's analysis of how a definition of a universal like 'table' proceeded by family-resemblance. With categorial concepts, we shall be concerned with special kinds of universals (unlike 'table') which can be detected as cutting across different communities of judgement. However, we may proceed to analyse these as Bambrough analysed 'table', and this we will now do.

Let us therefore examine some examples of categorial concepts. We begin with the concept of empirical 'explanation', though perhaps 'prediction' or 'description' would do just as well, involving, as these do, families of concepts overlapping and criss-crossing such as 'cause' and 'probability'. It is better to phrase matters in this way since the adoption of 'cause' as a categorial concept leads falsely to the assumption that quantum physics can be regarded as displacing classical physics. Let us take three examples of empirical explanation:

(a) If B invariable follows A, and B and A are necessarily related, then A caused B.
(b) If 95 per cent of Texans with Cadillacs are oil millionaires, then someone who is a Texan and owns a Cadillac is likely to be an oil millionaire.
(c) If you throw the dice six times, there is a one in six probability of number 5 being thrown.

Now, each of these statements is a statement about the physical world. If (b) and (c) appear only trivially so, they are worth considering since more complex though formally identical examples could be given in substitution from quantum physics in the case of (b) and (c). Statement (b) might be thought more appropriately an example of the historical/sociological form of knowledge, but it should be noted that no sociological or historical evaluations are required for its interpretation: it is a purely empirical, geographical description. Let us see what features are exemplified by each example:

(*a*)   Here two particulars (P) are named in causal relationship (C).
(*b*)   A *class* of particular events (L) are named and a particular man (P) in a relationship of probability (B).
(*c*)   A class of *general* events (E) is named and connected to a scheme of recurrence (S) in a relationship of probability (B).

The classes mentioned in (*b*) and (*c*) are different because the class of Texans who are oil millionaires refers to a conglomeration of individuals observable at a given time, whereas the class of recurring 5s makes reference to no such individuals. When we list these features we find:

(*a*)   P, C.
(*b*)   L, P, B.
(*c*)   E, S, B.

We see therefore that (*a*) and (*c*) have no common feature. What entitles us, however, to refer to them within the general category of empirical explanation or prediction is that b is also an empirical explanation and has P in common with (*a*) and B with (*c*). They are classifiable, therefore, within an empirical form of knowledge by means of family-resemblance, which enables not simply actual examples of empirical explanation to be subsumed within the class, but possible ones as well.

It is significant, moreover, to observe what results when one breaks the chain of resemblance. Supposing that in example a we were to deny that the relationship were causal, as Hume did (above, pp. 90–7) when he asserted that all records of past events were merely records of conjunctions of such events so that we were not entitled to make predictions. C would then be eliminated from a and replaced with no distinguishable relationship, since if conjunction is all there is and all other relations are illusions, then there is no point in making it a feature of a class of anything. Likewise, it would be possible to dispose of the probability relationship B in b, by denying that any particular (P) is named which is not already a member of the class with which it is linked with reference to this relationship. Statement b therefore would become simply a description of the intersection of the class of Texans who are oil millionaires with the class of Texans who are Cadillac owners. In c, it would be possible likewise to eliminate schemes of recurrence (S) and probability (B) by simply claiming that all that the statement amounts to is a description that the dice has six sides and that this applies generally to all six-sided figures. Such strategies of revolutionary displacement would result in the rewriting of the list of features possessed by (*a*), (*b*) and (*c*) as follows:

(*a*)   P
(*b*)   L
(*c*)   E

In fact it would have succeeded in precipitating the conceptual collapse of the concept of empirical explanation by breaking the links in the chain of family-resemblance. New concepts cannot be indiscriminately and haphazardly subsumed under the category of empirical explanation. New, possible instances of explanation can be added to open-class concepts in a rule-following method, which is not, however, that of exhaustive definition, which can only apply to actual and not possible classifications, as we have seen. Thus the method of definition by family-resemblance can enable us to rule out some candidates for classification as empirical explanations on the grounds that they are not linkable – their acceptance would break the links in the chain of family-resemblance. Some false moves, such as we have just given for (*a*), (*b*) and (*c*), are not unlike those made by proponents of revolutionary displacement theorists, such as Kuhn's paradigms, with whom we have seen Hirst has much in common.

We have already frequently quoted Waisman's analysis of mathematical categorial concepts in terms of family-resemblance (pp. 84–5 and pp. 329–30), and so we may pass on to an example of a moral categorial concept. Let us move on, then, to categorial concepts in the moral form of knowledge. Let us look, as we did with the empirical form, at three concepts of moral obligation ('ought') which are held by moral displacement theorists (like the Kuhnians in science) to represent different and mutually exclusive moral paradigms:

(*a*)   A ought to do x because x is universalisable.
(*b*)   A ought to do x because x is likely to contribute to the greatest happiness of the greatest number.
(*c*)   A ought to do x because love is the supreme moral principle and necessitates x.

Now the reason why displacement theorists refuse to include these within the 'same' category of moral justification may be seen from the way in which some moral practices are sanctioned by one concept but ruled out by others. Sometimes, moreover, particular moral practices lack the general applicability that they would have on one view of justification in comparison with another. Thus, if we substitute for 'x' in (*a*), (*b*) and (*c*) 'truth-telling' (T), 'promise keeping' (P) and murder' (M), we get the following results:

(*a*)   Here both T, P and M would be sanctioned by universalisability and no special exceptions made. If a *ceteris paribus* qualification is made, it points to general classes of exceptions.

(*b*)   Here neither 'truth-telling', nor 'promise keeping', nor 'murder' would necessarily constitute *general* moral judgements, at least from the standpoint of an *act*-utilitarian. In extreme circumstances, a particular broken promise (for example, one whose particular consequences had not been foreseen), a particular lie (for example, one where the truth might lead to a loss of morale) or a particular murder (of, say, a Hitler) might be sanctioned. Such acts, at least for an act-utilitarian, are not specifiable in advance nor generalisable. Each judgement is context-specific. If we try to generalise, then this becomes self-defeating since general lying to keep up morale and general avoidance of promises because of unforeseen outcomes leads to the opposite effects upon those who are lied to or to whom promises are made. Thus generalised, T, P and M meet their contraries in the case of b, and so we may write –T, –P and –M.

(*c*)   Here M is always wrong since love as the supreme principle rules out the taking of a man's life. But out of love one may sometimes lie (for example, to avoid hurt) or sometimes not keep promises (–T and –P). As with b, the last two are situation-specific.

Therefore we may list as examples of the properties of (*a*), (*b*) and (*c*):

(*a*)   T, P and M.
(*b*)   –T, –P and –M.
(*c*)   –T, –P and M.

Example (*a*), when exhaustively defined and compared with an exhaustive definition of (*b*), may not be classified as the 'same' but 'different' by the displacement theorists. But a shares M with (*c*) and (*b*) shares –P with (*c*), so that we are entitled to say that all three concepts are linked in the 'same' moral form of knowledge by family-resemblance. It is this open-ended character which enables actual moral categorial concepts but also possible new ones to be subsumed within the same category of moral explanation. Old ones are linked together and new ones are linkable with or within the conceptual web.

As we saw with the empirical form, so with the moral, certain concepts can be ruled out as invalid on the grounds that they would break links within the web of resemblance, precipitating collapse of the general conditions of moral intelligibility. All links would be broken if we tried to include within the open-class of categorial moral concepts something like:

(*d*)   A ought to do x because it represents the will of the stronger over the weaker.

We see, therefore, how Wittgenstein's insight into the family-resemblance aspect of universals can also yield a semantic test for validity while avoiding the pitfalls of classical essentialism. Example d would, after all, be one of the few examples which would instantiate a displacement theory of moral categorial change. A similar false move can also be detected by means of such an analysis when it is argued that either (*a*), or (*b*), or (*c*) represent the only valid moral theory. Such a move in the light of my argument would be as invalid as the displacement theorist's claims for quantum as opposed to classical paradigms in theoretical physics.

We pass now to some categorial concepts of the religious form, the means of identifying which will also mark a similar contrast with the means of identifying religious substantive concepts, discussed earlier in this chapter. Consider, then, the following examples:

(*a*)   God is beyond the world ('wholly other').
(*b*)   God is love.
(*c*)   God is immanent in nature ('immanence').
(*d*)   God is the hidden order in all historical events ('providence').

Let us, therefore, proceeding as we did with empirical and moral forms, list the features of each thus:

(*a*)   God is transcendent (T), not immanent (−I), and beyond emotion (−L).
(*b*)   God is transcendent (T), since otherwise he would be loving himself and is love (L), and therefore not immanent (−I).
(*c*)   God is immanent (I) but not transcendent (−T), nor is he always love (−L) because nature is sometimes hostile.

(*d*) God is immanent (I, –T) and also love (L), since the 'order' behind the chaotic flux of human affairs is equivalent to 'benign influence'.

Therefore we may list the properties of (*a*), (*b*), (*c*), (*d*) thus:

(*a*) T, –I and –L.
(*b*) T, –I and L.
(*c*) I, –T and –L.
(*d*) I, –T and L.

Feature (*b*) has no common features with c but is linked with a through T and –I, and (*c*) is linked with a through –L. Features (*a*), (*b*) and (*c*) are subsumable, then, within the same form of knowledge, and are describable as the 'same' kinds of concepts by means of family-resemblance analysis. Furthermore, d is able also to be added to the class because, though at an early period in the development of religious awareness it may not have been an instance of an actual religious concept, it was nevertheless a possible one. What made it a possible instance of a religious categorial concept was its capacity for being linkable with the web of family-resemblance. Feature (*d*) is linkable with b through L and with c through –T. Furthermore, the family-resemblance analysis leads to a similar semantic test for validity of religious categorial concepts in that certain concepts cannot validly be subsumed within the religious form because they are not linkable. Attempts to make such statements as 'God is dead' or 'God is ultimate concert' categorial to religious thinking fail because they fail to find links with the web of family-resemblance.

We pass to our final example of family-resemblance analysis, this time taken from the historical/sociological categorial concepts. Let us consider the following examples:

(*a*) Hitler was responsible for the mass-murder of the Jews.
(*b*) A bad winter and a poor harvest caused the French Revolution.
(*c*) Churchill tried to dissuade Stalin from wanting spheres of influence.

Each of these statements represents a version of historical explanation with underlying categories of historical cause or responsibility. Let us therefore try to identify the features of each example of historical explanation:

(*a*) An individual (I) and a class of individuals in a group relation-ship (G) are joined together by a means/end (M) explanation.

(*b*)   Natural events (N) and a group relationship (G) are joined together by means of a causal explanation (C).
(*c*)   Two individuals (I) are joined in terms of a means/end (M) explanation.

We may therefore list the features of (*a*), (*b*) and (*c*) as follows:

(*a*)   I, G and M.
(*b*)   N, G and C.
(*c*)   I and M.

Although b and c have no common features, they are nevertheless classifiable within the 'same' category of historical explanation, because (*c*) shares I and M with (*a*) and (*b*) shares G with (*a*). They are linkable within the web of family-resemblance represented by the historical/sociological form of knowledge. Furthermore, once again we find that family-resemblance analysis provides us with a semantic test for validity. Some forms of Marxist historical explanation would be ruled out which reduce all means/ends explanations (M) to causal ones (C), refuse to distinguish individual acts (I) from group ones, and then deny distinctions between objects (N) and persons (I). Here we observe the precipitation of a similar conceptual collapse that we observed earlier in connection with categorial concepts of the empirical form. Such a strategy, moreover, would not simply reduce the historical to the empirical form of knowledge, but to no form of knowledge at all and simply to the recording of isolated sensations. Thus we have, once again, examples of family-resemblances performing in language a function similar to that performed by morphemes in Chomskyan semantic theory.

We are now, in the light of the foregoing discussion, in a position to see how the incorporation of family-resemblance analysis into Hirst's theory leads us beyond the later Wittgenstein in the direction of an argument supportive of universals in a form of life. Family-resemblance analysis yields a view of categorial concepts which are not, like substantive concepts, subject to change. Though, on a superficial analysis, the categorial concepts of a particular form may appear to change into a different one, such concepts remain basically classifiable under the 'same' form of knowledge by means of identification by family-resemblance. This family-resemblance, moreover, unites the forms as categorial modes of awareness with common-sense judgements like, 'You made the chair fall' (empirical), 'You only gave me half' (mathematical), 'It's awesome' (religious), 'It's beautiful' (aesthetic), 'It's good' (moral), and 'It happened' (historical) with the developed forms of knowledge employed by specialists. It is this *continuity* which makes possible the application of forms of theoretical inquiry in informing common-sense judgements. This is why Dearden was wrong to talk of 'conceptual shift' and 'disjunction' between the forms and ordinary speech because his case rested upon some kind of putative possible exhaustive definition of both rather than on the detection of family-resemblances (above, p. 296). This is why, furthermore, it is wrong to claim a similar conceptual shift or disjunction between the languages of different cultures and different historical epochs regarding certain basic conditions of meaning. A displacement theory such as Kuhn's may require this, but we have seen how such theories rest upon a false understanding of the nature of open-class concepts or universals and how categorial concepts are to be ranked among their number. Between different languages, cultures and historical epochs, therefore, there can be discerned in terms of family-resemblance seven families of language-games that are the seven forms of knowledge which, *pace* Hirst, are the invariant givens of a human form of life. Such a theory, moreover, links up with Chomsky's view of semantic universals definitive of competence as opposed to performance, since the detection of such universals in terms of family-resemblance points to possible classifications which may not yet have been actualised in speech-acts.

Conclusions and Further Implications

At first sight it may appear that a theory of universals in a form of life, as I have outlined it, appears to make the forms of knowledge so vacuous that they cannot be used to settle any epistemological or curricular issue. Family-resemblance, by admitting so much within its ambit, simply and in a non-ironic sense 'leaves everything the same' and resolves no issues regarding what can or cannot be known. But this is not the case. Although the theory of semantic universals in a form of life cannot be used to settle every dispute regarding what is or is not true, it can, however, unravel certain errors of a fundamental kind. The theory tells us that whatever else a statement might be, it must be either empirical *or* moral *or* religious *or* aesthetic *or* historical/sociological *or* mathematical measured against the yardstick of six or seven distinct webs of family-resemblances spanning cultures and centuries whose logical relationship and distinctiveness are guaranteed by reducibility and irreducibility criteria. Thus fundamental errors, such as those of astrology and witchcraft, discontinuous with these conceptual webs, can be ruled out, as can some interpretations of historical, moral or quantum-mechanical methodologies of the present time, and some attempts to exclude religion as significant discourse by reductionist stratagems (above, pp. 119–24).

We have seen, moreover, how it is important to observe how, in this form, a theory of semantic universals in a form of life escapes certain interesting criticisms of Chomsky which were made by Hamlyn (above, pp. 303–8). First, this theory does not require that every idea be innate, but only that account be taken of what it is about human psychological make-up that enables language-users to move from actual to possible conceptual classifications and from actual propositional organisations to possible ones. Family-resemblance analysis as descriptive of what Chomsky means by competence as opposed to performance clearly rules out innate ideas understood in terms of paradigmatic mental images. Secondly, though some kind of innatist account of mind is implied, this cannot be seen as arising from an epistemology which asks how an individual builds up a picture of the world devoid of any social context. On my interpretation of universals in a form of life, Chomsky has posed a very different question, namely, what is it about human individuals that makes possible their agreement in social forms of life with their underlying agreement in a human form of life to which the trans-latability of human language points?

With the mention of the translatability of human languages, we focus finally on a further area of acute controversy regarding a theory of semantic universals. We saw earlier that Quine's thesis of radical translation denied that one human language was necessarily trans-latable into another (above, pp. 59–67). We also saw in this chapter (Section 8.4) that, albeit on different grounds, sometimes Wittgenstein's thesis about language-games was interpreted in such a way as to yield similar conclusions to those of Quine. When forms of life clash, there is no reason why necessarily issues between them should be able to be either understood or resolved in mutually comprehensible epistemology or ethical terms. Wittgenstein was thus interpreted as claiming that we can lose contact with a certain community of judgement or, as the result of changes in the social basis of objectivity, cease to understand the world and human life in a certain way. We have already argued that both views, that of Quine and, allegedly, that of Wittgenstein, are mistaken. We have argued that both views run counter to Wittgenstein's insight regarding family-resemblance in a way that in some moods perhaps Wittgenstein did himself. In the thesis of radical translation, we saw that, in Yudkin's words, Quine had to presume 'a pattern for exactness that only someone familiar with metaphysical hairsplitting in our own language could manifest'. It was thus a special kind of imprecision that we associated with a fully articulated doctrine of family-resemblance that would not allow categories of one language to form fully closed boundaries against another, as Quine's thesis required (above, pp. 63–4). In the theory of language-games, moreover, family-resemblance gave us the key for arguing a necessary irreformability (resulting from this special kind of imprecision) of categorial concepts that were, as such, the foundations of any human language, and that pointed to a general, human form of life.

Thus we see that on the grounds of the logic of any communicable form of human discourse, Katz is right to make the principle of 'effability' part of the case for a theory of semantic universals (Katz, 1972, pp. 20–21). Katz states his thesis, like Chomsky, in a way that we have claimed to be misleading, namely, as an empirical thesis describing facts that might have been otherwise and yet are (above, pp. 284–8). We saw that this was a misleading characterisation of such a thesis to call it 'empirical'. We argued that it logically and necessarily follows, given the facts of human languages (containing phenomena such as open-class universals, family-resemblances and so forth), that they are translatable because they cannot close their classes against each other. Granted that such necessity is contingent upon human evolution, the thesis, however, is not falsifiable, which makes the contingency a peculiar kind of contingency at best. Let us, however, having given the thesis logical rather than empirical support, describe the effability thesis according to Katz. We shall, as a result, be able to see how our analysis of categorial concepts as open-class family-resemblances will be able to take us some way towards satisfying the demands of such a thesis.

Katz considers the objection of the apparent implausibility of the effability thesis quite apart from Quine's objectionable example of radical translation with which we have dealt. How, after all, can we claim that communication is always possible, given cultural and historical distances and differences? Suppose we took an example of the communication system of an allegedly primitive society of South Sea islanders and of Western Europeans and compared the ability of the language of the latter in contrast with the former to deal with complex descriptions and concepts in science and technology. How can the doctrine of effability in the case of such examples be confidently asserted? Can the complex laws of modern physics, with approximate yet adequate equivalance of meaning, be translated into a language that hitherto has only dealt with categories that describe natural events as under the control of spirits? A similar problem, of course, confronts our thesis as to the sense in which it can be said that primitive man also divided his experience in terms of Hirst's forms of knowledge (see also Brent, 1978, pp. 176–95 ff.). Katz's example is of a native of the South Sea island community who, having learned both English and the exposition of modern physics, proceeded to return to his community and communicate in his native language what he had learned. Katz continues:

> What he must therefore do is either use English words for concepts not in his language or else make up words that more readily fit into the phonology of the language. In either case he will have to introduce a large stock of new words, but he will rely on the already existing semantic structure of the native language to define them on the already existing syntactic and phonological structure of the native language to make it possible to form sentences with them that express the laws of modern physics . . . We do not suppose that by so enlarging the vocabulary of his native language he has in fact changed the language essentially, just as we do not assume that English has changed essentially as a result of the increase in the number of vocabulary items brought about by the rise of science in the last hundred years. (Katz, 1972, pp. 20–21)

We believe the essential semantic structures of language to be characterisable partially in terms of what Hirst describes as categorial concepts grouped into six or so irreducible clusters called 'forms of knowledge, awareness, or understanding'. The creation of new substantive concepts like the creation of new vocabulary described in this passage do not affect or basically change the character of the categorial concepts. These are not new semantic representations but basically extensions of old ones of whose families, as it were, they remain part. Forms of knowledge are, as such, infinitely extendable in that they can generate new sentences bearing the same semantic representation as older ones. As such, our previous analysis of categorial concepts as forming chains which, when broken, destroy the semantic representation, is intended to provide material for the possibility of writing general semantic rules for such concepts in accordance with the effability principle of a theory of semantic universals. Our account thus conforms with Katz's formal enunciation of effability in the following terms:

> The concept of effability thus rests in the following principle about the conditions of linguistic stability and change: a language L cannot be said to have changed over the period from t_1 to t_2, even though the optimal grammar G_L at t_1 does not generate the set of sentences S and S is generated by the optimal grammar of L at t_2, if it is the case that merely the addition of a finite number of lexical items to G_L would enable it to generate S, where the notion of

adding lexical items is understood as adding as yet unused phonological possibilities. The syntactic features governing the distribution of the new lexical item in sentences and its semantic representation are not new but part of G_L. (Katz, 1972, p. 21)

In the light of our foregoing discussion, forms of knowledge can be and ought to be on the basis of their categorial concepts, incorporated into such a thesis so that, in this quotation, the following substitutions can be made: G_L = a form of knowledge, L = a new version of a form of knowledge, S = a particular proposition or group of propositions articulated and testable against a form of knowledge, 'unused phonological possibilities' is also extended to include 'unused morphological possibilities', and 'lexical item' is understood as 'substantive concept'.

We thus conclude our theoretical thesis developed in this book. For our final chapter we will turn our attention to the educational implications of our thesis in a brief survey.

Chapter 10

Conclusions: Multicultural Education and the Place of Religion

We began in Chapter 1 by offering some tentative account of the way in which conflicting social theories could be so reformulated as to provide a coherent model of the basis of which educational proposals could be generated. At the end of the day, and as a conclusion to a long and complex argument, we outlined how we saw a modified Chomskyan theory of semantic universals in forms of life as being capable of incorporating into a unified theory both a sociological theory of pedagogy, such as that of Bernstein, with a philosophical theory of curriculum foundations, such as that of Hirst. Our guiding principles throughout were derivable from the philosophical tradition of conceptual analysis, the analytic methods of which applied to the problems dealt with yielded a demonstration of the irreducibility or rule-following to rule-conforming models of explanation. In the course of our analysis, we saw that certain features, both of classical and phenomenological Marxism and Freudian psychoanalysis, were better handled within a new, rule-following framework than in their original frameworks, where they remained, to say the least, problematic.

There are, however, some objections to regarding the requirements of an adequate curriculum theory to be such as those that I have suggested. It will be well to deal briefly with some of these objections now. There is the objection that the basic guidelines for constructing educational theory should be not epistemological, as I have suggested, but rather ethical. As the problems with which I have dealt here are epistemological, namely, criteria for an adequate social-science theory of human action that can, in particular, account for truth-assertive (subject-predicate) languages, my enterprise is thus judged to be misconceived. (See, for example, White, 1978, pp. 364–5; Cooper, 1980, p. 171; Barrow, 1976).

It is my contention that epistemological or truth criteria here becomes as important as ethical criteria for the reasons that I have outlined. That the ultimate justification for curricular subjects is ethical is only true because the ultimate foundation of epistemology is a commitment that truth matters and *that* is the basis for curriculum judgements. *Prima facie*, Barrow's claim appears to be that subjects or curricular activities can have a variety of different forms and that the form to be chosen is the one that best satisfies the utilitarian criterion. Thus, too, specifically applied forms of subjects are ruled out because the very specialism may make students of them redundant in favour of more general forms that will enable students to use them in more than one area. Outside of purely economic considerations, there are general social areas in which the principle ought to work. Some forms of religious instruction, namely, those which lead to intolerance and bigotry and inter-denominational or inter-faith strife, should be ruled out in favour of other forms that do not. A similar case can also be made for some forms of history teaching in contrast to others. In the psychological sphere, which, in this respect, may be linked to outcomes of teaching subjects in the aforementioned social sphere, some forms of subject-matter in, for example, religion and the social sciences should be rejected on mental-health grounds, if, say, they produce feelings of repression in favour of others that do not. But there is a problem with considering that such decisions rest on ethical grounds alone without any reference to underlying epistemological theses. Such a procedure implies an epistemological relativism. What it implies is that there could be two or more equally valid epistemological forms of a subject and that the choice between them could be determined by an ethical argument alone.

We have demonstrated the grave difficulties that such an ethical solution to epistemological relativism must face (above, pp. 180–1). We saw, for example, how Marxists, following Marcuse, looked to phenomenology and Freud to solve problems of objectivity intractable within the classical Marxist model. They then sought for an ethical justification of one socially relative theory against another by looking for mental-health criteria derived from Freud, which, they believed, would ethically objectify their epistemological relativism and thus avoid its consequences. Curriculum theorists likewise justified one culturally relative curriculum proposal against another by reference to such mental-health criteria. Yet, in the final analysis, we saw that it was epistemological rather than ethical non-relative criteria that the essentially prescriptive character of social-scientific models required. The ethical prescriptions of mental-health criteria logically required a reality principle that, in turn, required the defensibility of a non-relativistic theory of knowledge. Moreover, our demonstration of the self-defeating character of too narrow a utilitarian criterion of curriculum selection is, in fact, as much an epistemological as an ethical demonstration. Too circumscribed developments and applications of disciplines of inquiry are false because they imply that such disciplines are only true (or important) for the circumscribed area to which they have been applied. The reason why what Peters described as 'cognitive overspill' as constituting the 'liberal' character of the curriculum is ethically imperative is because there are logical and epistemological connections between structures of thinking in applied areas and broader and more general schemes for interpreting nature and man's place within it (Peters, 1966, pp. 30–45 ff.). The ethical imperative of such a view of liberal education is founded, therefore, on an epistemological decision, namely, that it is the perpetuation of what is false to encourage the belief that the only application of basic modes of understanding is to a given type of production process in a given type of society that thereby finds such modes 'useful'. Thus we see that moral judgements about the curriculum are dependent upon the establishment of a prior epistemological position, and this has been the object both of my present and previous book.

Having therefore established in general terms our claim that curriculum theory requires an epistemological theory, let us now turn to a more specific area in order to illustrate the implications of what we have argued there. One of Barrow's objectives in providing an ethical criterion for curriculum selection was, as we saw, to obtain subjects that would lead to a multi-faith, multi-cultural community, learning through its school curriculum to live in peace with mutual respect. At first sight, this example would appear to be a purely ethical goal in which epistemological issues of truth or falsehood are not at stake. After all, are we not here in the realm of 'values' rather than 'facts', and is not such a recognition an essential prerequisite in framing programmes of multi-cultural education? It might be argued, say, that as all history is selective, isolated atrocities of early white settlers in Australia upon Aboriginals and vice versa should be played down in a multi-cultural studies' programme and examples of mutual support and assistance emphasised instead. The selection of material here would therefore appear to rest upon value-positions rather than epistemological ones. Furthermore, in the special case of a multi-cultural curriculum programme, a culturally relativistic position might appear, at first sight, to be the best hope of achieving such moral ends as mutual tolerance and forbearance through getting pupil recognition that one's way of life is not necessarily the only one, that it is, in Rousseau's words, 'impossible to live at peace with those whom we believe to be damned'. But there are two objections to this initially plausible-sounding proposal, one of which, in connection with mental-health criteria, we have already dealt with both in Chapter 5 and earlier in this chapter. An epistemological relativism cannot achieve ethical objectivity by appealing to either socially useful or mental-health criteria for distinguishing between culturally relative 'moral' or 'immoral' world views. This is because, as we have shown, in the final analysis definitions either of mental health or social utility have to take up some non-relative position on how what is useful or healthy connects up with some overall view of reality.

The second objection to such an approach to the justification of programmes for multi-cultural education was raised by Walking (1980). The enterprise of multi-cultural education is, after all, a good general description of those forms of history and religious teaching that, in Barrow's examples, were intended to fulfil the moral end of fostering respect and understanding between cultures. But, argues Walking, there is an epistemological requirement for such proposals in addition to ethical ones. This epistemological requirement is that, albeit in some minimal sense, cross-cultural understanding is possible. As Walking says:

> To understand a belief as a belief is to accept it as possibly correct or incorrect and to look for its grounds rather than its causes . . . The possibility of a pluralistic society depends upon the possibility of understanding people and their beliefs. It must . . . provide a dynamic context in which people's beliefs are exchanged, defended, argued about, converted, retained, assessed . . . all the reactions people have to beliefs of other people whom they take seriously. Extreme relativism or transmissionism in a curriculum imply a sort of cultural protectionism. (Walking, 1980, p. 94)

Furthermore, it is arguable that, since 'ought' implies 'can', the ethical 'ought of multi-cultural understanding through the curriculum implies an epistemological 'can'. In other words, it is pointless producing an ethical argument for why multi-cultural education is good both for the individual and society if our epistemology can establish no good grounds for why one culture can necessarily understand another. Walking has his own very carefully and schematically worked-out analysis of why multi-cultural educational programmes and their justification are hostage to what can or cannot be established on epistemological grounds in this area. Suffice it to say that it is on the basis of the cogency of such demands that I have been anxious, in this work on educational foundations, to object to such a thesis as Quine's on the indeterminacy of translation (above, pp. 63–8 and 298–300).

Furthermore, in analysing the epistemology of the later Wittgenstein, critical as this is for Hirst's curriculum theory, I have been similarly exercised by what is also a curriculum problem. I have been anxious not simply to show that charges of cultural relativism are misplaced, but that a much stronger thesis in terms of semantic universals is required if such a theory is to be capable of legislating on curriculum foundations. Unlike with Quine, the problem with the later Wittgenstein is, of course, one of working out precisely what his thesis is. In his posthumously published later work (1969 and 1974), he eschewed working out epistemological theories systematically and considered that philosophy was primarily a war against such systemisation, which he called the 'philosophic disease'. If I have used some of his insights (for example, 'family-resemblance') by interpreting them as supportive of a theory of semantic universals in a form of life, I may appear to have caught the disease. If so, then it was the doctor's treatment that gave it to me. His insights have proved too provocative in an opposite direction than the one he intended, but then, if he had no system, he ought not to have had such intentions anyway. At all events, I have been at pains to show that the acceptance of a culturally relative theory of language-games is potentially disastrous for an adequate justification of a multi-cultural curriculum. It is sometimes suggested that we can only understand another culture, in Wittgenstein's view, by taking over that culture's conceptual schemes and thus leaving our own. In that case, our own culture is no longer intelligible (Winch, 1964). We can, it is suggested, only participate in another community of judgement by ceasing to participate in our own. If this were the case, then similar conclusions as those of Quine's indeterminacy of translation would follow, albeit from different premises. It should by now be clear why, with an adequate theory of educational foundations in mind, we were at pains to resist such a conclusion as well as either Quine's or Wittgenstein's premises.

There are, however, further implications for the intelligibility of a programme of multi-cultural education if a culturally relative epistemology were to be sustainable. It was not simply epistemo-logical objectives such as 'understanding', but moral objectives such as 'respect between cultures' that were stated for such programmes. Moreover, such objectives are logically interrelated in a sense similar to that in which the ethical principle of respect for persons logically implies the concept of a person which is epistemologically defined. Briefly, it is arguable that not only is a basis in epistemology necessary for the notion of cross-cultural understanding, but that also, without such a notion, respect between different sets of persons inhabiting different cultures is a logical impossibility. In other words, the epistemological requirements of the moral concept of 'respect for persons' apply equally to the multi-cultural curriculum requirement of 'respect for cultures'. Let us briefly now sketch why this is so.

Fundamental to the concept of respect for persons is the

recognition that what it is that one is respecting exists on the same level of consciousness as oneself, and like oneself is a source of rational arguments and claims (Peters, 1966, pp. 208–13). When a child is born into the world, he begins ordering the booming, buzzing chaos that confronts him into categories among which are the categories of 'things' and 'people'. It is a distinction of fundamental importance for ethics. Upon this distinction rests the development of awareness that some objects external to him can only be pushed, pulled, hit or whatever, but that other objects (that are, in fact, not 'objects' but 'people') can also be addressed by means of language, entreated, persuaded and so forth (verbally or by gestures). The act of talking to such other persons implies commitment to the belief that they are able to listen, and as such represents the recognition of a fact about them, namely, that they are rational agents. They must hear and understand according to the same rule-following schemes by which we speak and understand. What is true here of understanding between individuals on which respect for persons is founded applies equally to the notion of multi-cultural understanding. There is no point in dialogue unless *ab initio* one is committed to there being grounds that will give such dialogue its point. Unless, therefore, there exists some commitment to the notion of a human community of judgement that can be justified as the presupposition of multi-cultural dialogue, then the goal of respect between cultures fostered by multi-cultural educational programmes is non-attainable. Thus we see yet again the indispensibility of adequate epistemological frameworks in social-scientific inquiry for an adequate curriculum theory.

I would like now finally to point to one further implication for theory of education in the argument that I have developed. I believe that the notion of a secular education that makes no reference to a religious understanding of human knowledge and experience (as opposed to religion as a social phenomenon) rests upon a powerful, ideological illusion. What sustains this secular illusion is an empiricist epistemology whose character in this regard I have frequently described as logical imperialism (above, pp. 121–3, 251–2, 280–2). A theoretical framework derivable from a sub-set of common-sense experience came to rule out other items of common-sense experience within the larger set. By applying criteria of reducibility and irreducibility, we have argued that logically this cannot be done and reference to the natural history of such forms of inquiry, in particular scientific inquiry, exemplify how excluded sub-sets reassert themselves, as did intuitions of chance and probability against those of cause (above, pp. 121–2). We have argued in family-resemblance a semantic continuity of religious statements behind all

changes, and that, under examination, we find in the continuity a
semantic residue guaranteed by semantic irreducibility and derivable
from one basic sub-set of common-sense experience. We have seen,
moreover, in this our concluding chapter, why, for an adequate
curriculum theory, it is necessary to have made this point. Unless
such a community of religious judgement is, in fact, not simply an
available option for general human understanding, but a normative,
transcultural necessity for such understanding, programmes for
transcultural understanding and mutual respect must fail since such
programmes include religious understanding. Nor will it do, in the
light of my general argument, to say that the presence of religious
understanding is simply a contingent fact about past and present
history. I have argued a necessity about religious judgements
comparable with the necessity of other kinds of judgements whose
basic categorial concepts have an irreformability or immunity to
change through their family-resemblance characters (above, pp.
338–43).

Thus what follows for curriculum foundations from claims about
how morally imperative multi-cultural studies in schools are is that
religion (not just the social study of religion, but religion as a form of
knowledge) must necessarily have its place in the curriculum. But
here we must add something about the true character of religious
indoctrination as distinct from the sense in which this term is used to
express a gut-feeling of disapproval. In this connection, we accept
the formal features of the Marxist view of indoctrination as 'that
which distorts reality', as against White's 'intentions' view of
indoctrination (White, 1972). As such, indoctrination is distinguishable from lying in that indoctrination involves the systematic
distortion of reality in which the interdependence of false
propositions leads to the indoctrinated person being deceived in a
generally consistent way over large and divergent areas of his
experience. Where we differ from Marxist understandings of
indoctrination, however, is that we do not see the systematic
distortion of reality in terms of what we have argued to be an
unintelligible dialectical view of reality that underpins descriptions
of indoctrination as that which freezes the given against real
alternatives that would change it (above, pp. 204–9). My definition
of reality distortion is that which confuses or attempts to nihilate part
or parts of a common framework of human judgements implicit in all
human speech-acts (above, pp. 292–303 and Brent, 1978, pp. 191–6).
The reality distortion that is indoctrination is therefore a distortion of
the reality processing structures that we have followed the
Chomskyans in both hypothesising from linguistic data and
hypothesising to be innate properties of human minds. There

follows, however, from such premises important practical conclusions about religious education and indoctrination. Those who would deny that religion is a form of knowledge and who would try to reduce religious understanding to social or psychological facts about religious believers, become, on our argument, the real indoctrinators.

But there are religious indoctrinators too. Those who, like Goss and others (above, pp. 159–61), regard religious claims as rivals to scientific ones and who try to nihilate or reduce the latter to the former, are similarly indoctrinators because they are distorting the common framework of human judgement. The knowledge of God, on our view, with constitutive schemes explanatory of the process of human life and man's eternal destiny, becomes a proper discipline of human inquiry. Such schemes are founded, like any other form of human inquiry, on certain basic and irreducible common-sense intuitions, and receive rational articulation into more developed patterns of explanation as the inquiry proceeds. The attack upon religion as a form of knowledge in our schools, well-meaning towards religion as this sometimes is in its desire to come to terms with modern, secular society, represents, unfortunately, a desire to come to terms with an illusion (see, for example, Cox, 1966; Hirst, 1974b, Chapter 5, with which cf. Harris, 1976). The secular society generated by empiricism's logical imperialism is a product, among other things, of the illusion of a causal, clockwork world. In such a world, modal expressions (representing the logic of 'choosing', 'deciding', 'intending' and other rule-following expressions) such as 'ought', 'necessary', 'possible', have no purchase. The logical arm of empiricist imperialism is extensional logic that claims to be able to cope with all such modalities (or 'intentions') by rewriting them as extensions (see, for example, Cooper, 1975, pp. 53–7; Quine, 1953, Chapter VIII). But there are philosophers who have found the writing out of modalities and their replacement by extensions unconvincing and have gone on then with specific arguments to defend the coherence of theism and to reach a religious understanding of the problem of evil (Swinburne, 1977, and Plantinga, 1974). Though we have not been able here to go into the technicalities of such modified essentialist arguments, our account of rule-following models and their irreducibility must be held to receive support from such sources. Suffice it to say that, as part of a theory of educational foundations, our specific argument for the validity of religious knowledge makes the role of the religious educator the role of one who needs to attack certain deep-seated fallacies in the thinking of contemporary secular man.

At this final and concluding point to my present argument, I will no doubt be accused of raising the spectre of metaphysics, so anathema to secular man. I must plead guilty, especially in view of a further book in preparation that is specifically a critique of the notion of secularism and entitled *The Secular Illusion*. Moreover, to have endeavoured to use in defence of my argument both methods of analytic philosophy and Chomskyan arguments, resonant as the latter are with the language of computer programmers, will, in the eyes of many, or even most of my contemporaries, have compounded my offence. I would, however, point out that the logical and linguistic phenomenon of the irreducibility of rule-following to rule-conforming models, when reformulated in terms of modal or intensional logic, has lead some contemporary philosophers to produce defences of religious statements in terms of such logic as we saw in our last paragraph. Since such a defence of modal logic is both an analytic and Chomskyan defence of a certain view of man, then such arguments can be regarded as generally supportive of our case, even though we have not in the present work been able to go into the technicalities of such logic. Our own argument within this general ambience of logical defences of religious arguments was briefly as follows, having, as will be plain, clear metaphysical implications in conclusion briefly spelled out. Whereas the existence of a universe of particulars in causal relationships presented no problems for an empiricist account of human understanding, a universe intelligible only in terms of general classes of statistically recurring probabilities was not (above, pp. 114–18). Such a universe, comprehensible in such terms, required on the part of the comprehender an innate data-processing ability with which the comprehender must be regarded as pre-programmed, and such an ability was described in such terms as the ability 'to transcend the particular', 'to form open-classes' and so forth. But here, of course, a metaphysical puzzle emerges in which the organisation of human understanding is isomorphic with the order of the world, but between which there can be no connections of a causal kind (Lonergan, 1957, pp. 431–2, pp. 53–68). The solution to the puzzle demands, I believe, the perspective of a religious metaphysic in which ultimate questions about the world and man's place within it can only be explained in categories analogically inferential with personal descriptions. Statistical patterns of probable recurrences are not, of course, personal descriptions. But we argued in the case of operant conditioning that, unless such statistical redescriptions of problems about human behaviour were reformulated in terms of intentions, choices, decisions and so on, that is to say, in categories analysable in terms of the modalities of necessity, possibility, probability and so on, they remained redescriptions and not genuine explanations. It is, however, possible, beginning with a study of man who, with his innate categories for processing reality is also seen in our metaphysical puzzle to be the measure of all things, to argue further about his application of those categories in his understanding of an external world, as Berger does, as follows:

> To say that religion is a human projection does not logically preclude the possibility that the projected meanings may have an ultimate status independent of man. Indeed, if a religious view of the world is posited, the anthropological ground of these projections may itself be the reflection of a reality that *includes* both world and man, so that man's ejaculations of meaning into the universe ultimately point to an all-embracing meaning in which he himself is grounded. (Berger, 1973, pp. 182–3)

It may therefore be that, having failed to produce explanations rather than redescriptions of his own psychological and social-psychological acts in statistical schemes of recurring probabilities, man's projection of such schemes derivable from sub-sets of his own common-sense experience may prove finally to be less than satisfactory as an explanation when applied to the external physical world. It is arguable, in other words, that a world redescribed in terms such as those of classes of recurring probabilities cannot be reached by human understanding without the inclusion of those personal categories applied, albeit analogically, by means of which religious statements about 'God's will' or 'God's love' are understood. To deny a child a genuine religious education would therefore, in my view, deprive him of a proper social context in which can be realised his innate endowment for understanding both the world and his life within it. But, for the moment, my argument must here rest until I publish in the future a more detailed exposure of the illusions of secular man.

Bibliographical References

Aristotle (1964), *Physics* (Harmondsworth: Penguin).

Aron, R. (1968), *Main Currents in Sociological Thought* (Harmondsworth: Penguin).

Ayer, A. J. (1940), *Language, Truth, and Logic* (Harmondsworth: Penguin).

Bambrough, R. (1968), 'Universals and family resemblances', in *Wittgenstein*, ed. G. Pitcher (London: Macmillan), pp. 186–204.

Baratz, S. S., and Baratz, J. (1972), 'Early childhood intervention: the social science base of institutional racism', in *Language in Education* (Milton Keynes: Open University Press), pp. 188–98.

Barrow, R. St J. (1976), *Commonsense and the Curriculum* (London: Allen & Unwin).

Bedford, E. (1956), 'Emotions', in *Proceedings of the Aristotelian Society*, vol. LVII, pp. 281–304.

Bennett, J. (1964), *Rationality* (London: Routledge & Kegan Paul).

Bennett, J. (1966), *Kant's Analytic* (Cambridge: Cambridge University Press).

Bennett, J. (1974), *Kant's Dialectic* (Cambridge: Cambridge University Press).

Berger, P., and Luckman, T. (1967), *The Social Construction of Reality* (Harmondsworth: Penguin).

Berger, P. (1971), *A Rumour of Angels* (Harmondsworth: Penguin).

Berger, P. (1973), *The Social Reality of Religion* (Harmondsworth: Penguin).

Bernstein, B. (1971a), 'Ritual in education', in *School and Society*, ed. B. R. Cosin *et al.* (Milton Keynes: Open University Press), pp. 160–5.

Bernstein, B. (1971b), 'Open school, open society', in *School and Society*, ed. B. R. Cosin *et al.* (Milton Keynes: Open University Press), pp. 166–70.

Bernstein, B. (1973), 'A brief account of the theory of codes', in *Social Relationships and Language*, ed. V. Lee (Milton Keynes: Open University Press), pp. 65–79.

Bloom, B. S. (ed.) (1956), *Taxonomy of Educational Objectives*, Vols. 1 and 2 (London: Longman).

Blum, A. F. (1971), 'The corpus of knowledge as a normative order', in *Knowledge and Control*, ed. M. F. D. Young (London: Collier Macmillan), pp. 117–32.

Brent, A. (1978), *Philosophical Foundations for the Curriculum* (London: Allen & Unwin).

Burnett, J. (1914), *Greek Philosophy*, Part 1, *From Thales to Plato* (London: Macmillan).

Chadwick, H. (1967), *The Early Church* (Harmondsworth: Penguin).

Chomsky, N. (1959), review of *Verbal Behaviour* by B. F. Skinner (New York, 1957), *Language*, vol. 35 (January–March), pp. 26–58.

Chomsky, N. (1965), *Aspects of the Theory of Syntax* (Cambridge, Mass.: MIT Press).

Chomsky, N. (1966), *Cartesian Linguistics* (New York: Harper).

Chomsky, N. (1968), 'Linguistics and philosophy', in *Language and Philosophy*, ed. S. Hook (New York: New York University Press), pp. 51–94.

Chomsky, N. (1972), *Language and Mind* (New York: Harcourt Brace Jovanovich).

Chomsky, N. (1975), 'Recent contributions to the theory of innate ideas', in *Innate Ideas*, ed. S. Stich (Berkeley, Calif.: University of California Press), pp. 121–31.

Chomsky, N., and Katx, J. J. (1973), 'On innateness: a reply to Cooper', *Philosophical Review*, vol. 83, pp. 70–87.

Cooper, D. E. (1972), 'Innateness: old and new', *Philosophical Review*, vol. 81, pp. 465–83.

Cooper, D. E. (1975), *Knowledge of Language* (Dorchester: Prism Press).

Cooper, D. E. (1978), 'Linguistics and cultural deprivation', *Journal of Philosophy of Education*, vol. 12, pp. 113–20.

Cooper, D. E. (1980), *Illusions of Equality* (London: Routledge & Kegan Paul).

Cox, E. (1966), *Changing Aims in Religious Education* (London: Routledge & Kegan Paul).

Dearden, R. F. (1968), *The Philosophy of Primary Education* (London: Routledge & Kegan Paul).

Descartes, R. (1911), *Rules for the Direction of Mind*, trans. E. Haldane and G. Ross (Cambridge: Cambridge University Press).

Dewey, J. (1944), *Democracy and Education* (London: Collier Macmillan).

Durkheim, E. (1915), *Elementary Forms of the Religious Life* (London: Allen & Unwin).

Durkheim, E. (1964), *The Division of Labour in Society* (London: Collier Macmillan).

Edgley, R. (1968), 'Innate ideas' in *Royal Institute of Philosophy Lectures*, vol. 3, 1968–9, ed. G. N. A. Vesey (London: Macmillan), pp. 1–33.

Einstein, A. (1969), 'Autobiographical notes', in *Albert Einstein: Philosopher-Scientist*, ed. P. Schilpp (La Salle, Ill.: Open Court), pp. 3–94.

Esland, G. (1971), 'Teaching and learning as the organisation of knowledge', in *Knowledge and Control*, ed. M. F. D. Young (London: Collier Macmillan), pp. 70–116.

Euripides (1954), *Electra*, trans. P. Vellacott (Harmondsworth: Penguin).

Evers, C. W., and Walker, J. C. (1980), 'The unity of knowledge', paper delivered at conference of Philosophy of Education Society of Australasia, August.

Flew, A. G. N. (1967), *Evolutionary Ethics* (London: Macmillan).

Freud, S. (1934), *The Future of an Illusion* (London: Macmillan).

Freud, S. (1966), *Two Short Accounts of Psycho-Analysis* (Harmondsworth: Penguin).

Freud, S. (1974), *Introductory Lectures in Psychoanalysis* (Harmondsworth: Penguin).

Freud, S., and Breuer, J. (1974), *Studies of Hysteria* (Harmondsworth: Penguin).

Gettier, E. (1963), 'Is justified true belief knowledge?', *Analysis*, vol. 23, pp. 121–3.

Goss, P. (1857), *Omphalos* (London: Rivington).

Greggory, I., and Woods, R. W. (1972), 'Indoctrination; inculcating doctrines', in *Concepts of Indoctrination*, ed. I. Snook (London: Routledge & Kegan Paul), pp. 162–89.

Guy, H. A. (1973), *The Story of Jesus of Nazareth* (London: Dent).

Hamlyn, D. W. (1970), *Theory of Knowledge* (London: Macmillan).

Hamlyn, D. W. (1978), *Experience and the Growth of Understanding* (London: Routledge & Kegan Paul).

Hand, N. (1976), 'What is English?', in *Explorations in the Politics of School Knowledge*, ed. G. Whitty and M. F. D. Young (Nafferton: Nafferton Books), pp. 9–18.

Harman, G. (1967), 'Psychological aspects of theory of syntax', *Journal of Philosophy*, vol. LXIV (February), pp. 75–87.

Harris, A. (1976), *Teaching Morality and Religions* (London: Allen & Unwin).

Harris, K. (1979), *Education and Knowledge* (London: Routledge & Kegan Paul).

Hirst, P. H. (1974a), *Knowledge and the Curriculum* (London: Routledge & Kegan Paul).

Hirst, P. H. (1974b), *Moral Education in a Secular Society* (London: University of London Press).

Hirst, P. H. (1979a), review of *Philosophical Foundations for the Curriculum* by A. Brent (Allen & Unwin, 1978), *Journal of Further and Higher Education* (Spring), pp. 103–6.

Hirst, P. H. (1979b), 'Human movement, knowledge, and education', *Journal of Philosophy of Education*, vol. 13, pp. 102–13.

Hodges, W. (1977), *Logic* (Harmondsworth: Penguin).

Hume, D. (1969), *A Treatise on Human Nature* (Harmondsworth: Penguin).

Irving, D. (1977), *Hitler's War* (London: Hodder & Stoughton).

Kant, I. (1939), *Critique of Pure Reason*, trans. H. Kemp-Smith (London: Macmillan).

Katz, J. J. (1972), *Semantic Theory* (New York: Harper).

Katz, J. J. (1979), 'Semantics and conceptual change', *Philosophical Review* (July), pp. 327–65.

Kenny, A. (1973), *Wittgenstein* (Harmondsworth: Penguin).

Kitcher, P. (1980), 'A-priori knowledge', *Philosophical Review* (January), pp. 3–23.

Kuhn, T. (1970), *The Structure of Scientific Revolutions* (Chicago, Ill.: University of Chicago Press).

Labov, W. (1973), 'The logic of non-standard English', in *Language in Education*, ed. V. J. Lee (Milton Keynes: Open University Press), pp. 198–212.

Lawton, D. (1968), *Social Class, Language and Education* (London: Routledge & Kegan Paul).

Lawton, D. (1973), *Social Change, Educational Theory, and Curriculum Planning* (London: Hodder & Stoughton).

Lee, V. J. (ed.) (1973), *Social Relationships and Language* (Milton Keynes: Open University Press).

Leibniz, G. W. (1968), *New Essays*, trans. M. Morris (London: Dent/Everyman).

Locke, J. (1975), *An Essay Concerning Human Understanding*, ed. P. H. Nidditch (London: Oxford University Press).

Lonergan, B. (1957), *Insight* (London: Darton, Longman & Todd).

Lukes, S. (1973), *Emile Durkheim: His Life and Work* (Harmondsworth: Penguin).

Lyons, J. (1977), *Chomsky* (London: Fontana).

Mackie, J. L. (1974), *Cement of the Universe* (London: Oxford University Press).

McDougall, W. (1932), *The Energies of Man* (London: Methuen).

McNeill, D. (1972), 'The creation of language', in *Language in Education*, ed. V. J. Lee (Milton Keynes: Open University Press), pp. 145–9.

Marcuse, H. (1954), *Eros and Civilisation* (Boston, Mass.: Beacon Press).

Marcuse, H. (1964), *One Dimensional Man* (London: Sphere).

Marcuse, H. (1968), *Negations: Essays in Critical Theory* (Harmondsworth: Penguin).

Nagel, T. (1969), 'Linguistics and epistemology', in *Language and Philosophy*, ed. S. Hook (New York: New York University Press), pp. 180–4.

Nagel, T. (1974), 'Freud's anthropomorphism', in *Freud*, ed. R. Wollheim (New York: Doubleday Anchor), pp. 11–24.

Pavlov, I. P. (1927), *Conditioned Reflexes* (Oxford: Oxford University Press).

Perry, L. R. (1965), 'What is an educational situation?', in *Philosophical Analysis and Education*, ed. R. D. Archambaut (London: Routledge & Kegan Paul), pp. 65–81.

Peters, R. S. (1958), *The Concept of Motivation* (London: Routledge & Kegan Paul).

Peters, R. S. (1966), *Ethics and Education* (London: Allen & Unwin).

Peters, R. S. (1972), 'Reason and passion', in *Education and the Development of Reason*, ed. R. F. Dearden, P. H. Hirst and R. S. Peters (London: Routledge & Kegan Paul), pp. 208–29.

Plantinga, A. (1974), *The Nature of Necessity* (London: Oxford University Press).

Popham, J. W. (1975), *Educational Evaluation* (Englewood Cliffs, NJ: Prentice-Hall).

Popper, K. (1959), *The Logic of Scientific Discovery* (London: Hutchinson).

Pring, R. (1971), 'Bloom's taxonomy: a philosophical critique (2)', *Cambridge Journal of Education*, vol. 96, no. 2, pp. 83–91.

Pring, R. (1972), 'Knowledge out of control', *Education for Teaching* (Autumn), pp. 19–28.

Pring, R. (1973), 'Curriculum integration', in *Philosophy of Education*, ed. R. S. Peters (London: Oxford University Press), pp. 123–49.

Pring, R. (1977), 'Common sense and education', *Proceedings of the Philosophy of Education Society of Great Britain*, vol. XI (July), pp. 57–77.

Quine, W. van O. (1953), *From a Logical Point of View* (New York: Harper).

Quine, W. van O. (1960), *Word and Object* (Cambridge, Mass.: MIT Press).

Quine, W. van O. (1973), *The Roots of Reference* (La Salle, Ill.: Open Court).

Quine, W. van O. (1975), 'Linguistics and philosophy', in *Innate Ideas*, ed. S. Stich (Berkeley, Calif.: University of California Press), pp. 199–201.

Reichenbach, H. (1969), 'Philosophical significance of relativity', in *Albert Einstein: Philosopher-Scientist*, ed. P. Schilpp (La Salle, Ill.: Open Court), pp. 287–311.

Richardson, J. T. E. (1976), *The Grammar of Justification* (Falmer: Sussex University Press).

Russell, B. (1912), 'On the relation of universals and particulars', *Proceedings of the Aristotelian Society*, vol. 12, pp. 1–24.

Russell, B., and Whitehead, N. (1962), *Principia Mathematica* (Cambridge: Cambridge University Press).

Ryle, G. (1949), *The Concept of Mind* (London: Macmillan).

Schilpp, P. (ed.) (1969), *Albert Einstein: Philosopher-Scientist* (La Salle, Ill.: Open Court).

Shipman, M. (1979), *In-School Evaluation* (London: Heinemann).

Skinner, B. F. (1953), *Science and Human Behavior* (New York: Collier Macmillan).

Skinner, B. F. (1968), *The Technology of Teaching* (Englewood Cliffs, NJ: Prentice-Hall).

Skinner, B. F. (1971), *Beyond Freedom and Dignity* (Harmondsworth: Penguin).

Skinner, B. F. (1978), interview, BBC Television *Man Alive* series, 'The Autobiography of a Non-Person'.

Sockett, H. (1971), 'Bloom's taxonomy: a philosophical critique (1)', *Cambridge Journal of Education*, vol. 96, no. 2, pp. 16–25.

Staniland, H. (1972), *Universals* (London: Macmillan).

Stich, S. (ed.) (1975), *Innate Ideas* (Berkeley, Calif.: University of California Press).

Strawson, P. (1959), *Individuals* (London: Methuen).

Swinburne, R. (1977), *The Coherence of Theism* (Oxford: Oxford University Press).

Swinburne, R. (1979), *The Existence of God* (Oxford: Oxford University Press).

Urmson, J. O. (1969), *The Emotivist Theory of Ethics* (London: Oxford University Press).

Virgil (1964), *Georgics*, trans. E. V. Rieu (Harmondsworth: Penguin).

Walking, P. H. (1980), 'The idea of a multi-cultural curriculum', *Journal of Philosophy of Education*, vol. 14, no. 2, pp. 87–96.

Watson, J. B. (1924), *Behaviorism* (Baltimore, Md: Johns Hopkins University Press).

White, J. (1972), 'Indoctrination and intentions', in *Concepts of Indoctrination*, ed. I. Snook (London: Routledge & Kegan Paul), pp. 117–30.

White, J. (1973), *Towards a Compulsory Curriculum* (London: Routledge & Kegan Paul).

White, J. (1978), review of *Philosophical Foundations for the Curriculum* by A. Brent (Allen & Unwin, 1978), *Journal of Curriculum Studies* (November), pp. 363–5.

Whitty, G., and Young, M. (1976), *Explorations in the Politics of School Knowledge* (Nafferton: Nafferton Books).

Whorf, B. L. (1956), *Language, Thought and Reality*, ed. J. B. Carroll (New York: Humanities Press).

Wilson, J. (1970), *Education and the Concept of Mental Health* (London: Routledge & Kegan Paul).

Wilson, S. (1971), *Introduction to Logic*, Pt. 2 (Milton Keynes: Open University Press).

Wittgenstein, L. (1961), *Tractatus Logico-Philosophicus* (London: Routledge & Kegan Paul).

Wittgenstein, L. (1969), *On Certainty* (Oxford: Blackwell).

Wittgenstein, L. (1974), *Philosophical Investigations* (Oxford: Blackwell).

Wright Mills, C. (1963), *Power, Politics and People*, ed. I. L. Horowitz (London: Oxford University Press).

Young, M. F. D. (ed.) (1971), *Knowledge and Control* (London: Collier Macmillan).

Young, M. F. D. (1976), 'The schooling of science' in *Explorations in the Politics of School Knowledge* (Nafferton: Nafferton Books), pp. 47–63.

Yudkin, M. (1979), 'On Quine's contretemps of translation', *Mind*, vol. 88, pp. 93–6.

Index